TWO FLIGHTS TO VICTORY

TWO FLIGHTS TO VICTORY

FROM THE DOOLITTLE RAID TO THE ENOLA GAY

DAVID G. STYLES

Spellmount

To Marie – My Inspiration

First published 2011 by Spellmount, an imprint of
The History Press
The Mill, Brimscombe Port
Stroud, Gloucestershire, GL5 2QG
www.thehistorypress.co.uk

© David G. Styles, 2011

The right of David G. Styles to be identified as the Author
of this work has been asserted in accordance with the
Copyrights, Designs and Patents Act 1988.

All rights reserved. No part of this book may be reprinted
or reproduced or utilised in any form or by any electronic,
mechanical or other means, now known or hereafter invented,
including photocopying and recording, or in any information
storage or retrieval system, without the permission in writing
from the Publishers.

British Library Cataloguing in Publication Data.
A catalogue record for this book is available from the British
Library.

ISBN 978 0 7524 6206 6

Typesetting and origination by The History Press
Printed in Great Britain

Contents

	Preface	7
	Introduction	11
1	James Harold Doolittle	15
2	The Foundations of Conflict	28
3	Preparing for a Secret Mission	42
4	The Doolittle Raid	54
5	After the Raid	69
6	Meeting in North Africa	80
7	Paul Warfield Tibbets Jr	96
8	The Manhattan Project	108
9	Bringing the B-29 to the 509th	115
10	At Wendover Field	124
11	On the Island of Tinian	134
12	Mission to Hiroshima	144
13	Mission to Nagasaki	160
14	After the Bomb	168
15	The Future of Strategic Bombing	176
	Appendix 1 People	178
	Appendix 2 Ships	209
	Appendix 3 Aircraft	214
	Appendix 4 Military Organisations	235
	Appendix 5 The Doolittle Targets	252
	Appendix 6 The Doolittle Raiders	258
	Appendix 7 The B-29s of the 393rd	270
	By the Same Author	280
	Bibliography	281
	Index	282

Preface

I was inspired to write this work by the late Colonel Chase Nielsen, one of the four Doolittle Raiders who survived 40 months of Japanese imprisonment in Shanghai. It was he who in a conversation in April 2003 at the Doolittle Raiders' Reunion in Fairfield, California, told me much about the connection between his idol, Lieutenant-Colonel Jimmy Doolittle, and a compatriot, Colonel Paul Tibbets. The conversation was the result of Colonel Nielsen having read material I had written as international correspondent to the 2003 Doolittle Raiders' Reunion in the lead-up to that event. Colonel Nielsen alluded to the connections with North Africa, how Tibbets and Doolittle's paths had crossed and how Doolittle had deliberately placed Tibbets in the position to be the obvious choice to lead the 509th Composite Group. Colonel Nielsen suggested that I research the subject and so I did. My greatest regret is that he did not live long enough to read this work.

This is the story of two great men and two great missions. One of those men had already achieved greatness before the Second World War and was to achieve greatness for a second time at its start. The other man's greatness was yet to come – very much at the hand of the first – and at the end of the conflict. Those two great men were James H. Doolittle and Paul W. Tibbets. Their missions are the subject of this story, the story of the only two air attacks on Japan during the Second World War to have been organised outside any wider battle plan. The first flight was aimed at delivering a 'bloody nose' to the Japanese to remind them that, after Pearl Harbor, the United States was not impotent, whilst the second, after the United States had become deeply embroiled in the war in Europe, North Africa and the Pacific, was aimed at bringing this awesome sequence of bitter battles to a final and abrupt end by destroying a whole city with a single weapon. The story tells of how the paths of the two men who commanded these two similar yet fundamentally different missions crossed in North Africa, and how Jimmy Doolittle was able to put Paul Tibbets into the position where he was almost certain to be selected to lead and carry out the dropping of the atomic bomb, an act that signalled the start of a whole new way of waging war.

I would like to acknowledge the help, support and encouragement I have received in the process of researching and developing this book. Without it this publication may not have reached fruition and almost certainly would not have been so complete. So I thank the actions, and now the memory, of Colonel Chase Nielsen, who inspired me to research and write it in the first place; Bob Fish, a trustee of the USS *Hornet* Museum at Alameda in California for his reading of my manuscript and guidance on matters of fact and dates; Lady Andrea White for her help and guidance in reprographics; Charley Wilcox and Ray Sestak of the 494th Bombardment Group Association for providing so much information about the two B-24s and their crews held in Hiroshima; George Nolta for his hugely valuable contribution on the Doolittle Raiders and the connection with Willows Airport; Professor Duo-Jiao Tan of Huazhong University of Science and

A 34th Bomb Squadron B-25 on an airfield hardstanding.

This view of B-25s on the deck of the USS *Hornet* shows the robust lashings required to keep the aircraft secure in heavy seas. Two of the aircraft are doing their daily engine run-ups.

PREFACE

Technology in Wuhan, People's Republic of China, for checking my China references; and lastly Marie Brooks for reading huge swathes of this work and making a valuable contribution to research.

Then I would like to publicly thank all those nameless people I have met along the way – librarians, bookshop staff and casual acquaintances who have given a few moments of their time without realising why. Finally, I have to say that seven years of research and painstaking study of detail will still not guarantee that there is not an error of fact somewhere in this book. I once read a quotation I'd like to repeat here: 'There are people whose pleasure comes from searching out mistakes in the published word. If you find mistakes in these pages, please believe that it is because, in this publication, I have tried to include something for everyone.' However, in all seriousness, the reader who finds genuine errors is asked kindly to forgive those oversights as innocent mistakes and tell me what and where they are. This story deserved and needed to be told – I hope I have done it justice.

This work acknowledges the memory of all the men, women and children of all nationalities who lost their lives in the Pacific Theatre of War between 1933 and 1945. We should hope that thirteen million people did not die in vain.

DGS

Introduction

Admiral Isoroku Yamamoto, Commander in Chief of the Imperial Japanese Navy and leader of the fleet that attacked Pearl Harbor on 7 December 1941 is on record as having said after that attack: 'I fear we have awoken a sleeping giant.' His period of service in the United States between the two world wars had given him the opportunity to get to know Americans and understand their psyche; hardly surprisingly, he was absolutely right.

After Pearl Harbor, President Roosevelt demanded action, and within four months the first of two significant air attacks on Japan took place. These two flights, the first on 18 April 1942 and the second on 6 August 1945, were the two most momentous flight missions of the Second World War in the Pacific. There are many parallels, the first being that these two missions (the latter being two flights), were mounted entirely independently of any major battle plan and in total secrecy. They were separate from all the major battles fought in the Pacific theatre of war, but they were the catalysts of victory. Doolittle's mission caused the Japanese to pull back some of their forces to the main islands in a defensive move, which allowed the United States and its allies a better chance of victory. Tibbets' mission, 40 months later, convinced the Japanese of their defeat, and sealed that victory.

Both men were lieutenant-colonels when they undertook their missions. Both men reached General Staff rank and both men carried with them a personal regret about the numbers of people who had lost their lives as a consequence of their missions. But both had simply done their duty on missions from which there was a strong likelihood they might not return. They did their jobs with great courage. James H. Doolittle retired from the United States Air Force in the rank of Lieutenant-General – the highest ranking Reserve officer in USAF history. Paul W. Tibbets Jr retired in the rank of Brigadier-General.

Sadly, General Tibbets retired in the wake of vicious press attacks which branded him the world's biggest killer (and almost certainly blighted his career) – a wholly unjust and cruel indictment of a man who had no part in the executive decisions which led to the hugely courageous mission he undertook for his country. In the author's view, these two men stand equal in their contributions to victory in the Second World War and in their immeasurable personal courage. Interesting then to reflect that the first of these two, after carrying out his mission with great success, should point the other on the route to his own momentous mission.

Paul Tibbets referred, in his autobiography, to his observations in the moments before the atom bomb was released on an unsuspecting Hiroshima. He wrote:

> In the buildings and on the streets there were people, of course, but from six miles up, they were invisible. To the men who fly the bombers, targets are inanimate, consisting of buildings, bridges, docks, factories, railroad yards. The

The mighty B-29 Superfortress.

tragic consequences to humanity are erased from one's thoughts in wartime, because war itself is a human tragedy' … As we viewed the awesome spectacle below, we were sobered by the knowledge that the world would never be the same. War, the scourge of the human race since time began, now held terrors beyond belief.

None of those 'unrecognisable specks' knew they were two minutes from death, and many had no idea what the war was about and did not want war at all. Many did not know about what Japanese soldiers had done at Nanking, the repercussions of the Doolittle Raid for the Chinese, the bestiality of the prison camps across the Pacific, the gruesome reality of the Burma Railway or the Battle of Iwo Jima. They were just people caught up in the actions of their leaders.

Naturally this weighed in the minds of President Truman and his Chiefs of Staff when making the decision to drop that bomb. They chose Hiroshima because it had a major military arsenal, a navy shipyard, a railway marshalling yard and there were two large army units stationed there. It had a higher than average proportion of military personnel in its population. It was an ideal target and its bombing with the inaptly named 'Little Boy' was a logical action to take in the process of trying to bring an already terrible conflict to an abrupt end.

The military experts of the time –Generals Douglas MacArthur and Holland M. Smith, Admirals Chester Nimitz and William Halsey and British Admiral Earl Mountbatten – all forecast that, if the war were to continue it would take up to four more years to win on Japanese soil, with a possible death toll of four million more as a conservative estimate. These men had seen firsthand the battles of Leyte Gulf, the Philippines, Tinian, Iwo Jima and Okinawa and they had seen the rising death toll as they moved closer to sovereign Japanese territory. In these circumstances, they were in favour of anything that could end this bloodiest of wars in days rather than years. And so the bomb was dropped.

1

James Harold Doolittle

Jimmy Doolittle was born in Alameda, the only child of Frank, a carpenter, and Rosa Shephard Doolittle, on the mainland side of San Francisco Bay in California in December 1896. As a young boy, he moved with his parents to Alaska and received his initial education in Nome. When the family returned to California he went to Los Angeles Junior College, where he met his lifelong love and partner, Josephine Daniels. He was already known as 'Jimmy', because of his diminutive size. The next step in his education was at the University of California School of Mines, but after only a year there, he enlisted as a flying cadet in the Signal Corps Reserve in October 1917 and trained at the School of Military Aeronautics at Rockwell Field, California. As a flight cadet, he had abandoned his education for service to his country. It was to be a career move he would never regret. He was commissioned a second lieutenant in the Signal Corps' Aviation Section in March 1918 and was assigned to Camp Dick, Texas, then Wright Field in Ohio, Gerstner Field in Louisiana and finally back to Rockwell Field, now as a flight leader and gunnery instructor. His next duty was at Kelly Field in Texas, firstly with the 104th Aero Squadron, then with the 90th Squadron on border patrol duty at Eagle Pass.

It was during this time that Jimmy Doolittle first carved his name in the annals of American aviation history. After a period over the Mexican border with the 104th Aero Squadron, he found himself assigned by no less a personality in that early Army Air Service than Brigadier-General Billy Mitchell, to a series of tasks which would cement his dedication to a career in aviation. The first was when he volunteered to recover a Curtiss JN-4 from Mexico after its pilot had miscalculated his navigation. This included taking mechanics to the site, repairing the aircraft and then flying it out. Next, he was involved in bombing trials which were set to prove that military aircraft could sink battleships and so better defend the country's coastline than surface defensive equipment. Next, when a fellow officer lost his life in an attempt to fly coast-to-coast across America, Jimmy Doolittle sought permission to make a fresh attempt, which was granted by General Mason M Patrick.

Doolittle took his DH-4 from Kelly Field to Camp Johnson, near Jacksonville in Florida, on 4 August 1922, with the intention of flying off Pablo Beach on Sunday 6 August. His wife, Joe, was there with him and she helped fuel up the aircraft. Ready to take off at 2140hrs, he started to roll along the beach. Then suddenly the left undercarriage wheel caught in a patch of soft sand and the aircraft turned turtle. Jimmy Doolittle thought he would have serious problems with his commanders but, surprisingly, he received a telegram from General Patrick telling him it was an unfortunate accident and better luck next time!

'Next time' was not long in coming and after repairing the nose, rudder and a wing strut, then remounting the engine and replacing the propeller, the DH-4 was ready to fly again. On 2 September, the aircraft was flown from Kelly Field to Pablo

An Airco DH-4 of the type flown by Jimmy Doolittle on his trans-America flight.

Lieutenant Jimmy Doolittle with his Curtiss R-3C after winning the 1925 Schneider Trophy.

Beach, ready for another attempt on 4 September. At 2152hrs Eastern Standard Time, Jimmy Doolittle started his epic flight, heading for Kelly Field, near San Antonio, Texas, a distance of 1050 miles. Because of the publicity put out by the US Army, he found himself accompanied at several stages of his trip by military aircraft from airfields along the way and as he approached San Antonio, he was escorted in by two aircraft appointed to ensure his safety. After refuelling, he headed for Rockwell Field in California, 2163 miles away.

Approaching Rockwell Field, he was escorted in by Captain William Randolph and Lieutenant C.L. Webber, though they had been flying around in circles for more than an hour over the Nevada state border before they saw him. Doolittle was elated to see them, as he was fighting very hard to stay awake. History was made on 5 September 1922 when Jimmy Doolittle crossed the Continental United States with just a single

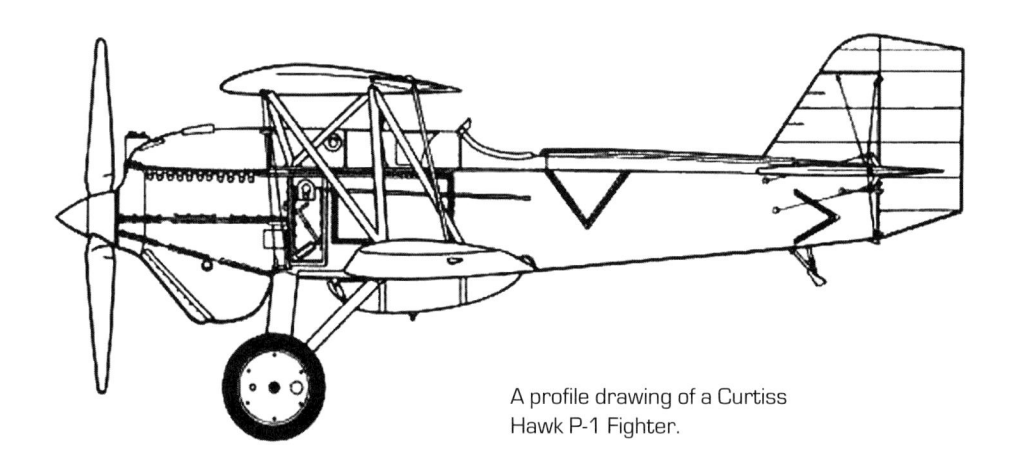

A profile drawing of a Curtiss Hawk P-1 Fighter.

30-minute stop, in 21 hours and 19 minutes. It was his first major internationally recognised flying achievement, but it would not be his last. For this achievement, Lieutenant James H. Doolittle USAAS was awarded the Distinguished Flying Cross, the first of three he was to receive in his career. In the same year he received his Bachelor of Arts degree from the University of California. In July 1923, Doolittle enrolled with Massachusetts Institute of Technology and graduated the following year with a Master of Science degree in Aeronautics, gaining his Doctorate of science a year later. He was one of the first men in the country to earn this degree.

In March 1924 he was transferred to McCook Field, to join in a programme conducting aircraft acceleration tests, then in June the following year he went to the Naval Air Station in Washington DC for special training with high-speed seaplanes. Then he served with the Naval Test Board at Mitchell Field, New York and, because of his outstanding flying skill, was selected to fly in the 1925 Schneider Trophy Race, an international race for seaplanes. Lieutenant Doolittle was the first US Army officer to fly in the race and was only the second American to win, with an average speed of 232mph flying a Curtiss R3C Navy racing floatplane. It was the fastest a seaplane had ever flown, and in the following year Doolittle received the Mackay Trophy for this feat.

In April 1926 Doolittle took a leave of absence to go to South America at the request of Glenn H. Curtiss, founder of Curtiss Aircraft where he gave a series of flying demonstrations; the company were aiming to sell their P-I fighter plane to the Chileans. Being a highly sociable crowd, the Chileans held a cocktail party in late May, to which Jimmy Doolittle was invited. He was introduced to what he described in his own words as a 'powerful drink called pisco sour'. Clearly, he found it quite palatable and as the evening wore on, conversation turned to motion pictures and the name Douglas Fairbanks came up, as it often did when Americans were part of the group.

Douglas Fairbanks, of course, had played the swashbuckling hero long before the arrival of Errol Flynn and, having submitted further to the influence of pisco sour than he was truly aware, Doolittle offered the comment that the various athletics for which Fairbanks had become famous were really nothing more than any able-bodied American could do. He was naturally challenged to prove it, and the acrobatic performance began with a couple of handstands and then a back flip. This didn't seem to satisfy his audience and so he did a two-hand stand on a window ledge, then a single hand stand. Responding to the applause, he gripped the inner edge of the two-foot window ledge and extended his body horizontally out of the window, using the support of the extended window ledge to hold him up.

But then disaster struck. The old sandstone of the ledge began to crumble and Doolittle plummeted fifteen feet to the courtyard below. He landed on his feet, and heard both ankles crack. His hosts quickly took him to hospital, where it was found that one ankle had a simple fracture, but that the other had a series of small breaks. Unfortunately, it all began to go wrong from this point. The X-rays somehow became confused and crossed over, so when Doolittle was taken to the plaster room, the wrong casts were placed on the ankles, setting them incorrectly. A few days afterwards the hospital realised the mistake and changed the casts, but one was now above the knee allowing no bending of the leg, so Doolittle could hardly walk, let alone fly. He was acutely embarrassed about his predicament – and about the predicament into which his antics had put Curtiss – so with no further thought, on the ninth day of inactivity, he told Boyd Sherman to get the P-1 ready for flight. Sherman was to bring a hacksaw to the hospital, with which they would reduce the above-the-knee plaster sufficient to allow him to bend his leg. Next, Sherman would fabricate a pair of clips, with which to secure the pilot's feet to the rudder pedals, so that Doolittle could operate the rudder with the minimum of pain.

Whilst it was a few years yet before Jimmy Doolittle proved beyond all doubt that an aircraft could be flown without rudder and turns achieved on ailerons alone, he certainly would have unwittingly practised some of that technique in his flight demonstrations in Chile. Before any demonstration could take place, Doolittle had to be comfortable with the modifications made to allow him to fly and to be equally comfortable in his plaster casts. So Boyd Sherman took him out to the airfield on 26 June and lifted him aboard the P-1. He took off and went through a light routine of aerobatics before trying a series of snap-rolls to test the strength of the casts. His right leg was the stronger, so he did a series of right-hand rolls first.

The cast cracked, but he carried on and did a sequence of left-hand rolls. This was much more serious. His leg was in great pain as the cast split. Sherman took him back to the hospital to get the casts repaired, but the hospital didn't want to know this 'crazy Yankee' and refused to see him. After a lot of searching they found an elderly German who made prostheses and who used, of all things, corset stays to reinforce them. He was persuaded to make new casts and to reinforce them to take the strains of aerobatic manoeuvres. But now, Doolittle couldn't walk without crutches.

A Curtiss P-1 Hawk Fighter.

Came the day of the first demonstration, the American duo reached the airfield and Sherman lifted Doolittle into the cockpit of the Curtiss. A German pilot, von Schoenebeck, was already airborne and putting his Dornier through its routine, winning a lot of applause for his performance. Doolittle took off and climbed to meet him, going through a stunt routine on the way up; then he made a pursuit pass. Von Schoenebeck took this as a challenge and tried to shake him off, but he was flying a 260hp plane and could not elude a 400hp one which was significantly more manoeuvrable into the bargain.

Von Schoenebeck broke off and landed. As he left the dogfight, Doolittle noticed that there was fabric loose on one wing. Back on the ground, Doolittle was accused of clipping the Dornier with a landing wheel. In fact, close examination showed that stress had split the German aircraft's wing fabric and so the Chilean government gave victory to the Americans, buying a number of Hawks from that demonstration.

Next it was on to Bolivia and typical of Jimmy Doolittle, there was a challenge to be met. With his crutches stowed in the machine-gun bays, he set off from Santiago and put up a new record for the flight time between Santiago and La Paz of 11 hours 25 minutes, with a single fuel stop at Antofagasta in northern Chile. Because there were anti-American and anti-Chilean demonstrations in La Paz, Doolittle took a piece of good advice and returned to Santiago, breaking his own record in the process and bringing it down now to 9 hours 55 minutes.

Argentina was the next stop on the itinerary. Flying over the Andes was another first, quite apart from the flight time from Santiago to Buenos Aires of 6 hours 45 minutes non-stop. A similar demonstration programme, with Jimmy Doolittle still clipped into his rudder pedals but without the distraction of Herr von Schoenebeck's Dornier, resulted in more Hawk sales. The trip was now complete and so Doolittle left the Hawk in Argentina and with Sherman sailed back to New York. As soon as he reached McCook Field, Doolittle requested sick leave to sort out his ankles, which seemed far from right. Sure enough, X-rays revealed that the bones had not healed correctly, though they decided not, after four months, to break them and start again. Instead, they put on new casts and rendered the patient immobile again for some months.

In the course of the South American trip, the Curtiss Aeroplane Exporting Company had achieved most of its sales goals, with the exception of Bolivia, Jimmy Doolittle had recovered his reputation and satisfied his temporary 'employers' and he had set two new time-and-distance records in the process. He had also entered his name in the record books as the first aviator to cross the Andes – and certainly the first to cross the Andes with two ankles in plaster, a record which is likely to remain in perpetuity.

Back in the United States he was admitted to Walter Reed Hospital for treatment, which took until April 1927, after which he went to McCook Field for experimental work and additional duty as instructor with the Organized Reserves of the Fifth Corps Area's 385th Bomb Squadron. During his recovery he had talked to some friends about outside loops and whether they were possible. An outside loop is, like a normal loop, a vertical circle in the sky, except that the pilot sits on the outside of the loop and pushes the stick forward, rather than on the inside, pulling the stick backwards. The manoeuvre had never been done before and Jimmy Doolittle was keen to be the first man to do it. Once at McCook he set about achieving his goal.

As any competent test pilot would, he did it in stages, so he could gauge how difficult it might be to come off the bottom of the loop on the outside. This was because he needed to establish, above all else, that he could push the aircraft on and upwards from the bottom end of the loop. He flew a Curtiss P-1 Hawk as secretly as he could, until he felt confident that he could actually perform the whole manoeuvre in one go and keep his hand pushing forward on the stick out of the bottom of the loop.

Four days after Charles Lindbergh made his famous first crossing of the Atlantic by air, Jimmy Doolittle gathered around him six test pilots to act as witnesses. Again, he put the Hawk into a normal loop first, then rolled at the top so that he was on the outside as he was about to dive into the first stage of this loop. Now, he had to concentrate on keeping the stick pushing forward and keeping the airspeed up to carry him round the bottom of the loop and into the climb. Soon, he was over the top of the loop and was still going. He'd just performed the world's first-ever outside loop flight and was justifiably excited about it. So were his six witnesses, who promptly told the press about it. One reporter asked him how he'd achieved it, which drew the wry quip: 'I don't know; I just thought of it on the spur of the moment.'

Upon his return to McCook Field, Doolittle has begun to seriously consider resigning his commission, and discussed the prospect of civilian life with his wife Joe (they had married on Christmas Eve 1917, so their entire experience of married life had been a military one). Then he got a call from Harry F. Guggenheim, the son of a multi-millionaire businessman and philanthropist, Daniel Guggenheim. Guggenheim Snr had set up a $2.5 million fund for the promotion of developments in aviation and Harry wanted Jimmy Doolittle to participate in a series of experiments flying in fog. As part of the Guggenheim development, an organisation called the Full Flight Laboratory was established at Mitchell Field on Long Island, New York, under the direction of a US Navy Captain Jerry Land. Land was asked to nominate someone to take over the Blind Flight Laboratory and nominated Jimmy Doolittle. And so Doolittle put thoughts of civilian life aside for the moment.

Two aircraft were purchased for the development of a full instrument flying set-up in an aircraft. The aircraft selected was a Consolidated NY-2, chosen for its all-round ruggedness and safety, as well as its inherent stability in flight. A canvas hood was made and fitted to the rear cockpit and a NACA cowl was tested to improve its air speed, as 98mph was too slow. An extra fuel tank was also fitted to improve its range. Many flights were made with the hood down to test the capability of the bank-and-turn indicator, but eventually it became apparent that something else was needed. That 'something' was a gyroscopic artificial horizon, which was ultimately developed by Elmer Sperry Jr in hand with Jimmy Doolittle. Here was the value of an engineer/test pilot versus just a test pilot, justifying Jerry Land's choice.

On 24 September 1929, Doolittle climbed aboard, with Lieutenant Ben Kelsey in the co-pilot's seat. The NY-2 was a trainer, so had two seats and two sets of controls, but Kelsey's role was simply as an observer. The aircraft had eleven different instruments in addition to those which gave information about the engine. They comprised: a magnetic compass; an earth inductor compass; a bank-and-turn indicator; a directional gyro; an artificial horizon; an airspeed indicator; an altimeter; a rate-of-climb indicator; an outside air thermometer; a vibrating reed homing range indicator; and a vibrating reed marker beacon indicator. The aircraft also carried a radio transmitter and radio receiver, two six-inch landing lights and a parachute flare – all essential equipment for the ultimate test. This was to take the aircraft off the ground, fly it for a predetermined distance and land it, all without seeing outside the aircraft's cockpit.

Doolittle lined himself up for a landing, still working entirely blind on instruments. As he came down on his glide-path, he veered to the right and looked set to fly into the path of a number of aircraft below, but then he corrected his course and put the Husky down on the airfield without touching another plane. Lieutenant James H. Doolittle had notched up another aviation first to his credit – the first recorded instrument flight in which an aircraft had been taken off, flown in a circuit and landed without the pilot ever seeing where he was going. Blind flying was here to stay. By the end of the year, the Guggenheim Fund was wound up, its mission accomplished and the project was taken over by the Department of Commerce and the US Army.

The aircraft used for the blind flying task, the Consolidated NY-2.

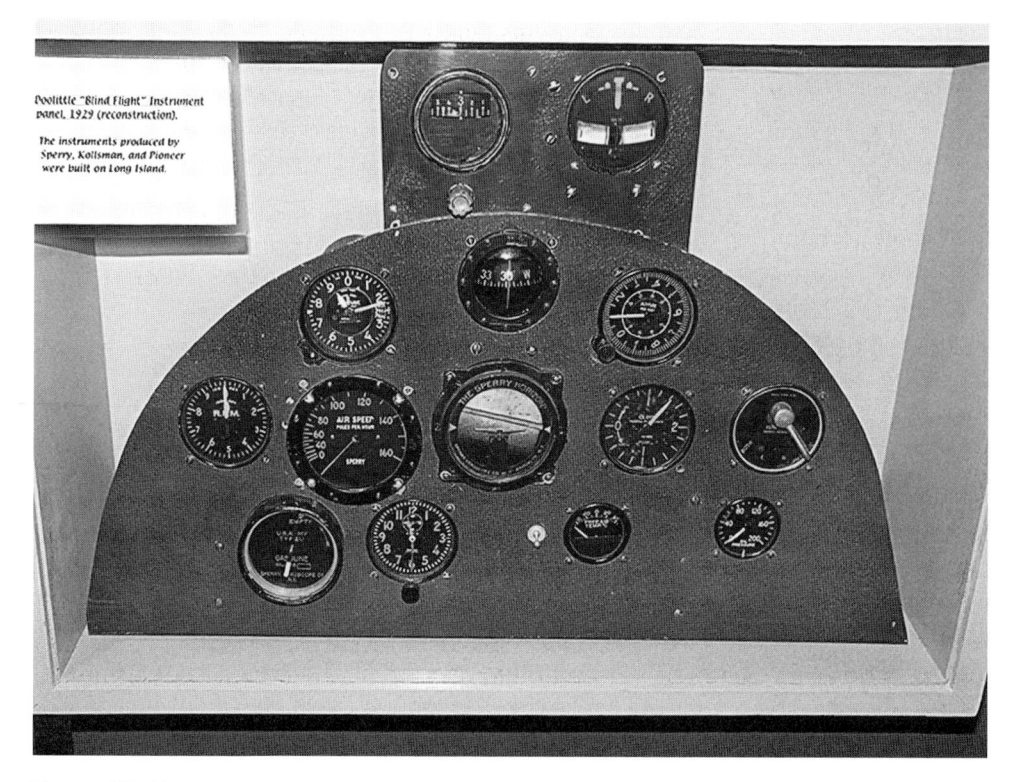

The modified instrument panel of the Consolidated NY-2.

Doolittle was awarded the Harmon Trophy for the experiments. He then resigned his regular commission to join the Shell Oil Company as manager of its Aviation Fuels Division, earning roughly three times what the US Army had paid him as a senior First Lieutenant. Soon after he was approached to join the Army Reserve in the rank of Major, which he did.

In 1931 Cliff Henderson, the organiser of the National Air Races in the United States, decided to set up an annual cross-country air race to promote and encourage American aviation achievements, not least to stimulate development as well as enthusiasm in the private aviation sector. Reliability and endurance would be just as important as speed if the competitors were to make a journey of around 2500 miles. Henderson sought out one of America's industry leaders, Vincent Bendix, to solicit backing for his idea and Bendix was clearly persuaded. The Bendix Transcontinental Trophy Race was born. Jimmy Doolittle took an immediate interest in the race, inaugurated to promote the fastest flight across the continent from Los Angeles to Cleveland. Shell Oil was clearly interested too, as Doolittle easily persuaded them to allow him to take part.

In this same period, an aircraft designer named E.M. Laird (known widely as 'Mattie') had been commissioned by the Cleveland Speed Foundation to produce a new aircraft for them, based on an already successful design known as the Laird 'Solution'. The new machine was to be called the Laird LC-DW500, or 'Super Solution'. The Laird 'Super Solution' was not an entirely new design, as Laird's racers had performed outstandingly well at the 1930 Chicago National Air Races, where a pilot named Speed Holman had won the Thompson Trophy Race in a Wasp Jr powered Laird 'Solution'. However, the 'Super Solution' was to gain even greater fame, as one called *Sky Buzzard* was to be flown by Doolittle. *Sky Buzzard* was painted green, with yellow wings and carried the racing number 400.

The Bendix Trophy Race took place on 4 September 1931; it was exactly nine years to the day after Doolittle had flown the first ever cross-country flight in his DH-4. It was a bright moonlit night. The start of the race was timed so that arrival at Cleveland would occur at the height of the afternoon's activities there. Crowds of spectators lined runway 15 and by 0100hrs the pilots had all climbed aboard, having done last-minute checks on weather, navigation needs and flight plans. The first aircraft rolled on to the runway and when Jimmy Doolittle's turn came, he closed the cockpit, checked the latches, checked his instruments, tightened his seat belt and rolled to the starting position. The engine cowling hid his view of the runway, but as the starter dropped his flag, Jimmy Doolittle pushed the throttle forward and was airborne in less than 500 feet. In just over ten years time that distance would have a profound significance for him, but in a far from sporting context.

Climbing rapidly, *Sky Buzzard* flew low over the mountains to the east and levelled off briefly at 5000 feet, while its pilot checked instruments and engine temperature gauges. Then Doolittle spotted the tail light of Beeler Blevens' heavily fuel-laden Orion climbing slowly. The 'Super Solution' flashed past Blevens. Blevens told the story some time later that he thought he was flying backwards (or was about to stall) as he saw *Sky Buzzard* pass him. Now Doolittle opened up the Wasp's throttle and aimed for 11,000 feet on a heading of 75 degrees. Flying over the Mojave Desert, he headed straight for Albuquerque, New Mexico. Now, it was time to set course for the first fuel stop, so a gradual reduction in altitude was called for, as Doolittle also checked his heading to ensure he had no need to change course. Every change in course would cost him time and fuel. Refuelling at Albuquerque, a speed and distance check confirmed that the 'Super Solution' had covered 674 miles at 228mph. As the aircraft's tank was filled, Doolittle climbed out to stretch his legs and down a glass of milk. Fuel caps secured, he climbed back into the cockpit, started up and lifted off to head for Kansas City, where he would make his next stop. As dawn broke, he climbed to 10,000 feet to head for

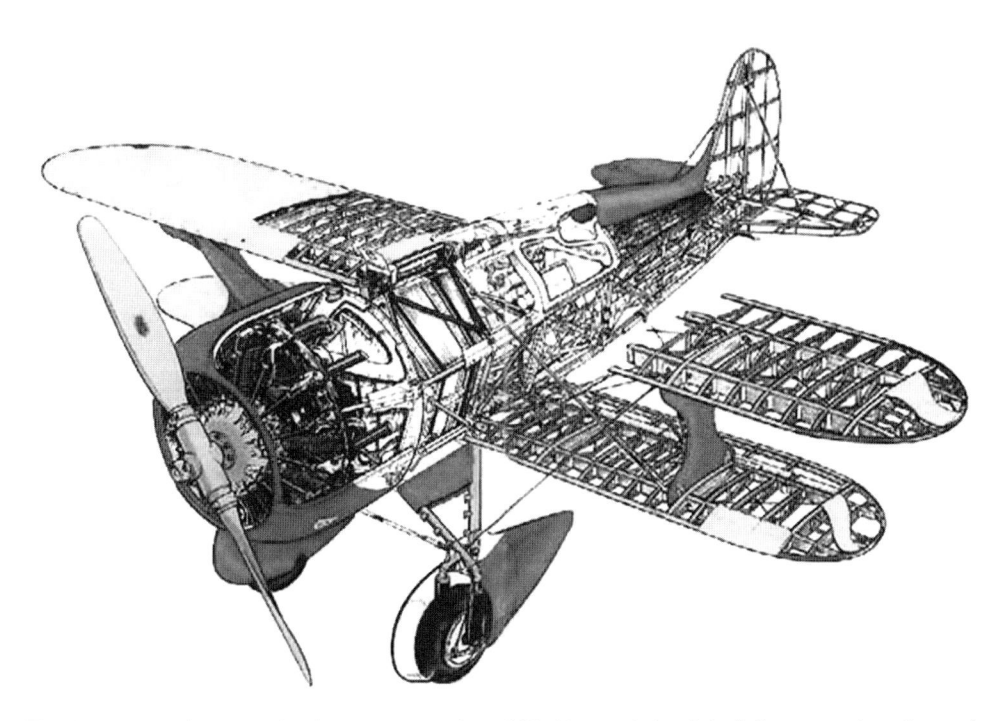

This illustration shows the intricate construction of *Sky Buzzard*, clearly built for strength and speed.

the prairies and his next fill-up. By this time Doolittle had built up a commanding lead, though he wasn't to know that yet. He had another three hours six minutes to cover 765 miles before learning he might be in front.

Jimmy Doolittle's stop at Kansas City lasted a brief ten minutes and he was back in the air. The sun was high in the sky and it was very hot. Turbulence was building up and pretty soon there were thunderstorms. It was clear to Doolittle that he would have to battle through a heavy squall to get to Cleveland, but as a pioneer of instrument flying he was not unduly worried. The storm lasted just over half an hour, then relief as *Sky Buzzard* flew into bright sunshine, and there it was: the red and white chequered pylon with 'Bendix' boldly displayed on it. Jimmy Doolittle had made his destination with less than two degrees drift in his navigation. His average speed was 223mph. But that was not the end of it, for Vincent Bendix had offered additional prize money for the pilot who could establish a new transcontinental record as well. Jimmy Doolittle just had to go on and take that record, so he did no more than fuel up again and head for Newark in New Jersey. He arrived at Newark just eleven hours, sixteen minutes and ten seconds after he had taken off from Burbank, having flown a total distance of 2450 miles at an average speed of 217mph.

James H. Doolittle was now not only the clear winner of the 1931 Bendix Trophy, his transcontinental record had clipped one hour eight minutes off the earlier record held by a flyer named Frank Hawk. It was a remarkable feat in which Doolittle had covered a slightly greater distance than he had covered back in 1922 in just over half the time. But for Jimmy Doolittle it didn't stop there. He had entered *Sky Buzzard* in the Thompson Trophy Race, which was due to start the next day. He had barely landed at Newark when he was off again, flying back to Cleveland to prepare for the race. By the time Doolittle landed back at Cleveland, there wasn't time to change the engine, as had been the plan, so the 'Super Solution' went into the Thompson Trophy Race with the longer distance direct drive engine still installed, instead of the geared drive version. The result was that *Sky Buzzard* withdrew with an engine that went down on power because of a scuffed piston. But the story of Jimmy Doolittle's next Thompson Trophy Race is another tale.

Having retired from the 1931 Thompson Trophy, Doolittle and the Laird team went to work on *Sky Buzzard* ready for the following season. During development trials, it was decided to convert the landing gear to retractable, as it was felt this would give better speed and handling. The aircraft also had a new paint finish, identifying it with sponsor Shell Oil, Doolittle's employer. It was bright yellow overall, with red tail surfaces and engine cowling, on both of which was painted the Shell logo. The racing number 400 was retained, now painted on the fuselage sides with a red lightning flash running through it. With its new retractable landing gear, Jimmy Doolittle took it for its first test flight on 23 August 1932 and found, as he was coming in to land, that he could not lower the gear because the slipstream prevented it from going down, so after several tries he decided to 'belly-flop' it on to the ground. Unfortunately, the damage was so extensive that *Sky Buzzard* wasn't going to be repaired in time for the race. Doolittle was without an aircraft, but not for long. The Granville brothers – creators of the Gee-Bee Racer – approached him and suddenly he had a flight in the Gee-Bee R-1.

The Thompson Trophy Race was established in 1930 by Charles Edwin Thompson of Thompson Products, Inc. of Cleveland and Detroit. They were manufacturers of aeronautical equipment, the most important product being sodium cooled valves. The race was an international free-for-all for male pilots only in aircraft equipped with engines of unlimited displacement. More than 60,000 spectators would witness the world's fastest, most powerful racers speed 10 times round the 10-mile course. In 1931 time trials preceded the main event. The qualification course was a straight path in front of the grandstands with each entrant flying two speed dashes in each direction. Qualifying speed was a minimum of 175mph, the objective being to keep as many of the entrants together in a pack during the race, adding to spectator excitement, but increasing the pilot risk factor.

Qualifying for the race would be an event in itself, for Doolittle saw it as a chance to go for the World Landplane Speed Record at the same time. In his first attempt, he flew through the 3km speed trap at an average of 293.19mph, comfortably breaking the 1924 record of 278.48mph. But he was disqualified for not having a barograph to indicate his maximum altitude. Irritated, Doolittle went up again, but the second attempt wasn't fast enough, so at noon on the Saturday before the big race, he came back for a last crack at the record. The weather was not ideal; it was hot and humid and there were high clouds, as well as an 8mph crosswind. Gee-Bees didn't like crosswinds at low speed, but that didn't bother Jimmy Doolittle – he wasn't planning to fly slowly. He went through the speed trap six times and set up a new qualifying speed for the race and a new World Landplane Speed Record at the same time – at an average speed of 296.287mph.

The 1932 race was due to start at 5.00pm and there were more than 50,000 people in the grandstand at Cleveland Airport. Jimmy Doolittle climbed into his Gee-Bee and fired up the engine – then pandemonium! The engine backfired and set light to the fuel in the carburettor and the cowling was ablaze. Doolittle scrambled out and the flames were quickly put out. A quick check showed only minor damage, so it was all put back together and Doolittle climbed back in, restarted and taxied out as though nothing had happened. Then the flag fell. Bob Hall's 'Bulldog' was in front, hotly pursued by Doolittle. Approaching the pylons, Doolittle recalled that during the Schneider Trophy Race he had dived into turns, so losing only 2mph. He repeated the manoeuvre, climbed between pylons and dived into turns outside the traditional racing line so as to catch Hall's more agile Bulldog and overtake it. Someone described

The Gee-Bee Racer soon took the lead at Cleveland.

the Gee-Bee as being like a bird of prey, its spatted wheels looking like a pair of talons hanging over the Bulldog. The two aircraft disappeared behind the treeline for the last time, then reappeared. As they drew closer, Doolittle had the lead and won the most prestigious short distance air race in America, even though the Gee-Bee had been trailing smoke for a couple of laps.

Doolittle returned to active duty as a Major in the Reserve in 1940, and in 1941 he was tasked with fixing a deadly problem. The Glenn L Martin Company had produced a twin-engine bomber, the B-26 Marauder, and it was being labelled a 'widow maker'; several young pilots had been killed in accidents while flying it after one engine had failed. Unusually the B-26 went into production straight from the drawing board, so there was never an XB-26. Initially it fell far short on range, but met every other aspect of the specification and so, unusually, on the promise that the Martin Company would bring the design closer to order specification, build was allowed to continue.

However, the death toll associated with the B-26 came to the notice of the General Staff in Washington and the US Army Air Corps' chief, General Henry H. 'Hap' Arnold. Arnold decided something had to be done and so Major Doolittle was summoned to his office and the problem was explained to him.

The B-26 was an aerodynamically advanced design and had a very sleek appearance – much prettier than the chunkier B-25, but seemingly far less stable in the air. It was powered by a pair of Pratt & Whitney Double Wasp engines turning large four-bladed propellers and had a landing speed of 130–135mph; many modern jets touch down at a similar speed, so the B-26 had a pretty rapid landing. Arnold had reached the end of his tether with this aircraft and its high accident rate. Doolittle's job was to investigate the allegations, test fly the machine and make recommendations – the principal one being whether or not the B-26 should even continue in production. He went to the Martin factory in Baltimore and checked out the design history, test pilots' reports and the aircraft itself. He pored over drawings, asked questions about in-flight handling on one engine and then examined the training programme for the pilots.

What Doolittle found led him to question whether the bomber itself was the problem, or was the training programme a clue to reducing the accident rate? It transpired that young pilots were progressing from primary trainers to basic trainers to advanced trainers before receiving their wings as pilots. All this was fine, except that every aircraft these young men had flown was a single-engined type; many had never even sat in

The early version of the Martin B-26A Marauder.

a two-engined aircraft. They were simply sent to a B-26 conversion school, sat inside with an instructor after ground school and led straight into flying the new bomber. Most had never flown an aircraft with tricycle undercarriage, or one as big as this. The few who had experience of twin-engine light-planes had fewer problems with the conversion to the bigger, more powerful B-26.

Doolittle's next move, typical of his flight testing thoroughness, was to interview pilots who had experienced the problems presented by the B-26 in flight and survived. The pilots said that the B-26 couldn't be flown on one engine and once on one engine you couldn't turn it into the dead engine without getting into trouble, and that it was virtually impossible to land on one engine. Doolittle's job now was to either prove them wrong or condemn the B-26. He was a man who believed that in general, all aircraft could be flown and there was nothing that good piloting skills and familiarity could not overcome. He thought it unlikely that the B-26 was inherently a killer, and indeed considered it potentially very useful. Now he had to set about proving that to serving bomber crews and newly trained bomber pilots.

He decided to test the aircraft himself, lining up a B-26 on the runway and feathering the left engine during the take-off run. He made a steep turn into the dead engine as he lifted off, then flew around the airfield circuit and landed, with the left engine still out. Shortly after that, he took off again and did the same thing to the right engine, turning again into the dead engine as he cleared the ground, brought it round again and landed. Without a co-pilot, that made quite an impact on the observing group. It also convinced them that the so-called 'impossible' manoeuvres were possible and even easy, as long as you knew what you were doing.

From this point on, there was no problem getting volunteers to fly the B-26. But Doolittle also made several recommendations for improvements in control characteristics and handling, including the introduction of twin-engine training for pilots who might be destined for multi-engined aircraft squadrons and the extension of training specifically on the B-26. The airframe didn't escape improvements either.

The wings were extended to improve wing loadings and lateral stability, and the fin was enlarged. Doolittle returned to General Arnold and recommended that the B-26 should continue in production, with the modifications he suggested.

Doolittle's next task was to travel to B-26 operational units and persuade their crews of the aircraft's true safety potential. Having proved that the aircraft did not kill people instinctively, he embarked on a brief training/familiarisation session to show pilots how to handle the dead engine problems which had been described by so many as lethal.

The B-26 now had a future and would ultimately turn in one of the best safety records of any bomber in the European theatre of operations. Jimmy Doolittle would soon have a much more important mission to prepare for – one which would not feature the B-26, rather an aircraft which had competed in the same specification bid, the North American B-25 Mitchell. He was promoted to Lieutenant-Colonel in January 1942 and was assigned to Headquarters Army Air Force in Washington DC.

2

The Foundations of Conflict

The seeds of Japanese military aggression in the Second World War were sewn in the seventh century, when a Chinese-style empire was established in Japan. This involved an attempt to integrate the many feudal territories of the country by the introduction of the Taika Reforms which brought, under the early shogunates, land re-distribution and a universal taxation system. In this same period, the Samurai was established as a group of warriors formed to protect landowners and their territories. Their role was purely military in nature and the Bushido Code was established in those very early days.

After many inter-tribal conflicts, the Heiji Rebellion of 1160 brought the Samurai to political power for the first time. After a period of relative stability, there was turmoil in the fourteenth century and many shifts of power, but the Ashikaga Shogunate re-established Samurai supremacy. However, more instability followed as the result of prolonged tribal territorial battles and it was not until 1603 that order was restored under the Tokugawa Shogunate, which lasted until 1868. During those years, the Emperor was effectively a puppet under the Shogun.

Throughout this period, Japan was a country closed off from the outside world, except for some trade. Portuguese explorers first landed there in 1542 and before the end of the sixteenth century, the port of Nagasaki had been opened to trade exclusively with the Portuguese merchants. Half a century later, British and Dutch merchants came and established a tenuous connection. However, in response to external pressures, especially from the US, the Convention of Kanghwa was endorsed by the Tokugawa in 1854, officially allowing foreigners *'gaijin'* into the country. At the same time activists and reform-minded Samurai who wanted to bring about political change launched the reform movement under the guise of restoring the emperor to power, thereby eliminating the power of the Shogun rulers. Imperial Rule returned under Emperor Meiji from the Tokugawa Shogunate, the 'Meiji Restoration' of 1868. Japan was moving forward politically and by the 1870s, realised that it had to open its doors to foreign trade if it was to develop and survive. The end of the Samurai era came with the Battle of Shiroyama in 1877. The Meiji Dynasty was firmly in place.

The Japanese embraced foreign trade with enthusiasm, although they were resistant to social and cultural change; the honour code of the Samurai remained in military circles after the ending of the Tokugawa Shogunate. The Japanese military code was built on the principles of the Samurai – courage, benevolence, respect, honesty, honour and loyalty. One aspect of the code was that a true Samurai would never kill an unarmed person. This is a significant point when reflecting on the conduct of officers and men of the Imperial Japanese Army in the years 1933–1945.

Japan's increased military prowess was made all too apparent during the First Sino-Japanese War of 1894–1895. Korea had been a point of contention between Japan and China for years; Korea was not a powerful country but was effectively under

The Meiji Revolution or Restoration brought about the return of Imperial rule in Japan in 1868, when the Emperor Meiji relocated to Tokyo to take power from the Tokugawa Shogun and open Japan to the world.

Chinese control, and projected from the Chinese mainland dangerously close to Japan. It also had valuable coal and iron ore deposits. Japan felt that whoever controlled Korea would be able to threaten Japanese security, and so from 1876 a series of political and military scuffles took place between Japan and China over the beleaguered country. The tipping point was when the Korean emperor requested Chinese troops to aid in the suppression of a rebellion. The Japanese objected to the Chinese influence and sent their own troops, who ended up seizing the emperor and installing a puppet government in Seoul. China objected and war broke out. Japanese ground troops routed Chinese forces on the Liaodong Peninsula and the Chinese navy was virtually destroyed in the Battle of the Yalu River. Troops also advanced through Korea into Manchuria as far as Weiheiwei and Yingkou, taking the port city of Lushunkou (Port Arthur). China was forced to sign the Treaty of Shimonoseki, which handed over the island of Formosa (Taiwan), Port Arthur and the Liaodong Peninsula of Manchuria to Japan.

Japan did not have the Liaodong Peninsula for long. Under pressure from Germany and France (encouraged by Russia) it relinquished the peninsula and Port Arthur to the Russians. The European countries supported the claim in the belief that a Russian presence would help stabilise the region and perhaps restrain Japanese ambitions. In fact, it aggravated the situation. Russia further consolidated its military position in Manchuria during the Chinese Boxer Rebellion of 1900, when troops from eight countries entered the country to relieve the international legations under siege in Beijing. Political friction between Japan and Russia continued, although there were negotiations to give Russia free control over parts of Manchuria in exchange for Japanese control of northern Korea. In the event, after being unable to come to an agreement, Japan severed diplomatic relations on 6 February 1904 and the Russo-Japanese War was declared on 8 February. Three hours before the Japanese made the declaration the Imperial Japanese Navy attacked the Russian fleet in Port Arthur. Some Russian ships attempted to escape the onslaught, but were sunk by the Japanese Navy under Admiral Togo Heihachiro in the Battle of the Yellow Sea. A year later, the Russian Baltic fleet was decimated in the Battle of Tsushima. This was the first modern war in which an eastern country defeated the forces of a European country, and was indicative of the new Japanese belligerence.

Japan turned its attention to Manchuria, the north-east district of China. Manchuria is the native home of the Jurchen people, who established the Chinese Qing Dynasty, which ran between 1612 and the end of Empire. Manchuria is made up of the three eastern provinces of Liaoning, Jilin and Heilongjiang. Across the Amur River and its tributary the Ussuri, the north eastern area meets the East Siberia district of Russia. Across the Yalu River, the southern area meets the Korean Peninsula. The western area is separated from the Mongolian Plateau by the Greater Khingan mountain range.

The Japanese made successful overtures to the Chinese Imperial administration and negotiated for the construction of the Manchuria Railway, the South Manchuria Railway Company being founded in 1906. This gave them a firm foothold in China, one they would turn into an iron grip which would last for over 40 years. The Japanese stationed military guards along the route to protect their investment, but there were many incursions by bandit Mongol groups and others from across the border in Imperial Russia. These were not state sponsored raids, but Russia did little to stop them – not least because Tsar Nicholas had his own problems to deal with. Russia was not politically stable and activists were making life very difficult for him and his government, so small

The three-year-old Pu Yi standing beside his father, Prince Chun, who is holding his infant brother Pujie.

The boy emperor Pu Yi in 1917, at the age of ten.

incidents out on the remote Chinese border – over 5000 miles away – were very low on the state's list of priorities.

By 1904, the last emperor of China in the Qing Dynasty, the child Pu Yi, had inherited the throne, but he had no power, firstly because his grandmother, the Dowager Empress Cixi acted as Regent, and secondly because control of China fell to General Chiang Kai-shek, who maintained the emperor only as a puppet of his regime. The instability on the Sino-Russian border meant that the growth of Japanese power in the region went almost unnoticed, as did the increasing cruelty meted out to the Chinese under its control.

In the process of expanding its empire, Japan's next move was the annexation of Korea in 1910. In 1914 it then took Shantung Province in China; this was supposedly an attack on Germany's leased naval base there, and therefore done in support of the Allies. However, after the war the Japanese insisted on keeping Shantung, which was accepted by the Allies who were desperate to include Japan in the new League of Nations, and who were in the process of drawing up the Treaty of Versailles. Their government's weak response to the Treaty (and the loss of Shantung) angered many Chinese, and on 4 May 1919 there were student protests across China, the first mass protest recorded in Chinese history. But it achieved little, for even though the Chinese refused to sign the Treaty, the Allies sacrificed China's participation in order to ensure Japan's enrolment in the League. China did not regain Shantung until December 1922.

Japan's support of the Allies during the First World War meant that the annexation of Korea was legitimised by the League of Nations in the 1920s, and China was effectively sidelined. In this situation, it is hardly surprising that resentment built up amongst Chinese influentials and academics. Had the League of Nations given support to China in the conclusion of the Treaty of Versailles, the balance of power in the Far East might have been different. But because the League did nothing to protect China's interests the Chinese began to look to Russia, which was going through a major turmoil itself after the Revolution of 1917. Russia's new regime was to be the model for a new China. Meanwhile Japan was able to fill the power vacuum.

The limited influence of the League of Nations was shattered by the Depression of the 1930s. When an alleged terrorist incident in 1931 (the destruction of a portion of the track of the South Manchurian Railway) was seized upon by the Japanese military

Pu Yi as the Emperor of Manchukuo under Japanese control. Here he is depicted in Japanese style military uniform for the international press, but in his own society he insisted on wearing traditional Chinese Imperial robes.

An express train of the South Manchuria Railway, using Japanese locomotive and rolling stock.

authorities as a pretext to invade Manchuria, China called on the League of Nations to intervene. But the Japanese claimed that China had violated treaty obligations and rejected any attempt at mediation, while the rest of the world stood by.

The major western powers, particularly Great Britain and France, did not consider it advisable to confront Japan, a fellow member of the League. Unless the interests of one or other of the leading western powers was directly affected to the extent that it was willing to go to war, the League was not prepared to stop an increasingly powerful nation from having its way with a weak, semi-colonial country, albeit one with huge untapped resources in manpower and raw materials that signalled far greater potential growth in the long term than the much smaller Japan could achieve.

The Manchurian Incident was a confrontation that gave Japan the opportunity to set up a puppet government in the area, renaming the region Manchukuo, a territory of Imperial Japan, in February 1932. During this period, an organisation called the May Fourth Movement was created, bringing a new wave of intellectual revolution by means of the New Culture Movement. Many of the leaders of this movement were bitterly disappointed by the betrayal of China by the western powers and turned to Marxism, going on to create what was to be known as the Chinese Communist Party.

Pu Yi was still nominally the Chinese Emperor, but now of the Manchukuo regime set up by the Japanese. The fact that Japan had sided with the Allies in the First World War meant that there was no western intervention during the hostile takeover. The League wanted Japan's membership, even at the cost of Chinese territorial rights, a decision it came to regret in the fullness of time because the Japanese military expansion in China grew at such an alarming and unimpeded rate.

The Second Sino-Japanese War started on 7 July 1937 with the Battle of Marco Polo Bridge, when Japanese and Chinese forces met near Tianjin. The Japanese Kwantung

The Rape of Nanking; a Japanese soldier surveys bodies that were dumped in the Yangtze River.

Army had been deployed at the west end of the bridge. They had claimed that one of their soldiers was believed to be hiding in the town and demanded that the army be allowed in to search for him, but the Chinese resisted. Some believe this incident was fabricated by the Japanese to provide a pretext for the invasion of central China. Whatever the cause, the Japanese did cross the bridge, and went on to take possession of Peking and Tianjin. With the fall of Peking on 18 August and Tianjin three days later, the North China Plain was helpless and unable to defend itself against Japanese mechanised divisions, which occupied it by the year end. The Japanese seized control of most of the major cities of China, which enabled them to secure virtual control of the whole country, even though there were Chinese people in the more remote parts of the country who never saw a Japanese face throughout the Japanese Imperial War of 1937–1945 (the Second World War in the Pacific).

It was on 9 December 1937 that the most infamous action of the Japanese invasion began: the Rape of Nanking. At first leaflets were distributed inviting the Chinese Army to surrender, with the assurance that they would be treated humanely if they laid down their arms. Many of the Chinese commanders had abandoned the city to the ordinary soldiers under the control of their NCOs and they had no idea how to handle the situation, and so they surrendered. The Japanese Kwantung Army then engaged in authorised genocide; the commander responsible for the bloodshed is said to have been Prince Yasuhiko Asaka, commander of the Yanagawa Corps, or 10th Army, who authorised instructions to 'kill all captives'. They rounded up the Chinese soldiers, bound them into groups and shot many of them in cold blood, dumping the bodies into the Yangtze River. Some were treated even more savagely, as they were tied up in groups of up to 50 and Japanese officers and soldiers set about beheading them with their swords. One Japanese press report told of two Japanese officers holding a contest to see which of them could behead 100

Women of Nanking blindfolded before their transportation to Japanese 'leisure camps'.

An article from December 1937, published in the Tokyo newspaper *Nichi Nichi Shimbun*, describing a contest to kill 100 Chinese using a sword. The picture shows Second Lieutenants Mukai and Noda. Mukai killed 106 people, while Noda's 'score' was 105. It goes on to talk about them going into a 'second innings'.

Chinese soldiers in the shortest time. Next came the turn of the civilian population. Thousands of women were held in Japanese 'leisure camps' to be raped and abused at leisure, and many more thousands of men women and children were killed out of hand. Over the six weeks of the Rape of Nanking the total death toll was estimated by the International Military Tribunal of the Far East to be 260,000, though the Chinese government's estimate from the Nanking War Crimes Tribunal was as high as 300,000.

Once Japan held China, the latter's huge resources were made available to the Japanese war machine, especially coal and foodstuffs. However, the Japanese were quite careful at this stage in their expansion to avoid confrontation with the western powers, even though they had withdrawn from the League of Nations in 1933. Western business interests in China were allowed to continue untouched for the time being, and the West seemed to take little notice of Japanese military growth. This was despite the fact that there were major US military installations in the Philippines, British installations in Hong Kong, Singapore, Malaya, Burma and India, and a large Dutch presence in what is now Indonesia. These were well placed to report on Japanese activities, not to mention the large ex-pat civilian population in the area; there were more British people in the Far East than any other foreign nationality.

The high point of Japanese military might came on 7 December 1941: the attack on Pearl Harbor. From Japan's perspective, the attack was justified by the increasing trading limitations placed by the countries of the Western Alliance on oil supplies and other international trading restrictions. The US had frozen Japanese assets after the Japanese annexation of Indo-China (the country now known as Vietnam), and had placed embargoes on the supply of oil and industrial raw materials to Japan, largely as a response to Japan's expansion of its empire into China and its annexing of Pacific islands. American aid and indirect military support of China had angered the Japanese government, especially Prime Minister General Tojo, who instructed that the islands of

Battleship Row, behind Ford Island, seen from the air by a Japanese aircraft during the attack on Pearl Harbor. In the centre background is the USS *West Virginia*, after being struck by a Japanese torpedo.

the Pacific should be secured by Japan so as to confirm mastery of the Pacific shipping lanes. There was also the issue of the American Volunteer Group, a fighter aircraft unit primarily based at Mingaladon in Burma, but tasked with the frustration of Japanese military aviation in south-west China. The group was commanded by the US military advisor to Chiang Kai-shek, General Claire Lee Chennault. The AVG became known as the 'Flying Tigers', and their motif, a winged cartoon tiger, was created by Walt Disney especially for the group. They operated the Curtiss Hawk Model 81, known elsewhere as the P-40 Tomakawk.

The AVG had been formed in the spring of 1941 and operated until the summer of 1942, when it was absorbed into the US Army Air Force as the 23rd Fighter Group, forming part of the 14th Air Force. By the time of the transfer the unit had destroyed 297 enemy aircraft, with a loss of only 14. Fifty years later the crews had their service credited as formal US military service, and in 1996 all the pilots were awarded the Distinguished Flying Cross and the ground crews were awarded the Bronze Star.

Today it is clear that a number of things could have been done to limit the severity of the attack on Pearl Harbor. It took place on a Sunday, and as was typical of western armies, most US personnel were off duty, many were off base and security was lax. The attitude was 'Who's going to go to war on a Sunday?' Admiral Isoroku Yamamoto, the Japanese Fleet Commander, had studied at Harvard between 1919 and 1921, then returned to the United States in 1925 on a diplomatic mission, so while he was not enthusiastic about going to war with the Americans, he knew their military habits and it was his decision to attack on a Sunday morning. He rightly suspected that there would be few personnel on base and his targets would be softer as a consequence.

The attack began at 0600hrs on Sunday 7 December, when 181 Japanese aircraft took off from their carriers, in a wave that consisted of torpedo bombers, dive bombers, normal bombers and fighters. The first opportunity for the US forces on Oahu to register that something was wrong was when a large number of aircraft were seen overhead, but they were thought to be friendly machines on their way into the harbour, as quite a number were expected.

The next warning sign was the sighting of an unidentified submarine entering Pearl Harbor. It was attacked and sunk by the destroyer USS *Ward* (DD-139), accompanied by a patrol plane. The report of this incident was treated casually by commanders and so no action was taken. At 0700hrs, a US Army radar operator at Opana registered a large block of aircraft approaching the islands. Being highly concerned, he reported his findings and his junior officer took it 'upstairs'. The senior officers thought it of no significance, assuming it to be an approaching group of US aircraft, and so once again no action was taken.

If these three incidents had been reacted to properly, then the attack on Pearl Harbor would have been much less significant militarily. But because these signs were ignored, no aircraft were scrambled before the Japanese arrived so there was no opportunity for any kind of advance defence. Battleship Row on Ford Island was virtually decimated, which could have been limited with proper command foresight alerting air defences. As it was, the US Navy bases at Ford Island and Kaneohe Bay were seriously damaged, as were the airfields at Ewa, Bellows, Wheeler's Field and Hickam Field, leaving the ships in the harbour at the mercy of the attackers.

There were over 90 ships at anchor in Pearl Harbor on that Sunday morning. The first wave of Japanese aircraft attacked at 0800hrs. By 0810hrs, all eight battleships in the harbour had been sunk or had taken damage. The USS *Pennsylvania* (BB-38) was in dry dock across the channel from Ford, but of the other seven, USS *West Virginia* (BB-48) went down, the USS *Oklahoma* (BB-37) sank, and USS *Arizona*'s forward magazine was hit and exploded, killing almost 1200 men. In addition, USS *California* (BB-44), USS *Maryland* (BB-46), USS *Tennessee* (BB-43) and USS *Nevada* (BB-36) were all damaged, some beyond immediate sailing. Despite it being damaged, however, USS *Nevada* managed to get under way and the intention was to put to sea to avoid further damage. However, another wave of 170 Japanese aircraft came into the area and focused an intensive attack on the *Nevada*. At this point, in order to keep the exit channel open, US Navy commanders ordered the ship to beach on Hospital Point, so keeping the exit waterway clear.

At 1000hrs the Japanese withdrew, leaving 21 ships of the US fleet damaged or sunk. In addition to the battleships already mentioned, the cruisers *Helena* (CL-50), *Honolulu* (CL-48) and *Raleigh* (CL-7), the destroyers *Cassin* (DD-372), *Downes* (DD-375), *Helm* (DD-388) and *Shaw* (DD373) were all hit. The seaplane tender Curtiss (AV-4), the target ship (formerly battleship) *Utah* (AG-16), the repair ship *Vestal* (AR-4), the minelayer *Oglala* (CM-4), the tug *Sotoyomo* (YT-9) and floating drydock Number 2 were also hit. Aircraft losses amounted to 188 destroyed, mostly on the ground, and 159 damaged but repairable. The American dead amounted to 2403, 68 of whom were civilians. 1178 people were wounded, while the Japanese lost only 29 aircraft.

If there can ever be any kind of upside to such a devastating attack, it was that the six US aircraft carriers were all at sea at the time. In addition, the attack failed to damage any part of their shoreside facilities, so they were able to return for servicing. Interestingly, only three ships were not restored to seaworthiness: the *Arizona* because it was beyond repair, and the *Oklahoma* and *Utah* because they were considered too old to be worth repairing and were therefore scrapped.

Amidst the horror of that day, some men shone. Cook 3rd Class Dorie Miller, a sailor aboard the USS *West Virginia*, was awarded the Navy Cross for his bravery. At the sounding of General Quarters, Miller went to his battle station, the anti-aircraft battery magazine amidships, only to discover that it had been destroyed by Japanese torpedos. He therefore went on deck, where an officer ordered him to carry the ship's captain, Mervyn Bennion, to safety. He then took control of an anti-aircraft gun, and although he had never been taught how to use it, continued firing until his ammunition ran out. Miller was the first Navy Cross nominee at Pearl Harbor, and the first African-American to be given the award. He died aboard the USS *Liscombe Bay* during the Battle of Tarawa on 20 November 1943.

The shockwaves sent through America on that December afternoon united the nation as never before. As far as the US was concerned, the action was taken without any declaration of war from the Japanese. A fourteen-part message *was* sent to the Japanese Embassy in Washington for delivery as a declaration of war to the State Department in Washington; the Embassy was instructed to deliver the declaration immediately before the attack was due to be launched on Pearl Harbor – that is 0800hrs Pacific Time. However, decoding the message took too long and the declaration was delivered long after the onslaught had begun. Some contend it was never delivered at all.

President Roosevelt addresses a packed Congress on 8 December 1941.

THE FOUNDATIONS OF CONFLICT

President Franklin Delano Roosevelt in a picture taken in 1933, the year he entered the White House.

> We, the Emperor, have now declared war upon the United States of America and Great Britain. The officers and men of our army and navy will concentrate their strength in engaging in battles, the members of our government will endeavour to carry out their assigned duties, our subjects throughout the Empire will employ full strength to perform their respective tasks. Thus uniting one hundred million hearts and discharging the fullest strength of the nation, we expect all our subjects to strive to attain the ultimate objective of this expedition.

On the afternoon of 7 December 1941, President Roosevelt was in the Oval Office with his chief foreign policy aide, Harry Hopkins, when their discussion was interrupted by a telephone call from Secretary of War Henry Stimson, who informed him that the Japanese had attacked Pearl Harbor and gave brief details of the scale of the assault and indicating that over 2000 Americans have died.

Roosevelt was beside himself with fury at the audacity of the attack and the fact that it was carried out with no declaration of war. He called a meeting of his military chiefs of staff; it was later said that despite being wheelchair bound, he raised himself to his feet to demand that they seek revenge for the unforgivable assault on US soil and personnel. The death toll particularly incensed the President and he sent the chiefs of staff away to start planning immediate reprisals.

At about 5.00pm he dictated to his secretary, Grace Tully, a request to Congress for a declaration of war. The speech was a brief, uncomplicated appeal to the American people rather than going through a thorough recitation of the Japanese attack and its lack of international integrity, as Secretary of State Cordell Hull had urged him.

The Chiefs at Staff at lunch, discussing the retaliation strategy for Pearl Harbor.

Mr. Vice President, Mr. Speaker, Members of the Senate, and of the House of Representatives:

Yesterday, December 7th, 1941 – a date which will live in infamy – the United States of America was suddenly and deliberately attacked by naval and air forces of the Empire of Japan. The United States was at peace with that nation and, at the solicitation of Japan, was still in conversation with its government and its emperor looking toward the maintenance of peace in the Pacific. Indeed, one hour after Japanese air squadrons had commenced bombing in the American island of Oahu, the Japanese ambassador to the United States and his colleague delivered to our Secretary of State a formal reply to a recent American message. And while this reply stated that it seemed useless to continue the existing diplomatic negotiations, it contained no threat or hint of war or of armed attack. It will be recorded that the distance of Hawaii from Japan makes it obvious that the attack was deliberately planned many days or even weeks ago. During the intervening time, the Japanese government has deliberately sought to deceive the United States by false statements and expressions of hope for continued peace. The attack yesterday on the Hawaiian islands has caused severe damage to American naval and military forces. I regret to tell you that very many American lives have been lost. In addition, American ships have been reported torpedoed on the high seas between San Francisco and Honolulu.

Yesterday, the Japanese government also launched an attack against Malaya.
Last night, Japanese forces attacked Hong Kong.
Last night, Japanese forces attacked Guam.
Last night, Japanese forces attacked the Philippine Islands.
Last night, the Japanese attacked Wake Island.
And this morning, the Japanese attacked Midway Island.
Japan has, therefore, undertaken a surprise offensive extending throughout the Pacific area. The facts of yesterday and today speak for themselves. The

people of the United States have already formed their opinions and well understand the implications to the very life and safety of our nation.

As Commander in Chief of the Army and Navy, I have directed that all measures be taken for our defense. But always will our whole nation remember the character of the onslaught against us.

No matter how long it may take us to overcome this premeditated invasion, the American people in their righteous might will win through to absolute victory.

I believe that I interpret the will of the Congress and of the people when I assert that we will not only defend ourselves to the uttermost, but will make it very certain that this form of treachery shall never again endanger us.

Hostilities exist.

There is no blinking at the fact that our people, our territory, and our interests are in grave danger.

With confidence in our armed forces, with the unbounding determination of our people, we will gain the inevitable triumph -- so help us God.

I ask that the Congress declare that since the unprovoked and dastardly attack by Japan on Sunday, December 7th, 1941, a state of war has existed between the United States and the Japanese empire.

Roosevelt's address made no reference to the Japanese declaration of war, if in fact he had seen it. The same day, at the request of the President, the US Congress declared war on Japan.

3

Preparing for a Secret Mission

The US Joint Chiefs of Staff came together on Monday 8 December and as the President was addressing Congress, they were debating methods of retaliation. Those present were headed by Fleet Admiral Ernest King, commander-in-chief of the US Navy, joined by General George C. Marshall, chief of staff of the US Army and Lieutenant-General Henry H. Arnold, chief of the US Army Air Corps. Any action would have to be a cooperative one between the navy and army, although at first it was unclear what was possible. No aircraft carrier active at the time could get near enough to the Japanese islands to make an effective strike and there was no land base in suitable proximity.

Admiral King's personal staff officer, Captain Francis Low, was present at the meeting. Low was a former submariner, not an obvious source of a solution to the problem. However, days after the meeting he was visiting Norfolk navy yard to check on the status of USS *Hornet*'s sea trials when, passing by the nearby naval air station, he saw US Army bombers making landing approaches on a runway marked out like an aircraft carrier. This gave Low the idea of using twin-engined bombers from an aircraft carrier, if an aircraft type, an aircraft carrier and crews could be brought together to do the job. He took his idea to Admiral King.

Admiral Ernest King had the reputation of being a 'hard old salt' who did not suffer fools gladly, but while he thought Captain Low's idea was a 'hare-brained' scheme, he was an aviator himself and called in Captain Donald Duncan, his air adviser, to investigate its feasibility. Duncan was convinced it could work, so Admiral King took it to General Henry H. Arnold, Commander-in-Chief of the Army Air Corps. General Arnold gave his endorsement and together they took it to the next meeting of the Chiefs of Staff. The Chiefs approved, subject to Lieutenant-Colonel James H. Doolittle's confirmation that the venture was operationally valid. Doolittle's response was 'Give me the equipment and I'll do the job'.

The USS *Hornet* (CV-8), photographed in its sea trials paint finish, before the zig-zag dual tone camouflage finish was applied.

PREPARING FOR A SECRET MISSION

It was nearly two weeks after the attack on Pearl Harbor when Jimmy Doolittle set about finding aircraft for his task; as far as he was concerned there were only three candidates: the Douglas B-23, the Martin B-26 and the North American B-25. The first pre-requisite for any bomber to be used from an aircraft carrier was good visibility from the pilot's seat, so the pilot could see the flagman at the bow end of the flight deck, who would give the cue for take off. This meant that only aircraft with tricycle undercarriages could be considered, which immediately discounted the Douglas B-23, already an outdated design, despite having only been introduced into service in 1936. The B-23 was a twin-engined bomber and was large and reliable, but with a 92-foot wingspan, was also likely to be too big and possibly too slow for the task in hand.

The Martin B-26 had just entered production, and was a much faster aircraft with a smaller wingspan of 71 feet, but it had a higher take-off speed and longer take-off run than the B-23. The B-26 was a type with which Jimmy Doolittle was already familiar, having had the task of evaluating it for production barely a year before. He wanted to give this type a second chance, because it was the fastest of the three aircraft under consideration, and it was spacious, allowing for the accommodation of extra fuel for the long flight to Japan from the *Hornet* and the longer onward flight to China. However, it had a high take-off speed. He calculated whether or not this speed would allow the aircraft to get off the ground in less than 500 feet, the likely space available on a crowded carrier. He concluded that it might stand a chance with a lot of preparatory work, but then having investigated the position of the centreline of the fuselage on the centreline of the flight deck of the *Hornet*, decided there wasn't enough safe clearance between the wingtip of the B-26 and the ship's tower. He was confident that he could miss the tower, but he wasn't confident that a young, recently trained pilot would. The B-26 was off the list.

The B-25, then, became Doolittle's sole choice of aircraft. Its 67-foot 6-inch wingspan was marginally less than the B-26 and it was significantly lighter, so stood a much better chance of getting off a carrier deck inside the requisite 500 feet. However,

The Douglas B-23 was much larger that the B-25 or B-26, and with a performance envelope that did not come near to Jimmy Doolittle's needs for the raid.

while Doolittle thought he only had three aircraft to choose from, the US Army Air Corps aircraft engineers had recommended a different aircraft altogether, the Douglas A20 'Havoc', which had been in squadron service for about a year. Like the B-25, it was powered by two Wright Cyclone 1650 engines, but it had a nominal maximum speed of 40mph more than the B-25, so could give Japanese fighters a real run for their money; the Mitsubishi 'Zero' fighter had a maximum speed of barely 350mph, against the A-20's 339mph.

As far as the engineering team was concerned, the A-20 was a better bet than the B-25, firstly because it was a lighter machine – they thought it would get off an aircraft carrier more easily than the B-25, despite its lesser wing area – and it was physically smaller than the B-25, so it would be easier to park 16 or more of them on the flight deck of the *Hornet*, which had been confirmed as the carrier for the mission. Its standing height on its landing gear was the same as the B-25, at 17 feet 7 inches, its wingspan was less at 61 feet, and its weight for the same bomb load was 27,600lbs versus the B-25 at 44,000lbs.

Having looked at the A-20, Jimmy Doolittle may have been tempted. He almost certainly could have coaxed an A-20 into the air inside that golden 500 feet with greater ease, carrying 2000lbs of bombs and enough fuel to get to Tokyo and on to China, and because of the lower take-off weight, the A-20 would probably have been able to get to China on less fuel. But the A-20 was designed as a short-haul bomber, whereas the B-25 was a medium range bomber. Crew numbers were the final key to Doolittle's choice. Recognising that the aircraft selected was going to have to fly at least 1800 miles from its carrier take-off position, that was going to take a lot of hours and the A-20 had a crew of only three. Using the B-25 would mean that there would be both a pilot and co-pilot on board to share the long hours of flying, and so the A-20 was dismissed.

Before confirming the selection of the B-25, Doolittle had to test it. It was decided to crane-load a couple of B-25s on the USS *Hornet*, as it ran its early acceptance sea trials in the western Atlantic. Both aircraft took off from the *Hornet* without incident, but

The Douglas A-20 had the same engines and bomb-load as the B-25, and was more than 16,000lbs lighter, but was not used for the Doolittle Raid as it had room for only one pilot.

The North American B-25B medium bomber selected for the Doolittle Raid.

they were not laden and had the full length of the deck for their take-off run. Doolittle's concern was whether a B-25 laden with bombs could take off successfully when it would have less than the length of the full flight deck to do so, as he was planning to use sixteen aircraft, each carrying 2000lbs of bombs (four 500lb bombs) and double the normal fuel load. He would have to get the best pilots for the job.

An additional benefit was that the B-25 had quite recently entered squadron service and so an operational unit could be used as the source of equipment and possibly of men. The aircraft were sourced from the 17th Bombardment Group, which consisted of the 34th Bomb Squadron, the 37th Bomb Squadron, the 89th Reconnaissance Squadron and the 95th Bomb Squadron. The 17th was based at Pendleton Field in Oregon, having moved up from March Field in California after re-equipment to the B-25 from the Douglas B-23. Doolittle now took a trip up to Pendleton Field and announced that he wanted 24 aircraft and crews to go 'on a special mission, the details of which he could not yet announce, except that it was a highly dangerous mission and there could be no guarantee that any volunteer would come home'. To a man, they stepped forward; 60 years later, one was asked by this author why he volunteered for such a dangerous mission: 'Why wouldn't we? This was Jimmy Doolittle, America's greatest aviator!' Doolittle's next task for was to inspect the service records of all the aircraft to choose the best machines. The aim was to take as near as possible six aircraft from each of the squadrons, to get an even balance and a good level of friendly rivalry, but not at the cost of expertise.

The next step was moving 24 aircraft and their crews to Owens Field at Columbia Army Air Base in South Carolina – now Columbia Downtown Airport – a B-25 aircrew training base. Aircraft often used to fly over the nearby Lake Murray and bomb an island on the lake, still known today as 'Bomb Island'. Columbia was where some of the aircraft modifications would take place, as well as crew training and work-up to the mission. The development and modification plan was given the cover name of the 'First Aviation Project' and the modifications carried out were somewhat adventurous. The aircraft were going to be required to fly 400 miles from their aircraft carrier launch to their Japanese targets, then on another 1000–1200 miles to an airfield in Chuchow in China. Therefore their range had to be 1600–1800 miles, carrying 2000lbs of bombs and approximately 600 extra gallons of fuel, so the fuel tankage on board was to be 1240 gallons as opposed to 694 gallons in the standard airframe.

To facilitate take-off in a short distance, all the B-25's armour plating was removed, then the remote-controlled under-belly gun turret was replaced with a 50-gallon additional fuel tank. A further tank was put in the forward bomb bay, while a collapsible fuel cell was put on top of the bomb bay. The cell was developed by the Goodyear Tire and Rubber Company at Doolittle's request; Doolittle reasoned that the Goodyear Blimp airship was covered in a fuel-proof fabric, so why couldn't a fuel tank be made from the same material? The Goodyear cell meant that another 160 gallons of fuel could be carried.

Painted broomstick handles were fitted to the tail of the aircraft as dummy guns to replace the standard .50 calibre machine guns, to deter Japanese fighters from launching a tail-on attack. The reduced armament meant that crew numbers could be five rather than seven, thus further reducing the weight and limiting the number of

A collapsible fuel cell was placed in the crawl space between the flight deck and the rear crew compartment, and in addition these metal fuel tanks were specially created to sit in the forward bomb bays of the Doolittle B-25s.

The top-secret Norden bombsight fitted as standard to the B-25.

PREPARING FOR A SECRET MISSION

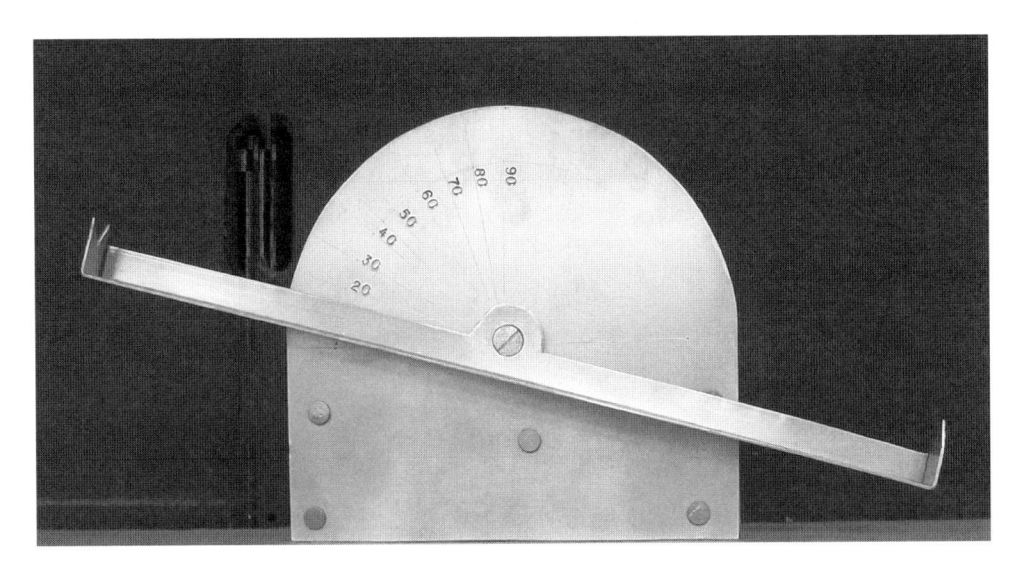

The 'Mark Twain' bombsight, made from 20 cents-worth of scrap alloy which saved 80lbs in weight.

lives at risk. As the raid was to be at low level, the top-secret Norden bombsight was removed and replaced with a simple post-and-notch sight made from a few pieces of metal and named the 'Mark Twain' bombsight, costing just 20 cents to manufacture. It was designed by Captain Ross Greening, the pilot of Aircraft Number 11.

After completion of the modification programme, the crews moved Eglin Army Air Field in Florida (still in use by USAF today) where training began in earnest. Eglin was chosen because the weather was better and because of the proximity of the Gulf of Mexico, unseen by inquisitive onlookers, of which more later. First the pilots and co-pilots had to come to grips with getting a laden B-25 off the ground, firstly inside a distance of 750 feet, then later of 500 feet. It was asking a great deal from the aircraft, let alone the crews, but in three weeks they had it working under the guidance of Navy Lieutenant Henry L. Miller. Miller's task was to teach them the basic principles of operating aircraft on a carrier. Apart from the issues of taking off in a short distance, they had to be taught the problems of deck pitch and possible roll, and the absolute necessity of watching and following the instructions of the flagman at the front of the deck, as he would know the best time to start the take-off roll, taking into account the movement of the carrier's deck. They would have to put their total confidence in the man whose task it was to get them into the air.

They had also to learn US Navy traditions at sea, so as to fit in with their hosts aboard the *Hornet* and avoid any inter-service conflict. Friendly inter-service rivalry was one thing, but friction was to be avoided at all costs. The airmen were accustomed to living in close quarters as a usual part of military life, but on the *Hornet* their personal space would be very limited; they would be completely thrown in with the US Navy men. It was vital that all personnel were conscious of the fact that this was a truly inter-service operation and that all would receive their share of the credit.

Once the basic take-off demands were satisfied, the next phase of training was flying low over water at a constant speed of 180 knots. The Gulf of Mexico was perfect for this part of the preparation, as there was virtually no air traffic in the region, and the crews could fly without being observed. The men had to become familiar with low-level over-water flying over long distances – one problem encountered in the past

```
ADDRESS REPLY TO
CHIEF OF THE AIR CORPS
   WAR DEPARTMENT
  WASHINGTON, D. C.
```

WAR DEPARTMENT　　　　　　　　　　JHD:mf
HEADQUARTERS OF THE ARMY AIR FORCES
~~OFFICE OF THE CHIEF OF THE AIR CORPS~~
WASHINGTON

June 15, 1942

1st Lieutenant Henry L. Miller
TS-2 Ellyson Field
Naval Air Station
Pensacola, Florida

Dear Henry:

   Thanks for your note of the 20th which, for some reason or other, I have just received.

   No information has been given out, as yet, on our losses, so I will have to ask you to keep the following "confidential": Corporal Factor, who was Gray's Rear Gunner, was killed. He was not hurt in action, but was found dead after the arrival in China. We don't know exactly what happened to him. In addition to Factor, we have four missing, six prisoners (in Japanese occupied China), one badly wounded and five slightly wounded. Thirty-two of the boys are on their way home, and the rest are being used for Combat or Transport Service in the Far East.

   I want to again thank you for the invaluable assistance you gave us during training and until the final take-off.

   With kindest personal regards and the hope that I may have the pleasure of seeing you again soon, I am

　　　　　　　　　　　　　　　As ever,

　　　　　　　　　　　　　　　J. H. DOOLITTLE

Soon after his promotion to Brigadier-General but before his move to North Africa, Jimmy Doolittle wrote this letter of appreciation to Lieutenant Henry Miller, the Navy pilot who trained the Doolittle Raiders to take off from a carrier deck.

was pilots suffering a form of 'snow blindness' and allowing their aircraft to sink below a normal horizon setting, dropping into the water. Doolittle wanted to prevent this, and also needed his crews to become accustomed to flying at a low cruise speed, then advancing the throttles to full power to climb to a safe level to drop their bombs. They would then have to fly out of Japanese air space as fast as possible, potentially have to avoid anti-aircraft fire and Japanese fighters. Dealing with the latter issues was not a part of the training programme; it was assumed that the men had been trained in these areas as part of their basic flight training. Doolittle's main concern was that the crews could get their B-25s off a carrier in 500 feet or less.

While his men did their work-up, Doolittle himself worked to make the B-25s' engines suitable for their mission. His aero-engineering expertise, combined with his vast flying experience, enabled him to set the carburettors on the two 1850hp Wright R2600 Cyclones of each aircraft to give maximum power on full throttle and maximum economy on cruise setting. The reason for these settings was that the aircraft had to cross 400 miles of Pacific Ocean in the approach to Japan and be unseen as far as possible, so the crews would have to maintain a very low altitude. Then, on reaching the target zone, the pilot would press forward on the throttle to maximum power and the aircraft had to lift to 1500 feet rapidly, so he could deposit his ordnance and escape the drop zone quickly, then fly out of Japanese air space as fast as possible. Doolittle personally supervised the modification of the fuel pumps and carburettors to provide the exact power settings required, and once the engines were adjusted to his satisfaction he banned any further changes without his personal approval.

In the middle of March 1942, Doolittle went to Washington to report on progress and to announce that the aircraft and crews would be mission-ready by the end of the month. At the same time he asked General Arnold if he could lead the mission. Arnold initially denied the request, but eventually said that if the Air Corps Chief of Staff, Major-General Millard Harmon, were willing to let him go, then he too would allow it. Doolittle instantly contacted General Harmon and applied a little 'spin' to the story by saying that General Arnold had said that it was okay with him if it was okay with General Harmon. In a phone call from General Arnold, General Harmon was then put in a position of having to say he had given his word to Doolittle; Doolittle had his place on the raid.

By 23 March 1942 the Doolittle squadron had been training at Eglin for only 20 days to prepare them for a mission they knew nothing about. That morning Jimmy Doolittle received a signal from General Arnold: 'Get on your horse!' He gathered the crews of the 17th Bombardment Wing and addressed them:

> Today's the day we move out. I'm going to tell you one more time what I've been harping on since we came to Eglin. Do not tell anyone what we were doing down here. Even if you think you've guessed what our mission is, just keep in mind that the lives of your buddies depend on your not breathing a word about this to another soul.

He then dismissed all but the 22 crews who were to move out (two of the original 24 aircraft had been damaged in training). The crews were instructed to fly their B-25s to McClellan Field, near Sacramento in California on the following morning, the first plane going off at 1100hrs. Once at McClellan the aircraft would be checked to ensure they were in the best possible flying condition in terms of their airframes, instruments, flying controls, glazing, hatch operations and undercarriage. The flight route was from Eglin to Kelly Field, near San Antonio in Texas. The next leg was to March Field in southern California and finally to McClellan. There was a bit of low flying and high spirits in that trans-continental run, but they all arrived intact and pretty much on time.

Doolittle Raider B-25 40-2297 being flown by Major John Hilger, over Texas en route to McLellan Field in California.

Jimmy Doolittle had taken off before the main group, refuelling at Kelly Field and then flying on instruments to McClellan directly over the Rockies. McClellan Field was a maintenance base and the intention was that all the aircraft would go through a final major sequence of checks and such repair work as might be found necessary, ready for the next stage of their mission, loading onto the aircraft carrier CV-8 USS *Hornet*, though of course the men did not know this was the plan.

On arrival at McClellan Field on 25 March, the B-25s were checked in for their major maintenance check. Doolittle had been assured that the maintenance centre at McClellan had been briefed that his B-25s would be arriving and were to be given priority over any other maintenance or refurbishment task. However, when the Doolittle aircraft arrived they were told they would have to wait for two weeks because of the backlog of work. The officer commanding McClellan Field told Doolittle that he had not been notified of the arrival of the B-25s and because most of the technicians working at McClellan were civilians, it would be difficult to persuade them to work the extra hours needed, as they were not subject to the same discipline as enlisted men. Having met the depot commander, Doolittle also learned that not all the materials necessary were available. The plexiglass navigational windows were to have been replaced with glass ones, as well as the fitment of new hydraulic valves to the gun turrets and the replacement of the propellers of all the aircraft. The collapsible rubber fuel cells had still to be installed and set against all this, there was a ship to catch.

Even once the work began there were problems. During the fitting of the propellers, Ted Lawson, pilot of *Ruptured Duck*, noted that when his propellers had been replaced, the crew had run up the engines so fast that the tips were picking up grit and suffering damage. Then, to add insult to injury, they sanded down the abrasions on the blade tips dry which, as Lawson observed, would make the tips go soft when exposed to salt water, so he told them to apply a film of oil. He would have had further replacement propellers fitted, but there were none available.

Jimmy Doolittle was furious that he could not persuade the workers or the depot commander of the urgency of getting his aircraft ready for flight quickly. Finally, an appeal to 'Hap' Arnold achieved the desired result, though not before at least one aircraft's engines had been tampered with, contrary to strict instructions. Doolittle had actually walked into the maintenance hangar as a technician was adjusting the mixture settings of the engines of Aircraft Number 8, captained by Captain Edward York. But there was no time to rectify the actions of the technician who had set the fuel mixture at Wright engine manual settings. This adjustment meant that York would be forced to divert to Vladivostok after the raid, as he ran dangerously low on fuel.

In the end it was even difficult to gain the release of the B-25s, because not all the scheduled work had been completed. But it was managed, largely thanks to the efforts of Major Jack Hilger, and they were flown from McClellan Field to NAS Alameda, where they would be craned aboard the waiting *Hornet*. In the 90 days since the Pentagon had commissioned the raid, to the men's departure for Alameda, the crews had trained for just six weeks.

There is a story that some of these aircraft, most probably four, were diverted to a little-known private airport called Willows Municipal Airport, in Glenn County, in northern California. The reason these aircraft went there, if indeed they did, was that they needed a little extra work and assurance that they could get off a deck in 500 feet. Why Willows? The owner of the time was a long-standing friend of Jimmy Doolittle, named Floyd 'Speed' Nolta. These two had befriended each other from their days in the Army Signal Corps at Rockwell Field back in 1918. And access from McClellan Field was quick and easy.

The problem was that some of the aircraft had been 'fiddled with' by the technicians at McClellan – even though Doolittle had ordered that all they were allowed to do was replace the spark plugs and check the integrity of the plug leads – and work on others had not been post-completion tested. It is believed that four aircraft found their way to Willows to be checked out technically, then take-off tested again to ensure they would be able to get off the deck of the *Hornet* in 500 feet. The story goes that the airfield was closed off for the time the B-25s were there. While there is no formal documentation to confirm their presence, a few residents of the area around Willows recall heavy aircraft engines being heard run up under high power settings and one lady, who worked for Nolta Air Service, was prohibited from leaving her office in the hangar one day while aircraft engines were being run up. She was only allowed to leave after the aircraft she heard had gone.

Of the aircraft that might have visited Willows, Ted Lawson's *Ruptured Duck* was one, for he had propeller problems and he notes in *Thirty Seconds Over Tokyo* – his record of the Doolittle Raid published in 1943 – that 'We spent a few more days in that area, practicing full-flap take-offs at small, almost deserted, airfields.' The eighth aircraft off the deck of the *Hornet* was Captain Ted 'Ski' York's machine, which had been tampered with by the McClellan technicians, who had changed the Doolittle selected carburettor jets for standard ones, thus undoing all the tuning work which had been carried out at Eglin in Florida. So, after whatever 'rescue' work was carried out on this aircraft's engines, it would certainly have needed testing again and so is a strong candidate for a visit to Willows.

The one man who came closest to confirming the diversion of aircraft to Willows was retired Rear Admiral Henry L. Miller who, as a Navy Lieutenant was attached to the Doolittle Raiders for the duration of their operation, even sailing on the *Hornet* with them. Miller's primary task was to work in the training programme for pilots to take off inside 500 feet, teaching them carrier take-off techniques. He also had to prepare

A Goodyear Blimp hovers over the *Hornet* a couple of days out to sea to deliver aircraft parts for the B-25s and a last mail delivery for the ship and aircraft crews.

PREPARING FOR A SECRET MISSION

the US Army personnel for sailing on an aircraft carrier. Miller recalled he accompanied aircraft to Willows for final take-off practices.

On 31 March, most of the crews flew their aircraft from McClellan Field and headed for Alameda Naval Air Station. On the approach, one of the B-25s decided to do a photo-shoot flying under the Bay Bridge. Initially, Ted Lawson's co-pilot Dean Davenport had suggested flying under the bridge 'because it was there', and as a 'hello and goodbye' to San Francisco. Davenport had control at that moment and Lawson decided it would be amusing. However, once they had got past the point of no return, it occurred to Davenport that there might be cables suspended under the bridge. In the event there were no obstacles. However, the navigator, Lieutenant Charles Mclure, was a keen cameraman and had brought with him his camera and a cassette of colour film. He wanted to film the flight but his camera had jammed, so he asked Ted Lawson to do the run again. It takes no imagination to imagine the reply.

The Doolittle Raiders' B-25s eventually arrived at Alameda, from where they were crane loaded onto the USS *Hornet*, moored on Pier 2. Only 16 aircraft were loaded, although all the crew members embarked in case back-ups were needed. Then the US Navy crewmen swarmed over the B-25s to lash them down to the flight deck ready for a journey to an unknown location.

Taken in 1945, this photograph clearly shows the wide runway of Stockton Field in California, designed to allow up to four aircraft to take off at one time without risk of contact so long as the pilots did so within the marked lines.

4

The Doolittle Raid

On 2 April 1942, the USS *Hornet* set sail on her maiden voyage as part of Task Force 16-2, a flotilla of eight ships. As they sailed under the Golden Gate Bridge, Captain Marc Mitscher, captain of the *Hornet*, announced to those on board that their destination was Tokyo. The response was an immediate unanimous cheer. However, Mitscher's announcement was not quite accurate; the bombers were to target several cities: Tokyo, Kobe, Yokohama, Yokosuka and Nagoya. These details were not revealed to the B-25 crews until they were well out to sea.

Task Force 16's flagship was the USS *Enterprise*, another aircraft carrier and sister ship to the *Hornet*, leading another group of eight ships – Task Force 16-1. On board was Vice-Admiral William 'Bull' Halsey, the overall Task Force Commander. The rest of the task force was made up of three heavy cruisers and one light cruiser, eight destroyers and two tankers to provide fuel for the round trip. The last two vessels of the 16-ship flotilla was a pair of submarines to patrol well ahead of the main flotilla to search for Japanese warships, so as to avoid the risk of their contact with the main force and potential scuttling of the mission. The two groups rendezvoused on 13 April, north of Midway Island, leaving as the single Task Force 16 heading for a point 400 miles from the Japanese island of Honshu, the site of Tokyo.

Task Force 16

Heavy Cruisers
USS *Salt Lake City* CA-25
USS *Northampton* CA-26
USS *Vincennes* CA-44

Light Cruisers
USS *Nashville* CL-43

Destroyers
USS *Baich* DD-363
USS *Fanning* DD-385
USS *Benham* DD397
USS *Ellet* DD-398

USS *Gwin* DD-433
USS *Meredith* DD-434
USS *Grayson* DD-435
USS *Monssen* DD-436

Fuel Tankers
USS *Sabine* AO-25
USS *Cimarron* AO-22

Submarines
USS *Thresher* SS-200
USS *Trout* SS-202

THE DOOLITTLE RAID

On board the *Hornet*, the air and ground crews of Doolittle's 16-aircraft squadron went through rigorous training and maintenance programmes, doing engine run-ups carrying out airframe checks and keeping the aircraft free from salt. There were water-protective coverings over the engines when they were not running, waterproof skirts around the landing gears and all hatches were closed and sealed, but even so the water got into most of the aircraft. The men also had to learn to work on a rolling vessel, especially difficult as the *Hornet* was a carrier: there were no guard rails to grab on to as they worked on the open deck.

Apart from this, there were various chores that Lieutenant-Colonel Doolittle devised to keep his ground crews occupied; he was not one to give them obviously pointless tasks, but he knew the importance of making them feel that they were doing vital work for their country and for Doolittle himself. The friendly rivalry Doolittle had built into

Doolittle's B-25s on the deck of the USS *Hornet*. The engine cowlings were covered to keep out salt when not running, and the ground crews did engine run-ups every day to ensure the aircraft were constantly serviceable.

Lieutenant-Colonel Jimmy Doolittle ties a Japanese medal to the tail of a 500lb bomb – to 'return with interest'.

the composition of the unit by selecting members from all four squadrons of the 17th Bombardment Group had turned into an intense loyalty towards him and his purpose.

On Wednesday 15 April, three days before the momentous take-off, a display was put on for the US Navy newsreel men, and Captain Mitscher and Lieutenant-Colonel Doolittle organised an array of the bombs each B-25 was to carry to its target to be displayed. Many Navy personnel at Pearl Harbor had handed in the Japanese medals they had received before the war, and several were tied to the bombs for the cameramen to capture on film. Mitscher then turned to the watching crews and said: 'Boys, return these medals with interest! Good hunting.'

Later in the day, after the cameramen had gone, Doolittle assembled the whole US Army Air Force contingent on the flight deck, adjacent to their aircraft, and read to them good luck messages from General Marshall, their Chief of Staff, General Arnold, Commander of the Army Air Force and Admiral King. Captain Ted Lawson recalled that it was a strange feeling to realise that so many high-ranking people back in Washington were rooting for them. He wrote that the enormity of the plan was too stunning to contemplate.

The original plan was to take off at around 400 miles from Honshu on the evening of Sunday 19 April. During an engine run-up on the 16th, one aircraft engine wrecked a blower, but the Navy carpenters quickly made a trestle platform to enable technicians to get up to the engine. They removed the engine, took it below decks, fixed it and had it back on its airframe in a couple of hours. This was the quality of inter-service co-operation that now existed between Army and Navy.

The crews were becoming edgy, so Doolittle had to devise more tedious but 'essential' tasks to keep them occupied. Navigation tests were run to ensure each pilot and navigator knew where his target was, how to reach it and how to escape from Japanese air space by the shortest and safest route. Each pilot was given a choice of one of the five target cities, but it was made very plain that no-one flying over Tokyo was to go near the Imperial Palace. That was to be avoided at all costs, though Yokosuka had been deliberately selected because of the location of the Imperial Naval College there. For the Americans, this was the equivalent of Annapolis, so the target was considered significant. Other targets selected were oil terminals, gasworks and factories. Each crew selected a number of targets, so that each of their 500lb bombs would make its mark. At least one of the bombs carried by every aircraft was an incendiary bomb, designed to cause maximum disruption on the ground by setting fires and divert attention from the explosive bombs disabling significant targets.

Between 16 and 17 April, the ground crews were busied with re-arranging the B25s on the *Hornet*'s flight deck to give maximum possible free distance at the front end of the deck. The aircraft right at the back had their rear fuselages and tailplanes hanging over the fantail of the carrier. Everything was now ready. Aircraft guns were armed up, bombs were winched aboard their planes, fuel levels were topped up and every machine was ready for the call to action. Doolittle gave one last briefing, in which he instructed Army crews to ensure they had nothing with them to connect them to the Navy, as the Task Force would be in danger for some time after they had left. He also instructed crews to use the loose cans of fuel each aircraft had on board as soon as possible, and to keep all fuel cans on board until the last was used and ditch them together. This would also help to prevent the Japanese tracing them back to Task Force 16.

On the 17th, as it happened only hours before take-off, Jimmy Doolittle called his crews together again and offered them the opportunity to withdraw if they felt uncomfortable about undertaking the mission. One individual did stand down and was replaced from the reserve crews brought along. Task Force 16 was about 1000 miles from Japan; the ships were refuelled by the tankers, who then turned for home. The carriers and their companion cruisers increased speed to 28 knots and made for the planned take-off position. Radar operators aboard the *Enterprise* spotted two small ships ahead, and fearing they might be Japanese and not wanting to make any kind of contact, Halsey had the ships take a starboard course to avoid the unknown vessels. As day dawned, a scout plane took off from the *Enterprise* to survey the scene.

Just before 0600hrs, the scout plane spotted what the observer was convinced was a Japanese patrol boat. They dropped a message back to *Enterprise* and the smaller task force continued on its way. A little after 0735hrs, lookouts aboard *Hornet* saw the Japanese boat;

Jimmy Doolittle taking off from the deck of the *Hornet*.

it was Patrol Boat 23, the *Nitto Maru*. USS *Nashville* opened fire and several shells later the boat went down, but not before getting a signal to Tokyo warning of the impending approach of an enemy task force. It has been said that the *Nitto Maru* would have gone down easier if the *Nashville* had simply rammed her. Now, all hell broke loose.

The Doolittle Raiders were still 600 miles from Japan and over 200 miles from their intended take-off distance. Admiral Halsey had a message flashed to Captain Mitscher instructing the bombers to take off. Army ground crews were still finishing loading fuel into the B-25s and the ship had to be turned into wind for take-off. Some of the Raiders were not pleased at being 'dumped' by the Navy, but Halsey had to take his flotilla out of harm's way, as there were Japanese ships and aircraft alerted to find Task Force 16. Aircrews were scrambled and Doolittle announced that they would now have to fly a further 200 miles than planned. With that, Jimmy Doolittle himself was first off the *Hornet*'s deck in 467 feet.

There was one mishap during the preparations for take-off. In the heavy weather the men were finding it difficult to even stand on deck, let alone move about. The last aircraft to take off – Lieutenant Bill Farrow's *Bat Out Of Hell* – was hanging over the fantail and it was difficult to get to the rear of the aircraft, so the deck handlers moved it forward on the rolling deck. As the aircraft in front was running up its engines, one of the seamen who had been helping manoeuvre the aircraft stepped aside, lost his footing and slipped into the path of the rotating propeller. The propeller scythed into Seaman Robert Wall's shoulder and severed his left arm as Bill Farrow sat in his cockpit and watched, powerless to do anything to prevent it. This was the only injury suffered before the B-25s left for their targets.

The weather was atrocious; the longitudinal pitch of the carrier, which had been turned into wind, was as much as 30 feet and the flagman at the front of the deck was lashed down to prevent him from being swept overboard. As Doolittle's aircraft lifted off it seemed to disappear, for he had taken off on the fall of the deck and as it rose again, he was out of sight. Some thought he had gone into the water, but as the deck went down again, there he was climbing out to do a circuit of the *Hornet*. It took another hour to get the rest of the sixteen planes off the deck, on the start of their momentous journey to repay the attack on Pearl Harbor.

When all sixteen B-25s were airborne, they were stretched out in a straggling line of about 150 miles, flying below 400 feet above sea level, maintaining the most economical speed of around 180 knots. No attempt was made to close into any kind of formation, for Doolittle had told each pilot that they were to seek out their own predetermined targets

THE DOOLITTLE RAID

and make for them as solo raiders. This would minimise the risk of groups of aircraft being shot down together, for nobody knew what kind of air defences would meet them. Nine aircraft would strike targets in Tokyo: three to the northern sector of the city, three to the central area and three to the south. Four aircraft would each strike a target in Yokohama and Yokosuka, the Yokosuka targets including the Naval Academy and the naval shipyard. The final three would strike selected targets in Nagoya and Kobe.

Once the last aircraft was off the deck of the *Hornet*, the five ships turned back to rejoin the rest of the task force and withdraw to Pearl Harbor. It was no longer safe to remain in waters so close to Japan. However, just as US officers had misjudged the signals leading up to the Japanese attack on Pearl Harbor, so the Japanese were now making similar errors as Doolittle's squadron of B-25s approached their shores. The first oversight came at 0945hrs, when a Japanese patrol aircraft spotted a twin-engined unidentified land-plane flying on a course towards Japan, several hundred miles offshore. It was Jimmy Doolittle's B-25. Japanese intelligence ignored the report as being of no significance. Japanese radio intercepts had also picked up radio signals between the *Enterprise* and *Hornet* long before they were in any position to be a threat, but the intelligence was similarly ignored, taking the view that any attacker would have to be within 200 miles of Japanese shores to get an air strike force off a carrier and inflict damage, then return to their ships. They had no idea that the aircraft on the *Hornet* were twin-engined bombers with a range of around 2000 miles; the Japanese assumed that they could take their time to prepare their defences.

A Japanese radar operator saw a series of unidentified dots on his screen as the Doolittle Raiders approached. Just like the US Army radar operator at Opama in Hawaii back in December, he reported the sighting to his immediate supervising officer. The officer passed it 'upstairs', where it was considered insignificant. The Japanese knew that there was a group of American ships heading towards them, but believed that no carrier-borne aircraft could be usefully operational at a distance of greater than 250 miles, as most single-engined aircraft had a range of approximately 500 miles.

As these observations were being ignored, B-25 40-2344, the first aircraft off the Hornet and piloted by Jimmy Doolittle, was approaching the Japanese coastline. It was around noon. The plan was for all 16 aircraft to drop their bombs and then head for the designated landing area, four small airfields around Chuchow, approximately 100 miles south of Shanghai and another 100 miles inland. It had been arranged for a radio beacon to be located at Chuchow main airfield to guide the B25s in once they crossed the Chinese coastline (Chuchow is today Quzhou City in Zhejiang Province). As we shall see, while the Raiders did make it to China, none landed at an airfield at all, let alone Chuchow. This was partly because the radio beacon never got there. The C-46 that was transporting it was shot down by the Japanese en route, and because the operation was shrouded in such secrecy, nobody was told. Nobody, that is, until Jimmy

Doolittle Raiders on their way to Japan. Note how low they were flying, partly to conserve fuel and partly to avoid detection. This loose formation of four aircraft soon split up as they approached enemy air space.

Target Yokosuka, bombed by the Doolittle Raiders on 18 April 1942.

Doolittle was radioed that the beacon was not there and that he and his crews were on their own. At least eight of the B-25s could have made the airfields had the beacon been there, as they flew further than Chuchow before crash-landing, while the remainder would not have made it due to lack of fuel. We shall now consider the actions of each of the 16 aircraft that took off from the Hornet. The fates of the crewmen after landing in China will be considered in greater detail in the next chapter.

Jimmy Doolittle crossed the coast about 80 miles to the northeast of Tokyo, then turned in towards his target. He decided to fly as low as he could to avoid radar and possibly detection from the air, because fighters would probably not be looking down for attackers. His hunch was right, for as he approached the city, he saw nine Japanese fighter aircraft about 1000 feet above him; he passed under them unnoticed. He flew over the Imperial Palace and found the complex of factories that was to be his target, the first direct attack on Japan in 700 years.

Doolittle took his B-25 to 1200 feet and aimed for the first bomb drop location. His bombardier, Lieutenant Fred Braemer, set up his 'Mark Twain' bomb sight, checked his map for accurate navigation points, returned to the bomb sight and pinpointed his target. Bomb doors opened and at 1230hrs, four 'pings' were heard as four incendiary bombs left the bomb bay. Seconds later, the factory was ablaze and Doolittle had to get out of reach. Anti-aircraft fire began to burst around the aircraft and Doolittle went back down to the rooftops and flew over the western district of Tokyo, then south and out to sea. The first of sixteen aircraft had reached its target, struck and flown out of Japanese airspace. By 2130hrs fuel was low and unable to find an airfield in the heavy fog, Doolittle ordered his crew to bail out in the mountains of China. He then followed them into the night, his B-25 crashing on a nearby mountainside in Haotianguan, where, today, Zhejiang Province meets Anhui Province. Doolittle stayed overnight in a water-powered trip-hammer in a paddy field until he was found by several young students, and was escorted to the Western Zhejiang Administration. There, he was joined by his crewmen who had been brought by Zhu Xuesan, a primary school teacher who spoke some English, and other villagers including a man named Zhang Gengrong. The only injury sustained by any of the Doolittle crew was a sprained ankle. Local Chinese people took them to Chungking from where they were eventually returned to friendly territory.

The second aircraft to take off from the *Hornet* was B-25 40-2292 captained by Lieutenant Travis Hoover, lifting off five minutes after Doolittle. His B-25 followed Doolittle's until it reached the shoreline, at which time Hoover veered off to bomb his own targets, two factory buildings and storehouses from a height of only 900 feet. He then trailed Doolittle most of the way to China where he managed to make a wheels-up crash-landing in a soft rice paddy near the port city of Ningbo, Zhejiang Province, which was then an area occupied by the Japanese Army. The crew set fire to the plane before evacuating westward with what they might need from the plane, staying overnight in a valley. Like Jimmy Doolittle's crew, they were also picked up by Chinese guerrillas and escorted to the Western Zhejiang Administration, although not before they had wandered around for three days. On 22 April they went by boat to Sungyao, then travelled by train and by foot to arrive in Chungking on 14 May.

Third off the deck was B-25 40-2270 nicknamed *Whiskey Pete*, from the 95th Squadron, captained by Lieutenant Robert M. Gray. He flew his B-25 through anti-aircraft fire to drop his bombs on industrial areas of Tokyo and strafe a military barracks before flying on to China. He failed to make out the Chinese coastline in the rainy night and it wasn't until he saw some lights through the cloud that he knew he had reached China. He dropped two candle bombs, hoping to find a place for landing, without success, so he ordered the crew to bail out at about 10.00pm, as the fuel was running out. The bomber was then flying over a mountainous area near Suicang County of Zhejiang province. They landed in a hillside and he and his bombardier, Sergeant A.E. Jones, were found and escorted by local farmers to Quzhou (Chuchow) the next morning. Co-pilot Lieutenant Jacob E. Manch landed on a hillside, while Lieutenant Manch went to sleep with the parachute as his quilt, rather than risk walking around in the darkness. At daybreak he

The deck of the USS *Hornet*, with aircraft on it, looking rearwards.

Lieutenant Ted Lawson flew B-25 40-2261 *Ruptured Duck* out of his target area successfully and headed for China.

walked down to a village at the foot of the hill and met a local farmer, who escorted him to Quzhou. Navigator-gunner Lieutenant Charles J. Ozuk's parachute was caught in a tree, and was only rescued the next by a local farmer named Liu Fang Qiao, who carried him to Quzhou. Corporal Leland Faktor died as he fell to the ground without a parachute, when his harness fouled on the escape hatch as he was bailing out.

The fourth aircraft off the *Hornet* was 95th Squadron's B-25 40-2282, piloted by Lieutenant Everett Holstrom. Once over Tokyo Holstrom learned that his aircraft's gun turret, mounted on top of the rear fuselage, had stopped rotating, so his gunner Corporal Bert Jordan had no firepower. Then he was surrounded by a squadron of Kawanishi 'Oscar' fighters, so he ordered the bombardier, Sergeant Robert Stephens, to dump the bombs in Tokyo Bay, and they made a run for it. The 'Oscar' was at that time a good high-speed lightweight single-engined fighter, but the B-25 was remarkably manoeuvrable for a twin-engined bomber. Despite him being greatly outnumbered, Holstrom's flying skills combined with the B-25's performance enabled him to fly south and out to sea with only minimal damage to the tail of his aircraft. The crew bailed out over China just as their fuel ran out.

95th Squadron's B-25 40-2283 was the fifth off the deck of *Hornet*, piloted by Captain David M. Jones. Captain Jones took off safely, despite a leak in the bomb bay fuel tank, and proceeded to Tokyo to score direct hits on a power station, oil tanks and a large manufacturing plant. Continuing on to China, he flew on instruments until he estimated he was in the vicinity of Chuhsien. His entire crew bailed out without injury and were the first of the raiders to reach Chuhsien.

95th Squadron's B-25 40-2298 *Green Hornet* took off sixth, captained by Lieutenant Dean Hallmark. Hallmark dropped his bombs on a steel mill north of Tokyo but no damage assessment could be made until after the war when Chase Nielsen was repatriated. The aircraft's fuel ran out and had to be crashed in the ocean. Sergeant Dieter and Corporal Fitzmaurice were drowned and Lieutenant Hallmark was slightly injured, but he swam to shore to meet up with the other two survivors, Lieutenants Meder and Nielsen. All three men were captured and interned as PoWs.

The seventh B-25 was 40-2261 *The Ruptured Duck*, also from the 95th Bombardment Squadron, captained by Lieutenant Ted W. Lawson. He and his crew successfully dropped their bombs on industrial factories in downtown Tokyo before racing out of Japanese air space for China. The aircraft eventually crashed on a beach in Sanmen County, Zhejiang Province, seriously injuring Lawson. Local villagers found the crewmen and took them to Haiyou Town for medical treatment.

B-25 40-2242, from the 95th Squadron was eighth to take off, piloted by Captain Edwards 'Ski' York. Captain York's B25 had suffered engine problems prior to the loading of the aircraft on the *Hornet*, and the flight to Japan compounded this. He had confirmed to Colonel Doolittle that on the flight from March Field to Alameda, he had encountered fuel problems and while on board the *Hornet*, he had expressed his fears about not having enough fuel to reach China. Despite heavy fuel consumption by both engines, York continued on course to drop his bombs on their assigned targets. Throughout the run the aircraft was defenceless with a top turret that failed to work. Without enough fuel to reach China, York elected to fly the shorter distance to Russia where he landed at a field near Vladivostok in hopes of refuelling to reach China. Instead, the still neutral Russians confiscated the bomber and interned the crew for thirteen months. The crew returned home in May 1943 after 'escaping' into Persia. The navigator of this aircraft, Lieutenant Nolan Herndon, told the author that he believed, and had evidence to show, that Captain York had been ordered to fly to Russia. Subsequent investigation reveals that Captain York had expressed misgivings about reaching China and so Colonel Doolittle had accepted, but not formally condoned, the likelihood of this aircraft diverting to Russia.

The ninth B-25, 40-2303 *Whirling Dervish* from 34th Squadron, was captained by Lieutenant Harold F. Watson. Lieutenant Watson and his crew bombed the Tokyo Gas and Electric Company on the shore of Tokyo Bay and virtually destroyed it, before flying on to China. Like all the crews before them, Crew Nine arrived in the dark and in heavy rain, so Watson ordered his crew to bail out 100 miles south of Puyong Lake. Watson was the only member of the crew injured, and he was carried to Hengyang in a sedan chair by friendly Chinese. He was hospitalised at Walter Reed Army Hospital in Washington, D.C. until the summer of 1944.

B-25 40-2250 from 89th Squadron was the tenth aircraft off the *Hornet*. Piloted by Lieutenant Richard Joyce, it originally intended to take off from the *Hornet* two days after leaving California to test the bomber's ability to do so safely. The test run was then cancelled and Joyce and crew joined the raid to bomb the Japan Special Steel

A crashed B-25 in China. This photograph was taken from the air by a reconnaissance aircraft.

Company and other targets. Joyce found himself-being pursued by six Oscars as he approached his objective, but managed to shake them off for just long enough to drop his bombs. He had to 'red-line' his engines to generate enough speed in a fast turn to slip away from them, flying at well over 300 miles an hour. Anti-aircraft fire was coming up, and some of it was hitting the Japanese barrage balloons; 40-2250 was the only plane to suffer any major damage over Japan (an 8-inch hole in the fuselage), but continued on to China where the crew safely bailed out. Local Chinese people helped the crew to reach Chuhsien in only four days and the entire crew remained in the region, operating missions well into 1943.

The eleventh B-25 was 40-2249 *Hari-Kari-er*, piloted by Captain C. Ross Greening. Upon reaching Japan, Captain Greening flew over an active enemy air base, and ten minutes later came under attack from four Japanese fighters. The gunner believed he shot down one of the enemy fighters and damaged another before the B-25 reached its targets to bomb a large oil refinery and storage area. The crew also fired on three enemy patrol boats at the mouth of Tokyo Harbour before heading west to China. The crew bailed out 200 miles inland from the coast. Lieutenant Kenneth Reddy the co-pilot, broke his kneecap and suffered a scalp wound and Sergeant Melvin Gardner, the engineer/gunner, sprained both ankles. *Hari-Kari-er* crashed in the mountains between Zhejiang and Anhui provinces and the crew were escorted to Shexian County

A B-25 on engine run-up on the deck of USS *Hornet*.

Lieutenant Bill Farrow from Darlington, South Carolina, was the last pilot off the deck of the USS Hornet, flying B-25 40-2268 *Bat Out of Hell*.

in Anhui Province. When Zeng Jianpei, an interpreter, asked them about their needs, Staff Sergeant William L. Birch, the bombardier, said he wanted a bottle of beer. Beer was extremely rare in China at that time, but to Sergeant Birch's surprise, Mr Zeng found him a bottle of Shanghai beer. Birch later said that the drink was 'the tastiest beer I ever tasted in my life.'

Twelfth off the *Hornet*'s flight deck was 37th Squadron's 40-2278 *Fickle Finger*, captained by Lieutenant Bill Bower. Lieutenant Bower and his crew bombed the Ogura refinery, two factories and a large warehouse alongside the docks at Yokohama. This was despite two enemy fighters trailing them inland, and a series of barrage balloons over their target. On the way to China they flew over a Japanese weather boat. They strafed and sank it before flying on to bail out. Sergeant Duquette broke his foot as he parachuted to the ground and was taken in a sedan carried by local Chinese as the entire crew travelled to join up with Lieutenant Joyce's crew from B-25 40-2250. Both crews reached Chuhsien four days later.

Jimmy Doolittle and Major John Hilger receive the Order of Yung Hui from Madame Chiang.

Jimmy Doolittle is promoted to Brigadier-General and awarded the Medal of Honor by President Franklin Delano Roosevelt.

B-25 40-2247 *The Avenger* from 37th Squadron was thirteenth off the deck, piloted by Lieutenant Edgar McElroy. *The Avenger* attacked the Yokosuka naval base to bomb enemy shipping and supplies. One Japanese ship took a direct hit and was seen to fall over on its side, and a second was sheathed in flames. McElroy also attacked the Imperial Japanese Naval Academy, then continued west towards China. The crew successfully bailed out over land and the only injury was a wrenched knee suffered by Sergeant Williams. The crew arrived at Chuhshei three days later thanks to help from local Chinese. The entire crew remained in that theatre of operations to fly missions for more than a year, and all five crew members survived the war despite an enviable record of combat missions.

Aircraft fourteen was B-25 40-2297 from the 89th Reconnaissance Squadron, piloted by Major John A. Hilger. Major Hilger spotted a Japanese patrol plane within hours of takeoff, but the enemy aircraft seemingly never saw the B-25, which continued west without incident to bomb the military barracks at Nagoya Castle and the Mitsubishi aircraft plant, just south of Nagoya. The effectiveness of their aim was evident as the aircraft continued westward. More than 30 miles from one of their targets, they could still see a plume of smoke rising into the sky. The crew safely bailed out of their bomber inside China, and were able to reach Chuhsien within two days.

The fifteenth B-25 off the *Hornet* was B-25 40-2267 *TNT* from 34th Squadron, piloted by Lieutenant Donald Smith. Lieutenant Smith and his crew were assigned to bomb targets in Kobe, south-west of Tokyo. They successfully dropped their bomb load on a large aircraft factory as well as around the dock yards, before flying on towards China. Smith decided to ditch his bomber in the waters near a small island near Sangchow and the whole crew left the aircraft safely before it sank, and paddled to shore in a life raft. For days the Japanese searched for them but the Americans evaded capture in a Chinese boat, thanks to help from the locals. En route to Chuchow, Lieutenant Smith learned of Ted Lawson's serious injuries and so he and his crew travelled on to meet up with him so Lieutenant White (the gunner, Thomas White MD) could render medical aid.

The last aircraft to leave the *Hornet* was from the 89th Squadron, B-25 40-2268 *Bat Out of Hell*, piloted by Lieutenant William Farrow. The plane left the carrier 59 minutes after Doolittle, so faced the prospect of a forewarned Japanese defence system. The ill-fated crew successfully bombed oil storage tanks and an aircraft factory despite enemy fighter attacks, then headed for China. With fuel running very low, Lieutenant Farrow instructed his crew to bail out even though he knew they were close to enemy-held Nangchang city. Within an hour Lieutenant George Barr, the navigator, was captured and before noon all five crewmen were prisoners. Lieutenant Farrow and the engineer/gunner Sergeant Spatz were executed by the Japanese along with Lieutenant Dean Hallmark, pilot of the sixth bomber, on 15 October 1942 at Kiangwan Prison Cemetery in Shanghai.

Of the 16 raiders, 15 had hit their designated targets and all escaped to safe air space. They followed the well-drilled tactic of flying in low, climbing to drop their bombs so as to avoid the risk of self-inflicted damage, then dropping again to near rooftop height to escape to the western coast of Japan. The story of the raid did not first appear in the US media, but rather was broken by the Japanese, who claimed that enemy bombers had done very little damage to Japanese property or military establishments and that eight of the planes had been shot down. Because the US government did not yet know the fate of the crewmen, it had no interest in publicising the raid until their whereabouts was known. It was a long time before the whole story emerged for public consumption.

When he got back to the United States, Jimmy Doolittle had been expecting to be court-martialed for losing sixteen B-25 bombers. Instead, when he arrived in

Washington, he was sent for by General Arnold and ushered into the White House Oval Office to meet the President. Roosevelt personally pinned the Medal of Honor to his chest for his gallantry, and Doolittle was also promoted to the rank of Brigadier-General. Every member of the 80 aircrew was awarded the Distinguished Flying Cross. Thomas White and David Thatcher were both awarded the Silver Star and all those injured were awarded the Purple Heart. The Chinese government of Chiang Kai-shek awarded the Order of Yung-Hui First Class to Jimmy Doolittle, Third Class to Major John Hilger and Fifth Class to all the other crew members. The Doolittle Raid was the greatest single act of courage in the air by American airmen, regardless of rank or status, up to that time. It would be followed by a similar act of courage some 40 months later.

5

After the Raid

The immediate result of the Doolittle Raid – apart from the destruction of vital Japanese targets – was that the 72 surviving airmen (Corporal Leland Faktor had died when bailing out) who had carried out their mission so successfully were now stranded in China, many of them injured, and were being pursued by the Japanese. We shall first consider some of their fates before moving on to the political aftermath of the raid.

As already described, the crew of the sixth B-25 off the *Hornet* (40-2298) had ditched in the sea off Shanghai; the impact was so violent that the pilot, Lieutenant Dean Hallmark, was thrown through the windscreen of the aircraft while still strapped to his seat; surprisingly, he wasn't seriously injured. Bombardier Sergeant Bill Dieter was in the nose and was submerged as the aircraft went in, but surfaced shortly afterwards to join the rest of the crew on top of the slowly sinking aircraft.

Lieutenants Hallmark, Meder and Nielsen rallied round to recover the aircraft's life raft and the CO_2 cylinder which would inflate it. But the pull-cord on the cylinder broke off flush with the cylinder and the only way to inflate the raft was by hand pump, a difficult task while being dashed by 12-foot waves. Sergeant Dieter and the rear gunner Corporal Fitzmaurice were in poor shape, and Lieutenant Nielsen, the navigator, had already rescued Dieter from the sea once. The second time Dieter went under, Nielsen could not save him; both Dieter and Fitzmaurice drowned. The life raft could not be inflated so the three surviving men swam for shore.

Separated in their swim, the officers were soon brought together again when all three were captured by the Japanese and taken to Shanghai. In a few days they were joined by the crew of the last aircraft to leave the *Hornet*, 40-2268, Lieutenants Bill Farrow, George Barr, Bob Hite and Sergeant Harold Spatz and Corporal Jake de Shazer. They were all incarcerated in Shanghai and in October 1942, Lieutenants Farrow and Hallmark, together with Sergeant Spatz, were executed by their captors for 'war crimes against the Empire of Japan'. The other five were kept as prisoners under 'commuted life sentences', mostly in solitary confinement. They kept their sanity by passing a bible between their cell windows, their only means of contacting each other. They were not allowed to speak to one another, but drew some twisted comfort from watching how the Japanese officers treated their ordinary soldiers out in the yard. All were kept on a starvation diet and Bob Meder succumbed to the effects of starvation and beri-beri and died in captivity. The others survived their ordeal, although Lieutenant George Barr suffered from severe psychological problems.

Lieutenant Ted Lawson, pilot of B-25 40-2261 *Ruptured Duck*, crashed his aircraft in a similar, though rather more drastic, fashion to the landing of Lieutenant Dean Hallmark. He had found the Chinese coastline and in a very brief respite in the storm, managed to see a beach. He concluded that this would be a good landing spot, as it looked reasonably smooth and he decided to try a three-point landing. Unfortunately

Jimmy Doolittle's B-25 after crash-landing in China, in a photograph taken by Sergeant Paul Leonard. Doolittle sits by the wing.

his engines died from fuel starvation and he landed in six feet of water. The aircraft dug in, somersaulted and threw him and his co-pilot, Dean Davenport, out through the plexiglass, both still attached to their seats. Rear Gunner Sergeant David Thatcher had been wearing heavier clothing than the others, so was less injured, though he had been concussed after being tossed around the rear section of the aircraft. He rescued Ted Lawson and got him ashore (an action that earned him the Silver Star), then tried to find medical help, because Lawson was in very bad shape. His left leg had had most of the flesh torn from it as he was ejected through the glass, his lower front teeth had been smashed out of his mouth and his lower lip hung loose off his face, which was badly cut in several places.

Meanwhile near the crash site of B-25 40-2267 *TNT*, Ma Liang Shui was playing cards with friends at home when suddenly he heard shouting outside the village. Flashlights were seen in the darkness at the far side of the village. In China at the time, flashlights meant enemy soldiers or pirates, so the Ma family fled to the mountain behind their house. Eventually Ma Liang Shui's father-in-law volunteered to find out what had happened, and returned saying that the noise came from foreigners. The Ma family returned home to find four white men in their pig pen. Ma took them to his house and his wife Zhao Xiao Bao found some dry clothes for them and lit a fire. Since no one in the village understood any English, it took the Chinese family quite some time to identify the foreigners, but with the help of a world map they finally established that the men were American flyers. At daybreak the following morning, Ma Liang Shui helped them find their fellow crewman, Lieutenant 'Doc' White who had been hiding under a large rock at the entrance of the village. White had gone back to the aircraft to try to recover his medical bag and medicine box, but was unsuccessful. He later said that if he could have recovered the medicine chest, Ted Lawson just might not have lost his leg. In the night, Ma Liang Shui and some friends dressed the airmen as Chinese fishermen and helped them through the Japanese blockade on a sampan.

The badly injured Lieutenant Lawson was transported to a small hospital by Chinese guerrillas. A doctor treated the wounds on his face with a strip of fabric and a strange poultice, which he advised Lawson not to remove but simply let it fall off in its own time. Remarkably, Lawson's lower jaw healed with barely a scar. However, there was still the matter of his mangled leg, which seemed beyond the scope of the hospital, as it was poorly equipped and the staff spoke little English. Lawson tried gesticulating to show he wanted someone to sew the flesh of his leg together, but to no avail.

At this point Lieutenant White (MD) from *TNT* arrived and decided that amputation was the only safe course, as gangrene had set in. He set up a crude

Ted Lawson in a photograph taken in 1943 by MGM Studios at the time his book *Thirty Seconds Over Tokyo* was made into a motion picture. Notice the minimal scarring on Ted's face around the mouth, resulting from the Chinese doctor's 'poultice'.

A Typical transportation method used to move Doolittle Raiders to Chungking. The armed escorts are regular Chinese soldiers and irregulars. The Chinese are carrying parasols to protect themselves from the sun.

operating theatre, and administered smuggled novocaine donated by the Chinese guerrillas in the form of a spinal anaesthetic. Nurses held Lawson's wrists and tried to comfort him as he watched White saw off his leg with a small surgical saw. Lawson was in great pain, but the novocaine helped and he later gave 'Doc' White credit for saving his life, since he gave him a blood transfusion from his own blood (not such a frightening prospect, if you realise that every aircrew member in the Army Air Corps carried a record of his blood group on his dog tags). Ted Lawson was later able to travel to Chungking with his fellow airmen, though he and the other injured men had to be carried in sedan chairs. Lieutenant White was to receive the Silver Star for his efforts.

Across the region, local Chinese helped 64 American aviators, some injured too badly to walk, to get to Chiang Kai-shek's capital of Chungking (now Chongqing) in southwest China so that they could be flown out back to US bases in the region. Some of the men were transferred to North Africa, others remained in the Pacific and yet others went back to the US, especially the injured. Before they left China, the men were feted by the people of the towns and villages they passed through. However, the aftermath of the raid for the local Chinese would be terrible.

Having located the fifteen aircraft at their crash sites, the Japanese proceeded to try to track down the Americans but took no more captives than the eight men from 40-2268 and 40-2298 they had already taken prisoner. If the Doolittle Raiders had been able to land at Chuchow airfield as they had planned, then they would have not have needed the help of the local people, as they would have been able to escape the region on their own. As it was, the Japanese decided to punish the Chinese for their collaboration with the enemy that had prevented the capture of the rest of the US airmen.

The Japanese methodically noted the location of the wreckage of each B-25 and then worked along the various routes to Chungking (where the stricken airmen had been taken by locals), massacring whole villages and towns as they went. Some 230,000 Chinese, men, women and children, were killed. Sometimes the Japanese staged public executions with firing squads; other times they resorted to more barbaric techniques. Many pregnant women had their stomachs slashed open and then witnessed their unborn babies cut to pieces before they themselves were murdered.

One incident which merits describing here is the fate of a village elder from Hsiangshan, Yang Shib-Diao. He found Lieutenant Dean Hallmark on the beach after he had swum ashore from his aircraft on the evening of 18 April. Hallmark was in need of medical attention and needed a place to hide until he could find the rest of his crew. Mr Yang took Hallmark to his home, then arranged for him to be fed and provided a hiding place where he could sleep. The next day, he arranged for Hallmark's crew to be moved secretly to Paishawan. Unfortunately, the Japanese had been tipped off by a Chinese soldier loyal to the occupiers. The soldiers swooped on the village and took the Americans prisoner. They then lined up the ten Chinese men who had been leading the airmen to safety and shot them. They next went to the nearby Chiachsi village in search of more, but found none. They killed the inhabitants anyway. Mr Yang had escaped at Paishawan, and had been arranging the burial of Sergeants Dieter and Fitzmaurice at Shatow. When he returned home it was to find his house destroyed, his family missing and signs of a deadly struggle. Being a man not in the best of health, the shock brought on a heart attack and he died.

The Reverend Charles Meeus, a Belgian missionary who had adopted Chinese citizenship, was travelling through Kiangsi and Chekiang Provinces and followed the path of a Japanese company of soldiers on their trail of destruction. He estimated that some 25,000 people had died in each of the towns he had passed through. The Japanese had warned townspeople everywhere they went that to help the Americans would result in their villages and towns being 'crushed into dust'. Reverend Meeus related the story he was told in a village near to Ihwang in Kiangsi Province. A village elder had given help to 'Doc' Watson just after his aircraft had crashed. The Japanese wrapped him in gasoline-soaked blankets, put a tyre around him so he could not move and then forced his wife to set light to him and watch him die. After that, they beheaded her. The horrifying brutality of the Japanese after the raid later caused Jimmy Doolittle to reflect that he would carry with him to his grave the bitter knowledge that for every one escaped American, almost 3600 Chinese people died. It was a horrifying price to pay – one which exceeded threefold the death toll of Hiroshima a little over three years later.

Back in the US, it was not until 12 March 1943 that the White House was informed by the Japanese of the executions of Lieutenants Farrow, Hallmark and Sergeant Spatz. President Roosevelt described it as 'utterly outrageous', and issued a statement to the Japanese government, to be delivered by the US Legation in Berne, Switzerland, to the Japanese Legation, for forwarding on to Tokyo.

> The American Government also solemnly warns the Japanese Government that for any other violations of its undertakings as regards American prisoners of war or for any other acts of criminal barbarity inflicted upon American prisoners in violation of the rules of warfare accepted and practiced by civilised

nations as military operations now in progress draw to their inexorable and inevitable conclusion, the American Government will visit upon the officers of the Japanese Government responsible for such uncivilised and inhuman acts the punishment they deserve.

On 21 April 1943, President Roosevelt publicly confirmed that the airmen had been executed by firing squad.

It is with a feeling of the deepest horror, which I know will be shared by all civilised peoples, that I have to announce the barbarous execution by the Japanese Government of some of the members of this country's armed forces who fell into Japanese hands as an incident of warfare.

The press has just carried the details of the American bombing of Japan a year ago. The crews of two of the American bombers were captured by the Japanese. On October 19 1942, this Government learned from Japanese radio broadcasts of the capture, trial, and severe punishment of those Americans. Continued endeavor was made to obtain confirmation of those reports from Tokyo. It was not until March 12, 1943, that the American Government received the communications given by the Japanese Government stating that these Americans had in fact been tried and that the death penalty had been pronounced against them. It was further stated that the death penalty was commuted for some but that the sentence of death had been applied to others.

This Government has vigorously condemned this act of barbarity in a formal communication sent to the Japanese Government. In that communication this Government has informed the Japanese Government that the American Government will hold personally and officially responsible for these diabolical crimes all of those officers of the Japanese Government who have participated therein and will in due course bring those officers to justice.

This recourse by our enemies to frightfulness is barbarous. The effort of the Japanese war lords thus to intimidate us will utterly fail. It will make the American people more determined than ever to blot out the shameless militarism of Japan.

The executions were considered justified by the Japanese as the government had introduced its 'Enemy Airmen's Act'. The act was declared law by General Shunroku Hata on 13 August 1942, four months after the two US crews were captured, but it was deemed to apply retrospectively. The act allowed for the execution of airmen or the commutation of the sentence to life imprisonment if the adjudicator decided that was appropriate.

The aftermath of the Doolittle Raid in Japan was firstly shock at the temerity of such an attack. General Tojo was angry that any country could violate Japanese territory, something which had not happened since 1287. How had the Americans reached Japan with twin-engined bombers? They could not have taken off from an aircraft carrier; they were too big and surely no carrier was long enough? Whatever the logistics, the Japanese High Command reasoned that the Americans had decided to bring the war into Japan's own back yard to avoid battles across the islands the Japanese had taken control of in recent years. Would they be able to resist a home island attack if this one raid were to be multiplied a thousand-fold? The answer had to be no – their forces were too thinly spread across the many Pacific islands. The decision was made to withdraw key units from the remoter islands and to reduce the occupying forces in remaining islands by up to five per cent, so as to secure the home

The Japanese aircraft carrier *Hiryu*, one of the four sunk by the US Navy at the Battle of Midway. The *Hiryu* is in its 'death throes', having taken serious forward damage.

islands if they should be attacked. The Japanese were now on the back foot and they had to ensure that news of the Doolittle Raid did not leak out to their occupying forces or to the Japanese fleet.

The Americans had no idea of the occupying force reductions made by the Japanese or the objectives of Admiral Yamamoto as he lured the US fleet into what went down in history as the Battle of Midway. Yamamoto's intention was to lure the US aircraft carriers into battle, so that he could destroy all six and then take total command of the air in the Pacific and at the same time eliminate any possibility of more aircraft carrier attacks on the home islands. On 4 June 1942, barely eight weeks after the Doolittle Raid, 8 American cruisers and 3 aircraft carriers faced 11 Japanese battleships, 23 cruisers and 4 aircraft carriers. Using aircraft that were often less than serviceable and crews who were totally inexperienced, the Americans faced a far superior force with a great deal of combat experience. In the first few hours, one US torpedo squadron was totally destroyed and all its aircrews lost; a 27-aircraft fighter squadron lost 21 of its number.

The battle should have been lost for the Americans, but the weather turned against the Japanese, with poor visibility on the surface. The Americans then threw in everything they had and sank all four Japanese carriers: the *Akagi*, the *Hiryu*, the *Kaga* and the *Soryu*. American losses at the end of the battle amounted to one aircraft carrier, the *Yorktown*, and one destroyer, plus 98 aircraft and 307 men. Japanese losses included all 4 aircraft carriers and 1 cruiser, plus a staggering 248 aircraft and 3057 men. For the Japanese, Midway was a shaming rout; for the Americans, it was the first of the string of victories that led them all the way to Japan.

One such victory, albeit a costly one, was the Battle of Guadalcanal, a small and insignificant island in the Solomons that had been taken by the Japanese in May 1942. They began to build an airfield to protect the southern approaches to the Solomons, so the US decided to secure it for American use and to prevent the Japanese from using it to sever their supply and communication lines. 1 August 1942 was the date set for the Americans to undertake an amphibious landing.

It was to be a bitter battle on two counts, firstly amongst the US commanders. The US Navy was nominally in overall command and the commander, Rear Admiral Richmond Turner, had significant disagreements with Major-General Alexander Vandegrift, the Marine commander, over who should control what once the Marines had landed. The situation was aggravated by the fact that these two men were of equal rank, though Turner was the senior in terms of time in rank. Turner was an old fashioned sailor who took the view that the Marines were subservient to the Navy. Vandegrift, on the other hand, knew well what assault landings were about and knew he needed to have total control of the beachhead and the land advance to be successful.

On the ground, it was a bitter battle in the real meaning of the term. The Navy thought it had softened up the beachhead and the Marines at first thought it would not be difficult to take the island, but then the Japanese opened fire as the landing craft left the shoreline. The next problem for the Marines was that Vice Admiral Frank Fletcher withdrew the aircraft carriers, and also therefore vital air support for the Marines on the ground, on 9 August. This infuriated General Vandegrift, because in such terrain air cover was essential, both to limit loss of life and to speed up the advance. As it turned out, it was February 1943 before Guadalcanal was secured by the Americans. In retrospect, American losses were relatively light, with 1600 dead and 4700 wounded, set against the Japanese losses of 25,400 dead and an indeterminate number of wounded. For his brilliant execution of command against massive odds, General Vandegrift was awarded the Medal of Honor and later became Commandant of the Marine Corps.

A few weeks after the American assault on Guadalcanal, US aircraft carriers met Japan's remaining carriers at the Battle of the Eastern Solomons on 24-25 August 1942. It was not a major skirmish, but another victory notched up for the Americans. The Japanese had observed that Vice Admiral Fletcher had moved his US carriers away from Guadalcanal, and like General Vandegrift, had considered that to be a premature move, but one that gave them an advantage and an opportunity to have a second confrontation with the American carriers. By the middle of 25 August, the Japanese realised that their efforts to displace the US carriers had once again misfired.

This Corsair gives an impression of the machine often described as the personal aircraft of Major Gregory 'Pappy' Boyington, White 86 *Lulubelle*. However, Boyington regularly flew the last available aircraft on the line, often the most 'beat-up' machine, just to demonstrate to his junior pilots that he expected no special favours. (JIS Models – Flying Mule Sales)

AFTER THE RAID

The Americans were in their stride and defeat after defeat came for the Japanese forces. After Guadalcanal came the Battle of the Bismarck Sea on 2–4 March 1943, then the Aleutian Islands Campaign (3 June 1942–15 August 1943), the Battle of New Georgia (20 June–25 August 1943), the bombing of Rabaul (2–11 November 1943) and the Battle of Tarawa (20–23 November). However many of the battles begun at this time were fought for years; Bougainville was taken on 21 August 1945, the battle for the island having begun on 1 November 1943.

During this time, too, one of the most distinguished fighting squadrons was making its mark with an aircraft designed for carrier operation, but not yet declared fit for such use. This was the Chance-Vought F4U Corsair. The Corsair's first operations from carriers in the region were performed by the British South East Asia Command in the Dutch East Indies. But it was as a land-based fighter operated particularly by VMF-214 (Marine Fighting Squadron 214), among others, that it gained enormous fame. VMF-214 was formed in June 1942 under the command of Major George Britt. Nicknamed 'The Swashbuckers', they fought in the Solomons campaign, flying Grumman Wildcats, then converting to the Corsair.

Britt handed over command to Major Gregory Boyington and the latter led the squadron into battle in August/September 1943. He had a reputation as a hard-drinking, hard-cursing, hard-hitting individual, and acquired the name 'Black Sheep' for his squadron (a name by which VMA-214 is still known). Having raised his personal total score of enemy 'kills' to 28, he was shot down and taken prisoner by the Japanese in January 1944, but not before he had created eight 'aces' in his squadron, who had between them shot down a total of 94 Japanese aircraft. For his endeavours, Boyington was awarded the Medal of Honor and the Navy Cross. He was the second highest scoring Marine Corps fighter pilot of the Second World War and retired in the rank of Colonel.

The Corsair aircraft merits mention here, because of its outstanding performance in the Pacific. In fact, it has the lowest loss-in-combat number of any aircraft in the Second World War. Of some 12,300 built, only 189 were lost in air-to-air combat.

The awesome scene that was Iwo Jima beach on the first day – Marines, alive and dead, spread across the landing beach.

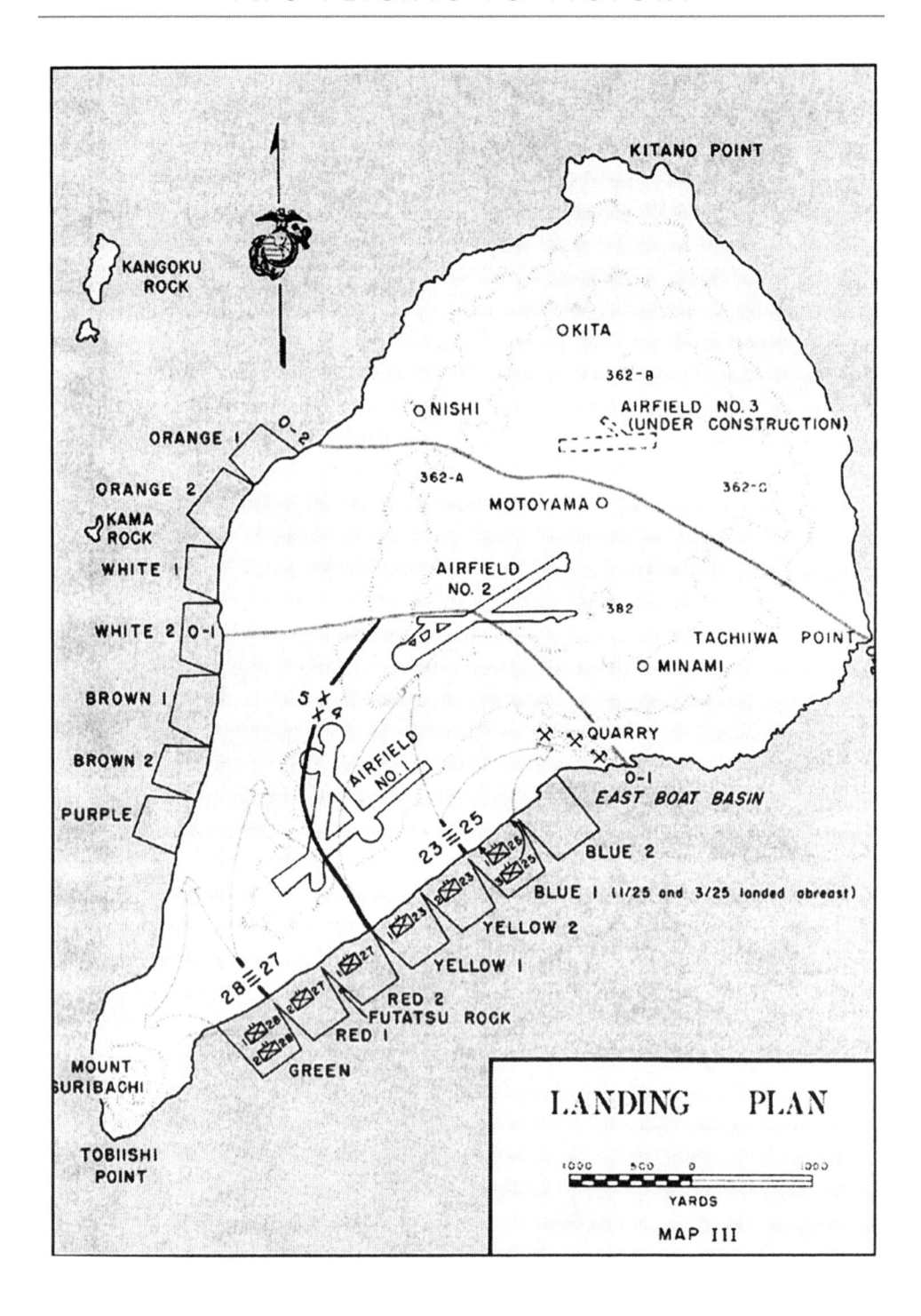

The US Marine Corps' landing plan for the assault on Iwo Jima – 'Sulfur Island' – a huge volcanic rock, but the first island of homeland Japan. The landing plan was almost certainly 'fathered' by Lieutenant-General Holland M. Smith, even though he thought it was a battle which could have been avoided by going straight for Okinawa instead. One can see Mount Suribachi at the bottom left.

It was the first naval fighter type to be capable of flying at more than 400mph and came to be known by the Japanese as the 'Whispering Death'. It also had the longest production record of any Second World War US fighter aircraft, continuing to be manufactured until 1953.

By the end of August 1944, US forces had achieved further hard-won victories in the Pacific, at Kwajalein (31 January–3 February 1944), Truk (17–18 February 1944), the Battle of the Philippine Sea (19–20 June 1944), Saipan (15 June–9 July 1944), Tinian (24 July–1 August 1944) and Guam (21 July–8 August 1944). The Battle of Leyte (20 October–31 December 1944) was the biggest naval battle in history and foreshadowed General MacArthur's promised return to the Philippines. The pace of victories was quickening as Iwo Jima (19 February–26 March 1945) and Okinawa (1 April 1–22 June 1945) fell. The Americans were closing in on Japan.

6

Meeting in North Africa

Once the euphoria of his Medal of Honor and his promotion to Brigadier-General was passed, Jimmy Doolittle was asked to travel the country promoting the US Army Air Force in a major recruitment and war bond campaign. Advertisements were placed in national publications such as *Life*; one was a full-page portrait of General Doolittle wearing flying gear, with a skyscape behind and the message: 'Do More For Doolittle'.

In August 1942, General Doolittle was called to Washington for a conference with General Arnold, who told him there was a new opening and he was to go to London to meet General Eisenhower, the commander of Allied Forces in Europe. They were to discuss America's contribution to the war effort in North Africa, as Eisenhower and the British government wanted to see a reversal of Allied fortunes there. The man on the ground was to be Major-General George S. Patton (affectionately known as 'Blood and Guts' Patton). Patton was a tank man and he had seen the carnage of badly managed tank battles. He was not about to make the same mistake in his command.

Doolittle met Patton in Washington and the two got on very well; they had a lot in common, yet they were worlds apart. Doolittle had been a reservist for half his career and had been a wartime recruit, so had not gone the West Point route, whereas George Patton had been a West Pointer, although he had graduated in 1909 47th in his class. He had wanted to go into the cavalry and was an excellent horseman, but his first wartime duty in the First World War was with tanks. He became a talented tank commander and strategist and it was to be with tanks that he would fight the new Operation *Torch*.

Patton and Doolittle met General Eisenhower in London on 7 August to discuss the plans for the North Africa operation. 'When Ike asked Georgie what action he proposed to take as ground commander, Georgie was all ready with a very positive, detailed invasion plan,' recalled Doolittle. When he had finished, Eisenhower nodded, obviously pleased, then turned to Doolittle for his plans. 'I replied with a very stupid answer,' he remembered. 'I will not be able to do anything until the air fields are captured and supplied with fuel, oil, ammunition, bombs, spare parts, and all the necessary ground personnel.' Doolittle realised that his pragmatic reply disappointed Eisenhower. 'It was a dumb thing,' he said, 'to tell a general with as much logistics experience and military service as Eisenhower.'

Subsequently Doolittle learned that Ike had cabled General George C. Marshall in Washington, who with Arnold was in charge of selecting the senior commanders for the operation, saying: 'Patton yes. Doolittle no.' General Marshall replied 'You may have anyone you prefer. We still recommend Doolittle.' This situation 'put Ike in a bad spot,' Doolittle said, 'and that made him dislike me even more. Although he finally agreed to accept me, it took me almost a year to really sell myself to him.' Despite this inauspicious beginning, Doolittle eventually became one of Eisenhower's boys. 'One

MEETING IN NORTH AFRICA 81

Brigadier-General Doolittle before leaving for North Africa.

Major-General George Patton pins a medal on a black GI. He is wearing his famous pair of ivory-handled pistols.

Despite being practically severed in half in a collision with a German fighter, this B-17, named *All American*, of the 97th Bomb Group, flown by Pilot Kenneth Bragg, limped back to its base in England, then broke apart on landing.

MEETING IN NORTH AFRICA

The Boeing B-17E Fortress I 41-2578. This aircraft was the oldest and longest serving B-17 in the Eighth Air Force. While with the 97th Bomb Group on 17 August 1942, it was the lead aircraft in the first Eighth Air Force heavy bombing mission, flown by Major Paul Tibbets. It was Colonel Frank Armstrong's craft and was named *Butcher Shop*.

Paul Tibbets and Colonel Hampton Atkinson at Biskra.

General Doolittle awards Colonel Hank Tillman and others the Purple Heart in front of the 414th Bombardment Squadron's B-17 *Sweet Chariot*.

Hell's Kitchen was a B-17 of the 414th Bombardment Squadron, one of the four comprising the 97th Bombardment Group, which brought European experience to North Africa.

thing that didn't exactly endear me to him was the fact that I had left the regular service in 1930. Then because I returned to the Active List as a reserve officer, he no doubt felt that somebody who had stayed in the army and been through all of the service schools would be more suitable as his air commander.'

While Doolittle was failing to impress Eisenhower, an American bomber group were preparing to make their first sortie in Europe. Constituted as the 97th Bombardment Group (Heavy) on 28 January 1942, as part of the Eighth Air Force, it was declared active on 3 February 1942, operating Boeing B-17E four-engined bombers – the famous Flying Fortress. The 97th had flown some anti-submarine patrols offshore, but in May the decision to relocate was made and by the end of July the squadrons (340th, 342nd and 343rd Bomb Squadrons) took off from Bangor, Maine, stopping in Labrador,

Greenland and Iceland en route to their new home at RAF Grafton Underwood in Northamptonshire. The commander was Colonel Frank Armstrong.

The 97th's first mission was due to take place on 9 August, but the weather was atrocious and a week of almost constant rainfall delayed it. It was 17 August before it could take place. Frank Armstrong's aircraft was named *Butcher Shop* and he would have flown the mission as aircraft captain, except that he had not yet been rated operational on the B-17, so he flew right seat with a certain Major Paul Tibbets, commander of 340th Squadron, in the left seat. *Butcher Shop* led the first daylight bombing raid by a US squadron over German-occupied Europe. On that morning, General Carl A. Spaatz, Commander of the Eighth Air Force, and a number of senior British officers watched the take-off of the 18 bombers, marking the first of over 300,000 bomber sorties the Eighth Air Force would make before May 1945.

Brigadier-General Ira Eaker, Commander of the VIII USAAF Bomber Command, also flew on this mission in B-17 *Yankee Doodle* and received official credit for 'leading' it. The aircraft took off just after midday, climbed to 23,000 feet and headed for France with an RAF Spitfire fighter escort. Three planes carried 1000lb bombs intended for the marshalling yards at Rouen and another nine carried 600lb bombs for the repair shops at Buddicum. The targets were destroyed and all the aircraft returned home; for the next few months the 97th flew regular sorties and continued training intensively, practising gunnery over the Wash.

Tibbets' B-17E was named *Red Gremlin*, the lead aircraft of the 340th Bomb Squadron and he took that aircraft on several sorties after the Rouen attack. He insisted that his crews dismantle their machine guns after use, wash them and treat them with light oil so as to reduce the risk of them jamming at 20,000 feet. Such was the thoroughness that Paul Tibbets applied to everything he did. Amongst the people he impressed with his professionalism was a man whose path he was to cross again in a couple of years' time, Colonel Curtis E. LeMay, then a bombing group commander in England, but destined to command the Twentieth Air Force in the Pacific.

In October 1942, as the Americans were preparing to launch the combined Operation *Torch*, the invasion of North Africa, Major Tibbets was called on to fly General Mark Clark on a secret mission to meet with the French commander in Algiers. He flew General Clark to Gibraltar in *Red Gremlin*, where a submarine picked him up and transported him to Algeria. Clark's mission was successful and numerous French units cooperated with the Allied landing forces. Apparently the senior staff were impressed with Tibbets' general-ferrying skills; on 5 November he flew General Eisenhower and a group of other senior commanders, including Major-General George Patton and Brigadier-General Jimmy Doolittle, from England to Gibraltar for the conference that preceded Operation *Torch*. It was a foggy morning and there was some discussion as to whether the flight should take place at all. Eisenhower was keen to get to Gibraltar but the weather conditions troubled him, so he consulted Tibbets. Tibbets' reaction was quite typical: 'Sir, we're going! You need to get to your conference and the fact that it's foggy means the Germans won't see us any more clearly than we'll see them!' With the plane crowded with staff officers, Eisenhower sat on a two-by-four board hastily installed in the cockpit, so he could get a pilot's eye view of the flight. This was the first time Doolittle met Tibbets and he observed even then that this young man had the makings of a general. By flying low and hugging the coast, except across the Bay of Biscay, Tibbets flew the generals to Gibraltar and home again without incident.

Eisenhower had finally accepted Doolittle as his air commander for North Africa, and so Doolittle became head of the newly formed Twelfth Air Force, working with Patton on the ground. Because Eisenhower and Patton had known each other since the First World War, Eisenhower decided that Patton should supervise Doolittle and report back if he failed to do his job effectively. As Patton and Doolittle got on well, Doolittle had little to fear, especially as Patton was in awe of the Doolittle Raid.

Brigadier-General Doolittle's first task in North Africa was to set up and organise the newly formed Twelfth Air Force and provide front line support for Patton on the ground. George Patton was appointed to lead the invasion force to take Casablanca, then to deputise for General Mark Clark. As it happened, Casablanca proved to be no battle, much to Patton's disappointment, for he was hoping to 'blood' his troops with a fairly easy skirmish against the Vichy French, in preparation for facing a much tougher adversary, Rommel's 17th Panzer Division. Instead Patton was, as he saw it, 'sidelined' in favour of General Lloyd Fredendall, who took command of II Corps in support of the British General Kenneth Anderson's 3rd Army. Shortly after came the Battle of the Kasserine Pass (19–25 February 1943), in which II Corps faced Rommel. Fredendall spread his tanks across a wide front to face the German onslaught and all Rommel had to do was drive straight through the middle of Fredendall's line, smashing II Corps in the process and heaping a humiliating defeat on the Americans. In all 2000 men died out of a total of 6500 US casualties and Fredendall was relieved of his command.

On 6 March 1943, George Patton took control of II Corps, with the task of recouping its honour. When Patton had examined the battlefield after Kasserine Pass he had been appalled at what he saw: undisciplined men shabbily dressed and with no respect for their officers. Patton took a grip of this situation very quickly, insisting that men shaved daily, dressed as near to uniform standards as they were able and saluted their officers. The officers were taken to task too. Next, he addressed the troops en masse and in his own profane manner, raised their morale and encouraged them to go out there and defeat the enemy they had come to meet.

Patton felt now that he had a score to settle with Erwin Rommel, the German Afrika Korps commander. However, Rommel was in Tunis awaiting medical evacuation to Germany, so Patton had to settle for General von Arnim, though he did not know that as his tanks went into battle. The outcome would almost certainly have been the same if he had faced Rommel, as the Americans drove the Afrika Korps back east and into the waiting hands of the British General Bernard Montgomery's Eighth Army. Between them then, the forces of Patton and Montgomery drove the Germans out of North Africa and across into Italy via Sicily.

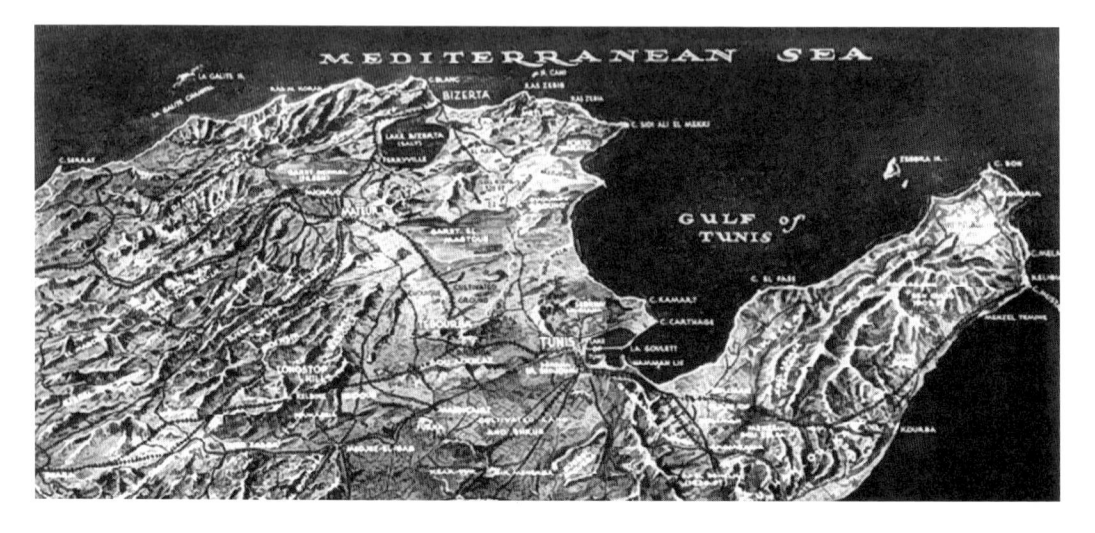

The main coast of Tunisia, the next recess in the coastline from the Gulf of Tunis. To the left is Bizerte.

MEETING IN NORTH AFRICA

Here is where the paths of Jimmy Doolittle and Paul Tibbets are set to cross, for Doolittle had asked for bomber squadrons with current battle experience to form the core of his new Twelfth Air Force in North Africa. His choices were very limited, because the only bomber groups and squadrons with experience were those in England – and not many of them had much of it. The obvious candidate was the 97th Bombardment Group, now split between Grafton Underwood and Polebrook. The whole Bomb Group was transferred from England to North Africa. Other units which joined the Twelfth were: the 1st Fighter Group, equipped with P38 Lightings; the 319th Bomb Group, the 320th Bomb Group and the 17th Bomb Group, all equipped with the Martin B-26 Marauder; the 340th Bomb Group, equipped with North American B25s; and the 99th Bomb Group which joined in April 1943, equipped with the B-17, like the 97th. In addition to this, a recently formed fighter squadron that would ultimately grow into a fighter group was assigned to the Twelfth Air Force – it was quite unique from all the other units joining the Twelfth because its entire manpower, pilots and ground-crew, were black. This was the 99th Fighter Squadron, soon to achieve great fame as the Tuskegee Airmen. Scorned by many for the colour of their skin, these men were to prove they could match the most outstanding combat records of any of their contemporaries.

Lieutenant-Colonel Paul W. Tibbets was still with the 340th Bomb Squadron as part of the 97th Bomb Group, now under the command of Colonel Hampton Atkinson, as Frank Armstrong had remained with the Eighth Air Force as executive officer to General Ira Eaker. 'Hamp', as Colonel Atkinson was known, had an undisclosed lung condition, which became progressively worse in North Africa. Tibbets made several attempts to persuade Atkinson to report sick but he stubbornly refused, making it very plain that the last thing he wanted was to be rotated back to the US on a 'sick ticket'.

Atkinson and Tibbets had become good friends, so Tibbets covered for him on several occasions over some seven weeks. He logged himself as co-pilot when in fact he was flying the mission from the left seat. There were times when Colonel Atkinson simply could not get out of his bed, but Tibbets told no one and did his Colonel's job, partly out of friendship and also because he thought it was the right thing to do.

The 97th was responsible for a whole chain of devastating bombings of the Tunisian port of Bizerte, the Germans' key supply line, and most of these had been led by Lieutenant-Colonel Paul Tibbets in the name of Colonel Atkinson. Eventually President Roosevelt heard about the successes and ordered the promotion of the commander, whose name he didn't know, to Brigadier-General. It was Jimmy Doolittle who had the task of making the promotion. This is when one of the most amazing stories of the Second World War unfolds, the connection between the first 'flight to victory' in the Pacific and the second.

When the President's message reached Brigadier-General Doolittle in Algiers, he obtained a pair of General's stars and flew personally to Biskra, where the 97th was located. Doolittle had made a habit of performing promotions of his senior officers and making medal awards himself, so this was nothing unusual. However, when he reached the 97th Bomb Group's headquarters hut, he found only Lieutenant-Colonel Paul Tibbets in the commander's office, who he recognised from when Tibbets had transported Eisenhower, Clark, Doolittle and others from England to Gibraltar for the Operation *Torch* conference. That flight had given Doolittle the opportunity not only tp rate Tibbets' flying skills, but also to observe the man's exemplary pre-flight inspection of the aircraft.

Asking the whereabouts of Colonel Atkinson, General Doolittle noticed a certain 'shuffling of feet', so guessed something wasn't quite right, especially when Tibbets said that Atkinson 'wasn't around', a response that was out of character from the man who had straight-talked Eisenhower. Doolittle made it plain that he expected the Group

Commander to 'be around' because all personnel were restricted to base and there was a war on. Doolittle could see that Tibbets was pretty uncomfortable, so he pressed the issue of Colonel Atkinson's whereabouts, only to discover that he was in bed.

Accompanying Tibbets to Atkinson's quarters, General Doolittle was appalled at what he saw – a man who had obviously not been fit to fly for quite some time. Atkinson clearly had flown only one or two of the bombing missions credited to him and General Doolittle made his displeasure very clear. The men had broken several rules, besides the fact that if Tibbets' aircraft had been shot down then both men would have been listed as missing while Atkinson was still safe in bed. Doolittle himself would have run the risk of censure for the actions of his subordinates. 'And now, on the President's orders, I have to promote you to Brigadier-General – a bit of a joke, don't you think?'

Colonel Atkinson had little to say. He explained that he fell sick on his arrival in Algeria and didn't expect to take so long to recover. He'd asked Lieutenant-Colonel Tibbets to cover for him, expecting it to be just for a few days, but the infection got worse. The two men had continued the deception until it was impossible to back out. Atkinson was honest enough to credit his promotion to Lieutenant-Colonel Tibbets. The new General Atkinson then told Tibbets that, since he was now a general, he was empowered to award a battlefield promotion and without further ado, he handed over his eagle rank badges to Tibbets and congratulated him on his promotion to full colonel. General Doolittle watched this little ceremony and thought better of his new Brigadier-General for his generosity. But good things rarely come free, as Tibbets was to discover.

Doolittle made it plain that he would keep Atkinson in his command and placed him in charge of the 5th Bombardment Wing in the Twelfth Air Force. Jimmy Doolittle was a straight talker and made it very plain that he never again wanted to be the victim of such a conspiracy. He then turned his attention to Tibbets and took him to pieces. First he laid into him for running the deception for so long. Besides the ramifications if Tibbets had been shot down while flying as Atkinson, there was also the issue of the officers who had flown co-pilot with Tibbets. They had not had their flying hours logged and would not have received medals due to them if they had done something to merit it. Tibbets is quoted as having reflected that he would not have been surprised if he'd finished the war as a second lieutenant!

Doolittle roasted Tibbets for falsifying the records, but did not court-martial him as he should have done; he openly admired Tibbets' loyalty and commitment to his job and to his commanding officer. Doolittle sent the new Colonel to pack his kit and Tibbets was ready for the worst, but then Jimmy Doolittle laughed out loud. The 'roasting' had gone far enough. Tibbets, with his reputation as a successful bomber operator, was to become the Twelfth Air Force Bomb Leader. He wanted the most experienced bomber man in his command at his Algiers headquarters. Thirty minutes later the two men were on their way to Algiers. But when Tibbets arrived, his recent battlefield promotion began to evaporate. It was at the headquarters that he met the man who was to become a serious adversary – and obstacle to his career progression – Colonel Lauris Norstad, the Command Executive Officer to Brigadier-General Doolittle. Norstad made it very plain that as long as he was there, he would be the only full colonel at Doolittle's headquarters. When Tibbets protested that he had been awarded a battlefield promotion, Norstad reminded him that a promotion board of three officers senior to the promotee had to ratify it and it had to be a unanimous decision. So far, so good, but then Norstad explained that he would form one third of that promotion board. Did Tibbets get his drift?

Soon afterwards, there was a mission planning session for a bombing run over Bizerte. Tibbets, as Bomb Leader, was in charge of the planning, but Colonel Norstad attended the briefing and decided to exercise his rank; he insisted that the run should be flown at 6000 feet. Tibbets explained that 6000 feet would be a disastrously low height because the aircraft would be wiped out by anti-aircraft fire; he urged a height of 20,000 feet. Norstad insisted on 6000 feet so Tibbets challenged him angrily to fly as his co-pilot and he would do the bombing run at that altitude. Norstad had never flown a real bombing mission and wasn't about to start now, so Tibbets won the day. But Norstad had been embarrassed in front of an audience of seasoned bomber crews and he wasn't going to forget it.

Hanging over the encounter was the fact that Colonel Norstad and Brigadier-General Hoyt Vandenberg were very close friends. Vandenberg had been appointed by Eisenhower as Doolittle's Chief of Staff and Vandenberg's uncle was the influential Republican leader of the time, Senator Arthur Vandenberg. The friendship between Vandenberg and Norstad extended so far that, as Vandenberg was promoted, his friend, just one rank step behind him, would go up a rung on the promotion ladder himself. Taking that into account, imagine the situation when Doolittle was confronted by Colonel Norstad, who demanded that Tibbets be court-martialed for insubordination for refusing to fly a mission at 6000 feet.

The fact that the bombing run in question was 100 per cent successful and not a single loss was sustained was of no interest to Norstad; he wanted revenge for being humiliated by Tibbets. Jimmy Doolittle was in a difficult situation, for the political influence Norstad wielded could cause him problems. However, Doolittle did remind Norstad that Tibbets was the Bomb Leader, besides being a highly experienced bomber pilot who had personally flown Eisenhower. The wind went out of Norstad's sails a little.

Doolittle's position with Colonel Norstad was a difficult one. Norstad had arrived in Twelfth Air Force before Jimmy Doolittle, and as Executive Officer had done an excellent holding job pending the latter's arrival. Doolittle was torn between Tibbets, the outstanding pilot and leader, and Norstad, a brilliant administrator. Furthermore, Norstad was a charismatic individual and was described by Tibbets himself as the kind of man to attract a following. After the war he would go on to become Commander of NATO Forces in Europe.

An early unmodified B-26, as can be seen from the shorter height fin and smaller wingspan.

41-17747, a B-26B Marauder of Doolittle's old Raiders bomb group, the 37th Bomb Squadron of the 17th Bombardment Group in the Twelfth Air Force. The aircraft was named *Earthquake McGoon*. Note the shot-up port engine nacelle.

Another issue that arose between Tibbets and Norstad was over the Martin B-26 'Widow Maker'. The B-26 equipped three medium bombardment groups, including Jimmy Doolittle's own old outfit, the 17th, from which he had taken the B-25s and crews that flew the Doolittle Raid. Indeed, some of his old crewmen, including Lieutenant Tom Griffin, who was soon to spend the rest of his war in captivity, were flying B-26s with the 17th Bombardment Group. The problem was that among the aircraft flying in North Africa were several early production examples which had not been modified according to Jimmy Doolittle's recommendations when he'd flown the aircraft back in 1940 (see Chapter 1).

Paul Tibbets, as Twelfth Air Force Bomb Leader, had taken this problem to Colonel Norstad who had waved the complaint aside, saying it was of no consequence and that Tibbets should not bother General Doolittle with it. But a number of crews had died as the result of flying accidents, so Tibbets felt he had to take it to Doolittle directly. Doolittle took Tibbets to a waiting B-26 and sat in the pilot's seat with Tibbets in the co-pilot's seat. Doolittle checked the battery master switch as he entered the aircraft, then flew it into a dead port engine, a dead starboard engine, looped it on one engine and put it back on to the ground. Paul Tibbets was astounded and retorted to Doolittle: 'You've flown this baby before!' to which Doolittle had to admit he had. Doolittle's test flight meant that modifications to the B-26s were begun and an extension of ten hours training was implemented. The B-26 went on to be one of the most respected and rugged bombers in operation.

Lieutenant-Colonel Tibbets had taken up the bomb leader's task with no predecessor, but a set of bombing performance statistics that looked pretty grim from any perspective. The benchmark was to get 80 per cent of a bomb drop inside a 400 foot circle. Tibbets was confronted with something like a 20 per cent performance as he took up his new job. One of the major problems that faced him was the large number of new crews in the Twelfth with only relatively basic training experience. They had no experience of ground fire and when they came under attack from anti-aircraft batteries, their resolve weakened and they tended to drop their load and run.

Tibbets' answer to the situation was to increase pre-flight inspection discipline and training, and to adopt a policy of mixing the men of inexperienced crews with combat veterans who had been stationed in England, especially with the 97th Bombardment Group. As a result, bombardiers in particular improved their performance. Crew mobility worked well, as the statistics showed; performance rose to 80 per cent. The Norden bombsight also played a significant role, in concert with Tibbets' intensive training regimes.

One example of the result of Lieutenant-Colonel Tibbets' rigorous training programme as Twelfth Air Force Bomb Leader was the attack on the island of Pantelleria on 18 May 1943. B-26s of the 17th Bombardment Group (Jimmy Doolittle's own old unit), accompanied by machines from the 320th, launched an air attack on Pantelleria, an Axis garrison of some 10,000 men positioned 62 miles south-west of Sicily. It was an obstruction to Generals Patton and Montgomery in their bid to take and secure the island, but the size of the garrison meant that an amphibious landing would be too costly in terms of infantry lives. The 99th Fighter Squadron (made up of only black airmen) was tasked with providing top cover for the bombers, who were charged with destroying all resistance from the air. Pantelleria did ultimately surrender on 11 June, as the result of the pounding it received from Twelfth Air Force B-26s, which dropped 6131 tons of bombs on the island.

This, the 99th Fighter Squadron's first mission, was flown with a collection of 'cast-off' Curtiss P-40 Warhawks. Three squadrons in the British 285 Wing – 112

The Boeing B-29 prototype in flight. Three of these aircraft crashed with engine fires, taking the crews to their deaths. This included Eddie Allen, Boeing's chief test pilot, with the result that Boeing wanted to cancel production, but General Arnold transferred flight testing to the US Army.

The first group of Tuskegee Airmen, the first all African-American fighter unit established in the USAAF. They started out as the 99th Fighter Squadron, commanded by Major Benjamin O. Davis (centre), and were assigned to Doolittle's Twelfth Air Force, then to the 15th Air Force to expand into the 332nd Fighter Group, the most highly decorated fighter group in that theatre of war.

Tuskegee Airman Lieutenant William Johnston. As bomber escorts, the Tuskegee Airmen never lost a bomber.

Squadron Royal Air Force, 5 Squadron South African Air Force and 27 Squadron Royal Australian Air Force – were already flying this aircraft type as the P40K 'Kittyhawk', with considerable success – but, of course, theirs had been delivered new. The 99th were given one week's 'initiation' into aerial warfare and North Africa before they were expected to perform and they were not allowed into the pre-flight briefing for the Pantelleria attack. Hardly surprising then, when they were 'jumped' by a large German fighter group coming out of the sun and had to fight for themselves individually, they were not much use. However, despite the accusations that the black pilots couldn't handle the complicated aircraft and that their ground crews couldn't keep the machines in the air, not one B-26 or P-40 was lost that day.

The 99th began its tradition of never losing a bomber under its escort. The Red Tails were becoming a force to be reckoned with and would soon be joined by three other squadrons to form the 332nd Fighter Group, under the command of Colonel Benjamin O. Davis. The 332nd Fighter Group, the 'Tuskegee Airmen' excelled in everything it did. The 332nd claimed the distinction of having never lost a bomber throughout their operations in North Africa and Italy. In a little over three years, the 332nd pilots between them were awarded 150 Distinguished Flying Crosses and 740 Air Medals.

By the middle of 1943, Tibbets had excelled in his task as Bomb Leader and delivered far beyond his commanding general's expectation, who had observed Tibbets' attitude to the preparation of the guns carried in a B-17 – like Tibbets, he knew that this attention to detail could make all the difference to a bomber's safe return. He wanted to reward Tibbets' efforts by getting him out from under Colonel Norstad, who remained a thorn in his side. Back in the US, events were in motion that would allow him to do so.

The B-29 super bomber, manufactured by Boeing under contract from the US Army, was having serious teething problems. Three aircraft had been lost in test flight incidents as the result of engine fires, which had burned through the seemingly inadequate firewalls and reached the main spar, causing a wing to fall off and the aircraft to plummet from the sky. Boeing's chief test pilot, Eddie Allen, had died in one of the accidents and Boeing contacted General Arnold to say they didn't want to build the B-29 any more or risk further loss of life. Arnold's response was that if Boeing pulled out then they could also return the $100 million they had been paid in design and development costs. A compromise was reached; the US Army Air Force would take over the test flight programme and Boeing would build to instructions. The ultimate result was one of the finest heavy bombers in history.

General Henry Arnold contacted his old friend Jimmy Doolittle and asked for his 'best damned bomber pilot – and quick' to run the USAAF testing. Doolittle didn't really want to lose Tibbets from an operational standpoint, but knew that if he remained in the Twelfth Air Force, Norstad would eventually engineer his downfall. Doolittle firmly believed that Tibbets was a man with great potential and handed him over to Arnold, giving him 24 hours to pack and return to Washington. There was a little more, however, to that decision than just handing over his 'best bomber pilot' to Arnold. Jimmy Doolittle knew something about the B-29's troubles and he was also aware of the Manhattan Project, to the extent that the B-29 was intended to play a role in ending the war in the Pacific by delivering a new weapon to a Japanese target. Doolittle also knew quite well that sending Tibbets to lead the test programme would put him directly in line to lead the planned bombing mission.

Jimmy Doolittle was to lose a valuable member of his team, but his own career path was changing too, because the Twelfth Air Force was being dismantled to create a new and bigger North Africa/Italy command – the Fifteenth Air Force – and Jimmy Doolittle was promoted to Major-General to lead it. The Fifteenth would absorb most of the flying units of the Twelfth, losing most of the Royal Air Force squadrons, but picking up a couple of B-24 wings to make up the numbers. The Consolidated B-24 was a

A B-29 in flight.

A B-24 Liberator drops its bomb load.

This B-24 *Strawberry Bitch* was one of the aircraft that took part in the Ploesti oilfield raids. It is now kept at the United States Air Force Museum at Wright-Patterson Air Force Base in Ohio.

four engined bomber in the same league as the Boeing B-17, but could carry a heavier bomb load and had a slightly longer range. It was already making a name for itself in the Pacific, where very long distances were being flown to and from targets.

Paul Tibbets left North Africa and Colonel Norstad behind, only to have a run-in with a customs officer on his arrival in the US. He had over $1000 in cash in his bag and the customs officer wanted to confiscate it, as many US servicemen had returned home with illicit cash (often made from the sale of government property or gambling), but Tibbets was bringing home two months' pay and some money for a friend's parents, the friend having stayed in North Africa. Paul Tibbets was not best pleased at being asked to surrender his money and it took a senior customs officer to defuse the situation. This done, he checked in with General Arnold and made his way to the Boeing factory in Wichita, Kansas.

7

Paul Warfield Tibbets Jr

Paul Tibbets was born on 23 February 1915 in Quincy, Illinois. His father had been a salesman in a family grocery business before progressing to selling real estate. His mother, Enola Gay Tibbets (nee Haggard), grew up on an Iowa farm and was named for a character in a novel her father was reading shortly before her birth. Paul Tibbets himself described the place of his childhood as Mark Twain country, although the steamboats were long gone.

The family moved to Miami in 1924, and at the age of twelve, young Paul was invited to take a ride with barnstorming pilot Doug Davis to drop Baby Ruth candy bars on Hialeah racetrack in a promotional stunt for the Curtiss Candy Company. From then on, he was captivated by flight and dreamed of a career as an airman, though his father wanted him to be a doctor. His mother, however, encouraged him to pursue his dream.

In 1928, he enrolled in the Western Military Academy in North Alton, and then progressed to the University of Florida at Gainesville in 1933. He transferred to pre-med studies at the University of Cincinnati in Ohio, but his love of flying eventually won the day and he joined the United States Army Air Corps in 1937.

As a flight cadet he first flew the Consolidated PT-3, the same aircraft type that Jimmy Doolittle first flew 'blind' back in 1929, though Doolittle's aircraft was the Navy version, the NY-2. Successfully completing his primary flight training, Lieutenant Tibbets graduated to the North American BT-9, a fixed undercarriage precursor of the internationally famous North American AT-6 Texan (or Harvard in British service). The general shape of the wing plan, the fin, the tailplane and the fuselage of the BT-9 were all similar to the Texan, though the aircraft was slower. Receiving his wings in February 1938, at Randolph Field in Texas – the site of Jimmy Doolittle's stopover in his heroic trans-America flight in 1922 – Paul Tibbets scored the highest cumulative grades of his class, but chose to fly observation aircraft types instead of fighters, which would have been a natural choice for many a high-scorer.

Transferring to Fort Benning in Georgia, Lieutenant Tibbets started his flying career with the Douglas O-46, a parasol-wing observation type that was outdated as it rolled off the El Segundo production line. The next observation type that he flew was the more up-to-date North American O-47, a rather pot-bellied mid-wing monoplane with windows in the floor of the fuselage to allow photography from inside the aircraft pointing almost straight down. In fact, it was possible to fix a K-20 flight camera, a photographic device that used five-inch wide film, into an exactly vertical position for reconnaissance purposes. It could be connected to a remote control and electric drive motor so the photographer didn't have to be sitting next to it.

Next on Paul Tibbets' flight list was the Martin B-10, a mid-wing twin-engined bomber with enclosed cockpit and retractable undercarriage. This aircraft was quite advanced for its time, introduced into service in 1935/36. It could fly at 230mph and carried up to 2500lbs of bombs. He was always meticulous in his adherence to

The two-year-old Paul Tibbets on his father's knee. At the time his father was a Captain in the US Army, fighting in the First World War.

The young Paul at the age of five.

Cadet Tibbets, as depicted in the West Point Military Academy Yearbook in 1933.

Lieutenant Tibbets with his newly awarded wings after graduating from flying training at Kelly Field, Texas.

The Douglas O-46, an obsolescent aircraft from the day it entered service.

The North American O-47, notable for its 'pot-bellied' appearance, to accommodate a vertical camera.

The Martin B-10 twin-engined bomber, the first all-metal bomber in the US inventory and an aircraft capable of keeping pace in airspeed with its fighter/pursuit counterparts.

the rules of aviation and engagement and it was probably this aircraft, more than any other, on which he honed his skill and dedication to perfection in the air, and his considerable bombing skills.

While at Fort Benning, Paul Tibbets met and became friendly with George Smith Patton Jr. Patton was a colonel in 1938, and Tibbets a second lieutenant, and Tibbets never called him anything other than 'Colonel Patton', even when they went shooting together. Not long after his arrival at Fort Benning, Patton decided that he should have an observation aircraft assigned to him as a personal machine to go up and observe his battle tank groupings in field exercises. Hardly surprisingly, Headquarters Army Air Corps didn't authorise such an operation, so Patton bought his own aircraft. It was a Stinson Voyager and Tibbets and a friend were persuaded to fly it, although as it was a civilian aircraft they had to get civil pilot's licences to legally fly Patton over his tank battles.

During this time a friend set Tibbets up on a blind date with his girlfriend's friend. The lady was named Lucy Wingate and she and Tibbets quickly fell in love. Married in Holy Trinity, Alabama, a short distance from Fort Benning, on 19 June 1939, Lucy presented her husband with a son, Paul Tibbets III, on 19 November 1940. Not long after this, the Army Air Corps began to search for pilots with 1000 hours or more on their log books for advanced flying training in anticipation of the possibility of the US being drawn

A Stinson Voyager, registered in Britain in the early post-war years.

Stinson L-5 Sentinel

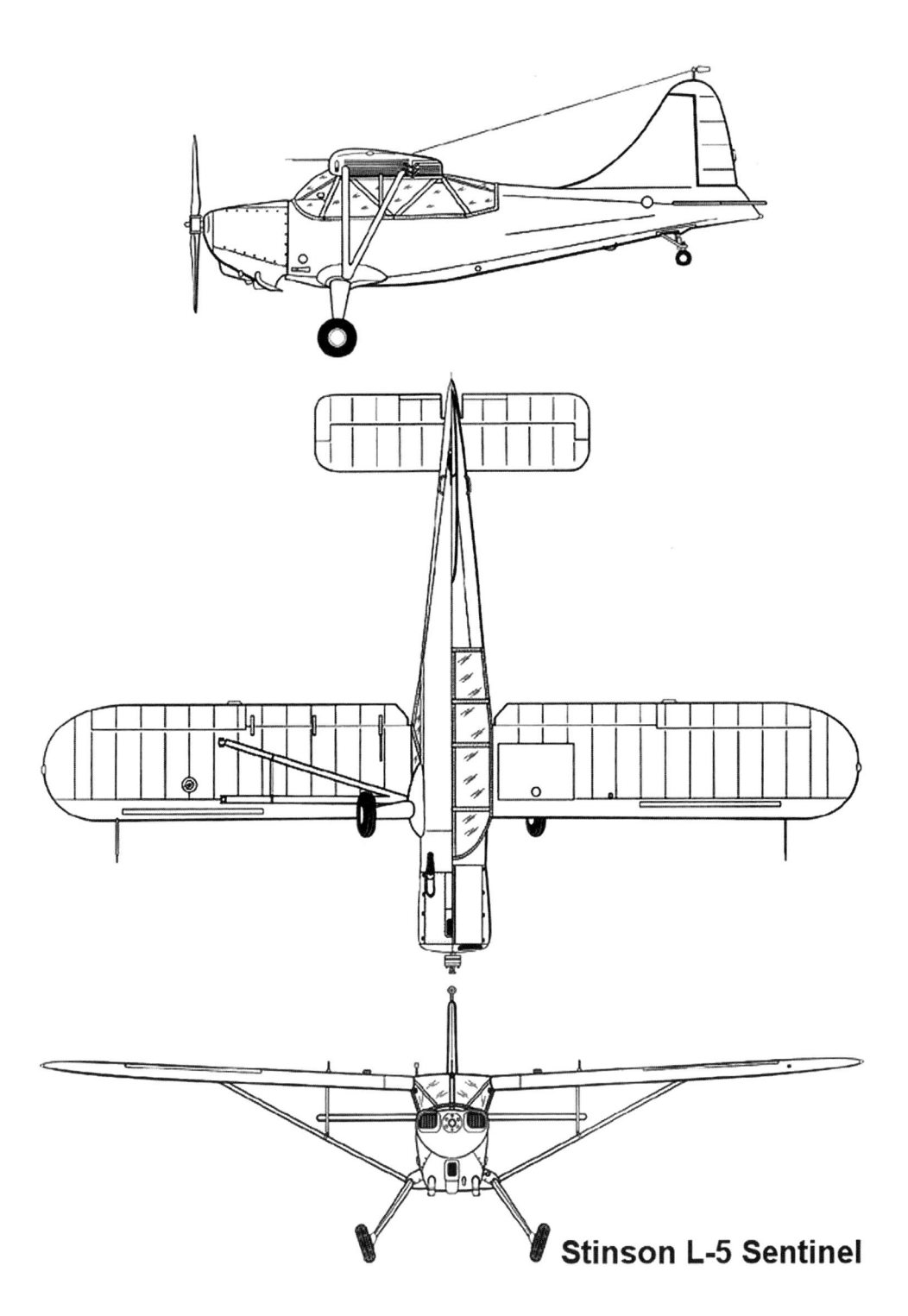

A Stinson Voyager 105/Sentinel, the aircraft model bought by Patton so that Paul Tibbets could fly him over his tank formations.

into the war in Europe. Tibbets was chosen and at the beginning of 1941 he moved to Randolph Field, near San Antonio in Texas, for flight training on the Douglas A-20 Havoc light bomber/ground attack aircraft.

In April 1941 Tibbets took up the post of Engineering Officer with the 90th Squadron, Third Attack Group at Hunter Field in Savannah, Georgia, covering the introduction of the Douglas A-20. The A-20 was powered by two Wright R-2600-A5B 'Double Cyclone' engines. The Double Cyclone was a fourteen-cylinder double-row radial engine and was expected to be entirely reliable, as was the reputation of all Wright engines. However, such was not the case this time, as Paul Tibbets discovered. The A-20 was a low-level attack aircraft and low level to the Third Attack Group meant at or below 100 feet, but at that altitude engine crankcase back-pressure occurred; when a pilot throttled back for an approach and landing, he would find oil being pumped out of the oil cooler breather. A pressure relief valve introduced into the oiling system solved the problem, but the root of the problem was that the A-20 had been designed for intermediate altitudes.

The training needed to operate the A-20 was quite different from any the US Army Air Corps had instituted before. Pilots had to learn to fly at 100 feet in case they were called on to fight in Europe; Britain's Royal Air Force pilots were flying the A-20 at that altitude and below, because that was the height of German flak towers. If an aircraft could fly below the towers it would leave the defenders powerless and have a greater chance of reaching its target, and the pilots also had to learn to use the local terrain as cover. As Paul Tibbets said, 'We were expected to have chlorophyll on our propeller tips. If there were trees, we'd fly alongside them. If there were hills, we'd fly between them. And all this with your wing tucked in close to the one next to you.'

On Saturday 6 December 1941 the 90th was sent to take part in manoeuvres at Fort Bragg in North Carolina, flying attack missions on ground troops. They flew back on the Sunday at leisure. Paul Tibbets made his way to Savannah and homed in on a local radio station to pick up a marker for his radio compass. Suddenly, the music in his headset stopped and a voice broke in to announce that the Japanese Navy had attacked Pearl Harbor.

The Douglas A-20 was not originally ordered by the USAAC, but France bought 270. When the US joined the war in Europe, some 6,000 were delivered.

The Douglas B-18 was the 'in-fill' aircraft while deliveries were awaited of the Boeing B-17, so Paul Tibbets found himself flying this type until the 340th Bombardment Squadron could be formed with the B-17. The greatest legacy of the B-18 was its flying surfaces design emerging in the C-47 Dakota.

With war at America's door, Paul Tibbets, with his extensive log of hours on the A-20, was selected for training on the new, bigger bomber that many said should have been ordered instead of the B-18. This was the Boeing B-17 'Flying Fortress'. However, there was a shortage of B-17s to fly, so as a temporary measure, the Douglas B-18 twin-engined bomber came to Savannah and Tibbets and his fellow crews flew patrols up and down the Atlantic Coast, tasked with destroying German submarines.

The B-18's greatest quality was that it was a stable aeroplane to fly, though it was very slow and could only climb comfortably to 12,000 feet. But it could fly for a long time and nine-hour patrols became commonplace. Every B-18 in US Army Air Corps service was transferred to Savannah to equip the coastal patrol group, with the result that a new squadron was formed and located at Fort Bragg. Captain Paul Tibbets had the task of organising the relocation of aircraft and men.

The aircraft Tibbets should have been flying, the Boeing B-17, was designed by a team led by Clair Egtvedt, who visualised a four-engined bomber that could match the speed of most contemporary fighter planes. This was Boeing's Model 299 and was the largest land-plane of its day. As the B-17 went into volume production at factories all over the US, Captain Tibbets was ordered to McDill Field to finally commence training on the type. He was the first officer to join the newly formed 97th Bombardment Group (H) and was given the job of receiving new crews and aircraft and work out a training programme to bring his fliers up to operational standard. Most of his new pilots were second lieutenants with minimal flying experience, and their conversion to multi-engine flying had consisted of 20 hours or so in the Cessna UC-78 'Bobcat', a communications and command six-seat twin.

Tibbets decided that the best way to familiarise the young green pilots would be to give them three six-hour transition sorties in a B-18, then bring them up to a series of six-hour cycles in a B-17 as quickly as possible, so the Group could move up to Sarasota to pick up its own equipment and transfer to a theatre of operations. As commander of the 340th Squadron, he was responsible for bringing the flight crews up to readiness, not just the pilots. This included navigators, flight engineers, gunners, bombardiers and radiomen; all had to be combat ready and prepared to ship out as quickly as possible. During this time he often did not see his wife and son in Tampa for days at a time.

The move to Sarasota had to take place inside six weeks, during which time all crews, aircraft and support equipment, including a range of spare parts for the aircraft, had to be ready to move. He then learned that they would be given a further six weeks at Sarasota to be ready to ship out overseas. Next came an instruction to fly to Fresno in California. On the way, they were to route through Ellington Field, near San Antonio in Texas. By the time Paul Tibbets had gathered his wits at Ellington, he discovered that almost every airfield in Texas had a B-17 on it! This was a poor testament to the navigation training his crews had received, but such had been the drive to train the pilots to fly the B-17, formation flying and navigation had been somewhat overlooked. He approached the commander of the bombing and navigation school at Ellington to ask for an intensive course for his crews. There were lectures day and night and navigators were taken onto rooftops to practise the use of sextants, while gunners had to be able to strip a machine gun blindfold.

Then came a surprise; the 340th flew to Fresno as instructed, only to be told that plans had changed and they were not going to the Pacific as expected, but were to fly to Bangor in Maine. By this point the 97th Bombardment Group consisted of four squadrons, two at Bangor and the two at Westover Field in Massachusetts. The 97th was going to England. As previously mentioned, the Group was initially located at Grafton Underwood in the South Midlands county of Northamptonshire. So began Major Paul Tibbets' role in the Second World War, the details of which are covered elsewhere in this book, but suffice to say, after his time in North Africa he returned to the US to lead the 509th Composite Group, formed to drop the as yet unfinished atomic bomb. The Group was stationed on the island of Tinian in May 1945, from where the now Colonel Tibbets flew the historic flight that resulted in the destruction of Hiroshima.

With the war in the Pacific over and debates raging over the morality of dropping the atom bomb, the 509th Composite Group and its squadrons left Tinian and returned to the US. The decision had been made that the 509th would continue to exist and Colonel Tibbets would, for the time being, remain in command. The location chosen

The Boeing B-17E finally formed the equipment of the 97th Bombardment Group, which originally was intended for the war in the Pacific, but was actually assigned to operate from England.

One of the Douglas C-54 'Skymaster' aircraft of the 320th Troop Transport Squadron. Colonel Tibbets flew this aircraft regularly between Washington, Alamogordo, Wendover and Tinian in the work-up of the atomic bomb programme. Some referred to this aircraft as 'Tibbets' Taxi'.

for the 509th's new home was Roswell in New Mexico, a remote location that would protect the airmen from media scrutiny.

In the wider world the Soviet Union was isolating itself from the West and was working on its own version of the B-29. It materialised as the Tupolev Tu-4 and was a remarkably good copy of Boeing's giant. The Russians were also developing their own nuclear weapons, and in response US leaders such General Curtis LeMay (see Chapter 6) – now based at the Pentagon after his return from command of the Twentieth Air Force – believed that America had to retain nuclear supremacy to counter the Soviet threat. The Cold War had begun.

The first step in US post-war nuclear testing was to take place in the Bikini Atoll, located in the western end of the Marshall Islands chain. Colonel Paul Tibbets was instructed by General LeMay to report to General Street at Bolling Field, to learn about Operation *Crossroads*, a test programme for the further development and refinement of the atom bomb, a joint Army-Navy project. A target of 70 various naval vessels, including an old German warship and one from Japan, were formed in a circle, with the USS *Nevada*, now redundant from Navy service and painted bright orange as a target for the bomber crew to see from 30,000 feet. The obvious choice for the drop would have been Tibbets and his Hiroshima crew, but political manoeuvring meant that another team were chosen, who declined Tibbets' advice. The result was a disaster.

The test bomb fell some 1800 feet from its target, the *Nevada*, and sank a merchant ship, the *Gillian*. General LeMay was furious to learn that much of the test equipment placed on board the ships in the ring had been so damaged as to be unreadable, as the vessels were too close to where the bomb fell, which they would not have been if it had hit its target within the estimated 300 foot drop point. LeMay wanted to know why the drop was so wide and he wanted Paul Tibbets to tell him. It turned out that the crew had put in the wrong ballistic information into the bombsight. LeMay had Tibbets and Ferebee sent to Washington, where they presented their findings to General Carl Spaatz. It did not go down well.

In 1947 Paul Tibbets had a new challenge. After a period as a student at the Air Command and Staff College at Maxwell Air Force Base, Alabama, Colonel Tibbets was assigned to the Pentagon, where he was appointed Director of the Strategic Air Division. As the bomber branch chief he worked closely with Boeing during the development of their new six jet engine powered, swept-wing bomber, the B-47 Stratojet, until February 1952. He flew with the legendary Boeing test pilot, 'Tex' Johnson, who taught Tibbets what the B-47 could really do in the air.

Following a stint at the Air War College in 1955, Tibbets was appointed Director of War Plans, Allied Air Forces in Central Europe at Fontainebleau in France. In 1956 he returned to the US to command the 308th Bomb Wing at Hunter Air Force Base in Georgia. In just one year, under Tibbets' strict discipline and leadership, the 308th went from a lowly unit to the top of the ratings. In January 1958, Tibbets was reassigned to MacDill Air Force Base in Florida, where he assumed command of the ailing 6th Air Division. With this command came the star of a brigadier general. Again, the new general whipped the base into shape with strict discipline and ruthless personnel changes.

From February 1961 until mid-1964, General Tibbets was assigned to Headquarters Air Force as director of management analysis. During his last two years of service he

After the war was over, the 509th Composite Group and all its aircraft were transferred back to the US, this time to Roswell Army Airfield in New Mexico.

The last official photograph of Brigadier-General Paul W. Tibbets. A quite remarkable man who maintained to his dying day that what he did was right.

travelled to New Delhi in India as part of the US military mission there; he was mobbed and vilified as a mass murderer because of Hiroshima.

Brigadier-General Paul W. Tibbets made his final visit to the *Enola Gay* in 2005. While in the cockpit he recounted stories of how he loved his crewmen and how well they had executed their mission – a mission that heralded the end of the Second World War. His personal views of the 509th Composite Group mission accomplishment never changed during his lifetime. 'I am content that we did what reason compelled and duty dictated.' Paul Warfield Tibbets Jr died at his home in Columbus, Ohio on 1 November 2007, at the age of 92.

8

The Manhattan Project

The Germans had been researching the use of Uranium-235 as a weapon material for some time before the US began work on it. The Allies had little detailed knowledge of Axis research, beyond that it was headed by Werner Heisenberg, one of Nils Bohr's pre-war colleagues, and that some research was conducted in Japan, but with little progress. At one time it was feared that Hitler's scientists were very close to developing the bomb, although a number of German scientists expressed surprise to their Allied captors when two bombs were detonated in Japan. They were convinced that talk of atomic weapons was merely propaganda. The Nazi reactor effort had been severely handicapped by Heisenberg's belief that heavy water was necessary as a neutron moderator; they never discovered the secret of purified graphite for making nuclear reactors from natural uranium.

The Germans controlled a heavy water production facility outside Rjukan in Tinn, Norway, built by Norsk Hydro in 1934 as an expansion to the Vemork hydroelectric power plant, which had opened in 1911. It was the first purpose-built facility, and had a production capacity of 12 tons a year. In 1940 (before the German invasion of Norway) the French government had purchased the plant's entire stock of heavy water, after discovering that Germany had already offered to do so, the French concluding that they were researching an atomic bomb. The *Deuxième Bureau* (French Secret Service) contacted three local agents – Captain Muller, Lieutenant Mossé and Lieutenant Knall-Demars – to obtain the plant's stock (185kg/188 litres). This they did with the help of the Swedish and Norwegian resistance, and it was then transported to England on the SS *Broompark*, just before the German invasion in April 1940. The heavy water was stored at the Tower of London for a time, before being taken to Cambridge; it could not be sent to France as Germany had invaded the country in May.

The Allies then decided to destroy the Vemork plant, and on 18 October 1942 four Norwegian SOE (Special Operations Executive) agents were parachuted near the plant to perform reconnaissance, a mission codenamed Operation *Grouse*. On 19 November 1942 British paratroopers attacked the Vemork plant in an attempt to destroy it and permanently cut off German supplies of heavy water, a raid known as Operation *Freshman*. However the raid failed when two of the three gliders crashed, killing their occupants, and the men on the third glider were executed by the Germans. Operation *Gunnerside* in February 1943 saw six Norwegian SOE agents parachuted to join their comrades from *Grouse*, and on 28 February they destroyed the heavy water section of the Vemork plant, along with 500kg of heavy water. These operations effectively ended the German nuclear research programme.

However, as the Allies did not know exactly how far German nuclear development had gone, and with the necessity of ending the protracted war in the Pacific to consider, President Roosevelt authorised unprecedented scientific and military expenditure to give the US the atom bomb first. He knew from intelligence reports that the Germans had high-grade uranium compounds, a nearly complete cyclotron, combined with what was then probably the greatest chemical engineering industry in the world.

The Manhattan Project was America's answer to German research, initiated to develop nuclear fission and fusion, the ultimate objective being to produce a new weapon. The theory was that nuclear fission – the splitting of atoms – would create a destructive force greater than anything seen before, an atomic bomb. The Manhattan Engineering District of the Corps of Engineers was give the job of developing the new weapon, and on 17 September 1942, Colonel Leslie R. Groves (promoted Brigadier-General just six days later to match the perceived authority level required to lead the project) was appointed to establish and run it, with a budget of more than $2 billion.

Leslie Groves was born in Albany, New York, on 17 August 1896. He studied at the University of Washington for one year and progressed to the Massachusetts Institute of Technology for another two years before entering the US Army Academy at West Point, from which he graduated in 1918. He was commissioned in the Corps of Engineers and took courses at the Engineer's School, Camp Humphreys (now Fort Belvoir), Virginia, 1918–20 and 1921, with time out for brief service in France during the First World War.

In 1931, Groves was attached to the Office of the Chief of Engineers in Washington and was promoted to Captain in October 1934. In 1936, he graduated from the Command and General Staff School, Fort Leavenworth, Kansas, and from the Army War College in 1939, after which he was assigned to the General Staff in Washington. He was promoted to Major and Temporary Colonel in July and November 1940 and

Major-General Leslie Groves in an unusually leisurely pose at his desk in Washington DC.

The Manhattan Project sites.

assigned first to the Office of the Quartermaster General and then to the Office of the Chief of Engineers where his responsibility for the oversight of army construction projects included supervision of the building of the Pentagon, which was completed in under 18 months. It was this impressive ability to deliver that won him the leadership of the Manhattan Project.

Groves was charged with the task of securing a site in Tennessee for manufacture and another location for the development team. He moved the Manhattan Project itself to Washington and secured priority ratings for the procurement of construction and raw materials. When he took command in 1941 he made it very clear to his scientists that by late 1942 he expected them to be in a position to decide what processes would produce a bomb in the shortest period of time. The needs of war, he said, required scientists to move from laboratory research to development and production in record time. Though traditional scientific caution might have been short-circuited in the process, there was no alternative if a bomb was to be built in time to be used. As everyone involved in the Manhattan Project soon learned, Groves would never lose sight of his goal and would make all his decisions with that single objective in mind.

The Manhattan Project was authorised to build full-scale gaseous diffusion and plutonium plants and the compromise electromagnetic plant, as well as heavy water production facilities. It was reported that bombs could possibly be produced during the first half of 1945 but despite presidential and military pressures, it was the clear view of the Manhattan team that earlier delivery was highly unlikely. There was no way of guaranteeing that the US would overtake Germany in the race for the atomic bomb.

THE MANHATTAN PROJECT

When General Groves took command of the project, he was answerable only to the Secretary of State for War, Henry Stimson, who was the liaison between Groves and President Roosevelt. Roosevelt and Stimson, thanks to detailed FBI security vetting, knew more about Leslie Groves than about any other man in the Officer Corps, even down to his love of tennis and candy bars and his ability to perform complicated mathematics in his head. They also knew that he worked a 15-hour day, was a tough negotiator, and would cut corners but not take risks, having a remarkable capacity for getting the job done on time and within budget.

Groves' team spent its $2 billion on production facilities in Tennessee, New Mexico and Washington DC. Vast sums were also spent on research into areas that proved to be blind alleys, but such was the urgency of making progress. There was naturally a great deal of secrecy surrounding the project, which appears to have irritated many of the civilian scientists, but it did mean that it was possible to make decisions with little regard for normal peacetime political considerations. Groves knew that as long as he had the backing of the White House, money would be available and he could devote his considerable energies entirely to running the bomb project. Such was the level of subterfuge that many people working for the organisation did not know what they had been part of until they heard about the bombing of Hiroshima.

Unfinished research on three separate processes had to be used to freeze design plans for production facilities, even though it was recognised that later findings would inevitably dictate changes. The pilot plant stage was eliminated entirely, violating all manufacturing practices and leading to intermittent shutdowns. The problems of compressing the stages between the laboratory and full production created an emotionally charged atmosphere with optimism and despair alternating with alarming frequency. And whilst the development work was continuing, there was the task of finding an aircraft to carry the new bomb, a target to hit, and a bombing group to do the job.

Paul Tibbets had joined the B-29 test programme in March 1943. By the end of the summer of 1944, he had flown around 1400 hours in the B-29, first as a test pilot then as a flight instructor, and knew it better than any other pilot in the US Army Air Force. It had become clear to those in command that Tibbets was the obvious choice to lead the group that would eventually drop the yet unfinished weapon.

Meanwhile the Manhattan Project nearly came off the rails. On 26 August 1944, Nils Bohr went to see President Roosevelt without informing Groves. It appears that he wanted to discuss with the President the issue of sharing the knowledge he and his colleagues had acquired with the world's scientific community. In making this approach, he could not possibly have been thinking of the security of the US, and even today it is hard to understand his reasoning. Thankfully the President denied his request and the project remained secret. When General Groves discovered this, he was utterly furious. That Bohr had approached the President with such a ludicrous proposal was, to Groves, unthinkable.

There was also the issue that the project's scientists were not as united as they should have been. US intelligence had established that the Nazis did not have the resources to produce an atomic weapon in the foreseeable future, and the scientists began to divide into two groups, those who wanted to work on the bomb, and those who felt they were no longer certain it was necessary. Some suggested that, since the Germans had not yet surrendered, Hitler's scientists could still be working in the heart of rural Germany, and could yet surprise the world, but others considered the manufacture of such a deadly weapon to be unethical if it was no longer needed.

General Groves was willing to allow such discussions to take place, but clearly expected them to remain very much behind closed doors. His task was very clear to him – to see through the construction of a useable nuclear weapon that could be

The German submarine U-234 in dock at Kiel, prior to its only voyage into enemy waters.

Kapitanleutnant Johann Fehler comes aboard USS *Sutton* to formally surrender his ship, its passengers and contents. The two Japanese officers on board committed suicide.

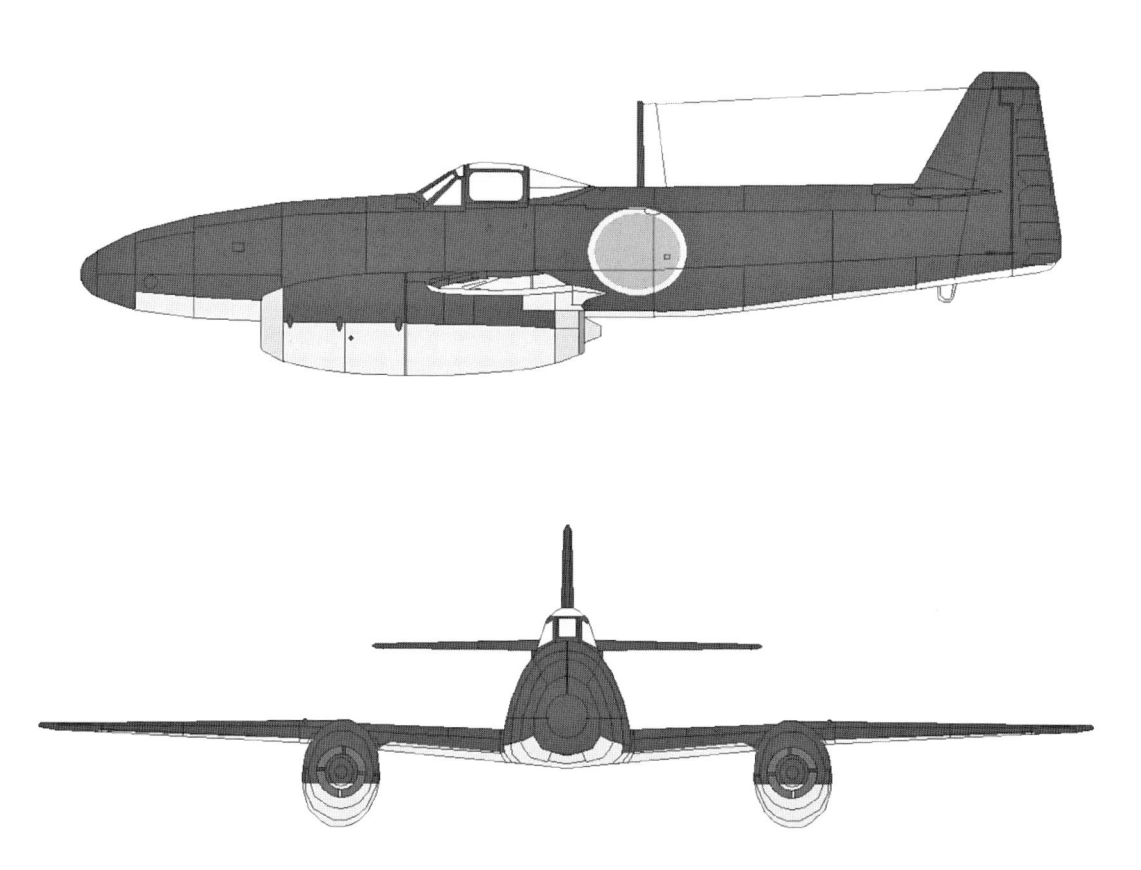

The Nakajima Kikka was closely modelled on the Messerschmitt Me-262 and was in development at the time of the Japanese surrender.

brought to bear on Japan to bring them to the point of surrender. Nothing less would satisfy him, for he knew that nothing else would satisfy his President. Now was not the time to stop work on the weapon he believed could end the war. He knew exactly which side of the controversy each of the project's scientists supported. His vast number of security agents kept him informed, although they had failed to anticipate that Bohr would go to Roosevelt. Groves had never experienced such effrontery since taking command of the project on 17 September 1942. It would not happen again. Security was further tightened at all sites.

Vindication of Groves' philosophy came with a discovery in May 1945 of German-produced Uranium-235. Germany's largest U-boat, the 1700-ton Type XB minelayer *U-234* – was at sea when the European war ended, on her way to Japan. It surrendered in mid-ocean to a US Navy destroyer escort. Her cargo included two complete ME-262 jet fighters in kit form with complete technical data and 550 kilograms of uranium oxide, labelled 235, packed in lead.

The surrender of *U-234* came about as its captain, Kapitan-Lieutenant Johann Fehler, picked up a radio signal that Germany had surrendered to the Allies. Realising that he was now in contravention of the Geneva Convention, he instructed that his ship should surface and sent out a surrender signal. Rendezvousing with the American destroyers USS *Grand Banks* and USS *Sutton*, he surrendered his vessel, its cargo and twelve passengers, who included a German general and a nuclear scientist. *U-234* was then escorted by the two US destroyers to its final destination at Newport News in Virginia.

The cargo of *U-234* might not have influenced the ultimate outcome of the Second World War in the Pacific, but Me-262s over Japan would have been a serious deterrent to the American bombing campaign. The possession of uranium in weapon-building quantities could also have been a serious threat to international stability. But the US got there first.

9

Bringing the B-29 to the 509th

As Lieutenant-Colonel Paul Tibbets left North Africa for the US, the Manhattan Project was well under way, though he would not be aware of it for another year. General Jimmy Doolittle did know about it, but none of the detail, just that America's biggest bomber, the B-29, would carry a weapon to its target. And he had sent Tibbets to work on the B-29 in the knowledge that his best bomber pilot would almost certainly make the drop.

Tibbets took a period of leave before taking up his new job, to spend time with his wife Lucy and their two sons. He then made his way to the Boeing factory in Wichita.

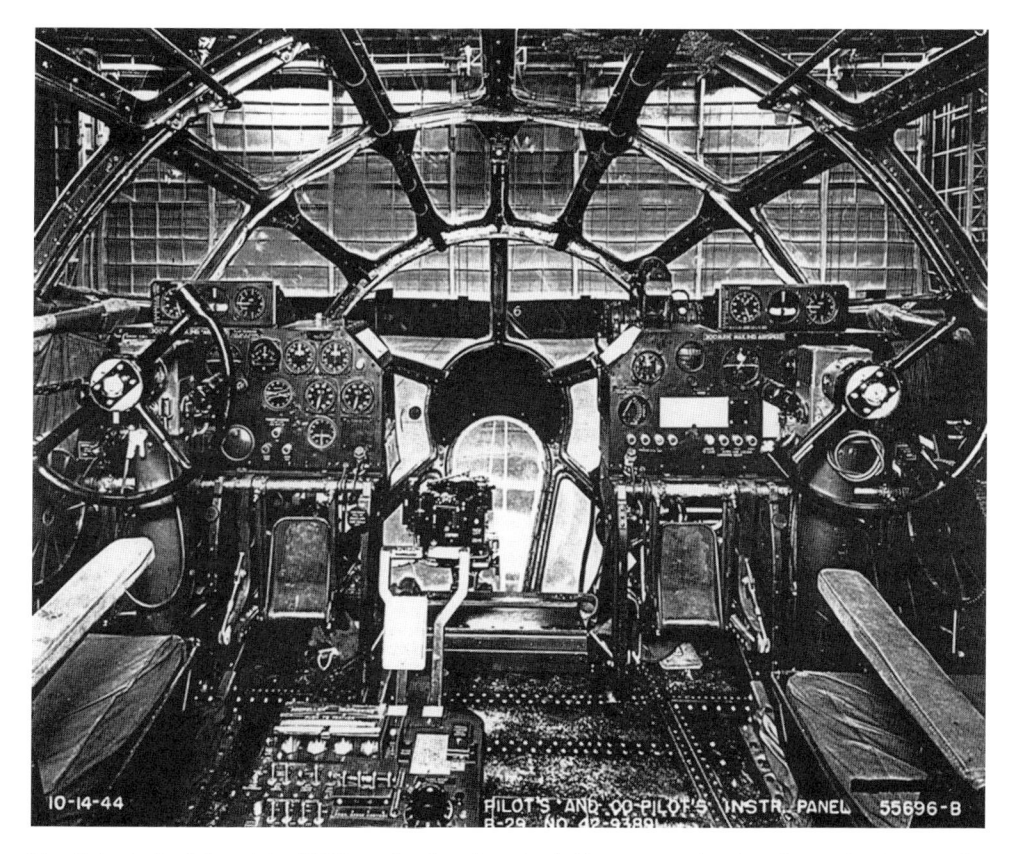

The flight deck of the mighty B-29, at the time America's biggest ever bomber. It was fundamentally different from any aircraft that preceded it.

A pilot sits in at the flight deck of the B-29.

His first task was to meet the Boeing team he would work with, familiarise himself with the factory site and then learn all he could about his new charge, the Boeing B-29 Superfortress. He studied drawings and specifications, and asked questions of all levels of people, from the senior executives down to the shop-floor assemblers, trying to establish the reasons behind the three accidents in testing. He wanted to know why the three airframes had gone down and particularly, he wanted to know all about the aircraft the chief test pilot Eddie Allen went down with. He needed to understand that everything possible had been done by the aircrews to prevent the crashes, so he could pin each crash down to a particular technical fault as far as possible. He was going nowhere near the inside of a B-29 until he had a much better understanding of the machine and its nasty habits.

Originally drawn up in its operational form as early as 1940, the B-29 was a highly innovative aircraft, truly a 'leading-edge' machine. It had a fire control system that enabled one gunner to operate five pairs of machine guns, a pneumatic bomb bay door, and completely pressurised crew compartments which were interconnected (front and rear) by a crawl-through tube. It also had a tricycle landing gear, was bigger and faster, could fly higher and further, and with a far bigger bomb load than the old faithful B-17. It was also the largest bomber yet built, powered by four 18-cylinder double-row radial Wright R-3350 Double Cyclone engines, which were themselves a problem, as they frequently failed or burst into flames.

B-29s in build at the Boeing plant at Wichita, Kansas.

Female workers in an American factory. Women like these were the inspiration for the famous image of 'Rosie the Riveter'. The crawl tube shows how confined much of the work was.

The aircraft was designed to carry a bomb load of 20,000lbs over a distance of 5800 miles at an operational altitude of 30,000 feet without refuelling. The all-up weight was 120,000lbs by design and airframe design sketches began on the project, the Boeing Model 345, back in the late 1930s. A mock-up of the aircraft was built in 1941 and the US Army ordered fourteen development prototypes, followed very quickly by a production order for 250 more for squadron service. The first prototype flew in September 1942 and testing continued until 18 February 1943, when the second prototype crashed after an in-flight engine fire burned through the wing structure and caused the aircraft to break up in the air, killing the crew and 19 people on the ground. It was at this point that Boeing threatened to pull out and USAAF took over the testing (see Chapter 6).

In March 1943, Lieutenant-Colonel Paul Tibbets started work, analysing the existing flight test programme and assessing the task ahead. There were long meetings with the Curtiss-Wright Corporation, investigating all aspects of how an engine sets itself on fire, checking fuel lines for suspect connections which could leak in service and create an opportunity for combustion, checking valve timings to ensure accuracy, checking all engine seals and gaskets and bolt torque settings to reduce the possibilities of gasket creep and thus leakages. No engine rotated on Tibbets' B-29s until all these things were checked and then checked again. The test flights weren't going to start in earnest until all these factors were signed off and Tibbets was satisfied that he stood a 99 per cent chance of getting a B-29 off the ground and back to base on four engines.

The Wright 3350 compound radial engine that powered the B-29. Engine problems centred largely around the fact that the exhaust valves were sodium filled to facilitate cooling. In the early stages of the B-29's career, these valves were breaking stems and the valve heads dropping into the cylinders, breaking up the pistons and allowing the combustion flame to reach down the magnesium crankcase, with disastrous results.

The B-29 demanded a great deal of attention to the engines in its development stage and into operational service.

His next task was to investigate issues in the airframe design. Feedback from Curtiss-Wright's engine specialists suggested a close look at the main wing spars and the engine mountings. Tibbets wanted there to be adequate fire-walling between the engine mounts and the spars, not least to prevent another accident such as that which had killed Eddie Allen. That crash had occurred because of an engine fire, which might not have happened if there had been closer liaison between Wright and Boeing, because the Wright engineers contended that if a certain modification recommended by them had been implemented, the fire would not have reached the main spar.

Clearly there were several design issues with the B-29, but they were difficult to resolve because the aerodynamic shape had to remain as designed in order to maintain the prospect of it achieving its design envelope performance, but one of the key problems with the 3350 engine was that it overheated inside the cowlings of the B-29. The air induction apertures were made as large as possible inside the basic cowl design shape and the cooling outlet shutters were made much bigger than the original design. This meant that in hot climates the maximum speed at 30,000 feet was reduced, but fewer engines burst into flames.

Curtiss-Wright finally had to insist on Boeing reducing the maximum power setting of the 3350 in order to reduce the risk of overheating. Boeing had done all it could with the cowlings. They introduced a lined firewall between the engine and its back mounting plate, they enlarged exhaust valves in a hope of dissipating heat more quickly, and they introduced sodium-filled exhaust valves. The object of this was that a hollow valve filled with elemental sodium as a coolant would function more efficiently and keep the operating temperature down. But sometimes the valve head burned out and the slimmer, hollow stem would break, letting the valve head hit the piston as the engine ran. This would punch a hole into the piston and then neat fuel was pushed into the crankcase where it would ignite, the fire made worse by being inside a casting made from 300lbs of magnesium. If the fire wasn't controlled almost the instant it started, it would rage back into the wing spar and at the very least weaken it, which had led to the accident which killed Eddie Allen. However, under Tibbets' guidance the B-29's engine and airframe issues were resolved, and it finally took to the air. Tibbets logged over 400 flying hours to make sure of its reliability.

The flight test programme in co-ordination with Boeing and Air Materiel Command continued until March 1944 at which time Lieutenant-Colonel Tibbets, having completed his work and signed the aircraft off, was assigned to Grand Island in Nebraska, to become Director of Operations under his old commander from his days with the 97th Bombardment Group, now Brigadier-General Frank Armstrong, who had been given the task of setting up a B-29 instructor transition school and a basic flight training unit for new combat pilots. Tibbets spent six months there, giving him a total of 18 months with the B-29 and making him the most experienced B-29 pilot in USAAF. It made his next assignment inevitable.

Summoned to Second Air Force headquarters on 1 September 1944, Tibbets reported firstly to Colonel John Lansdale, who simply introduced himself as himself as 'Lansdale, Intelligence'. He asked Tibbets to step into the washroom, adjoining the office of General Uzal G. Ent, the commanding general of Second Air Force. Tibbets assumed it was not to be a traditional security interview. 'Have you ever been in trouble with the police?' Tibbets was an honest individual and his instincts told him that this man already knew the answer to the question, so replied in the affirmative. He had been arrested by the North Miami Beach police as a youth, having been found in the back of a car with a girl. He'd spent a few hours in a cell, while a friend of his father, Judge Curry, gained his release and managed to suppress the whole incident.

Lansdale then took him to General Ents' office. Besides the general there were two other men in the room, US Navy Captain William 'Deak' Parsons, an explosives expert, and Harvard physicist Professor Norman Ramsey. Ramsey asked Tibbets if he had heard of atomic energy; Tibbets explained that he had majored in physics in college. 'So what do you know of atomic energy and why it might be of interest to military organisations?' Tibbets looked at Ent for guidance, but found nothing but a deadpan face. Ent had been cautioned only a few days before this meeting, when he first become aware of Project Manhattan, that he risked being court-martialed if any leak of information was traced to him. Tibbets looked to Lansdale, who gave the tiniest of nods. Tibbets stated that he understood that the Germans had been experimenting with the creation of heavy water, which they had taken over from the Norwegians, with the intention of splitting the atom. Ramsey seemed pleased and went on then to explain that the US had split the atom and was working on creating a bomb that would use atomic energy for its explosive power. He predicted that it would have the force of 20,000 tons of TNT. General Ent then told Tibbets that he had been selected to drop that bomb.

Professor Ramsey and Captain Parsons started to give Tibbets a thorough briefing on the history and problems associated with building the bomb, but Lansdale interjected: 'Colonel, I want you to understand one thing. Security is first, last and always. You will commit as little as possible to paper. You will tell only those who need to know what they must know to do their jobs properly. Understood?' Tibbets replied that he understood perfectly. General Ent explained that Tibbets would take command of the 393rd Bombardment Squadron (VH), currently based in Nebraska. It would form part of a larger unit, which would make it a totally self-contained and self-sufficient group, to be known as the 509th Composite Group. The 393rd Bombardment (H) Squadron already existed as a B-17 unit and had been ready to transfer to Europe

BRINGING THE B-29 TO THE 509TH

A cross-section of the Hiroshima bomb 'Little Boy', showing the gun-type mechanism.

Wendover Field in Utah. A remote, unfriendly place, but perfect for preserving the essential secrecy of the 509th Composite Group.

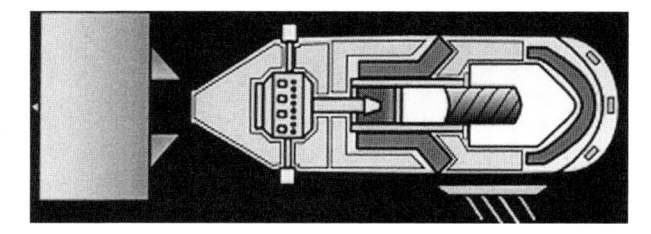

before General Ent stepped in and designated it the world's first atomic strike force. The training base would be at Wendover Field in Utah. The code name for the US Army Air Force's involvement in the project would be 'Silverplate' and Colonel Tibbets would be empowered to use this code word to acquire anything he needed.

Tibbets was finding it hard to believe that one bomb dropped from a single aircraft could equal the force of 20,000 tons of high explosive. In terms of current squadron operations, it would take over 400 bombers to deliver that firepower. But if it was really going to happen, he wanted to work with the men he knew and trusted from his days in Europe and North Africa. In order to ready them he would have to set up an intensive flying training programme for his crews; they would have to learn not only how to fly the B-29, but how to deal with a new weapon.

It took a little getting to grips with the unusual title of 'Composite' for the 509th, but it was a wholly self-contained group of a kind not seen before in US Army Air Force history. Entirely self sufficient, it had a heavy bombardment squadron (the 393rd, serving the principal function of the Group), a heavy transportation squadron (the 320th), an engineering squadron, a support squadron (the 390th Base Service Squadron) a medical group and even a military police unit. The 509th could operate in total isolation from any other unit.

A Boeing B-29 to 'Tibbets Spec' of the 393rd Bombardment (VH) Squadron.

Colonel Paul Tibbets aboard a C-54, prior to take-off for another trip to Wendover and Alamagordo.

In order to outfit the new Group, Tibbets travelled to the Martin Aircraft factory in Omaha, Nebraska to select and prepare the fifteen Boeing B-29s that would be allotted to the 393rd Bomb Squadron. Every aircraft was inspected by Tibbets inside and out. The surface finish of each aircraft had to be as super-smooth as a flush-rivetted airframe could be. The pressurised crew compartments had to be tested to ensure they would work at 35,000 feet without the slightest hitch. The bomb doors had to operate smoothly. The engines had to be tuned at the factory to each match the other three for start-up, running and power output. All the remotely controlled gun barbettes had to be removed so only the tail gun was left, and the wing spars had to

BRINGING THE B-29 TO THE 509TH

Major Paul Tibbets and his crew from *Red Gremlin*, the B-17 he flew with the 340th Bomb Squadron in England. Most of this crew rejoined him to fly with the 509th Composite Group from Tinian.

be checked for integrity down their whole length to avoid any risk of damage in a tight turn. The chosen aircraft were then flown to Colorado Springs Army Air Force Base, where Headquarters Second Air Force was located. This was so they could meet up with the rest of the components of the 509th Composite Group ahead of its move to Wendover Field, because the fifteen were not delivered in one lot.

Lieutenant-Colonel Tibbets arrived at Wendover Field on 8 September 1944 to set up his headquarters and organise the airfield to meet his needs. On 11 September, according to Colonel Tibbets' own record, the B-29s of the 393rd Bombardment Squadron were the first part of the 509th to arrive at Wendover. The next aircraft to arrive were the six Douglas C-54 Skymasters to equip the 320th Troop Carrier Squadron. Moving to Wendover was a huge undertaking, and Tibbets knew that his men would hate the place; it was remote and there were few diversions off the base. He would have to keep them occupied with essential work until they were ready to ship out to a location closer to Japan. The officers – aircrew and ground crew – arrived first, and were tasked with ensuring that everything was in place to enable their teams to go straight to work. Group cohesion was important to Tibbets, because there were several teams of men, ostensibly serving in different squadrons, but all part of the 509th Composite Group. They had to become a single unit. He had been given the pick of the US Army Air Force's best crews to form his unit and the first thing he did was to search out a number of the men who had flown with him on the 340th Bomb Squadron in England and North Africa. Amongst those he selected were Tom Ferebee, his former bombardier, Staff Sergeant George Caron, his tail-gunner, Dutch Van Kirk, his navigator and Staff Sergeant Wyatt Duzenbury, his flight engineer. The 509th Composite Group was declared formed on 9 December 1944 and activated at Wendover Field on 17 December to being its work-up to operational readiness status.

10

At Wendover Field

While the 509th Composite Group was formally activated as a unit of the US Army Air Force on 17 December 1944, it was not yet declared operational; there were some months of training to be done before that day came. During that time security was of the utmost importance, and a specialist team of 30 special agents was brought in, led by William 'Bud' Uanna, with the task of infiltrating every unit of the 509th, made up of 1800 men, to ensure there were no leaks. Every man's service record was checked, looking for notes that might suggest that he was prone to loose talk, and mail, telephone calls and off-duty conversations were monitored.

In late December Tibbets was given the opportunity to test the men's adherence to the strict security guidelines. In late December he granted a mass leave for Christmas to all but a skeleton crew essential to keeping Wendover free from prying eyes. Uanna's men posed as civilians at the nearby airport and bus and rail stations and engaged the airmen in conversation to see if they would reveal anything about their posting. Those who divulged information received a telegram on arrival home, recalling them to base immediately, and scaring the wits out of them in the process.

One sergeant who failed the test was called before Tibbets to answer for why he had not respected the security instructions he had been given at Wendover. Protesting his innocence, the sergeant was reminded that he had sat next to a stranger in the bus station at Salt Lake City and that the man had discovered that the sergeant was based at Wendover Field and that the B-29 was being flown there. Colonel Tibbets put him under close arrest for 24 hours and warned him of the risk of being court-martialed for a breach of security. The sergeant was then recalled and told that it would be a great inconvenience to court-martial him at this time, so he was being let off with a caution, but that the incident would be put on his record and any future breach of security, however mild, would see him face a court-martial board and the prospect of the rest of his war behind bars. The scare had the desired effect and the sergeant put the word around; soon the whole unit knew what could be the result of loose talk.

The men were also made aware that their every move was monitored by Uanna's team openly listening in on telephone conversations; if a man was rung by his wife to tell him she was pregnant, the man would be congratulated before he had time to reveal the good news to his comrades. Eventually the crews began to compare Wendover with Alcatraz, so Tibbets decided to take a gamble that would make the need for security clear, but also boost morale. He gathered the Group in the base auditorium and explained: 'You have been brought here for a very special mission. Those of you who stay with the 509th will be going overseas. You are going to take part in an effort that could end the war.' The men began to realise why they were being subjected to such security precautions, and were cheered at the thought that they would be making a significant contribution to peace.

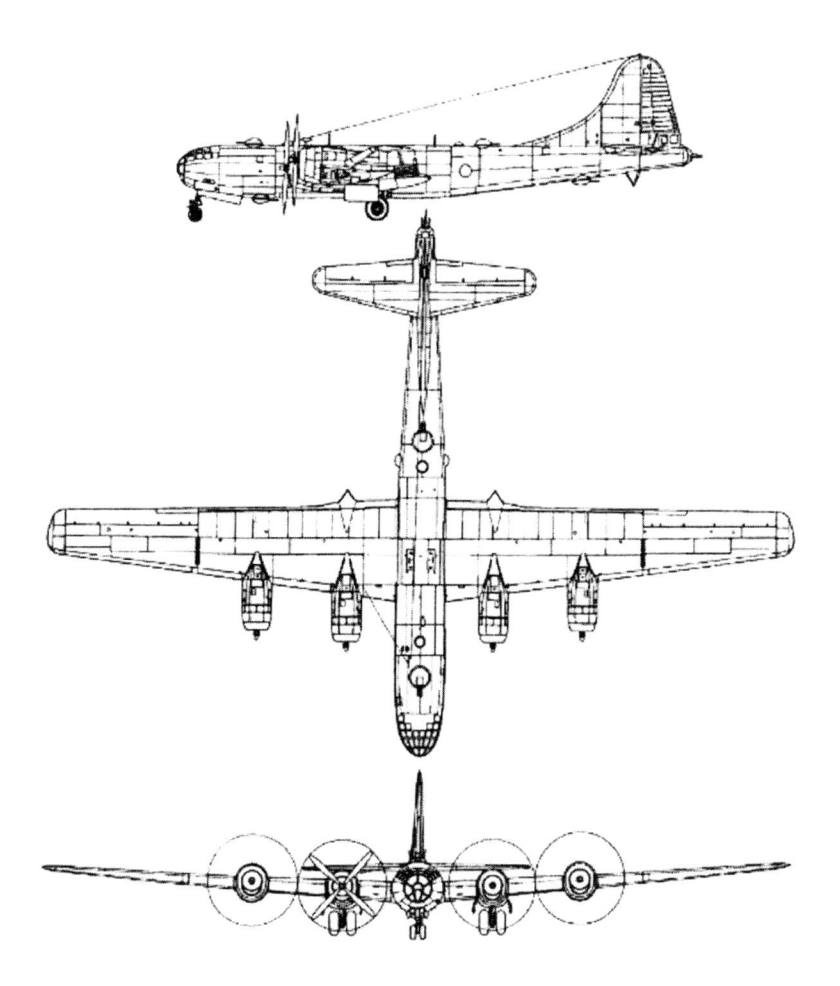

The Boeing B-29 Superfortress. The standard specification had four 4-gun barbettes, two on top of the fuselage and two below. There were two rear-firing machine guns and a 20mm cannon. The aircraft of the 393rd Bombardment Squadron had no guns or armour plating, reducing weight and improving aerodynamic efficiency.

Beyond security, Tibbets had another problem – that of training up men who had been drafted into his various units with high levels of skills, but limited or no experience of the B-29. However, every section had a core of men who knew something of the B-29 and had received at least one training course on the aircraft in their particular field of expertise. The solution was to run a series of on-the-job training programmes, using those with experience to train those with none. Soon the levels of technical efficiency were up to the standard that Tibbets needed. The same system was used for operational training.

There were two particular aspects of flying the B-29 that were new to all the pilots of the 393rd Squadron. The first was taking off with a single 10,000lb weapon in the bomb bay, for whilst it was only half the weight the aircraft could carry, none of the new pilots had any experience of taking off in the B-29 with a bomb load, which affected the handling quite significantly. The other technique that had to be learnt was the 'escape' manoeuvre; Tibbets knew that once the bomb was dropped, the pilot would have to get away from the drop zone as quickly as possible, as the Manhattan Project scientists predicted a large shock wave after the explosion. He devised a manoeuvre in which the pilot put his aircraft into a 155-degree right turn, diving at the same time so as to maximise the use of speed to turn and fly away. The turn had to be to the right because the engines of the B-29 rotated anti-clockwise, so it was easier to turn the aircraft into the direction of the engine rotation and the resultant rate of acceleration was greater. The manoeuvre would cause the aircraft to lose about 5000 feet, but it was as rapid a turn as many a fighter could make. It would allow the aircraft to travel eight miles (the distance required to ensure the survival of the crew) in the two minutes or so that it would take for the bomb to reach its detonation point. The atom bomb was a 'stand off' type, meaning that a pressure fuse would set off the explosion train at somewhere around 2000 feet; this meant that no explosive energy would be lost in impact, but also that the aircraft would have less time to make its escape. The pilot training was especially important to Tibbets because any of the crews could be chosen to make the historic drop; everybody had to perfect the take-off technique and the diving turn.

In order to get the required rate of speed for the escape tactic, the B-29s had been stripped of all non-essential gear, including armour plating and all guns except the tail gun. General Frank Armstrong – Paul Tibbets' old friend and group commander in England, who was now commander of the 315th Bomb Wing, of which the 509th Composite Group was nominally a part – queried the lack of defensive firepower but Tibbets explained that most Japanese fighters were 'getting out of breath' at the B-29's operating altitude, so were a minimal risk, and in any case the B-29 would be able to handle almost as well as a fighter when it carried less weight. It would be able to put any fighter behind it, a natural line of approach for an attacking fighter anyway, and then use the tail gun. General Armstrong left it to his old friend, but was still apprehensive.

The next phase of training demanded that the pilots and bombardiers perfect the art of dropping a bomb from a height of 30,000 feet to hit a target in a circle 400 feet in diameter. This was a tall order for men whose initial bombing training did not feature such precision bombing, and practise was the order of the day. To aid them the bombardiers had one of the finest pieces of equipment at their disposal, the Norden bombsight. It was known as the 'pickle barrel' bomb sight, the implication being that using it meant one could drop a bomb into a pickle barrel at high altitude. Meteorologists were also part of crews so they could aid bombardiers; without compensations for wind direction and speed, a bomb could land half a mile off target.

A B-29 of the 393rd Bomb Squadron without gun barbettes. Only the tail gun remained.

A 'pumpkin' bomb; the only difference between these bombs and 'Fat Man', the second atomic bomb, was that these were all 10,000lb high-explosive weapons, used for practice and operational missions where a city was a designated potential target. Note the three impact fuses on the nose of the bomb.

Bombing training had only just started when Tibbets realised that his crews were not getting the feel for the task in hand; he concluded that it was because the practice bombs were not giving a true picture. The trajectory of a conventional practice bomb weighing around 1000lbs is not the same, and does not follow the same route, as a weapon weighing ten times that, so Tibbets asked for a supply of dummy bombs of the same size, shape and weight as the weapons they were going to drop for real. General Groves was not happy because of the cost, and he questioned the necessity. But Manhattan Project scientist Dr Ernest Lawrence supported Tibbets, saying that it was important to know the likely trajectory of the bomb. General Groves relented and so approximately 200 dummies were delivered. Tibbets wanted no aerodynamic surprises on a mission of such importance.

Besides training for take off and escape, the airmen had to perfect their navigation skills; Tibbets had learned that navigating over water for a long period of time could disorientate a navigator. Every navigator had to learn to trust his instruments implicitly, which in turn had to be unfailingly accurate. For this reason a comprehensive instrument team formed part of the 509th Composite Group. The problem was that many pilots would navigate by instruments when there was nothing else to navigate by, but if they saw a landmark they would lock onto that instead. This was not necessarily an issue, but if he did not verify his position with the instruments and the landmark was not what he thought it was, the result was that the aircraft got lost. There were several embarrassing incidents of this nature during the training programme at Wendover so Tibbets decided to run an exercise in Cuba to raise standards, and also give the crews some much needed rest and relaxation.

Aircraft were sent to Batista Field, near Havana, five at a time, on a ten-day training exercise. They practised island hopping in the Gulf of Mexico, so getting experience of transiting from overland to over-water navigation, as well as practising the escape technique devised by Tibbets. In addition to that, each crew and ground team was allowed leave in Havana —the first true break they'd had since arriving at Wendover back in December. It was a highly successful 30 days and the crews returned happier and better trained.

In the same period, Lieutenant-Colonel Tibbets found an opportunity for a little rest and relaxation of his own. He had been summoned to Washington for one of his regular briefings with General Groves and he managed to secure permission to fly one of the 320th Squadron's C-54 troop transports back to Wendover, with a diversion to Salt Lake City to pick up his mother, who travelled there from Miami via Chicago on United Airlines. He had promised her that if possible he would fly her back to Wendover to see his son, Gene, on his first birthday. Tibbets picked up the C-54 at and flew alongside her aircraft all the way to Salt Lake City, at which point she joined him.

In order to save his mother the tiring inconvenience of the disjointed return flight, Colonel Tibbets contacted General Williams at Second Air Force and asked if he could take his mother back to Miami on his flight to Havana to oversee the navigation training exercise. They placed Mrs Tibbets in the 'jump' seat between pilot and co-pilot for the one-stop flight from Wendover to Miami. They ran through cold weather just before landing at Oklahoma City, where ice, breaking from the de-icing wing leading edges, clunked against the fuselage, and the flight across the Gulf of Mexico took them through a series of thunderstorms. Apparently Mrs Tibbets thoroughly enjoyed the flight and was asking questions all the way.

Part of the 'night navigation exercises' for the bomber crews of the 393rd Bomb Squadron was, in their eyes, finding the best night spots in Havana! Sloppy Joe's was a favorite haunt, because it had a resident photographer who recorded scenes like this, of the crew of *Top Secret* enjoying a little relaxation.

'Tibbets' Taxi', the C-54 he used for travelling between Wendover, later Tinian, and Alamogordo in New Mexico for the continuing conferences and update meetings leading up to the Hiroshima and Nagasaki missions.

Back at Wendover, training continued with the new dummy bombs, nicknamed 'pumpkin bombs' by the crews for their short, dumpy shape. The first ones were filled with concrete rather than explosive and all the aircraft carried movie cameras to record the accuracy of the drop. Bombardiers were under extreme pressure to get their pumpkins inside the 400-foot target from 30,000 feet every time. Drops were made at the Salton Sea bombing range in California, as well as various locations in Nevada and Utah; the long journeys to the ranges meant that the crews got more navigation practice. Tibbets was heavily involved in this practice and training, despite having to make almost bi-weekly trips to Alamagordo for conferences about the timing of production of the first bomb, the tactics required to protect the crew, and how the bombs were predicted to explode. The last issue was naturally the subject of educated guesses.

For the crews of the 393rd Bombardment Squadron (VH), the continuous training soon became tedious, although the detachment to Cuba had been something of a relief. It had been a wake-up call for the navigators, who had not realised just how easy it was to become disorientated when switching from navigation over water to over land. There was also the issue that the bombardiers were still not up to standard. Tibbets himself realised this on a training flight with his own crew – seasoned from their experience in Europe and North Africa – when Captain Tom Ferebee, in Tibbets' eyes 'the best damned bombardier in the Air Force', missed the 400-foot target circle on a number of occasions.

Tibbets decided to watch Tom Ferebee in the approach and release phases of dropping a bomb; he was sure that if Ferebee's bombs were not hitting their target, then it was due to an outside influence, as both Ferebee and the Norden bombsight were the best of their kind. Watching the bombardier in the approach phase, he saw Tom set up his bombsight with co-ordinates, wind drift and bomb trajectory set, and then final pin-pointing. Then, just as he was setting up for the release, he shifted his body, with the result that the pinpoint aim changed, enough to take his bomb out of the 400-foot circle. On the next run Tibbets instructed Ferebee to get in a comfortable position from the start so he wouldn't have to move, and sure enough the 'pumpkin' hit its target. That message was passed across the squadron and accuracy soared; by February 1945 the navigators, bombardiers and pilots of the 509th were up to standard.

The last unit to join the 509th Composite Group at Wendover Field was the 1st Ordnance Squadron (Special, Aviation), a unit that would be in charge of the atomic bomb once the Group moved to their jump-off location in the Pacific. Declared active on 6 March 1945, the team was made up of machinists, metallurgists, electronics experts and other engineering personnel. The Squadron was set up under Project Alberta, an extension of the Manhattan Project, which was tasked with providing trained personnel and special equipment to the Squadron, on behalf of the 509th Composite Group, to enable it to assemble atomic weapons at the 509th's operating base, so allowing weapons to be transported more safely in their component parts.

Project Alberta began to operate in October 1943 as Group E-7 of the Ordnance Division at Los Alamos, headed by Professor Norman Ramsey, the leading scientist of the Manhattan Project. The military aspect of this work was conducted by the USAAF's 216th Base Unit at Wendover, under the name Project W-47. Initial tasks included designing the exterior casings for the bombs and establishing the ballistics information necessary to achieve reasonable accuracy. This unit also took part in developing the delivery tactics which could best assure the survival of the crew from the resulting blast. For these activities, the initial 'Silverplate' B-29 modification, known locally as the Pullman B-29, was used in flight tests at Muroc Army Air Field in California (Now Edwards AFB) between March and June 1944.

Many of the 1st Ordnance Squadron personnel had worked at Alamogordo on the finely machine tooled components and modifications of the bomb, such as the detonation fuses which had been adjusted several times, both after test explosion at Alamogordo and during the use of pumpkin bombs in trials by the 393rd Bombardment Squadron. The selection process for staffing the Squadron was rigorous; there was an 80 per cent failure rate. There were many volunteers, some of whom raised the head of security 'Bud' Uanna's suspicions. This was due in large part to the fact that they did not complain of the strict security surrounding the Squadron. From the very beginning the

The 1st Ordnance Squadron (Special, Aviation).

The 1st Ordnance Squadron's main base area, showing a workshop and vehicle parking.

security was very high level; everything the Squadron did was classified as top secret. The men were not allowed to mix with locals and were escorted by FBI security agents when they travelled to and from Wendover. When on base with the other squadrons of the 509th, they were not allowed to share barracks with them, and once in the Squadron they could not request a transfer out.

The fact that some of the Squadron didn't appear to mind the security restrictions appeared strange; the majority of the men objected to such treatment. Digging into their service histories, Uanna realised why they found the strict living no hardship: they had spent time in prison, convicted of various felonies (including manslaughter, rape and assault) and even murder. Uanna went to Tibbets with his findings, who said he would see each of the men in question, starting with the murderer. He showed each man his official file – the only one in existence that revealed the man's true past – and told each that as long as he continued to do an excellent job, at the end of the war he would be given the file and a match and the matter would never be raised again! One should reflect that of the 225 personnel of the 1st Ordnance Squadron, only about 20 men had questionable backgrounds; it was not a band of brigands as some histories have it. All the men were highly skilled and Tibbets decided that this was the most important consideration.

On 10 March 1945, a few days after the 1st Ordnance Squadron arrived at Wendover, one of its second lieutenants named Morris Jeppson found himself on board one of the new B-29s on a bombing test run with the man credited by many as being the best bombardier in the 393rd Bombardment Squadron. He was there as a weapons specialist, as the flight was to run a test on the detonation fuse of a 'pumpkin' bomb; it was vital that the fuse functioned at 2000 feet above the ground. To aid with bombing accuracy another bombing instrument observation and control panel had been added to the aircraft to allow a young flight engineer to observe and control the release of the bomb if the bombardier was not able to use his release mechanism.

Airborne over the small town of Calipatria in southern California, and approaching the Salton Sea bombing range now so familiar to the 393rd crews, everything was running perfectly. Tom Ferebee announced 'two minutes from aiming point' and called on the pilot Captain Bob Lewis for a minor adjustment to his heading. The adjustment was made and 'One and a half minutes to AP' came the message, then suddenly the aircraft lurched upwards, freed of its 10,000lb burden a minute and a half too early.

Ferebee was enraged, as the bomb was plummeting down towards Calipatria and yet he had not personally operated the release mechanism. It turned out that the young flight engineer had misheard Ferebee and had released the bomb himself, using the additional control panel. The bomb missed Calipatria by only half a mile, burying itself ten feet into the ground. Soon military police cordoned off the area and a crew from 1st Ordnance Squadron recovered the bomb. Within 24 hours, nobody even knew a bomb had dropped on that spot, but the flight engineer was removed from Wendover that very afternoon.

On 22 March, Captain William Parsons arrived at Wendover with a set of drawings that illustrated exactly how the fusing of the atomic bomb would work. He had brought the drawings to explain the process to Tibbets and Captain Charles F. Beggs, the Commander of 1st Ordnance Squadron. Lieutenant Morris Jeppson was also in attendance at the meeting, as the only 1st Ordnance officer to have flown a practice mission with the 393rd. Tibbets was amazed at the seeming simplicity of the bomb triggering process, which involved a uranium core weighing just 22lbs. It consisted of two segments of Uranium-235 six feet apart, separated by a device called a 'tamper', which was a neutron-resistant shield sitting in the space between the unequally sized pieces of uranium inside a cannon barrel, which itself was encased inside the bomb. The smaller unit of uranium weighed 5lbs and was the bullet element of the cannon. At the moment the fuse was triggered, the bullet would be fired at the larger body of uranium to cause the nuclear explosion.

Parsons ordered tests to ensure the smooth operation of bombing runs and to avoid the occasional mishaps of previous practice runs. The information gathered from the earlier test flights was consolidated and closely studied by Captain Beggs and Lieutenant Jeppson, so as to minimise the potential for miscalculations or accidents. When they had completed their study they discussed the ultra-fine instrument work that would have to be carried out in the 1st Ordnance workshops, checking that the adjustments were feasible before further test runs.

On 19 April, the next test was ready to be run. Major Charles Sweeney, flying with his regular bombardier Captain Kermit Beahan and Crew Number 15, took up another 'pumpkin' with 100lbs of explosive inside to give a visual register that it had arrived on target around 30,000 feet below and to check the fuses. Sweeney took his aircraft up to 32,000 feet to locate a makeshift target which had been constructed by the men of the 1st Ordnance Squadron just a few miles from Wendover out in the Utah desert. Down below, in a shelter positioned as near the Aiming Point as safely possible, was a group of observers from the 1st Ordnance Squadron, led by Major Charles Beggs, a group of scientists from Alamogordo and Captain 'Deak' Parsons. They were there to film the descent of the bomb from the aircraft's bomb bay all the way down to where the fuse should detonate at 2000 feet. In the event the bomb detonated only 100 feet or so below the aircraft and spread its shattered components across several miles of desert. The fuse had somehow read the wrong pressure, or the bomb had run through a wave of unusually high pressure, enough to blow it up. The 1st Ordnance team now had a major recalculation on their hands to prevent that from happening again.

On the same day as the failed fuse test, Captain Bob Lewis was also in the air; his mission was to test whether a pilot could land gently enough to put his aircraft and cargo back on the ground safely, if for some reason the crew could not release their

1st Ordnance Squadron's domestic and administrative area, backing on to the motor pool and workshop area.

Captain Bob Lewis with *The Great Artiste*.

bomb. It was always possible that an aircraft would have to return to US territory with a nuclear weapon still in the bomb bay. Lewis took off with a 9000lb ballast-filled 'pumpkin'; he did not fly his own B-29 but rather *The Great Artiste*, Victor Number 89. Lewis was Tibbets' own co-pilot and highly competent, so Tibbets reasoned that if he couldn't do it, then there would be little chance of anyone else being able to. Lewis put the B-29 down without the slightest puff of smoke from the tires. It truly was a perfect three-point landing, but one the men fervently hoped they would never have to do for real.

At 1535hrs on Thursday 12 April 1945, Franklin Delano Roosevelt, 32nd President of the United States of America, collapsed and died. He was the longest serving US President. Many military personnel, including those of the 509th Composite Group, felt his loss and were suspicious of his successor, Harry S. Truman. In fact they had little to fear, as Truman stood behind the Manhattan Project.

At Wendover Field the strain of repetitive training and little action began to tell on the men. On Monday 23 April, Colonel Paul Tibbets faced a barrage of complaints about the conduct of his crews; there were stories of men chasing naked women along hotel corridors, bar brawls in Salt Lake City, dangerous car chases, damage to local buildings and generally unacceptable behaviour. To Lieutenant-Colonel Tibbets, the message was clear – it was time to move. He already knew that arrangements had been made for a transfer to an island near Japan, Tinian, and so he made a call to Washington, using the 'Silverplate' codeword. It was arranged for the ground crews and non-flying elements of the Group to embark at Seattle on Monday 6 May. The aircrews would fly the B-29s and the C54s to Tinian a few days later, so the arrival of aircrews and ground crews would coincide. Barely had he made this arrangement than he had a call from General Leslie Groves telling him to fly to Washington immediately. He started by censuring Tibbets for his temerity, then burst into laughter. 'At last' he said, 'You've got us moving. Nobody now can stop us! And the scientists can't play with their toys any more!' The 509th Composite Group was getting closer to its mission and the 393rd Bombardment Squadron (VH) would soon be putting its long weeks of training into use. The end of the Second World War in the Pacific was approaching.

11

On the Island of Tinian

From 24 July to 1 August 1944, the island of Tinian, one of the Mariana Islands in the Pacific, was the scene of fierce fighting between US and Japanese troops. It was valuable territory as it had two airfields, North Field (destined to be the home of the 509th) and West Field. Troops from the 2nd and 4th Marine Divisions, commanded by Lieutenant-General Holland M. Smith, landed on Tinian, supported by a naval bombardment and artillery firing across the strait from the island of Saipan, which had been taken on 9 July. A successful feint for the major settlement of Tinian Town diverted the Japanese from the actual landing site on the north of the island, although the USS *Colorado* was hit by shore batteries 22 times, killing 44 men, and the destroyer USS *Norman Scott* was hit six times, killing the captain, Seymore Owens, and 22 of his shipmates. However, the Marines' advance was inexorable; the battle saw the first use of napalm in the Pacific.

General Holland M. 'Howlin' Mad' Smith, commander of the 2nd and 4th Marine Divisions, a master and pioneer of amphibious landing. The 2nd and 4th secured Tinian Island in nine days.

ON THE ISLAND OF TINIAN

A burned-out Marine Corps landing craft, a symbol of the ferocity of the battle for Tinian.

North Field on Tinian. This was the huge airfield built by the Japanese.

On 6 May 1945, two thirds of the 509th's personnel boarded the troopship SS *Cape Victory* at Seattle, bound for Tinian. They arrived on 29 May and began unloading equipment into North Field. The advanced air echelon had arrived on 18 May, so had ten days to work on the layout of the 509th ramp area and domestic site. The actual construction of the site was not complete when they arrived – the runways of North Field had to be extended to 8500 feet, enough to get a fully laden B-29 into the air – but it soon was and the eighteen B-29s arrived on the island during the first week of June. By late June all the units of the 509th Composite Group had arrived on the island.

Before the 509th could formally take over its part of North Field, Tibbets inspected it. He paid special attention to the workshops, where the 1st Ordnance Squadron would be based, as without the best possible conditions their vital work might be jeopardised.

Major Charles Beggs (commander 1st Ordnance Squadron) accompanied him around the workshops as his endorsement was essential.

Once the inspections were over, Tibbets announced that the 509th would take possession of the compound on 8 July. The 1st Ordnance Squadron settled in and began preparing bombs for practice runs over the nearby island of Rota, still occupied by the Japanese, but isolated by the Americans so that no Japanese Navy ships could reach it and no Japanese aviator would dare approach it. The Japanese troops trapped on the island were subjected to daily bombing raids designed to test the modified fuses fitted to dummy bombs.

1st Ordnance Squadron's Lieutenant Morris Jeppson was now waiting for the arrival of the components of the real bombs, a Uranium-235 weapon and the other a plutonium device. On 14 July an unmarked black truck, escorted by several unmarked cars containing heavily armed guards, drove out of Los Alamos compound and headed for Santa Fe, then the airfield at Albuquerque. Major Robert Furman and Captain James Nolan were members of that convoy, US Army scientists who were to accompany the fifteen-foot long crate which contained the major non-nuclear parts of a bomb together with a single completed uranium projectile; the uranium target was still incomplete and would be sent later. The uranium bomb was 'Little Boy', destroyer of Hiroshima. Loaded aboard a C-47 Dakota, the men and their cargo flew from Albuquerque to Hamilton Field, outside San Francisco. From here they travelled to Alameda Navy Yard – the same location from where the USS *Hornet* had sailed with Jimmy Doolittle's Raiders just over three years earlier. Here, the USS *Indianapolis* was waiting to take the two men and their hugely valuable cargo to Tinian.

Charles Beggs and Morris Jeppson were eagerly awaiting news that the *Indianapolis* was in sight on the morning of Thursday 26 July. Sure enough, the ship had made its journey safely and they stood on the quayside, ready to go out and collect the weapon components and the two men accompanying them (the harbour was too shallow for the *Indianapolis* to dock). On the same day the three sections of the uranium target assembly were flown from Kirtland Army Air Force Base near Albuquerque, New Mexico in three C-54 Skymaster aircraft operated by the 509th Composite Group's Green Hornet squadron, the 320th Troop Transport Squadron, who also carried a second unit of uranium and segments of plutonium for the 'Fat Man' bomb – one in

The USS *Indianapolis*, the battle cruiser charged with delivering the components of 'Little Boy' to Tinian.

each aircraft on the grounds of safety. Within a couple of days, once the 1st Ordnance Squadron had completed its work, there would be two fully assembled atom bombs.

Having dropped off its precious cargo, the *Indianapolis* now set sail for Leyte, in the Philippines. She had no escort, and on 30 July, she was spotted by the captain of the Japanese submarine I-58, Lieutenant-Commander Mochitsura Hashimoto. The submarine fired a succession of four torpedoes and quickly sank the 10,000-ton vessel, killing over 300 American sailors almost immediately. 880 men found themselves in the sea, afloat for 110 hours, picked off by sharks attracted to the blood in the water. Eventually, on 2 August, the sailors were spotted by a patrol boat and were picked up by the *Doyle*. Only 316 men survived.

Even before the delivery of the atom bomb explosive components to Tinian, General Carl A. Spaatz, recently appointed Commander of the Strategic Air Forces, and therefore most senior air officer in the Pacific, had met General Thomas Handy, Acting Commander-in-Chief of the US Army, together with Major-General Leslie Groves. He was briefed on the existence of the atomic bomb, its intended use over Japan on a selected day after 3 August and its potential destructive power. Spaatz was completely in accord with the objectives, but hesitated on learning that the result could be a Japanese death toll of 100,000. General Spaatz asked for his order, as the responsible commander, to be in writing, offering the explanation that if he was going to be responsible for 100,000 deaths, he wanted it on paper.

Proceeding to his new Guam headquarters, General Spaatz called a meeting with the key personnel attending. They included Lieutenant-General Curtis LeMay, Captain Parsons, Colonel Tibbets, Colonel Blanchard and the senior command meteorologist. Weather, it was confirmed, would be the final determinant of the date of the mission. Having discussed all the relevant details, General Spaatz announced that he had the mission order from the Pentagon in writing.

> To: General Carl Spaatz, CG, USASAF:
>
> 1. The 509 Composite Group, Twentieth Air Force will deliver its first special bomb as soon as weather will permit visual bombing after about 3 August 1945 on one of the targets:
> Hiroshima, Kokura, NIIgata and Nagasaki. To carry military and civilian scientific personnel from the War Department to observe and record the effects of the explosion of the bomb, additional aircraft will accompany the aircraft carrying the bomb. The observing planes will stay several miles distant from the point of impact of the bomb.
> 2. Additional bombs will be delivered on the above targets as soon as made ready by the project staff Further instructions will be issued concerning targets other than those listed above.
> 3. Dissemination of any and all information concerning the use of the weapon against Japan is reserved to the Secretary of War and the President of the United States. No communiqués on the subject or releases of information will be issued by commanders in the field without specific prior authority. Any news stories will be sent to the War Department for special clearance.
> 4. The foregoing directive is issued to you by direction and with the approval of the Secretary of War and of the Chief of Staff, USA. It is desired that you personally deliver one copy of this directive to General MacArthur and one copy to Admiral Nimitz for their in formation.
>
> Signed: Thos. T. Handy, General, G.S.C.
> Acting Chief of Staff

A PBY-5 Catalina flying boat patrol aircraft of the type that saw the *Indianapolis* and began to pick up its survivors.

Next came the task of advising the Commander-in-Chief US Land Forces in the Pacific, General Douglas MacArthur, who had been kept completely in the dark up to this point. MacArthur would be the one to follow the atom bomb attack, or attacks, with land forces into the Japanese Home Islands.

Whilst the political preparations were going on and the 1st Ordnance Squadron busied themselves in their workshops, the 393rd Bombardment Squadron was able to do further training exercises and undertake a few real missions, although they had to be low risk. The last thing Tibbets wanted was for one of his aircraft to end up in Japanese hands; they would be extremely curious about a B-29 with only one set of bomb hooks for a very large bomb. The fact that the 393rd did low risk missions fuelled resentment amongst the other bomb groups on the airfield, who considered the 509th an oddball outfit and didn't understand why it was even on Tinian.

Much of the 393rd's training was now being done under the supervision of Lieutenant-Colonel Tom Classen, Paul Tibbets' immediate deputy and the original commander of the 393rd. This was because Tibbets was spending more time travelling between Guam, Washington and Los Alamos. On one trip to Guam to liaise with General Curtis LeMay and his staff at Headquarters Twentieth Air Force, he met Brigadier-General John Davies, commander of the 313th Bombardment Wing and co-ordinator of all B-29 flight training on Tinian. He wanted the 393rd crews to attend his flight training programmes to ensure that they were 'up to scratch'. To avoid an argument, Tibbets sent three of his crews for training. He was soon asked whether all his crews were like them. When he answered in the affirmative he was told not to send any more, because they were demoralising the school; they knew more about aircraft, navigation and bomb-aiming than the instructors.

The issue of aircraft maintenance then arose. The 21st Bomber Command of the Twentieth Air Force had adopted a policy of centralised aircraft maintenance for all the B-29s on Tinian and General LeMay had approved the ruling on the basis of better standards, better time control and reducing wastage. Bill Ervine, LeMay's Director of Materiel had passed the instruction across to Tibbets, who, for obvious reasons, resisted the instruction and found himself summoned to LeMay's office. LeMay had learned of the atomic mission and knew that the 393rd Bombardment Squadron was officially listed as part of the 315th Bombardment Wing, but he knew nothing of the

A B-29 ready for take off during the continuation training programme set up by Lieutenant-Colonel Tom Classen.

specialist nature of the Squadron's task. Tibbets put him straight, without divulging anything more than had already been decided General LeMay should know. LeMay backed Tibbets and the 393rd continued in its routine.

On 16 July Colonel Tibbets was in Washington for a conference, and had planned to then fly to Alamogordo in New Mexico to see the test firing of a bomb, before returning to Tinian. He then received an urgent message from Major Tom Ferebee, his bombardier, asking him to return to the island immediately. He abandoned his trip to Alamogordo and headed for Tinian, only stopping overnight at Cincinnati on his westbound journey. He had barely landed his C-54 at Tinian than Ferebee was at the door of his aircraft. It seemed that efforts were being made by Colonel William Blanchard, the Twentieth Air Force operations officer, to switch the atom bomb operation from the 509th Composite Group to a regular Twentieth Air Force squadron. General LeMay had divulged what little he knew about the 509th's special mission to Blanchard and Blanchard wanted one of the established units on the island to do it. He had no idea of the extent of development and training preparations or the possible consequences of his actions.

Tibbets flew to Guam to see General LeMay, and explained as carefully as he could without divulging secret information that his aircraft had been specially prepared and that his crews had been specially trained, not just to fly the B-29, but to perform certain manoeuvres that were essential to a classified mission. Blanchard was questioning the proficiency of the 509th's crews, so Tibbets offered to take him on a demonstration flight. Instead LeMay instructed that Blanchard go on a real mission. Tibbets himself flew a B-29, with Captain Bob Lewis as his co-pilot and Major Tom Ferebee as the bombardier, with Blanchard in the jump seat. Captain 'Dutch' Van Kirk navigated the aircraft to the island of Rota, and Ferebee pin-pointed his target and let the 'pumpkin' go. With the sudden loss in weight and Tibbets' sharp turn to the right in his 155-degree 'escape' turn, Blanchard was severely shaken and glad to get out the aircraft. The 509th was left to do its job.

Part of this job was to get the Japanese used to the appearance of one or two aircraft over their airspace, so that when the day came for the real drop, the aircraft would go unchallenged. Several daylight runs were made, dropping 'pumpkin' bombs, and the tactic worked. Each time a couple of B-29s appeared over a potential target, the air raid sirens would sound, but there was no pursuit by fighter aircraft and no attempt to shoot them down with anti-aircraft fire, as it wouldn't have reached the 30,000 feet altitude at which the B-29s were flying.

Peace was not to return for too long. Tibbets was making frequent trips to Washington DC for conferences with General Groves and the scientists from

393rd Bombardment Squadron (VH) Bombing Missions

Aircraft	Crew	July 1945 20	July 1945 24	July 1945 26	July 1945 29	August 1945 6	August 1945 8	August 1945 9	August 1945 14	Sorties
Full House	A1	•	•	•	•	•		•	•	7
Laggin' Dragon	A2					•				1
Next Objective	A3	•	•				∆			4
Strange Cargo	A4	•	•				•		•	4
–	A5	Back to the US to collect an atomic bomb								0
Jabit III	B6	•		•	•	•	•			5
Some Punkins	B7	•	•	•			•		•	5
Top Secret	B8	•	•	•	•		•		•	6
Enola Gay	B9		•	•		*		•		4
Up An' Atom	B10	•		•	•		•		•	5
Straight Flush	C11	•	•	•	•	•			•	6
Big Stink	C12	•		•		•		•		4
Bock's Car	C13		•	•	•			*		4
Necessary Evil	C14		•	•	•	•				4
The Great Artiste	C15	∆	•		•	•		•		5
		10	10	10	8	8	6	5	7	64

• 'Pumpkin' bomb   * atomic bomb   ∆ weather observation

the Manhattan Project, to discuss issues such as the test explosion that had been carried out on 16 July, and the trajectories of the two bomb types: 'Little Boy', the Uranium-235 bomb that would be dropped on the first target was a different shape to 'Fat Man', the plutonium bomb to be dropped, if necessary, on the second target. The targets themselves were not yet agreed on. The first target was either to be Kyoto, Hiroshima, Yokohama or Kokura, but then Secretary for War Henry Stimson intervened, saying that it would be a bad idea to strike at Kyoto, because it was a very historic city with many important Japanese shrines. Wanting to minimise the civilian backlash, it was agreed that Kyoto should be withdrawn from the target list altogether and replaced with Niigata. Then Kokura came under review and Nagasaki replaced it as having greater military significance.

Besides the issue of where to drop the bomb, there was also the debate as to whether it was necessary to drop it at all. Some of the scientists argued that the war in Europe was over, so there was less justification to drop this bomb on Japan, as with Germany having surrendered there would be more Allied troops to invade the Pacific. General Arnold, Chief of the US Army Air Force, rejected that point of view, citing Generals MacArthur and Smith's predictions that defeating Japan would take four more years and cost four million lives. Eventually all were persuaded.

On 26 July there came the publication of the Potsdam Declaration to Japan, the result of the Potsdam Conference, in which the Allied leaders had met to discuss ending the war in the Pacific. President Truman revealed its contents as it was dispatched to the Emperor of Japan.

A drop-model of 'Little Boy', a fission-type weapon, which used a gun device to bring about the explosion.

JULY 26, 1945

WE—THE PRESIDENT of the United States, the President of the National Government of the Republic of China, and the Prime Minister of Great Britain, representing the hundreds of millions of our countrymen, have conferred and agree that Japan shall be given an opportunity to end this war.

1: The prodigious land, sea and air forces of the United States, the British Empire and of China, many times reinforced by their armies and air fleets from the west, are poised to strike the final blows upon Japan. This military power is sustained and inspired by the determination of all the Allied nations to prosecute the war against Japan until she ceases to resist.

2: The result of the futile and senseless German resistance to the might of the aroused free peoples of the world stands forth in awful clarity as an example to the people of Japan. The might that now converges on Japan is immeasurably greater than that which, when applied to the resisting Nazis, necessarily laid waste to the lands, industry and the method of life of the whole German people. The full application of our military power, backed by our resolve, will mean the inevitable and complete destruction of the Japanese armed forces and just as inevitably the utter devastation of the Japanese homeland.

3: The time has come for Japan to decide whether she will continue to be controlled by those self willed militaristic advisers whose unintelligent calculations have brought the Empire of Japan to the threshold of annihilation, or whether she will follow the path of reason.

4: Following are our terms. We will not deviate from them. There are no alternatives. We shall brook no delay.

5: There must be eliminated for all time the authority and influence of those who have deceived and misled the people of Japan into embarking on world conquest, for we insist that a new order of peace, security and justice will be impossible until irresponsible militarism is driven from the world.

6: Until such a new order is established and until there is convincing proof that Japan's war making power is destroyed, points in Japanese territory to be designated by the Allies shall be occupied to secure the achievement of the basic objectives we are here setting forth.

7: The terms of the Cairo Declaration shall be carried out and Japanese sovereignty shall be limited to the islands of Honshu, Hokkaido, Kyushu, Shikoku and such minor islands as we determine.

8: The Japanese military forces, after being completely disarmed, shall be permitted to return to their homes with the opportunity to lead peaceful and productive lives.

9: We do not intend that the Japanese shall be enslaved as a race or destroyed as a nation, but stern justice shall be meted out to all war criminals, including those who have visited cruelties upon our prisoners. The Japanese Government shall remove all obstacles to the revival and strengthening of democratic tendencies among the Japanese people. Freedom of speech, of religion and of thought, as well as respect for the fundamental human rights shall be established.

10: Japan shall be permitted to maintain such industries as will sustain her economy and permit the exaction of just reparations in kind but not those which would enable her to re arm for war. To this end access to, as distinguished from control of, raw materials shall be permitted. Eventual Japanese participation in world trade relations shall be permitted.

11: The occupying forces of the Allies shall be withdrawn from Japan as soon as these objectives have been accomplished and there has been established in accordance with the freely expressed will of the Japanese people a peacefully inclined and responsible government.

12: We call upon the government of Japan to proclaim now the unconditional surrender of all Japanese armed forces, and to provide proper and adequate assurances of their good faith in such action. The alternative for Japan is prompt and utter destruction.

Negotiations with Japanese representatives of the Emperor had been taking place in Berne, in Switzerland for a surrender of Japan to the Allies for several weeks beforehand. The Japanese already knew they were beaten, but the sticking point in the negotiations was the perceived invincibility of the Emperor. Emperor Hirohito was regarded by many of his people as a demi-god and his removal from the throne was unthinkable. The Japanese were therefore pressing for the retention of the Emperor, his autonomous government and his armed forces – in other words a truce without disarmament. To China, Great Britain and the US this was wholly unacceptable and so the Potsdam Proclamation was issued to the Japanese government through their ambassador in Berne. Because there were no positive signs from either, preparations continued on Tinian.

In the early hours of Sunday 29 July, an assembly of aircrews of the 393rd Bombardment Squadron were called together for a briefing. This was to be the fourth practice mission with 'pumpkin' bombs. As it turned out, it would be their last practice mission. Colonel Hazen Payette, the 509th's Intelligence Officer, chaired the briefing and gave each of the nine crews designated to fly that day their individual targets. All the pilots started their engines and waited their turn to roll. Major James Hopkins was piloting *Strange Cargo* and behind him was Captain Bob Lewis aboard *The Great Artiste*.

Hopkins suddenly encountered a problem – his blockbuster had come loose on its hook mountings and dropped into the bomb doors, forcing them open and dropping on to the tarmac in front of Bob Lewis. Then came the niftiest piece of recovery work ever carried out by the men of the 1st Ordnance Squadron. A team appeared as if from

The 1st Ordnance Squadron's bomb assembly building, the only fully air conditioned structure on Tinian.

nowhere and, knowing that a false move could kill them all, gently took control of the bomb and trolleyed it away from *The Great Artiste*. The control tower then advised all crews that they could relax, to which Bob Lewis replied: 'I'm going on a mission!'

Meanwhile, also on 29 July, General Carl A. Spaatz was appointed Commander Strategic Forces in the Pacific, based on Guam. He brought with him the authorisation order for the dropping of the 'special bomb' on one of four target options – Hiroshima, Kokura, Nagasaki or Niigata. No date was given for the drop, other than it should be after 3 August. Tibbets was asked about the state of readiness of the 393rd Bombardment Squadron (VH) by Generals LeMay and Spaatz and he assured them that two bombs had been fully assembled in readiness for use, except that the uranium and plutonium rods were stored away from the bombs in the interests of safety.

The 393rd had already performed twelve 'special missions' with dummy bombs and so were ready for action. The targets were again reviewed by the two generals and Tibbets and it was agreed that Hiroshima should be the primary target, because it had a significant naval shipyard, a large military garrison, a major ordnance depot and mixed industry. Colonel Tibbets prepared a report and recommendation to General LeMay, modelled on one he had received from General Groves, setting out the primary target, Kokura as the secondary and Nagasaki as the third. Signed off by General LeMay, it came back as Special Bombing Mission Number 13 (in sequence with the twelve 'pumpkin' raids already carried out) and the date selected was 6 August.

The final countdown to the world's first atomic mission began on 1 August, when Colonel Paul Tibbets sent a copy of his order for the mission to General Curtis LeMay. It explained that seven aircraft would be used. Three would fly well ahead of the rest to check weather conditions over Hiroshima, Niigata and Yokosuka. One would fly to Iwo Jima and stand by there in case the aircraft carrying the bomb ran into problems and had to divert to Iwo Jima to transfer the bomb. The other two would be the instrument recorder aircraft and the photo recording aircraft and these two would accompany the primary aircraft, what in the end would be the *Enola Gay*.

The last test mission took place on the morning of Sunday 5 August, when Major Charles Sweeney took an inert dummy bomb up to 30,000 feet over the ocean and let it go. The objective of the flight was to give the fusing mechanism one last test, and 1st Ordnance had worked into the night to make it happen, but it didn't. The sequence of switches operating the fusing mechanism should have sent out a puff of smoke to indicate that the barometric pressure switch had activated the nuclear 'cannon', but the bomb went into the water without a trace of smoke. After a lot more midnight oil had been burned, Captain Parsons made the announcement that he would fuse the bomb the next day, 6 August 1945.

12

Mission to Hiroshima

On 5 August 1945, an artist spent 30 minutes painting the name *Enola Gay* on the nose of B-29 airframe number 36-MO-44-86292. This was the aircraft Colonel Paul Tibbets had designated as 'his' aircraft when it arrived from the Martin factory in Omaha. Meanwhile Tibbets called a briefing of the crew commanders chosen to go on the first atomic bombing raid, as well as General Thomas Farrell, Admiral William Purnell, Captain William 'Deak' Parsons, Commander Fred Ashworth, Professor Norman Ramsey and Professor Robert Brode. Tibbets would fly the bomb-carrying aircraft with Captain Bob Lewis as his co-pilot; Lewis had always thought he would and should be the aircraft captain and was furious to discover the name *Enola Gay* on its side, which clearly meant his boss would be flying the mission.

The three aircraft that would fly ahead to check the weather conditions would be *Straight Flush*, *Jabit III* and *Full House*. *Top Secret* was the aircraft selected to fly to Iwo Jima, in case the primary aircraft needed to hand over the bomb. Accompanying the *Enola Gay* would be *The Great Artiste*, the instrument recorder aircraft, and *Necessary Evil*, carrying observers and camera equipment to photograph the blast.

Captain Parsons sent a ripple of apprehension through the group by saying that he was not happy about the *Enola Gay* taking off with a live and fused weapon on board. He had seen several accidents in which heavily laden B-29s had failed to take off and crashed in balls of fire, a serious thought given that the B-29 in question would be carrying enough explosive power to destroy Tinian. His solution was that he would fly

The most famous B-29, *Enola Gay*, named after Paul Tibbets' mother.

Side view of *Enola Gay* with her final markings.

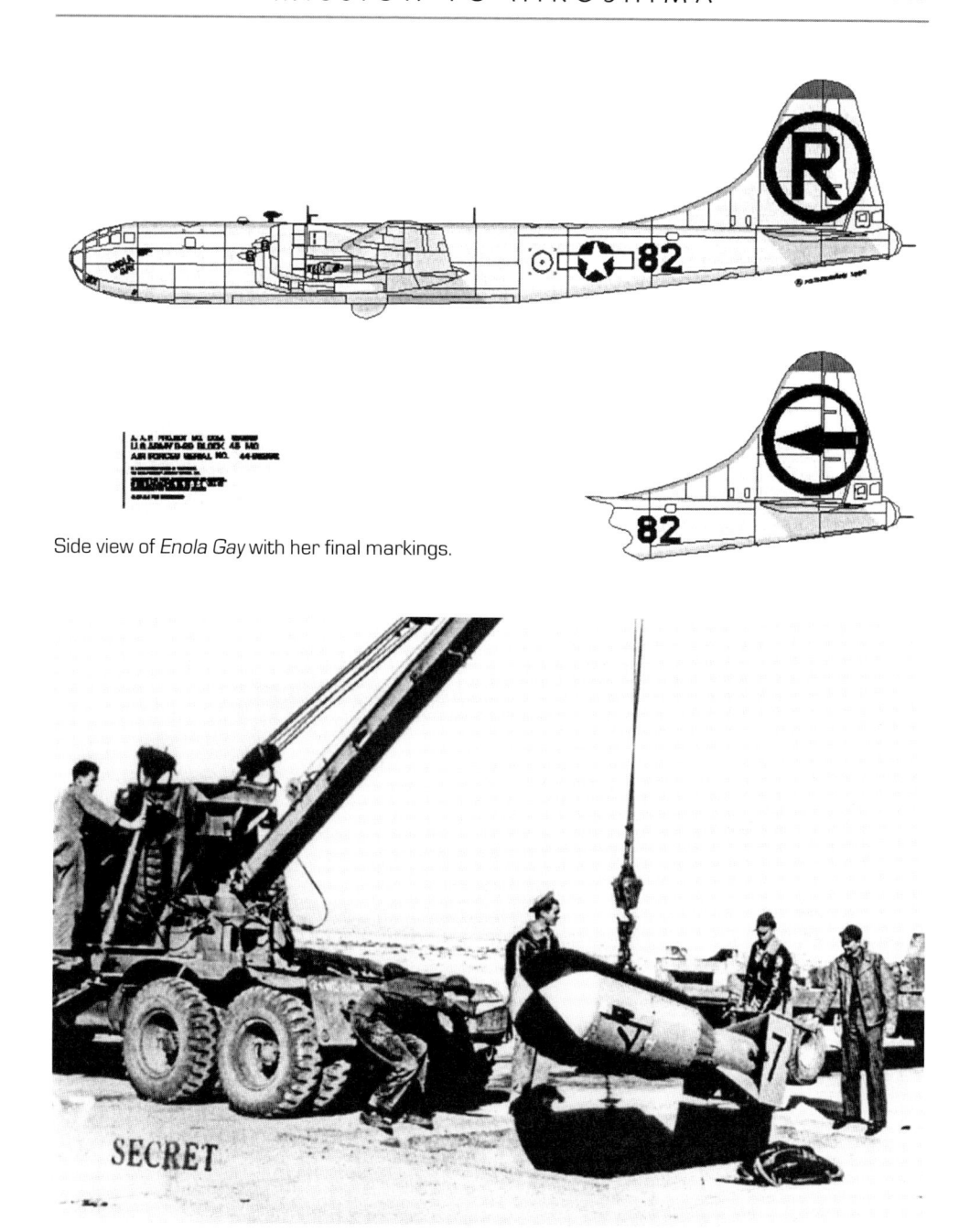

'Little Boy' being lowered into the loading pit.

as a member of the crew and would personally install the explosive charge and the stick of uranium into the bomb after take-off. Asked if he was sure he was capable of doing that, he replied: 'No. But I've got all day to learn!' Lieutenant Jeppson also practised the procedure in case the task should fall to him.

After the meeting Tibbets went out to the apron on which his aircraft was standing and did the first of several walk-around pre-flight checks. He noticed that the painter had not only put his mother's name on the aircraft, he had also complied with the request to replace one of the 509th arrowhead markings on the fin of the aircraft with the letter 'R', which the other B-29s on Tinian wore. This was to confuse any enemy aircraft they might meet on the way, though such a meeting was unlikely. The same marking change was applied to the other six B-29s which would accompany the *Enola Gay* on its momentous journey.

At 3.30pm the unfused 'Little Boy' bomb, shrouded in tarpaulin, was placed on a trailer and hauled to the loading pit on the aircraft dispersal area. The pit was necessary, because the bomb was too big to place underneath a B-29, being 28 inches in diameter and twelve feet long. Several of the ground crew took the opportunity to write messages on the bomb – a common practice even though the recipients would never be able to read them. The most poignant was 'From the Boys of the *Indianapolis*'; the news of the sinking had just reached Tinian and the loss was keenly felt. The *Enola Gay* was then rolled over the pit and the bomb was winched up into the bomb bay. The doors closed and a heavily armed guard was posted around the aircraft until take-off. 1st Ordnance had done its job for the time being. All its team could do now was wait to see how successful their year's work had been.

As soon as the bomb was in place inside the bomb bay of *Enola Gay*, Captain Parsons went to work practising arming the bomb as though it was in the air. As he had never done this before, he and everybody around him was of course apprehensive. He put the uranium and explosive charge in, then took them out and put them back in again. It was over 100 degrees Fahrenheit and he consoled himself with the thought that it would not be that hot at 31,000 feet, but he would still have to work in very cramped conditions. His hands and coveralls were smeared black with graphite lubricant and his fingers and the backs of his hands bled from cuts he sustained from the sharp edges, but eventually he was confident.

While Parsons was wrestling with fuses, Tibbets was introduced to William Lawrence, the science correspondent for the *New York Times*. Lawrence had taken leave from his newspaper to work for the US government, his task being to write the story of

Commander Fred Ashworth numbers and checks the final 'Little Boy' bomb in the 1st Ordnance Squadron's bomb assembly building, prior to its loading into *Enola Gay*.

'Little Boy' in position in the bomb bay of *Enola Gay*.

The crawl tube used by crew members to go from the flight deck to midships in the B-29. Captain Parsons had to go through this tube to reach the bomb, through the round hatch below, in order to fuse it.

the atom-splitting process from the very beginning of the Manhattan Project to its conclusion with the nuclear bomb. Lawrence was to gently introduce the public at large to the new atomic age by releasing pre-prepared items to the world's press after the planned Hiroshima mission. This was all on the assumption that, while a second attack was prepared for, Japan would see the awesome destruction of Hiroshima and surrender immediately. Lawrence had hoped to accompany the flight, but it was too late to find him a space.

Tibbets also received an answer from US intelligence to a question he had posed some time before: whether there were any American prisoners of war in Hiroshima. He was told there were not, though in fact two B-24 crews had been shot down on 28

Nose art of *Taloa*, shot down over Hiroshima.

Nose art of *Lonesome Lady*.

July and, unknown to the Americans, were being held in Hiroshima. The aircraft B-24 44-40680 *Lonesome Lady* and B-24 44-40716 *Taloa* had been part of a group sent to destroy the Japanese battleship *Haruna* in Kure Harbour, and were hit by anti-aircraft fire after dropping their loads. While the captain of *Lonesome Lady*, Lieutenant Tom Cartwright, was taken for questioning in Tokyo, the remaining 13 airmen, along with ten other US prisoners, were held in Hiroshima Castle, where they died on 6 August. Tibbets was to discover this some time later; he was asked if he would have still dropped the bomb if he had known about the prisoners. His reply was a yes, explaining that however regrettable the loss of American lives, the attack was for the greater good.

On the evening of 5 August Tibbets and the seven crews that would make up the mission to Hiroshima had their evening meal, then assembled for the first pre-flight briefing. The usual aspects of any pre-mission briefing were covered – the route, the altitudes for each leg of the flight, the radio frequencies to be used and a weather briefing. The latter was very important as it was to be a long flight, with the potential for meteorological variation, so there was extensive coverage of the weather they were likely to encounter on the way. Tibbets changed his radio call sign from Victor to Dimples and he announced that the first leg would be at 5000 feet. This would allow Captain Parsons to arm the bomb in a reasonably comfortable unpressurised environment.

Every aircraft of the 393rd Bombardment Squadron carried a single vertical camera to record images of the ground below in each mission, including 'pumpkin' missions.

The Great Artiste.

The final pre-flight briefing took place at 2300 hours; this was for the three crews who would be making the 13-hour flight together – the *Enola Gay*, *The Great Artiste* and *Necessary Evil*. Details were gone over again, and for the first time Tibbets explained the significance of the weapon they would be dropping, one with the explosive force of 20,000 tons of TNT. The aircraft would fly separately to Iwo Jima where they would meet up and make their way together to Hiroshima.

Tibbets finished the briefing with another run-down on the sequence to be followed when the three aircraft reached the target area. Tibbets would fly under instruction from his bombardier, Major Tom Ferebee. Ferebee's selection of the aiming point had been discussed and approved in an earlier meeting at Guam with General LeMay, so there was no question of the aiming point being anything other than Ferebee's choice. Dependent upon wind direction, his favoured approach was from the east, so that he could see clearly the bisection of the river crossed by the Aioi Bridge. The Aioi Bridge was the aiming point, a 'T' shaped bridge, crossing from east to west at the head of the 'T', while the leg of the 'T' went south into the Nakajima delta between the two estuaries of the Ota river. If the aircraft had to approach from the west, they would be flying into the sun, making Ferebee's job that much harder, but flying from the north or south would be acceptable, though east was still the best option. The crewmen were instructed to wear their special-issue goggles when the bomb went off, as a precaution against the expected huge flash. Then Chaplain William Downey said a prayer for their safe return.

Tibbets' crew on the *Enola Gay* was as follows: Captain Bob Lewis (co-pilot); Captain Theodore 'Dutch' Van Kirk (navigator); Major Tom Ferebee (bombardier); Tech Sergeant Wyatt Duzenbury (flight engineer); Sergeant Joseph Stiborik (radar operator); Private First Class Richard Nelson (radio operator); Staff Sergeant George Caron (tail gunner); Lieutenant Jacob Beser (radar countermeasures officer); Captain William Parsons USN (weaponeer and ordnance officer); Second Lieutenant Maurice Jeppson (assistant weaponeer).

The three weather aircraft *Straight Flush*, *Jabit III* and *Full House* had already taken off. Their task, ahead of *Enola Gay* and its companions, was to check the weather and advise of conditions and visibility over the target areas (there were two back-up targets should Hiroshima prove impossible). Major Claude Eatherly's *Straight Flush* would cover Hiroshima; Major John Wilson flew *Jabit III* to Kokura, while Major Ralph Taylor took *Full House* to a position over Nagasaki. This was the continuation of days

Top left: *Necessary Evil.*

Top right: *Straight Flush.*

Centre left: *Jabit III.*

Centre right: *Full House.*

Left: *Top Secret.*

of weather surveys by B-29s over the potential targets, and their reports had dictated the date chosen for the historic drop.

Top Secret, commanded by Captain Charles McKnight, was assigned to fly to Iwo Jima and park on a guarded apron by a specially constructed pit. This was a precaution against the possibility of *Enola Gay* encountering problems in the air which might call for it to divert to an alternative landing ground. If necessary the bomb could be winched out of *Enola Gay* into the pit, the two aircraft changed over and the reserve aircraft, *Top Secret*, would take the bomb and go on to the target.

Just prior to boarding their aircraft, Tibbets and his crews did a last run through of the bombing manoeuvre. The bomb would be released and the *Enola Gay* would do the 155 degree turn to the right. Major Sweeney would mirror the turn to the left in *The Great Artiste* after releasing the instrument sets which would be parachuted to record shock effect, flash readings and radioactivity. Captain George Marquadt in *Necessary Evil* would lag far enough behind the other two aircraft to be out of danger, so could turn normally into a gentle arc to photograph events.

As the crews walked to their aircraft they had to run the gauntlet of photographers, and the strip was bright with floodlights. After pictures had been taken, Colonel Tibbets requested that the floodlights be turned off, so he and his crew could 'go to work'. As the crew of the *Enola Gay* climbed aboard in the early hours of the morning of 6 August, General Farrell stopped Captain Parsons and reminded him that he had no personal firearm; he'd forgotten to sign one out of the armoury. A military policeman came up and proffered his weapon, which Parsons accepted.

Sergeant George Caron, the tail gunner, had planned to take his camera on the mission but in all the turmoil of preparation he had left it behind. He had an Air Force K-20 five-inch film handheld camera which was issued to him for the task of photographing the bomb-drop, but not a personal camera. As it happened, he still had a chance to take photographs of the event, because a US Army captain came up to him as he was boarding and handed him an Argus C-3 camera in the hope of getting some photographs for his album. The camera was a 35mm film camera, the first such still camera made in the US. George Caron took some of the most historic pictures, but unsurprisingly he was relieved of both cameras as he landed back at Tinian.

The crew of the B-29 *Enola Gay* photographed before take-off in the very early hours of 6 August 1945.

An Argus C3 35mm camera.

A K20 handheld air camera.

Everybody was aboard, strapped into position and ready to go. All the final instrument checks were done and Tibbets called to the flight engineer Tech Sergeant Duzenbury for confirmation. The engine starting sequence was begun, each engine rotated three full turns, to prime them for starting and to circulate the oil so they weren't dry when fired.
Number 3 went first, the inboard starboard engine, then Number 4, the outboard starboard engine, then Number 1, the outboard port engine and finally Number 2, the inboard port engine. All four engines were then run up for a few moments to ensure smoothness and oil circulation.
Making sure the brakes were set, Colonel Tibbets signalled to the ground crewmen to pull the chocks away. The aircraft was laden with 7000 gallons of fuel and more than 9,000lbs of atomic bomb; there was tension in the air as the aircraft prepared to taxi. Tibbets called the control tower: 'Dimples Eight Two to North Tinian Tower – ready for take-off on Runway Able.' The Tower replied: 'Dimples Eight Two – cleared for take-off'. He held the brakes on as the engines were run up to full power, then released them, and the *Enola Gay* began to roll along the two miles of runway. It was 0245hrs as she began to climb into the sky.
500 miles out and at 4700 feet, the 1st Ordnance Squadron men 'Deak' Parsons and Morris Jeppson climbed down to the bomb bay and let themselves into the cramped space on the platform just behind 'Little Boy'. Jeppson held the powerful flashlight while Parsons went to work assembling the triggering device. He checked that the green safety plugs were installed, removed the rear plate and the armour plate,

The island of Iwo Jima, with Mount Suribachi in the foreground. The main airfield where *Top Secret* would land as standby to *Enola Gay*, is in the background.

inserted a breech wrench into the breech plug, unscrewed the breech plug, inserted the four-section charges with their red ends facing the breech, inserted the breech plug and tightened it in place, connected the firing lead and re-installed the armour and rear plates. The men removed their tools and climbed back up the catwalk; it had taken 25 minutes.

After over two hours flying, the navigator 'Dutch' Van Kirk reported that Iwo Jima should be somewhere below. Sure enough, at 0555hrs Tibbets saw it through a hole in the cloud and reduced height to 10,000 feet, circling the island. Sweeney's *The Great Artiste* and Marquadt's *Necessary Evil* were about ten miles behind, so Tibbets circled over Mount Suribachi, waiting for them to take up position on his wingtips. At 0607hrs the three aircraft set course for Hiroshima.

While in the air, Tibbets and his crew were radioed to confirm the selection of Hiroshima as their target, after which radio silence was applied. Now was the time for Morris Jeppson to make his way down to the bomb bay for a second time. He removed the green safety plugs – designed to prevent premature detonation – and put them in his pocket. The weapon was now live.

The *Enola Gay* passed over the island of Shikoku and the Iyo Sea and Tibbets climbed to his operational altitude of 30,700 feet. Soon those members of the crew who could see out of the aircraft concurred that the city they saw below was Hiroshima. Now, they had to pinpoint the aiming point. There was a southerly 10-knot wind as Tom Ferebee was setting up his Norden bombsight. Flying almost due west, the heading was 264 degrees. At 17 seconds after 0814hrs, just a minute before the due drop time, Ferebee flicked a toggle switch, which activated a high-pitched radio tone. Everybody put on their darkened goggles and at 0815hrs from 31,060 feet, 'Little Boy' left the bomb bay of the *Enola Gay*. 43 seconds later, at 0816hrs local time, a great expanse of Hiroshima disappeared into oblivion.

In the first second or so after the explosion, a spot of red-to-purple light expanded at alarming speed to a great glowing fireball hundreds of feet wide and rising rapidly.

The scene of destruction at Hiroshima.

At the same time, a blinding flash spread for miles from the epicentre and disappeared almost as quickly as it had appeared. The ball of fire continued to expand into a huge mushroom cloud nearly 30,000 feet high and the blast of the weapon spread from the centre. At the core of that fireball the temperature reached 300,000 degrees Celsius.

Enola Gay and *The Great Artiste* had broken away as they had practised so many times, but the occupants of both aircraft reported that they were tossed around like feathers in a breeze as the blast struck them. In their wake 62,000 buildings had been obliterated and approximately 82,000 people vaporised, a quarter of Hiroshima's population.

In his autobiography, Tibbets recalled the sight.

> At the base of the cloud, fires were springing up everywhere, amid the turbulent mass of smoke that had the appearance of bubbling hot tar. If Dante had been with us in the plane, he would have been terrified! The city we had seen so clearly in the sunlight a few minutes before was now an ugly smudge. It had completely disappeared under this awful blanket of smoke and fire.

Staff Sergeant George Caron described the spectacle as 'like a peep into hell'. He wrote down his observations while still in the *Enola Gay*, about 11 miles from the drop.

> A column of smoke rising fast. It has a fiery red core. A bubbling mass, purple grey in color, with that red core. It's all turbulent. Fires are springing up everywhere, like flames shooting out of a huge bed of coals. I am starting to count the fires. One, two, three, four, five, six ... fourteen, fifteen ... it's

The explosion of 'Little Boy' caused this mushroom cloud to rise to 30,000 feet in seconds.

impossible. There are too many to count. Here it comes, the mushroom shape that Captain Parsons spoke about. It's coming this way. It's like a mass of bubbling molasses. The mushroom is spreading out. It's maybe a mile or two wide and half a mile high. It's growing up and up and up. It's nearly level with us and climbing. It's very black, but there is a purplish tint to the cloud. The base of the mushroom looks like a heavy undercast that is shot through with flames. The city must be below that. The flames and smoke are billowing out, whirling out into the foothills. The hills are disappearing under the smoke. All I can see now of the city is the main dock and what looks like an airfield. That is still visible. There are planes down there.

Caron also took many photographs of the mushroom cloud, still iconic images today, as did Lieutenant Russell Gackenbach, navigator of *Necessary Evil*, the observation aircraft. One of Gackenbach's images shows a complete and perfectly formed mushroom cloud high in the sky, above the darker, continuing blast cloud. By this time, the mushroom cloud had reached 45,000 feet.

Radio operator Richard Nelson had by now sent the message given to him by Colonel Tibbets that the mission was a success. However, Captain Parsons handed him a second, official, message: '82 V 670. Able, Line 1, Line 2, Line 6, Line 9.' When de-coded it would tell General Farrell, who would be waiting in the 509th Operations Room on Tinian, the news he had been waiting for hours to hear:

> CLEAR CUT. SUCCESSFUL IN ALL RESPECTS. VISIBLE EFFECTS GREATER THAN ALAMOGORDO. CONDITIONS NORMAL IN AIR PLANE FOLLOWING DELIVERY. PROCEEDING TO BASE.

The Hiroshima mushroom cloud at its height, photographed by Lieutenant Russell Gackenbach.

The press prepares its cameras and reflector boards and dignitaries await the landing of *Enola Gay* back at Tinian.

General Farrell could now send the news to General Leslie Groves in Washington, who in turn reported it to President Truman, who was aboard the USS *Augusta* on his way home from the Potsdam Conference.

After a third and final circle around Hiroshima, Tibbets put the *Enola Gay* on course for Tinian. *The Great Artiste* and *Necessary Evil* formed up behind, and the three bombers headed down the 'Hirohito Highway'. There was time to relax – the US had total control of the air away from Japan itself – so Paul Tibbets stuck a pipe in his mouth. Others ate their flight rations while Bob Lewis wrote observation notes. It had been an easy mission.

Enola Gay returning to Tinian after dropping 'Little Boy'.

General Carl Spaatz, Commander of all US Air Forces in the Pacific, pins the Distinguished Service Cross to Colonel Paul Tibbets' flying suit after Tibbets climbed down from the flight deck of *Enola Gay*.

Later that day, President Harry S. Truman broadcast a statement, aimed primarily at the Japanese government.

> The Japanese began the war from the air at Pearl Harbor. They have been repaid many-fold. If they do not now accept our terms they may expect a rain of ruin from the air, the like of which has never been seen on this earth.

As the *Enola Gay* landed back on Tinian, they were greeted by a mass of press men, photographers and military dignitaries. Colonel Paul Tibbets came down the ladder to solid ground after the longest fourteen hours of his life. He was greeted by General Carl Spaatz, Commanding General, Strategic Air Forces, who immediately pinned on Tibbets' now shabby flight coveralls the Distinguished Service Cross. All of the rest of his crew were awarded the Silver Star. The men were exhausted, but posed for photographs. The security team descended on Staff Sergeant George Caron and predictably relieved him of his two cameras. He never saw them again, but his images became internationally famous.

Having escaped the photographers, the crews of the *Enola Gay*, *The Great Artiste* and *Necessary Evil* were treated to a spread laid on by Mess Officer Charles Perry, who had been working the kitchen staff on Tinian since 1030hrs, the time he heard of the mission's success. At hearing the news he had turned to his cooks and shouted, 'The party's on!' Perry's staff prepared hundreds of pies, cooled scores of crates of beer and lemonade, made thousands of hot dogs, sliced beef and salami for open sandwiches, mixed potato and fruit salads. Perry even prepared a programme to mark the occasion.

509TH
FREE BEER PARTY TODAY 2 P.M.
TODAY—TODAY—TODAY—TODAY—TODAY
PLACE—509TH BALL DIAMOND
FOR ALL MEN OF THE 509TH COMPOSITE GROUP
FOUR(4) BOTTLES OF BEER PER MAN
NO RATION CARD NEEDED
LEMONADE FOR THOSE WHO DO NOT CARE FOR BEER
ALL STAR SOFT BALL GAME 2 P.M.
JITTER BUG CONTEST
HOT MUSIC
NOVELTY ACTS
SURPRISE CONTEST—YOU'LL FIND OUT
EXTRA—ADDED ATTRACTION, BLONDE, VIVACIOUS,
CURVACEOUS, STARLET DIRECT FROM ???????
PRIZES—GOOD ONES TOO

AND RATION FREE BEER
FOOD GALORE BY PERRY & CO. CATERERS
SPECIAL MOVIE WILL FOLLOW AT 1930, 'IT'S A PLEASURE'
IN TECHNICOLOR WITH
SONJA HENIE AND MICHAEL O'SHEA

CHECK WITH YOUR ORDERLY ROOM
FOR MORE DETAILS
WEAR OLD CLOTHES WEAR OLD CLOTHES
6 AUGUST 1945
WELCOME PARTY FOR RETURN OF
ENOLA GAY FROM
HIROSHIMA MISSION

On Tuesday 7 August the *Enola Gay*, with Bob Lewis in command, took part in a follow-up attack on Japan using conventional bombs. Meanwhile Colonel Tibbets flew to Guam where, on 8 August, he attended a major de-brief on the Hiroshima flight with Generals Spaatz and LeMay. He also took part in a press conference, during which his answers were limited to facts of the mission; he ignored or sidetracked questions which tried to gauge his emotional response to the bombing.

The *Enola Gay* comes to rest in front of the waiting press and VIPs.

In Washington the Chiefs of Staff were discussing whether or not the Hiroshima bomb might harden Japan's will to continue the war, despite the awesome damage done. It was debated whether Japan thought that the US had more bombs, and whether the 'Fat Man' bomb should be used. To do so might convince Japan that US nuclear capabilities were greater than they actually were, that they had a large supply that could be used to systematically destroy every Japanese city. It was decided to drop another bomb if Japan did not surrender. General LeMay asked Colonel Tibbets to lead the second attack, but Tibbets was quick to respond that he would rather pass it to another crew, saying that they could all do the job as well.

13

Mission to Nagasaki

With no Japanese surrender 48 hours after the destruction of Hiroshima, Tibbets was busy organising the second mission. The target was either to be Kokura or Nagasaki, dependent on weather conditions and visibility. Both cities were on the island of Honshu, south-west of Hiroshima. Major Charles Sweeney would pilot the primary aircraft, *Bock's Car* (so named because it was usually flown by Captain Frederick Bock), and amongst those on board would be Jacob Beser, the only man to accompany both atomic bombs to Japan, as countermeasures officer. Sweeney's regular aircraft, *The Great Artiste*, would once again carry instruments to record the blast, while *Big Stink* would carry the photographic equipment. The mission was set for 9 August 1945. All that was needed was the order to go.

All the cautious preparatory work that had been carried out on *Enola Gay* was now lavished on *Bock's Car*. Short of stripping them down, every engine was checked over, every spark plug replaced, ignition and valve timings checked, bolts torqued to specified settings, cylinder barrels examined for leaks, propeller drives examined and prop blades inspected for surface or edge damage. The crankcases were checked for even minor imperfections and oil leaks, and the engine cowlings were gone over to make sure that all the cooling shutters opened and closed in unison when the required temperatures were reached.

Once the engines were considered to pass muster, the airframe was next. Every single flush rivet was checked over, the cover panels where the upper and lower gun barbettes would have been fitted to the standard B-29 models, the hinged flying surfaces, horizontal and vertical, were inspected for smoothness and function. The other hinged panels – the undercarriage doors and the bomb doors – were checked and

Bock's Car, the B-29 that carried the 'Fat Man' bomb to Nagasaki on 9 August 1945.

double checked with the aircraft on support jacks. The unique bomb release mechanism came in for very special attention, because not only did the huge hook need to hang on to its precious cargo, but it needed to let it go precisely at the moment of release and break the electrical connections – its 'umbilical cord' as it left the aircraft. The aircraft was then polished to give it the greatest possible aerodynamic advantage in the air.

While *Bock's Car* was being prepared for its mission, the US Army Air Force was dropping leaflets by the million, addressed to the Japanese people in their own language and aimed at motivating a surrender. They featured a reproduction of one of George Caron's photographs of the Hiroshima mushroom cloud to illustrate the power of the atomic bomb.

> To the Japanese people:
>
> America asks that you take immediate heed of what we say on this leaflet.
> We are in possession of the most destructive explosive ever devised by man. A single one of our newly-developed atomic bombs is actually the equivalent in explosive power to what 2,000 of our giant B-29s can carry on a single mission. This awful fact is one for you to ponder and we solemnly assure you that it is grimly accurate.
> We have just begun to use this weapon against your homeland. If you still have any doubt, make inquiry as to what happened to Hiroshima when just one atomic bomb fell on that city.
> Before using this bomb to destroy every resource of the military by which they are prolonging this useless war, we ask that you now petition the Emperor to end the war. Our President has outlined for you the thirteen consequences of an honourable settlement. We urge that you accept these consequences and begin the work of building a new, better and peace-loving Japan.
> You should take these steps now to cease military resistance. Otherwise, we shall resolutely employ this bomb and all our other superior weapons to promptly and forcefully end the war.
> Evacuate your cities now!

The pre-flight briefing for the Nagasaki mission followed the pattern of the earlier mission, except that there were extra passengers. Two were British observers, representatives of the British government, who had wanted to go on the first flight but had been unable to due to lack of space. They were Group Captain Leonard Cheshire VC and William Penney, and they would travel in *The Great Artiste*. Cheshire was a leading British bomber pilot and the youngest Group Captain (equivalent to full Colonel) in the RAF. He had succeeded Wing Commander Guy Gibson to command the famous 617 'Dam Busters' Squadron. Another observer would be Bill Lawrence, the *New York Times* journalist. The briefing set the primary target as Kokura, because it was the home of a huge munitions arsenal, with Nagasaki as the secondary. The weather forecast for the time between 0800hrs and 0900hrs was said to be 'satisfactory' with good visibility.

Major Chuck Sweeney's crew on *Bock's Car* was as follows: Captain Charles Albury (co-pilot); Second Lieutenant Fred Olivi (regular co-pilot); Lieutenant James Van Pelt (navigator); Captain Kermit Beahan (bombardier); Master Sergeant John D. Kuharek (flight engineer); Staff Sergeant Ray Gallagher (gunner, assistant flight engineer); Staff Segeant Edward Buckley (radar operator); Sergeant Abe Spitzer (radio operator); Sergeant Albert Dehart (tail gunner); Lieutenant Jacob Beser (radar countermeasures officer); Commander Fred Ashworth (weaponeer); and Lieutenant Philip Barnes (assistant weaponeer).

'Fat Man' was firmly tucked away in the bomb bay and everybody was ready to go. However, during final checks from the cockpit, Major Sweeney came across a fault that demanded some rapid arithmetic. The fuel pumps delivering fuel from the forward bomb bay tank, containing 600 gallons of fuel, had failed to function, so leaving *Bock's Car* with 600 gallons of fuel less to cover the round trip and the weight of that 600 gallons as unwanted ballast. After doing his sums and cross-checking them with flight engineer Master Sergeant John Kuharek, Sweeney decided that they would have almost two hours of fuel to spare, so the decision was still 'go'. However, the take-off was delayed by nearly half an hour, while the two planes that were to accompany *Bock's Car* over the target, *The Great Artiste* (Captain Fred Bock) and *Big Stink* (Major Jim Hopkins), took off on time. As during the Hiroshima raid, the weather aircraft had already left. One man who should have been in the air was Dr Robert Serber, from Project Alberta, who had been allotted a place on *Big Stink* along with the British observers. However, he forgot his parachute and there were no spares on board, so Major Hopkins caused quite a stir by ordering him off the aircraft – even though they had already taxied onto the runway – on the grounds of safety. It was not a popular decision amongst the scientists, but a perfectly logical one. However, since Serber had been the only person on board who knew how to operate the high-speed camera, Major Hopkins had to be instructed on its use by radio from Tinian.

Having got round the fuel problem, Major Sweeney was faced with another when he reached Yokohama, the area designated as the rendezvous point for the three planes. He arrived to find that he could only locate *The Great Artiste*, and after waiting 40 minutes the two aircraft decided to head for Kokura. However, the delay gave time for a change in weather; when they arrived it was to find Kokura obscured by haze. After three passes they had failed to find the aiming point, and headed for the city of Nagasaki.

The weather over Nagasaki wasn't much better than over Kokura, but the bombardier Captain Beahan did eventually spot a small break in the cloud and through it he recognised the central sports stadium. There were signs of anti-aircraft fire exploding

'Fat Man', the atomic bomb dropped on Nagasaki. This was a fusion type of weapon and a more powerful device than 'Little Boy'.

Big Stink, piloted by Major James Hopkins, carried the two British observers, Group Captain Leonard Cheshire and Professor William Penney to witness the Nagasaki bombing, but because of a rendezvous error, they were late on the scene.

below and the radar countermeasures officer Jacob Beser noticed signs of activity on the Japanese fighter-control circuits he was monitoring. There were fighters coming up to intercept; there was no time to lose. However, Beahan was questioning the visibility of the target.

Eventually the fuel situation made Charles Sweeney's decision for him. The bomb had to go down on Nagasaki or it was going nowhere. A second run across the target area produced no better visibility than the first and so Captain Beahan decided that he would use radar for the drop. It wasn't a very accurate method, but the blast would be such to make it unimportant. Beahan called for minor course corrections and then released the plutonium bomb. It fell almost half a mile wide of the intended aiming point, but at 1102hrs, at an altitude of 1650 feet, 'Fat Man' exploded over the north-west section of the city, taking out the Mitsubishi torpedo plant and the Mitsubishi steel and armaments works nearby.

As 'Fat Man' fell, Major Sweeney swung his B-29 into the much-practised 155 degree right diving turn. Just as at Hiroshima, *The Great Artiste* also did its sharp diving turn to the left after releasing its instruments to record the statistics of the impact. This time they knew what to expect as a flash preceded a blast, followed by a mushroom cloud rising quickly to 30,000 feet. This was followed by the shock wave, which shook the aircraft even at a distance of ten miles.

Almost too late, but not quite, *Big Stink* finally reached Nagasaki, not in time to see the most spectacular parts of this bomb drop, but in time to see the immediate aftermath, the mushroom cloud, now risen to 50,000 feet, the blast damage on the

Nagasaki was laid waste in much the same way as Hiroshima, though the damage was not quite as extensive.

The crew of *Bock's Car* after landing back at Tinian after their fuel scare.

ground, the massive fires and a view of utter destruction. However, Leonard Cheshire and William Penney were both disappointed not to have seen the initial explosion.

In *Bock's Car*, Major Sweeney decided he had no time to circle around Nagasaki for too long. His fuel level was critical and he had no access to the 600 gallons in his bomb bay tank. He knew that he would not make it to Iwo Jima, the designated landing place, but he and Sergeant John Kuharek worked out that they could just get to Okinawa. Navigator James Van Pelt set course for Yontan airfield on Okinawa, where *Bock's Car* arrived with only a few gallons of fuel left. After refuelling the crew flew back to Tinian, where Tibbets praised their achievement against the odds. Privately he decided that should another atomic attack prove necessary, he would lead it himself.

Although the plutonium bomb used on Nagasaki was considerably more powerful than the uranium bomb used on Hiroshima, it did less damage and caused fewer casualties, mainly because it exploded over an industrial area, and hills shielded portions of the city from the blast. The explosion affected around 43 square miles, but approximately 8.5 of those square miles were water, and 33 more were only partially settled. A significant number of roads and rail tracks escaped major damage and in some areas electricity was not knocked out, and fire breaks helped to prevent the spread of fires into the south.

The destruction at Nagasaki has generally received less attention than that at Hiroshima, but it was still pretty extensive. Almost everything up to half a mile from ground zero was completely destroyed, including even the earthquake-hardened

The mushroom cloud of smoke and fire over Nagasaki rose to 50,000 feet.

concrete structures, some of which had survived at comparable distances at Hiroshima. According to a Nagasaki prefecture report 'men and animals died almost instantly' within just over half a mile of the point of detonation, and overall it has been estimated that 40,000 people lost their lives. Almost all homes within a mile and a half were destroyed, and dry, combustible materials such as paper instantly burst into flames as far away as 10,000 feet from ground zero. Of the 52,000 homes in Nagasaki, 14,000 were destroyed and 5400 more were seriously damaged. Only 12 per cent of homes escaped unscathed.

The official Manhattan Engineer District report on the attack termed the damage to the two Mitsubishi plants 'spectacular'. Despite the absence of a firestorm, numerous secondary fires erupted throughout the city. Fire-fighting efforts were hampered by water line breaks, and six weeks later the city was still suffering from water shortages. A US Navy officer who visited the city in mid-September reported that, even over a month after the attack, 'a smell of death and corruption pervades the place.' As at Hiroshima, the psychological effects of the attack were considerable.

On the day after the Nagasaki drop, Emperor Hirohito overruled his generals, many of whom still wanted to fight on, and moved to accept the conditions of the Potsdam Declaration. He made a radio broadcast to his people on 14 August, thus signalling Japan's surrender to the Allies.

> To our good and loyal subjects: After pondering deeply the general trends of the world and the actual conditions obtaining in our empire today, we have decided to effect a settlement of the present situation by resorting to an extraordinary measure.
>
> We have ordered our Government to communicate to the Governments of the United States, Great Britain, China and the Soviet Union that our empire accepts the provisions of their joint declaration.
>
> To strive for the common prosperity and happiness of all nations as well as the security and well-being of our subjects is the solemn obligation which has been handed down by our imperial ancestors and which we lay close to the heart.
>
> Indeed, we declared war on America and Britain out of our sincere desire to insure Japan's self-preservation and the stabilization of East Asia, it being far from our thought either to infringe upon the sovereignty of other nations or to embark upon territorial aggrandizement.
>
> But now the war has lasted for nearly four years. Despite the best that has been done by everyone – the gallant fighting of our military and naval forces, the diligence and assiduity of our servants of the State and the devoted service of our 100,000,000 people – the war situation has developed not necessarily to Japan's advantage, while the general trends of the world have all turned against her interest.
>
> Moreover, the enemy has begun to employ a new and most cruel bomb, the power of which to do damage is, indeed, incalculable, taking the toll of many innocent lives. Should we continue to fight, it would not only result in an ultimate collapse and obliteration of the Japanese nation, but also it would lead to the total extinction of human civilization.
>
> Such being the case, how are we to save the millions of our subjects, nor to atone ourselves before the hallowed spirits of our imperial ancestors? This is the reason why we have ordered the acceptance of the provisions of the joint declaration of the powers.
>
> We cannot but express the deepest sense of regret to our allied nations of East Asia, who have consistently cooperated with the Empire toward the emancipation of East Asia.

The thought of those officers and men as well as others who have fallen in the fields of battle, those who died at their posts of duty, or those who met death otherwise and all their bereaved families, pains our heart night and day.

The welfare of the wounded and the war sufferers and of those who lost their homes and livelihood is the object of our profound solicitude. The hardships and sufferings to which our nation is to be subjected hereafter will be certainly great.

We are keenly aware of the inmost feelings of all of you, our subjects. However, it is according to the dictates of time and fate that we have resolved to pave the way for a grand peace for all the generations to come by enduring the (unavoidable) and suffering what is insufferable. Having been able to save and maintain the structure of the Imperial State, we are always with you, our good and loyal subjects, relying upon your sincerity and integrity.

Beware most strictly of any outbursts of emotion that may engender needless complications, of any fraternal contention and strife that may create confusion, lead you astray and cause you to lose the confidence of the world.

Let the entire nation continue as one family from generation to generation, ever firm in its faith of the imperishableness of its divine land, and mindful of its heavy burden of responsibilities, and the long road before it. Unite your total strength to be devoted to the construction for the future. Cultivate the ways of rectitude, nobility of spirit, and work with resolution so that you may enhance the innate glory of the Imperial State and keep pace with the progress of the world.

The final confirmation of surrender was broadcast to the American people on 15 August 1945 and the formal declaration of surrender was signed on board the USS *Missouri* on 15 September. The Second World War in the Pacific was over.

A soldier walks through the ruins of Nagasaki, 1945.

14

After the Bomb

The immediate aftermath of the bombings of Hiroshima and Nagasaki was the incredible death toll, hundreds of thousands of Japanese vaporised in seconds. These deaths were caused by the flash and blast, the sheer power of the heat and explosion. But in the longer term more were to die as the result of radiation, an unseen, indiscriminate and enduring killer. In August 1945, very few people had any real idea – including the scientists of the Manhattan Project – of the long term consequences of an atom bomb explosion. It was believed that, because the two atom bombs exploded above the ground rather than on impact, the radiation would go upwards with the mushroom cloud. It was in this belief that only days after the bomb exploded over Hiroshima, there were rescue workers and scientific teams all over the city, oblivious to the possible harm that could befall them in years to come.

The Genbaku Dome was designed by a Czech architect named Jan Letzel and was built in 1915 as the Hiroshima Prefectural Commercial Exhibition, renamed the Hiroshima Prefectural Industrial Promotion Hall in 1933. Today, it stands as the key memorial of the Hiroshima Peace Park and is a UNESCO World Heritage site.

Immediately after the blasts, the US Army, with support from the Navy, Marine Corps and the International Red Cross, went into the stricken cities and began an extensive rescue operation. They monitored radiation levels and were surprised to discover the levels were not nearly as high as they had expected. Colonel Ashly Oughterson, the surgical consultant to General MacArthur, saw the need to conduct an extensive medical study, which he devised at the end of August 1945. By September, an American team persuaded the Japanese government to work with them on a collaborative investigation to study the residual radiation effects of the bombs. The research team focused on the medical consequences of radiation, seeking answers to three main questions: what were the immediate effects; did radiation result in an increase in cancer incidence over the long term; and how did radiation influence the future generations of survivors?

For months after the bombings, in addition to having extensive burns, survivors developed puzzling symptoms: blood abnormalities, fever, chronic fatigue, diarrhoea, vomiting, hair loss and depression. 'Radiation sickness' and 'Acute Radiation Syndrome' were names given by doctors to describe these symptoms that presented themselves sometimes within hours of the blasts. The aforementioned burns were caused by the thermal energy released from the nuclear explosion; thermal or 'flash' burns were the result of direct radiation, secondary or 'flame' burns were the result of objects igniting and engulfing an individual. Over 90 per cent of the victims' burns in Hiroshima and Nagasaki were 'flash' burns. The burns were often deadly as radiation impairs the immune system, thus leaving the victims open to infection. This was particularly true in Hiroshima as medical care did not arrive for five days, too late to save many.

Three months after the initiation of Colonel Oughterson's research project, in January 1946, the team concluded that the vulnerable area for those killed instantly

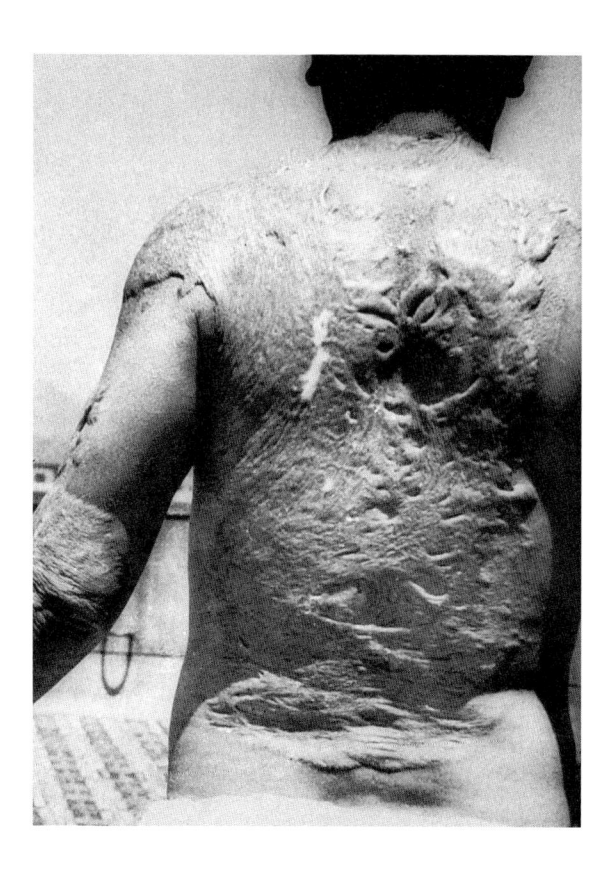

A victim of the atomic bomb, whose flesh was melted by flash burns.

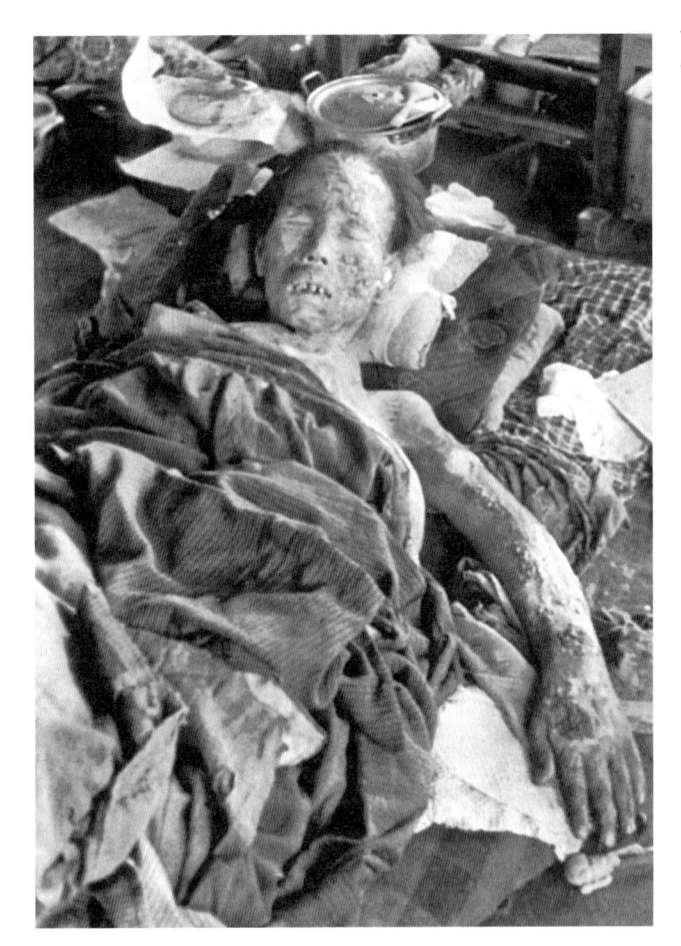

The human cost of ending the war in the Pacific.

was approximately 2.9 square miles from ground zero, and for all casualties (those dying soon afterwards from severe injuries), 9.4 square miles. Even ten miles from the hypocentre, the sheer force of the bomb had caused fatal injuries.

Hiroshima and Nagasaki rebuilt their communities after the war, with a great deal of outside help. But the survivors were not left unscathed. Both cities suffered an increase in cases of leukaemia due to radiation exposure, rates peaking in 1948. In 1956 the Japanese physician Gensaku Oho persuaded the cities' medical associations to set up tumour registries for a closer analysis of the rate of development. In addition to that, the joint team of American and Japanese researchers also began examining cancer rates. They concluded that while radiation caused more cancer, it did not do within a younger age range than usual, rather increased cases in the age range in which cancer was most likely. They also concluded that radiation did not induce a specific 'radiation-type' cancer, but rather increased the rate of all cancers.

In the interests of political stability, the US encouraged its allies to endorse the reconstruction of Japan as a political and industrial entity. The Allied Control Commission was set up to control and oversee its political and economic recovery, and to ensure that military growth was curtailed. Japan's defence forces were allowed to reconstruct and equip, but at nothing like the scale previously. By the time of the Korean War – during which US bases in Japan were used for bombing raids on North Korea – the Allied Control Commission was relaxing its controls on Japanese industry

Hiroshima laid waste by 'Little Boy'.

The destruction wrought by 'Fat Man' on Nagasaki.

and by the end of 1952 was promoting collaborative arrangements between Japanese manufacturing industry and western companies.

The motor vehicle industry was a key area of growth in Japan after the Second World War. Nissan went from buying kits from Austin to manufacture the British cars in Japan, to being a world leader in the motor industry, completely eclipsing Austin itself and opening plants in Europe. Similarly Japan's optical industry grew, with two significant camera makers, Canon and Nikon, selling cameras to US troops based there and building up the nation's foreign exchange fund. Japan is now a world leader in these industries, as well as electronics.

Over the years Japan has made several attempts to apologise to the countries it invaded and the people its soldiers mistreated during the Second World War, the first official apology coming in 1957. As recently as June 2009, Japanese Prime Minister Hashimoto offered 'an expression of deep remorse and heartfelt apology to the people who suffered in the Second World War'. However, many recipients of those apologies have treated them with scepticism, largely because they have seen no attempt by Japan to compensate the survivors for their suffering. Some of those survivors felt this was not adequate, since they were not, in their view, properly compensated for what they endured. The fact is that it is almost impossible to determine what is 'adequate compensation'.

In military terms, Japan has redeemed itself in the eyes of the world. Today, the Japan Self Defence Forces are made up of the Ground Self Defence Force, the Maritime Self Defence Force and Self Defence Force, Air – the Koku Jietai. By a treaty signed shortly after the Second World War, the Japanese military are primarily restricted to the military function simply of self defence, as their titles imply. However, in recent years, the JASDF has been involved in several peacekeeping missions, providing air transport in combined UN service operations around the world.

In the wider world, the defeat of Japan gave the western powers the opportunity to restore stability in China, so long under Japanese control. However, the opportunity was squandered, and as money poured into the reconstruction of Japan, the Chinese were left to fight amongst themselves to decide who would take the place of the Japanese oppressors. On one side the Nationalists, led by General Chiang Kai-shek, and on the other the Communists led by Mao Tse Tung. Mao won the mainland battle for China and Chiang Kai-shek was driven out to Taiwan, what was then Formosa. The US made attempts to resolve the civil war by offering to fund a coalition to the tune of half a

The Nissan GT-1 Class car fielded at the Le Mans 24 Hours Race in France; a symbol of the Japanese recovery.

The young Chiang Kai-shek as an officer cadet.

billion dollars, encouraging General Chiang to democratise his Kuomintang regime and accept the Communists into a political coalition which would, the US thought, endure until true democratic elections could take place. The attempt failed, in part due to the efforts of US politicians who did not want to encourage any kind of communist regime, which undermined American credibility in Chinese eyes. It was to be 1972 before any positive step was taken by the US to establish what might be described as 'normal' relations between the West and the People's Republic of China, when President Richard Nixon visited the country.

Over the years there has been much debate as to whether the attacks on Hiroshima, and more particularly Nagasaki, were justified; it has been said that the Japanese were on the brink of surrender before 6 August, through the negotiations in Switzerland. However, if that were true then surely it should have taken only one bomb to convince them. It has also been said that the US was looking for the opportunity to test its new weapons and jumped at the chance. Many books have been written along this line, saying that the bombings did not need to take place, an easy stance so many years after the event. The fact is that the US admirals and generals who knew most about the

Mao Tse-Tung in 1921 at the age of 27, when he first joined the Chinese Communist Party.

Taken at a railway bridge in Shangtang, this photograph shows Mao Tse Tung's People's Liberation Army attacking a Nationalist Kuomintang defensive position.

subject at the time agreed to a man that it was the most effective and least expensive way (in terms of lives, materials and time) to end the war.

And what of the men of the 509th? After the mission to Nagasaki, combat operations continued until the official Japanese surrender, at which point the men flew training missions until standing down. The Group returned to the US on 6 November 1945, moving to Roswell Army Airfield in New Mexico, where the 1st Ordnance Squadron was commended by Brigadier-General Thomas F. Farrell and Commodore William S. Parsons, prior to the engineers being dispersed.

> The undersigned wish to commend the members of the 1st Ordnance Squadron (Special, Aviation) for meritorious service all have given to the atomic bomb programme to bring it into being as a successful war weapon.
>
> It is felt that without your hard work, technical service and careful heed to the military security placed upon the programme, the project could not have succeeded as it did. We are fully cognizant of the problems faced by you as a result of the new type of work and the acceleration with which it had to be carried out. Without your steadfastness and devotion to duty, the outstanding success of the atomic bomb would have been impossible.
>
> You may feel that the influence the atomic bomb has had in bringing the world conflict to a successful conclusion is a direct result of your efforts. For this you have our profound appreciation.

There was one thing left for Colonel Paul Tibbets to do: fulfil the promise he had made to those felons who had managed to get themselves assigned to the 1st Ordnance Squadron, despite all the security screening. He sent for the men in turn and handed over their official file that he had held since Wendover Field, and gave each one a match. Colonel William H. Blanchard replaced Tibbets as commander on 22 January 1946, and oversaw the 509th Bombardment Group becoming the core of the newly formed Strategic Air Command.

15

The Future of Strategic Bombing

Since the end of the Second World War, there has been constant debate about the best type of strategic force to have available against the risk of major conflict. *Enola Gay* and *Bock's Car* certainly demonstrated the enormous value of long range strategic bombing back in 1945, but the argument continues – should a strategic strike force be airborne or seaborne? Since those historic flights, the closest thing to a major conflict was the Korean War, where all the ingredients of the previous war were present – the open battlefield, strategic and tactical bombing and air-to-air combat. Interestingly, quite a lot of air cover was provided from aircraft carriers and ship-to-shore bombardment also took place. It might be argued that the ship-to-shore batteries were 'strategic', but it could never be argued that aircraft carrier-to-target operations were anything other than tactical. The arguments about the merits of seaborne battle groups versus long-range strategic bombers have passed through the Vietnam conflict and continue to the present day without resolution.

One key argument is that of unit cost; one B-2 Spirit costs $1 billion, a huge sum even before one factors in the cost of having a whole squadron comprising up to ten aircraft with a crew of three per aircraft and a ground crew of up to 200. The operational unit cost is therefore very high, and one which prompted Congress to cancel 114 B-2s before they were built, leaving the US with only 21, 20 after one was lost in a take-off accident. While there is no official data, one might conservatively estimate that two squadrons of B-2 Spirits have cost the US some $40 billion to operate for 20 years.

How does that compare with the seaborne alternative? The latest US Navy carrier to put to sea is the Nimitz Class CVN-77 USS *George H.W. Bush*, at a cost of almost $7 billion. Less than a squadron of B-2 Spirits? Yes, but that does not take into account the costs of the ship's crew of 3200 and the estimated Air Wing personnel complement of 2800. There is also the matter of the aircraft, likely the new F-35, 60 of which would cost a total of $12 billion. All that is without any helicopter force, of which 30 would be envisaged. Therefore the cost of one ship and its air group would be around $20 billion before it even put to sea.

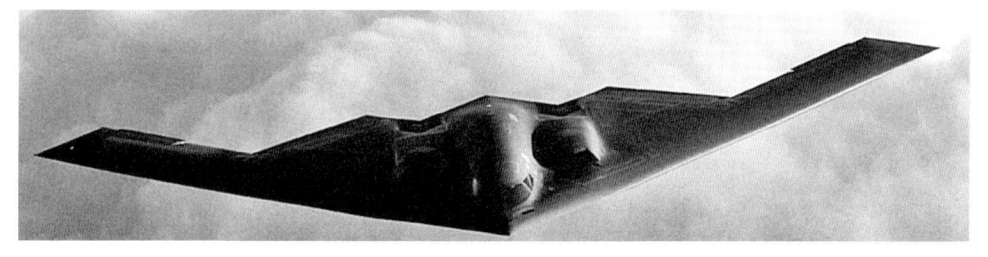

The next generation of bomber: like a giant bat, the B-2 Spirit travels at high speed with very low radar recognition to deliver its ordnance.

THE FUTURE OF STRATEGIC BOMBING

The USS *George H.W. Bush*, with a complement of aircraft on board.

The mighty 'Buff' – the Boeing B-52 'Stratofortress' – the biggest all-jet bomber ever built. This B-52H is 48 years old and expected to fly on until 2040.

The capital and operating costs of these two alternatives are not even the whole story; a more pressing issue is what provides the greater national security, an argument that is raging in Britain as well as the US. Should the Navy or the Air Force be responsible for maintaining a strategic strike force? Can a seaborne force actually perform the task? Given the huge costs, it seems the answer is probably no, as several ships would be needed. Also a modern seaborne strike force essentially uses shorter range aircraft – the Doolittle Raid would be impossible today – and takes longer to reach its target area. A squadron of B-2 Spirits could deliver 80 nuclear weapons – or 500,000lbs of conventional high-explosive bombs – to a target 6000 miles away in ten hours. A Naval Task Force, with a top speed of 30 knots would take more than seven days to reach he same target distance.

In the final days of the Pacific campaign, the strategic activity was the long range bombing of Japan, culminating in the atom bombing of Hiroshima and Nagasaki. The tactical element was Admiral Mitscher's Fast Carrier Force which had the job of striking short range targets from carriers to 'soften up' the approaches for battle force landings. The Long Range Strategic Bomber is here to stay, because there is nothing better at carrying out a fast-response, long-range precision strike that maintains some element of surprise in the approach. A Doolittle Raid today would be unnecessary, because an aircraft could be on its target halfway round the world within hours. Fast-reaction strategic strike is reliant on the long-range bomber. But the tactical value of the aircraft carrier remains; both have their place in a military arsenal.

As a footnote, consider this. There are 76 B-52H 'Stratofortresses' in service with the USAF; all have been in service for more than 40 years and may continue to serve for 30 more. The B-52 can carry even more than the B-2 'Spirit' – 70,000lbs of bombs. It can reach a target 6000 miles away in approximately twelve hours and can bomb from 40,000 feet. The B- 52s cost $9.8 million each to build in 1962, and have certainly proved to be value for money. The good old 'Buff' continues to fly. What a heritage the B-29 has left.

Appendix 1

People

LIEUTENANT-GENERAL FRANK A. ARMSTRONG

Frank Armstrong was born in Hamilton, North Carolina in 1902 and joined the Army Air Corps in 1928. He graduated from Wake Forest College with a law degree in 1923 and a bachelor of science degree in 1925. His early career took him to a bomber squadron and then he became a flight instructor. in 1934 he joined a group of pilots under the command of Captain Ira Eaker who delivered mail by air, and in December he was transferred to a pursuit squadron. In December that year, he was flying a twin-engined amphibian aircraft when one engine blew up in the air and the wing caught fire. He successfully landed the aircraft and was awarded the Distinguished Flying Cross.

In March 1937, Captain Armstrong transferred to the 13th Attack Squadron, Barksdale Field, Louisiana, part of the 3rd Attack Group, flying Northrop A-17 attack planes. He became its commander on 7 May 1939, and continued in command of the squadron on 1 July 1939, when it became the 13th Bombardment Squadron (Light), converting to B-18 Bolo bombers. Armstrong commanded the 13th BS until 5 October 1940

Captain Armstrong was attached to the Royal Air Force in England from November 1940 to February 1941 as a combat observer. He returned to the US to command the 90th Bombardment Squadron in Savannah, Georgia, and was promoted major on 15 March, then lieutenant-colonel in January 1942. He was appointed as the Assistant Chief of Air Staff, A-3 (Operations) at Army Air Forces Headquarters in Washington DC, when he was selected on 24 January 1942 to accompany General Eaker to England with five other officers to establish the VIII Bomber Command,

Eighth Air Force, where he became its operations officer and was promoted to colonel on 15 March 1942.

Armstrong commanded two B-17 Flying Fortress groups and a wing each of B-17 and B-29 Superfortresses in combat operations against Germany and Japan. He personally led, though not as lead pilot because he was not yet rated to fly the B-17 solo, the first USAAF strategic bombing attack from England in August 1942 (his pilot was Major Paul W. Tibbets in Armstrong's own aircraft *Butcher Shop*). He also led the last strategic raid on Japan three years later.

General Armstrong's commands included: 13th Attack Squadron, 97th Bomb Group, 306th Bomb Group, 1st Bomb Wing, 315th Bomb Wing, Second Air Force and Alaskan Command. His careers decorations included the Distinguished Service Cross, the Distinguished Service Medal, the Silver Star, the Legion of Merit, the Distinguished Flying Cross, the Air Medal and the Royal Air Force Distinguished Flying Cross. He was the first US officer to receive the RAF's DFC. His flying ratings included Command Pilot, Combat Observer and Technical Observer.

After the Second World War, General Armstrong was involved in the B-47 Stratojet flying programme. He was later appointed Commanding General Second Air Force and ended his active career in the post of Commanding General, Alaskan Command.

GENERAL HENRY H. ARNOLD

Henry H Arnold was born in Gladwyne, Pennsylvania on 26 June 1886. He entered the US Army Academy at West Point Military Academy in New York in the summer of 1903 and graduated in 1907, being commissioned as an infantry second lieutenant. He was assigned to the Philippines, but so disliked his infantry role that he volunteered to assist Captain Arthur Cowan in the task of mapping the island of Luzon. When Cowan returned to the US to take up the post of Chief of the Aeronautical Division of the Signal Corps, he sought out two lieutenants to train as pilots and Henry Arnold was one of them.

Arnold was taught to fly at the Wright Brothers Training School and gained Military Aviator's Certificate Number 2 and FAI Pilot Certificate Number 29. While serving as a flight instructor, he set two world altitude records and was the first pilot to carry US mail. Captain Arnold was prevented from going to France in the First World War, because it was decided that experienced aviators were needed to train new pilots, so he was promoted to major and appointed Information Officer for the Aviation Division of the Signal Corps. Within two months, he was promoted to full colonel to take up the post of Executive Officer for the Aviation Division.

After the war, Henry Arnold reverted to the rank of major and found himself on the staff of General Billy Mitchell; when Mitchell was court-martialled for 'insubordination' in expressing his views on the need for air power, Arnold and a couple of close friends gave evidence in favour of the General. In 1931 Colonel Arnold took command of March Field in California. December 1935 brought a promotion to brigadier-general with the appointment of Assistant Chief of the Army Air Corps. In 1938 he was promoted major-general and assumed full command of the Air Corps. The Second World War required the reorganisation of the Army Air Corps, raising the profile of military aviation and Arnold; in December 1941, after Pearl Harbor, he was made a lieutenant-general.

In March 1943, his promotion to full general reflected his position in the Chiefs of Staff. He personally oversaw the introduction and operation of the huge B-29 force launched against Japan and had a leading hand in giving Colonel Paul Tibbets the level of authority to bring about the raids on Hiroshima and Nagasaki.

In December 1944, recognising his achievements and significant contribution to the success of the Allies in the Second World War, General Arnold was promoted to five-star General of the Army, alongside General Marshall and later General Eisenhower. Henry Arnold's claims to distinction include winning the air war in the Pacific, contributing to the winning of the air war in Europe and being the only five-star general in two arms of the US forces – the Army and the Air Force, for he was the founding Commanding General of the US Air Force in 1947.

General Arnold died on 15 January 1950 and was buried in Arlington National Cemetery in Virginia, but his remains were later transferred to the grounds of the US Air Force Academy in Colorado Springs. For the USAF Academy Class of 2012 General Arnold was nominated Exemplar in recognition of his career-long achievements.

LIEUTENANT-GENERAL JOSEPH H. ATKINSON

Atkinson was born in Dublin, Texas in 1900. He received his early schooling in Dublin and attended a business college in that city. He enlisted in the US Army on 20 December 1922, became a flying cadet in September 1923, and earned his wings and commission as a second lieutenant on 13 September 1924 after completing training at Brooks and Kelly Fields, Texas. After receiving his commission, Atkinson was assigned to the 16th Observation squadron at Fort Riley, Kansas. He also served with the 12th Observation Squadron, commanded by Major Henry Arnold. One of Atkinson's duties was to fly the presidential airmail from the summer White House in Superior, Wisconsin to Chicago, with the squadron operating from what he called a 'typical cornfield operation.'

Atkinson attended the Air Corps Technical School, Maintenance Engineering Course at Chanute Field, from October 1929 to April 1930. He became a flying instructor, first at Brooks Field and later at Randolph Field, both in Texas. He was promoted to first lieutenant on 6 November 1933, and in September 1934 was assigned as adjutant of the 29th Pursuit Squadron stationed at Albrook Field, in the Panama Canal Zone, becoming commanding officer of the squadron in December. He became Captain Atkinson on 15 March 1935 and on 14 January 1936 was assigned as flight commander (later commander) of the 11th Bombardment Squadron stationed at Hamilton Field, California. He served with this squadron until January 1940, interrupting his service from 1 June to 26 August 1939 to attend the Air Corps Tactical School at Maxwell Field, Alabama.

Atkinson's next assignment was with the 24th Bombardment Squadron at Eglin and Orlando Fields, Florida, beginning on 18 February 1940, as its commanding officer. He was promoted to major on 1 February 1941. In September 1941 he was appointed assistant chief of staff, A-3, at Headquarters Army Air Forces. On 23 January 1942 he was promoted to lieutenant colonel and then on 9 May 1942 he was promoted to colonel. His next assignment was as commanding officer of the 97th Bombardment Group, beginning in September 1942, whilst the unit was stationed in England, taking over from Colonel Frank Armstrong, then transferring to North Africa.

In the last weeks of 1942 and the early days of 1943, Atkinson suffered from a chest infection that kept him in bed. Not wanting to report sick and be rotated back to the US, a series of bombing raids was carried out over Tunisia in his name by Lieutenant-Colonel Paul Tibbets, his executive officer in the 97th Bombardment Group. On 18 January 1943, Atkinson was promoted to brigadier-general by Presidential Order and made commanding general of the 5th Bomb Wing, stationed first in Africa and later in Italy. He credited the award of his first star to the performance of Paul Tibbets, his 'exec'. Then, while in Italy, General Atkinson was designated as deputy commanding general of the Fifteenth Air Force in February 1944. He remained in that assignment until July 1944 when he was designated as commanding general of III Bomber Command at MacDill Field, Florida.

In May 1945, General Atkinson was assigned to the Alaskan Department at Fort Richardson. He was appointed deputy commanding general of Alaskan Air Command on 20 January 1946 and on 1 October was appointed commanding general. He was promoted to major general on 24 January 1948. In February 1949 he became commanding general of the 311th Air Division in Topeka, Kansas. He remained with this organisation until 31 October; on 1 November he was assigned as commanding general, Second Air Force, at Barksdale Air Force Base, Louisiana.

In November 1952, he was appointed vice-commander and later commander-in-chief of the Alaskan Command (with the additional duty of commander, Alaskan Air Command, from 24 February to 17 September 1956) at Elmendorf Air Force Base. He was promoted to lieutenant general on 3 March 1953. In September 1956, he was appointed commander, Air Defense Command at Ent Air Force Base, Colorado, until his retirement on 28 February 1961.

During his service in the European theatre in the Second World War, General Atkinson earned many decorations including: the Distinguished Service Medal with oak leaf cluster; Silver Star with oak leaf cluster; Distinguished Flying Cross; Air Medal with five oak leaf clusters; and French Croix de Guerre with palm. Other decorations awarded were: the American Campaign Medal; European-African-Middle Eastern Campaign Medal; National Defense Service Medal; and Air Force Longevity Service Award with seven oak leaf clusters.

MAJOR-GENERAL CLAIRE LEE CHENNAULT

Claire Lee Chennault was a controversial character who was born in Commerce, Texas, and went to China with a number of other Americans as a flying instructor. Arriving in China as a Captain, Chennault was promoted temporary Major and soon assumed the title of 'Colonel'. He was noticed by General Chiang Kai-shek, who was impressed by his flying style and flamboyant presence. Madame Chiang, Soong Mei-Li, was also impressed by 'Colonel' Chennault and he was recruited into the Chinese Army as a Brigadier-General and appointed Chiang's Air Chief of Staff.

As the American Volunteer Group came into existence, Chennault was elevated to major-general and took direct command of the group, recruiting a number of old Army Air Corps friends. The loyalty shown by most of the pilots to Chennault and his undoubted personal flying skills was very much what made the reputation of the 'Flying Tigers'. Their Curtiss P-40s were technically inferior to the Japanese Mitsubishi A6M 'Zero', but many Japanese pilots were brought down by the Americans, including Lieutenant Gregory Boyington, a US Marine pilot who shot down six Japanese aircraft during his short tour with the AVG, and who later commanded the famous 'Black Sheep' Squadron.

General Chennault had a flamboyant and sometimes abrasive manner, though he did not like to take risks: he played to win. He had wanted to concentrate all his squadrons in Kunming, but Chiang Kai-shek overruled him because he wanted to ensure that American lend-lease supplies continued to move up the Burma Road into China. So Chiang decided to loan the AVG 3rd Squadron to the British for the defence of Rangoon. Ultimately, of course, Burma fell to the Japanese, but not before the 'Flying Tigers' had put up a valiant fight.

With the decision to absorb the AVG into the regular US Army Air Force, Chennault returned to US service in the rank of Brigadier-General and was appointed Commanding General of the 14th Air Force. He retired in 1946 as a Major-General and was promoted to Lieutenant-General only days before his death in 1958 for services to his country. He is buried in Arlington National Cemetery.

Major-General Claire Lee Chennault, from a painting by J.C. Leyendekker in the Haggin Museum, Stockton, California.

GENERAL IRA C. EAKER

Ira Clarence Eaker was born in Texas in 1896, the son of a tenant farmer, and enlisted in the Army Reserve in 1917, gaining his commission and finding himself assigned to the 64th Infantry Regiment, which was deployed to France as part of the 7th Infantry Division. In March 1918, Lieutenant Eaker was detached to Kelly Field in Texas for flight training. Graduating as a pilot, he was assigned to Rockwell Field. In 1929 he flew the *Question Mark* with his friend Carl Spaatz to establish the viability of in-flight refuelling. After Jimmy Doolittle established the viability of 'blind flying', Ira Eaker flew 'blind' across the US in 1930.

Eaker had connections with a squadron that later came under the command of Colonel Jimmy Doolittle, the 34th, while it was still a pursuit squadron. He was appointed to command it in October 1934, then was detached to the US Navy in the early summer of 1935, before entering the Air Corps Tactical School at Maxwell Field in Alabama. After graduating he moved on to the Command and General Staff School at Fort Leavenworth in Kansas. Appointed Assistant Chief of the Information Division in the office of the Chief of the Air Corps, he then returned to flying by taking command of the 20th Pursuit Group (later to gain fame as the 20th Tactical Fighter Wing) at Hamilton Field in California.

At the beginning of 1942 he was promoted to brigadier-general and command of the VIII Bomber Command of the Eighth Air Force. Eaker was the man who sought and gained Winston Churchill's approval to fly daylight precision bombing raids over Europe while the Royal Air Force flew night raids. It was as a result of this that Colonel Frank Armstrong and Major Paul Tibbets flew the first USAAF bombing mission in Europe over the Rouen railway yards. General Eaker flew with that mission in B-17 *Yankee Doodle* from Grafton Underwood. At the end of 1943, promoted to lieutenant-general, Eaker took over command of the air forces of North Africa and Italy, as Lieutenant-General Jimmy Doolittle moved north to take over an expanded Eighth Air Force. Eaker was not happy about the bombing of Monte Cassino, as he doubted its value as a military target.

Appointed Deputy Commander of the Army Air Force on 30 April, as well as Chief of the Air Staff, until his retirement in August 1947, USAAF placed him on its retired list in the rank of permanent lieutenant-general in 1948. In 1985 he was awarded his fourth star (the same time as Jimmy Doolittle) in recognition of his services to his nation and his significant contributions to the development of aviation.

Lt Gen Ira C. Eaker, USAF (Ret)

FLEET ADMIRAL WILLIAM F. HALSEY JR

William Halsey was born in Elizabeth, New Jersey in October 1882. His father was Captain William F. Halsey and so he tried to enter the US Navy, but was unable to gain admission to the Naval Academy at Annapolis, so went to the University of Virginia to study medicine, on the theory that he would gain entry as a doctor if he couldn't do it any other way. However, after just a year in Virginia Halsey entered Annapolis and graduated in 1904, being promoted directly to the rank of lieutenant.

Halsey served aboard battleships during his early career, then chose to specialise in the field of torpedoes and torpedo boats. By 1912, he was commanding the First Group of the Atlantic Fleet Torpedo Flotilla. During the First World War, Lieutenant Commander Halsey took command of the USS Shaw, earning the Navy Cross. Serving as Naval Attache to Berlin between 1922 and 1925, he then went back to sea aboard USS Dale on a European cruise. By 1930, Captain Halsey was leading two destroyer squadrons, after which he attended a senior command course at the Naval Academy.

Halsey's next command was to be an aircraft carrier, but he had to qualify as an aviator before taking command of the USS Saratoga, then NAS Pensacola in Florida. By 1938, he was commanding carrier divisions as Rear Admiral and by 1941 was elevated to the rank of Vice-Admiral, commanding the Aircraft Battle Force. After Pearl Harbor, Admiral Halsey was given command of Task Force 16, a 16-ship flotilla which included the USS Hornet, the vessel that carried Doolittle's squadron of sixteen B-25 bombers.

LIEUTENANT COMMANDER MOCHITSURA HASHIMOTO IJN

Mochitsura Hashimoto was born in Kyoto in October 1909, the son of a Shinto priest. His father had expected him to follow in the family tradition, but he joined the Imperial Japanese Navy in 1927. Graduating from the Naval Academy in 1931, he first served on destroyers, then volunteered for service aboard submarines. His first submarine assignment was I-24, which he joined in 1941. As Torpedo Officer he was responsible for the launching of the midget submarine which managed to enter Pearl Harbor when Admiral Yamamoto's attack took place on the morning of Sunday 7 December.

After Pearl Harbor, the young Hashimoto served in a number of Pacific campaigns and in 1944 was assigned to command a new submarine RO-44. This vessel was launched in 1943 at Tamano and operated out of Truk, until it fell into American hands. In February 1944, newly promoted Lieutenant Commander Hashimoto was instructed to approach Miji with the task of intercepting approaching US carriers, but the American ships had more speed and Hashimoto was unable to intercept.

In April, RO-44 and RO-42 were both waiting in harbour for instructions at Truk, when an American B-24 Liberator spotted them and inflicted light damage on both. RO-44 returned to Kure Navy Yard for repairs. Lieutenant Commander Hashimoto was relieved of command, but in May he assumed command of I-58, patrolling the seas off Leyte.

On 30 July 1945, Lieutenant Commander Hashimoto was patrolling when he saw a US battleship with no escorts. At 0015hrs, I-58 released four torpedo salvoes in the direction of the battleship, the USS *Indianapolis*, which sank in twelve minutes. The commander of the *Indianapolis*, Captain William McVay (see below) was court-martialed for the loss of the ship, and Hashimoto was called to court as a prosecution witness. Hashimoto joined the campaign for the exoneration of McVay and wrote a letter to US Secretary of the Navy John Warner. Hashimoto spent the rest of his days as a Shinto priest, dying close to his birthplace in 2000.

EMPEROR HIROHITO OF JAPAN, 1901–1989

Hirohito was born in 1901, son of the Taisho Emperor, Yoshihito. That age of the Japanese empire was known as the 'Chrysanthemum Throne' and the young Hirohito was installed as Crown Prince in 1916. His father had been in poor health for many years and so those with military ambitions had a free hand to expand their territorial aims in the Emperor's name, especially in China.

Hirohito observed events, but was in no position to influence them, even as Crown Prince. That changed in 1926, with the death of his father and his assumption of the Crown in his own right. He took the name 'Showa' for his tenure of power and modelled his Imperial rule on that of his grandfather, Emperor Meiji, he who had defeated the last Samurai, Saigo Takamori, in 1876, making himself very popular. Hirohito admired his grandfather's achievements and his stand on the adoption of western dress was a key part of his style of rule. Western clothes were worn by his armed forces, politicians, civil servants and businessmen.

One of Hirohito's staunch supporters was General Hideki Tojo, who opposed a coup attempt on the Japanese Imperial Throne in February 1936 and was ultimately rewarded firstly with command of the Kwantung Army in China and later being made Vice-Minister of the Army in 1938, then appointment as Prime Minister in 1941. Tojo was a great advocate of expanding into China, and Hirohito supported this and Admiral Isoroku Yamamoto's attack on Pearl Harbor.

After the war, US strategy in the Pacific was to establish a strong peace. Hirohito remained as emperor, but with a freely elected government. Whilst blame for the Japanese atrocities during the war was shifted from Hirohito to his military-style government led by General Tojo, Hirohito had been a part of many cabinet meetings that had laid out the Japanese military strategy.

FLEET ADMIRAL ERNEST J. KING

Ernest J. King was born in Lorain, Ohio on 23 November 1878. Graduating from the Naval Academy at Annapolis in Maryland in 1901, he had already seen war service in the Spanish-American campaign aboard USS *San Francisco*. As a junior officer, he served on various small ships and as an instructor at the Naval Academy. He commanded the destroyer *Terry* (DD-25) and a torpedo flotilla, and from 1915–1918 he served on the staff of Admiral Henry Mayo. After another tour at the Naval Academy, Captain King went on to command a submarine flotilla and the New London, Connecticut submarine base.

In August 1928, after flight training and more sea service, King became Assistant Chief of the Bureau of Aeronautics. Thereafter he took command of Naval Air Station at Hampton Roads, Virginia, and in 1930 became captain of the large aircraft carrier USS *Lexington* (CV-2). Promoted to Rear Admiral in 1933, he was made Chief of the Bureau of Aeronautics. During the later 1930s he commanded

Admiral King was a naval aviator himself. As a Rear Admiral, he had just flown himself in a Curtiss Seagull to Richmond, Virginia.

the Battle Fleet's aircraft carriers and in early 1941, became commander of the Atlantic Patrol Force. His next appointment was to command the newly-recreated Atlantic Fleet, until Pearl Harbor was attacked by the Japanese.

Admiral King was transferred back to Washington DC as Commander in Chief, US Fleet in December 1941. He also became Chief of Naval Operations in March 1942, holding both positions throughout the remainder of the Second World War. As a member of the Joint Chiefs of Staff, he was instrumental in obtaining sufficient resources to begin and sustain offensive operations against Japan, despite a grand strategy of directing the bulk of America's sea power in the Atlantic and European theatres of operation.

King was promoted to the new rank of Fleet Admiral in December 1944. A year later, after victory was secured over Japan, he left his wartime offices, though remained in an advisory role. After several years of ill-health, Fleet Admiral King died on 25 June 1956.

GENERAL CURTIS E. LEMAY, USAF

Curtis Emerson LeMay came from a poor family; his father was an odd-job man who moved his family around the US as he looked for work. Young Curtis was born in Columbus, Ohio, and returned there to study in local high schools before finally securing a place in Ohio State University to study civil engineering. While at Ohio State, he joined the National Society of Pershing Rifles, which kindled an interest in the prospect of a military career.

In 1929, at the age of 23, LeMay gained a commission in the Army Air Corps Reserve and in the following January, transferred to the Regular Service. Becoming a pursuit pilot, he was stationed in Hawaii, where he was selected for training in aerial navigation and in August 1937, was flying as navigator in a Boeing B-17 in a navigational exercise and located his target, the battleship USS *Utah*. In 1938 he and his squadron of B-17s were tasked with finding the Italian liner *Rex* in the Atlantic, a distance of 610 miles from land.

When the US joined the Second World War, Major LeMay led the 305th Bombardment Group to England in October 1942. By September 1943, he was commanding the 4th Bombardment Wing, which became the 3rd Air Division. He personally led mass bombing raids, such as the 146 B-17s he took to Schweinfurt-Regensburg, going well beyond the range of escort fighters and taking his remaining 122 bombers on to North Africa.

Transferring to China in August 1944, Major-General LeMay commanded the XX Bomber Command, which was operating Boeing B-29s out of China, 'over the hump'. But then, in January 1945, General Carl Spaatz transferred LeMay to Guam, where he took command of the XXI Bomber Command, which was building up rapidly on Tinian Island. The precision bombing techniques employed in Europe were not working in the Pacific, partly because of unpredictable weather over Japan. LeMay developed night-time incendiary bombing and sent B-29s in at low level with considerable success.

Within LeMay's XXI Bomber Command was the 509th Composite Group, commanded by Lieutenant-Colonel Paul Tibbets. LeMay knew about the 509th

General Curtis E. LeMay as a four-star general and Chief of Staff of the USAF.

and Tibbets, but did not know exactly what the 509th's mission was until General Henry Arnold told him. From that point on, General LeMay gave Colonel Tibbets his wholehearted support and facilitated Tibbets' activities.

General LeMay became the youngest four-star general in the US Air Force at 44 years of age and gained great fame as the architect and creator of Strategic Air Command. He later became Chief of Staff of the US Air Force, from which post he retired in 1965. Another significant achievement in his career was that he remains the longest-serving four-star general in the US Armed Forces, with 21 years in rank. Amongst his many decorations are the Royal Air Force's Distinguished Flying Cross.

REAR ADMIRAL FRANCIS S. LOW, US NAVY

Rear Admiral Francis Stuart Low was born in Albany, New York in 1894. He graduated from the US Naval Academy at Annapolis in 1915. During the First World War, he served in submarines and later worked on submarine and torpedo research. In 1923 he joined the staff of Rear Admiral M.M. Murray, Commander Control Force and Submarine Division 13, from where, in 1926, he attended the Naval War College. From 1932 to 1935 he served on the staff of Submarine Squadron 5 and later assumed command of USS *Paul Jones*. He then became Commander of Submarine Division 13 in 1937.

Low was the man who was inspired by a visit to Norfolk Navy Yard in Virginia, when he saw Army bombers practicing attacks on the chalked outline of a carrier deck. From this he got the idea of a joint navy/army operation launching army bombers from a navy ship to strike at the heart of the Japanese Empire. He hurried back to Washington to sell the idea to Admiral King, the Commander-in-Chief of the US Fleet, and after consultation the Doolittle Raid was authorised.

Low later commanded the cruiser USS *Wichita* in Operation *Torch*, the Allied invasion of North Africa, and the Battle of Round Island in the Pacific. In early 1943 he was recalled to serve on Admiral King's staff in which position he was a key architect in the planning and implementation of Tenth Fleet. While Admiral King was the nominal commander of Tenth Fleet, the daily operations were in the hands of Rear Admiral Low, a command he held until January 1945. Again entering the Pacific war, he took command of Cruiser Division 16 during the Okinawa invasion and later that year became Commander of Destroyers, Pacific Fleet. In 1947 Rear Admiral Low was Commander of Services Pacific, and Deputy Chief of Naval Operations (Logistics) in 1950. In 1953 he became Commander of Western Sea Frontier.

GENERAL DOUGLAS MACARTHUR

General Douglas MacArthur was born in 1880 at Little Rock, Arkansas, the son of an Army officer who was to rise to become Lieutenant-General Arthur MacArthur Jr. Douglas entered the US Military Academy at West Point in 1898 and graduated in 1903 to become a second lieutenant in the US Corps of Engineers. His first tour of duty was in the Philippines as aide-de-camp to his father. He visited Japan during the Russo-Japanese War of 1905 and was then despatched to Washington DC as ADC to President Theodore Roosevelt.

When he left Washington in 1907, MacArthur worked on Corps of Engineers projects in Kansas, Milwaukee and Washington DC. He was assigned to the General Staff in 1913, where he remained until 1917, though he was detached to take part in the Vera Cruz Expedition of 1914. Here, he distinguished himself and was recommended for the Medal of Honor, though it was refused on that occasion on the basis that he was exceeding orders. He was promoted full colonel in 1917 and transferred from the Corps of Engineers to the infantry.

He went to Europe to take part in the fighting and was promoted to brigadier-general and ultimately commanded the 84th Infantry Brigade. MacArthur's courage was never in doubt; he was the second most decorated American officer of that war, receiving a Distinguished Service Medal, two Distinguished Service Crosses, seven Silver Stars and two Purple Hearts. His military policy was to lead from the front. He shunned protective clothing and hand guns, always carrying a riding crop. In one event, the Hundred Days Offensive, MacArthur asked why the America battalion involved had been almost wiped out and was told that the problem was a lack of artillery cover. The artillery officer chastised by General MacArthur was one Captain Harry S Truman, the man who would many years later relieve MacArthur of command for insubordination.

MacArthur's first post after the First World War was as Superintendent of West Point Military Academy, where he made major curriculum and disciplinary changes, adding politics and economics to the programme. He then moved to the Philippines for a tour, after which he returned to the US on his promotion to Major-General. He was a member of the court martial board that tried and convicted Brigadier-General Billy Mitchell, the man who advocated an independent US air force.

TOP SECRET

DECLASSIFIED
E.O. 11652 Sec. 3(E) and 5(D)
WHITE HOUSE PRESS RELEASE 4/10/51
By NLT/6C, NARS Date 3-7-75

PROPOSED ORDER TO GENERAL MacARTHUR TO BE SIGNED BY THE PRESIDENT

   I deeply regret that it becomes my duty as President and Commander in Chief of the United States military forces to replace you as Supreme Commander, Allied Powers; Commander in Chief, United Nations Command; Commander in Chief, Far East; and Commanding General, U. S. Army, Far East.

   You will turn over your commands, effective at once, to Lt. Gen. Matthew B. Ridgway. You are authorized to have issued such orders as are necessary to complete desired travel to such place as you select.

   My reasons for your replacement, ~~which~~ will be made public concurrently with the delivery to you of the foregoing order, ~~will be communicated to you by Secretary Pace.~~ and are contained in the next following message.

   Harry Truman

TOP SECRET

Douglas MacArthur retired as a Major-General in December 1937, but when the President of the Philippines asked him to form a Philippine Army, he opted to remain on the active list in order to be 'more effective'. His subordinates during his years in the Philippines included Lieutenant-Colonel Dwight D. Eisenhower, whom he described as 'the best clerk I ever had'. In July 1941, MacArthur became a lieutenant-general and was given command of the US Armed Forces in the Far East, based in Manila. With the Japanese invasion of the Philippines he was driven out, but made his most famous quotation 'I shall return'. Three years later, he did and for his courage he was awarded the Medal of Honor by President Roosevelt.

After the Battle of Leyte Gulf MacArthur set up his headquarters in Manila, from where he planned the invasion of Japan. This never came, but he did have the privilege of receiving the Japanese formal surrender on 15 September 1945. After the end of the war, General MacArthur supervised the reconstruction of Japan, the war crimes trials and ultimately the US entry into the Korean War.

In September 1950, MacArthur orchestrated an amphibious landing, with close air support and naval gunpower, at Inchon, far north of the 38th Parallel. The UN Forces outflanked the North Koreans and drove them further north in chaos. As they approached the Yalu River, bordering China, MacArthur proclaimed that the war was over and that the Chinese were not coming. Mao Tse Tung was furious and so, as his foreign minister, Zhou En Lai issued warnings to the UN via India. Chinese troops had already crossed the river in large numbers and struck out at the UN force, taking it by surprise and driving it south almost to the tip of the Korean Peninsula. This was when MacArthur asked permission to strike at Chinese bases in Manchuria. When refused, he wrote several letters to politicians seeking support for his views and incurred the wrath of President Truman, who relieved him of command and recalled him to the US.

REAR ADMIRAL CHARLES BUTLER MCVAY III USN

Charles McVay III was born in Ephrata, Pennsylvania on 30 July 1898. His father, Charles Butler McVay Jr, was a naval officer and had commanded the tender, USS *Yankton* during what was known as the cruise of the Great White Fleet. He was promoted to admiral in the First World War and in the earlier 1930s he served as Commander-in-Chief of the US Navy's Asiatic Fleet.

Charles III was a 1920 graduate of the US Naval Academy at Annapolis. Before taking command of the USS *Indianapolis* in November 1944, Captain McVay was chairman of the Joint Intelligence Committee of the combined chiefs of staff in Washington DC, the Allies' highest intelligence unit. Earlier in the Second World War, he had been awarded the Silver Star for displaying courage under fire.

After undergoing a major overhaul, the *Indianapolis*, under the command of Captain McVay, joined Vice-Admiral Marc Mitscher's Fast Carrier Task Force – the 5th Fleet's Task Force 58 – in readiness for the attack on Iwo Jima in February 1945, in which the *Indianapolis* played the vital role of support ship to Mitscher's carriers, blasting shore installations while the carrier fleet downed 499 Japanese aircraft for only 49 losses.

The next task for Captain McVay and his ship was the invasion of Okinawa in March. *Indianapolis* had rejoined Mitscher's Task Force to take part in that fierce battle, and after successful attacks the anti-aircraft guns of *Indianapolis* brought down seven Japanese aircraft on the morning of 31 March. However, on the same day a kamikaze aircraft struck the ship, killing thirteen men, wounding many others in the process and penetrating the hull. Damaged and without fresh water, the *Indianapolis* limped home to Mare Island in California for repairs.

After repairs had been made Captain McVay took his ship to the San Francisco Naval Shipyard at Hunter's Point to transport the components of the atom bomb 'Little Boy' to Tinian. After making its delivery the *Indianapolis* sailed to Guam, where she was put under orders to sail to Leyte in the Philippines, to take part in the liberation of the country. Captain McVay received an assessment of the trip which would normally have called for an escort, because Japanese submarines were likely to be in the area, so he asked for one and was refused.

There was no requirement for the *Indianapolis* to follow the traditional zig-zag pattern (a technique used to avoid torpedoes), so in order to conserve fuel, it did not. The determined sailing speed was given to Captain McVay as 15.7 knots to allow his arrival at Leyte on Tuesday 31 July at 1100hrs. He never kept that rendezvous, because the Japanese submarine I-58 sank the ship with four well-aimed torpedoes. Captain McVay was court-martialled for losing his ship by negligence.

Contrary to the court-martial's findings, three SOS signals were sent out from the *Indianapolis* as it was going down and it is known that they were received at three different shore stations. At one location, the officer of the watch was drunk. At a second, the officer of the watch didn't believe the signal and chose to ignore it, while the third simply thought it was a hoax call from the Japanese. Some 800 men were left floating on debris in the sea for 110 hours, and when they were finally spotted it was only by coincidence; a radio man in a Catalina flying boat patrolling overhead had repaired an antenna on his aircraft and while in the rear of the aircraft, happened to look down from one of the Catalina's fuselage 'blisters' and spotted a huge oil slick with men floating in it. The Catalina circled and Lieutenant Adrian Marks, the pilot, made an open-sea landing, an action which contravened regulations, but at least it drove off sharks and allowed him to pick up some survivors. The Catalina sent a signal to Guam and the USS *Cecil J. Doyle* was sent to the rescue. There were only 316 survivors.

Upon his retirement in 1949, McVay received a 'tombstone promotion' to rear admiral, so as to re-establish his standing and increase his pension. However, he lived with the awful consequences of the loss of his ship and the serious injustice of his court-martial until 1968, when he shot himself with his US Navy revolver. As history now tells us, it was the endeavours of a 12-year-old schoolboy named Hunter Scott from Pensacola, Florida, working diligently on a school history project over 50 years later that brought the injustice to light. After the boy gave evidence to Congress and submitted over 800 documents for review, President Clinton signed the document that exonerated Captain McVay in October 2000. However, the record of that court-martial remains on his file.

ADMIRAL MARC MITSCHER, US NAVY

Marc Andrew 'Pete' Mitscher was born in Hillsboro, Wisconsin in 1887. When he was two years old, his family moved to Oklahoma City, where his father became an Indian Agent and later the second mayor of that city. Marc was educated in Washington DC and then moved on to the US Naval Academy, from where he graduated in 1910. He served aboard the USS *California* during the Mexican Campaign in 1913, then took up aviation training at the Naval Aeronautical Station Pensacola, in Florida, in 1915. He graduated as Naval Aviator Number 33.

Promoted to lieutenant commander in 1918, he commanded the second largest seaplane training station in the US, NAS Dinner Point at Coconut Grove, Florida. In 1919, Mitscher took off from Newfoundland in a Curtiss NC flying boat to take part in a naval trans-Atlantic flight expedition. Landing in the Azores in heavy fog, he was unable to take off again to complete the flight, but was awarded the Navy Cross for his part in the historic event.

Between the wars, Mitscher had shore commands and served aboard the carriers *Langley* and *Saratoga*. In 1941 he was transferred from the post of Assistant Chief Bureau of Aeronautics, to fit out and assume command of the US Navy's newest carrier, USS *Hornet* (CV-8). The *Hornet* was ordered to complete sea trials and then go to San Francisco, where Mitscher would meet the Doolittle Raiders.

After the Doolittle Raid, the *Hornet* was assigned to the task force that fought the Battle of Midway. Among *Hornet's* aircraft complement was VT-8, Torpedo Squadron 8, flying obsolescent Douglas Devastators. In one attack on Japanese carriers, Lieutenant Commander John C. Waldron, commander of TB-8, led his aircraft without fighter escort (it had been held off to cover dive bombers to be used later in the attack). The result was that all of TB-8, except for one man, Ensign George Gay, was lost, shot down by Japanese fighters. But the actions of TB-8 did enable dive bombers from the *Enterprise* and *Yorktown* to sink the Japanese carriers *Hiryu*, *Soryu* and *Akagi*.

Mitscher handed over command of the *Hornet* to Captain Charles P. Mason in June 1942. He was transferred to shore commands until March 1944, when he was promoted to Vice-Admiral and given command of the Fifth Fleet's Task Force 58. This Task Force also doubled as the Third

Fleet's Task Force 38, and was also known as the Fast Carrier Task Force. Mitscher inflicted severe damage on Japanese installations and his aircrews destroyed most of the Japanese defending aircraft. In the Battle of the Philippine Sea in June 1944, he ordered his ships to turn on deck landing lights to allow pilots to find their way back on to decks. This defied US Navy procedure, but brought home many pilots who would otherwise have been lost.

After the war, Mitscher returned to the US and ultimately was appointed Admiral, Commander in Chief of the Atlantic Fleet. He died at Norfolk, Virginia, in 1947 while holding that post. It is interesting now to read Admiral Arleigh Burke's tribute to Mitscher after his death:

> He spoke in a low voice and used few words. Yet, so great was his concern for his people – for their training and welfare in peacetime and their rescue in combat – that he was able to obtain their final ounce of effort and loyalty, without which he could not have become the pre-eminent carrier force commander in the world. A bulldog of a fighter, a strategist blessed with an uncanny ability to foresee his enemy's next move, and a lifelong searcher after truth and trout streams, he was above all else – perhaps above all other – a Naval Aviator.

FLEET ADMIRAL CHESTER W. NIMITZ

Chester William Nimitz was born in Fredericksburg, Texas, in 1885. Spending a significant part of his youth with his grandfather, who ran an unusual hotel shaped like a ship, at first he wanted to join the US Army, even though his grandfather had taught him a great deal about seamanship. When he was given the opportunity to take the entrance examination for Annapolis, the US Naval Academy, he took his grandfather's advice and went for it.

Graduating from Annapolis in 1905, coming seventh in a class of 114, he was assigned to his first command. His ship was the USS *Decatur*, an old destroyer somewhat past its best and out of commission when he took it over. He assembled crew and armament in two days and set sail for the Philippines, where had been despatched because of a war scare with Japan. With little knowledge of the local waters and only very sketchy charts, the inexperienced Ensign ran his ship aground and found himself facing a court-martial. It took him some time to live that down, but his case was helped by being awarded the Silver Life Saving Medal for saving a seaman whilst aboard the USS *Skipjack*.

By 1910, all had been forgiven, for he was promoted full lieutenant and in 1916 was promoted again to lieutenant commander. He spent the First World War on the staff of the Commander of Submarines and in 1918, rose to the rank of commander. Between the wars, he commanded the battleship USS *South Carolina* and the cruisers USS *Augusta* and USS *Chicago*, before transferring to the submarine base at Pearl Harbor. He was by this time a rear admiral. In 1939 he was appointed Chief of the Bureau of Navigation, and was serving in that post when Pearl Harbor was attacked. President Roosevelt picked Nimitz from 28 flag officers senior to him to relieve Admiral Kimmel at Pearl Harbor, making him an admiral at the same time.

Admiral Nimitz became Commander-in-Chief Pacific Fleet (CINCPAC) and effectively managed the naval battles of the Pacific, starting with the Battle of Midway, right through the Battle of Leyte Gulf, the largest naval battle in history. Nimitz was a man of great honour and commitment to his beloved Navy and would tolerate no abuse of the institution from any quarter.

One very significant action he took was the forgiving of Captain Charles McVay, commander of the USS *Indianapolis* who was the only US Navy officer to be court-martialled for the loss of his ship during the Second World War. Nimitz told McVay that

Admiral Chester W. Nimitz pins the Navy Cross to the chest of Mess Steward Dorie Miller for his action at Pearl Harbor.

he understood all too well his predicament, having experienced the problem himself many years earlier. Nonetheless, McVay was convicted, though Nimitz regarded it as unsound and had McVay's sentence remitted in 1946, then restored him to active duty.

REAR ADMIRAL WILLIAM PARSONS

William Parsons, known as 'Deak' to those who worked with him, entered the Naval Academy at Annapolis in 1918. He graduated in 1922 and first served aboard the USS *Idaho*, but when that cruise came to its end, he entered the Navy Postgraduate School in Washington to study ordnance. He then served a tour aboard the battleship *Texas*, before returning to Washington as Liaison Officer working between the Bureau of Ordnance and the Naval Research Laboratory. His next tour of duty was at the Navy Proving Grounds, where he took part in the creation of the radio proximity fuse for anti-aircraft shells fired from ships of the US Fleet.

In 1943, he was assigned to the Los Alamos Laboratory of the Manhattan Project as the Ordnance Division Director, also taking over Project Alberta. He was the military link between the Manhattan Project scientists and the operational development and workup of the 509th Composite Group, under the command of Colonel Paul Tibbets.

Parsons was a vital link between Los Alamos and the 509th, and as Tibbets flew almost weekly flights for liaison meetings with the scientists, it was Parsons who frequently smoothed out differences and ultimately inspired Tibbets' decision to move the 509th from Wendover to Tinian, thus bringing to an end the hesitations of the scientists who seemed constantly to want to implement 'just one more improvement'.

During the final stages of the work-up to the Hiroshima raid, Captain Parsons spent a great deal of time at Tinian, ensuring that the bomb fuse in 'Little Boy' was as it should be and when the aircraft took off, he it was who actually fitted the fuse as *Enola Gay* made its way to the target.

After the war, Parsons rose to commodore, then rear admiral, that rank being confirmed as permanent in July 1948. It was while he was serving as Assistant Chief of the Navy's Bureau of Ordnance, that he died from a heart attack, on 5 December 1953.

GENERAL GEORGE SMITH PATTON JR

George Patton was born in 1885 in San Gabriel, California. Strictly speaking, he was George S. Patton III, because his father was Jr, but he assumed the 'Junior' appendage out of respect for his grandfather, who was a colonel in the Confederate Army and died in battle at Opequon Creek in Virginia in 1864, the most important of the battles of the Shenandoah Valley. Colonel Patton's promotion to brigadier-general had been approved the day after his death, so it never took effect.

Patton's father was not a military man; he was a politician, a Democrat and one of Woodrow Wilson's protégés. He did graduate from the Virginia Military Institute in 1877, but went on to serve as Los Angeles County District Attorney and the first City Attorney for the city of Pasadena, California, afterwards becoming the first mayor of San Marino, California. The family was wealthy and young George was sent to the Virginia Military Institute, which he attended for one year, rushing through VMI's chapter of the Kappa Alpha Order, then transferring to the United States Military Academy at West Point.

The Academy instructed him to repeat his first, 'plebe', year because of his poor performance in mathematics. Such was his motivation for military success that he repeated that year with honours and was appointed Cadet Adjutant (the second highest position for a cadet). Instead of graduating in 1908, his due year, he was commissioned as a cavalry officer in the rank of second lieutenant in 1909.

The Fifth Modern Olympiad took place in 1912 and Second Lieutenant Patton was selected to represent the US in the pentathlon, which then was open to military entrants only. He finished fifth and won accolades from his superiors and the public. He was then appointed the US Army's youngest-ever 'Master of the Sword' and was based at the Mounted Service School at Fort Riley in Kansas. Whilst there, he improved and modernised the Army's cavalry sabre fencing techniques and designed a new sabre which became generally known as the 'Patton Sabre'.

Patton's first 'blooding' in battle was under the command of Brigadier-General John J Pershing in the Mexican Expedition, otherwise known as the Mexican Revolution. Patton launched the first-ever armoured vehicle attack, using three armoured cars in a raid on General Julio Cardenas's headquarters, killing two senior Mexican commanders. They brought their bodies back strapped to the fronts of their vehicles in the manner used by deer hunters.

When the US entered the First World War, Major-General Pershing took Patton with him and promoted him to captain, placing him in charge of the Tank School and Centre at Langres, then later he was given a battle command to lead the 1st Provisional Tank Brigade. In September 1918 he was wounded in the left leg whilst leading six men in an attack on a German gun position in the Battle of Saint Mihiel. He and his orderly, PFC Joseph Angelo, were the only two survivors and both received the Distinguished Service Cross. Patton was also awarded the Distinguished Service Medal and the Purple Heart.

Reverting to the rank of captain after the war, Patton was transferred to Washington DC where he befriended Captain Dwight D. Eisenhower. Together, they were the architects of the tank warfare strategy used in the Second World War. Patton was now a tank professional and probably one of the best authorities on tank warfare, acknowledged even by his former commander General John J. Pershing. It was in the 1930s, while at Fort Benning, in Georgia, that the then Colonel Patton met and took a liking to a young Army Air Corps Lieutenant named Paul W. Tibbets, who flew him in his air observations of simulated tank battles.

When the Second World War began, Major-General Patton was commanding the 2nd Armored Brigade of the US Second Armored Division. Eisenhower requested an appointment to serve under him, but General Marshall refused. In 1942 Patton was instructed to take and secure Casablanca from the Vichy French at the beginning of Operation *Torch*. He achieved that objective with minimal gunfire and losses, though his tactics were criticised by some of his peers and commanders. When General Lloyd Fredendall was relieved of command after the disastrous Battle of Kasserine, Patton was given II Corps and began his rampage across North Africa, to meet up with British General Bernard Montgomery and join the assault on Sicily and Italy.

After the unfortunate incident involving a soldier with battle fatigue, who Patton slapped before ordering him back into the front, Patton was relieved of command for almost a year. He was then appointed by his old subordinate General Omar Bradley to take part in the Battle of the Bulge. It was to be his finest hour.

Despite Patton pleading for a field command in the Pacific after the end of the war in Europe, he was promoted to four-star general and appointed Military Governor of Bavaria and, notoriously, retained all the former Nazi officials in administrative office on the basis that 'These men know how to run civic services in Germany efficiently and besides that, I know where they all are!' Patton anticipated the massive growth in military presence and strength in Germany of the Russians and held the firm view that the German Army should be retained and reinforced against the risk of a conflict with a far worse adversary. Eisenhower was furious and relieved Patton of all command. As a result Patton openly accused Eisenhower of caring more about his political future than his duties as a commanding general. Their friendship effectively came to an end.

Patton died as the result of a car accident in December 1945, just over a month after his sixtieth birthday. Characteristically, he was buried in the Luxembourg American Cemetery and Memorial in Hamm, along with many of his men from the Third Army, in preference to the traditional Arlington National Cemetery. However, on 19 March 1947, his body was moved to its current prominent location at the head of his former troops.

FRANKLIN DELANO ROOSEVELT

Franklin Roosevelt was born in 1882 in Hyde Park, New York to a wealthy family. He was first elected to the New York Senate in 1911 and served there until 1913, when he became involved in national politics. He had been nominated as Presidential Candidate for the Democrat Party as early as 1920, but it was 1932 before he finally secured office to succeed Herbert Hoover. He made his mark during the Great Depression, creating the New Deal to provide relief for the unemployed, reforming the economic and banking systems in the US. It was he who instigated the National Recovery Administration, the Agricultural Adjustment Administration, the Federal Deposit Insurance Corporation and the Social Security System.

Whilst the US was taking an isolationist stance over developing events in Europe, 'FDR' had strong views about the necessity for allies to pull together and support each other in times of hardship. He saw the threat of Hitler's Germany and wanted to do more for Britain than Congress would allow, so he found ways of providing aid, including ultimately the 'Lend-Lease' programme.

President Roosevelt authorised nuclear research – the splitting of the atom – for military use in December 1941, with the formation and first meeting of the Office of Scientific Research and Development; the Manhattan Project had begun. Thus the atomic bomb was in its infancy even as the Doolittle Raid was being planned. After the raid Roosevelt awarded Doolittle the Medal of

Honor, and had him promoted to brigadier-general, surprising Doolittle who had thought to be court-martialed for losing his aircraft.

Roosevelt considered victory over Japan to be the absolute goal, but he did not live to see it. He died on 12 April 1945; the final victory came under his successor, Harry S Truman.

GENERAL HOLLAND M. SMITH

Holland McTyeire Smith was born in 1882 to John Wesley and Caroline Smith in Seale, Alabama. As a child, he set his sights on a military career and enlisted in the Alabama National Guard as he was working towards his Bachelor of Science degree from Auburn University. He followed this up with further studies to achieve a Bachelor of Laws from Alabama University and practised law until 1905, at which point he sought a commission in the Army. In the event he was actually commissioned as a second lieutenant in the Marine Corps. He sailed for the Philippines in 1906 and joined the 1st Marine Brigade. It was in this period of his service that he acquired the nickname 'Howlin' Mad'. He returned to the US in 1908 and was assigned to the Marine Barracks at Annapolis, Maryland, the home of the Naval Academy. In April 1914 he left the 1st Brigade to take command of the Marine detachment aboard USS *Galveston* until July 1915.

After a period of service at the US Navy Yard in New Orleans, then a year in Dominica with the 4th Marine Regiment, the First World War loomed large and after sailing to France at the beginning of June 1917, Captain Smith was appointed commander of the 8th Machine Gun Company of the 5th Marines. Next came a transfer to the US Army General Staff College at Langres in France, from where he graduated in February 1918. He transferred to the 4th Marine Brigade as adjutant, followed by a place on the Staff of I Corps.

He returned to the US to do another training programme at the Naval War College, followed by a tour in Washington DC at the War Plans Section of the Office of Naval Operations, where he was the first Marine officer to serve on the Joint Army-Navy Planning Committee. Up to April 1931, Lieutenant-Colonel Smith had several shore station duties before returning to sea aboard the USS *California* as Force Marine Officer and Aide to the Commander of the Battle Force US Fleet. After roles as Commandant of the Marine Barracks in Washington, then Chief of Staff of the Department of the Pacific, he was promoted to colonel and assigned as Director of Operations and Training, Marine Corps.

The Second World War brought further promotion and senior command, from Commander 1st Marine Brigade to Commander 1st Marine Division in the rank of major-general. After a stint as Commander Amphibious Force, Atlantic Fleet., where he proved his mastery of amphibious warfare, he transferred to the Pacific Fleet, where he oversaw the amphibious training of the 2nd and 3rd Marine Divisions, as well as the 7th Army Division. Promoted to lieutenant-general in March 1944, his command of V Amphibious Corps proved hugely successful.

Under Holland M. Smith's overall command, the islands of Tarawa, Kwajalein, Saipan and Tinian were taken from the Japanese and he led the fiercest battle of the Pacific campaign, Iwo Jima, a battle he always thought need not have been fought. Smith's final assignment was as Commandant, Marine Training and Replacement Command, based at Camp Pendleton in California. He was promoted four-star general in May 1946, then retired after 41 years as a Marine.

GENERAL CARL A. SPAATZ USAF

General Carl Andrew ('Tooey') Spaatz picked up his nickname because of a physical resemblance to another West Point cadet whose name was Toohey. Graduating from West Point in 1914, he transferred to the Aviation Section of the US Army Signal Corps in late 1915. Serving under General John J. Pershing in the 1916 Mexican Expedition, he joined the 1st Aero Squadron and was promoted to first lieutenant in 1916, then a year later to captain.

When the US joined the fighting in Europe, Captain Spaatz was given command of the 31st Pursuit Squadron in the American Expeditionary Force. Within a few months he was serving with the 13th Aero Squadron and had shot down three German aircraft. In 1918, he was promoted to temporary major, but after the war reverted to his permanent rank of captain when he became Assistant Air Officer for the Western Department of the Air Service. In July 1920, he was promoted major again.

After leaving the Office of the Chief of the Air Corps in 1929, he was appointed commander of the 7th Bombardment Group. This was just after he and two other Army aviators – Captain Ira C. Eaker and Captain Elwood Quesada (both later Army Air Force Generals) – flew a Fokker Tri-Motor named *Question Mark* over the Los Angeles city district for 150 hours, proving the value of in-flight refuelling. Returning to Washington after a spell with the Second Air Wing, Colonel Spaatz returned to the staff of the Chief of the Air Corps, from where he was sent to London as an observer in 1940, then returned to promotion to brigadier-general and command of the Materiel Division of the Air Corps.

When the US entered the war in 1942, Major-General Spaatz was appointed to establish and command the Eighth Air Force. He also commanded the Twelfth Air Force and then the 15th Air Force, both of which had been established by Lieutenant-General Jimmy Doolittle. By the time Doolittle took command of the Eighth Air Force, Carl Spaatz was overall Commander of the Strategic Air Forces in Europe. In March 1945, General Spaatz was promoted to temporary general and in July that year, after the war in Europe had ended, he took command of the Strategic Air Force in the Pacific, which included the Twentieth Air Force. The atomic bombing of Hiroshima and Nagasaki took place under his command and he personally pinned the Distinguished Service Cross on the flying coveralls of Colonel Paul Tibbets.

After the end of the Second World War, General Spaatz was appointed Commander-in-Chief of the US Army Air Force and in 1947, on the formation of the US Air Force as an independent service, he became its first Chief of Staff, thus becoming the first four-star general to be chief of two independent arms of the US Armed Forces. He retired in 1948 and died in 1974, aged 83.

GENERAL HIDEKI TOJO

Hideki Tojo was born into a family of influence in 1884. His father was Lieutenant-General Tojo in the Imperial Japanese Army and was born in Iwate, a son of the Nanbu Clan Samurai, Hidetoshi Tojo. He served under the Meiji Dynasty at the time of the battle of the last of Samurai in 1876, but there is no record of him having been involved in that battle – perhaps not surprisingly, being the son of a samurai himself.

Young Hideki graduated from the Imperial Japanese Army Academy in 1905 and went on to the Imperial Staff College in 1915. After the First World War, he was sent to Germany as a military attaché. A brief period at home brought him promotion to major and then a return to Germany for another year.

By 1929, Tojo was a lieutenant-colonel and was becoming involved in army politics, serving in a conservative moderate group, which enhanced his military career and his political ambitions. Promoted to major-general in 1933, he served as Chief of Personnel in the Army Ministry, which took him to China as commander of an infantry brigade. September 1935 brought further progress, to commander of the Kempeitai in the Kwantung Army, then he became Chief of Staff of that army.

Tojo was recalled to Tokyo in 1938 and appointed Vice-Minister of the Army; at the end of the year he became Inspector-General of Army Aviation, followed

One of the most important members of the Nanbu Clan was Nanbu Nobonao, the family head in the Azuchi-Momoyama era during the sixteenth century.

by the appointment to Army Minister. On 18 October 1941 he became Prime Minister, and was soon planning the attack on Pearl Harbor. On 1 December, Emperor Hirohito approved the decision to go to war with the US, Great Britain and Holland.

Being the grandson of a samurai, Tojo understood well the traditional principles of the Bushido Code, but corrupted them to suit his own ends, by giving his army and the people of Japan the impression that it was a Bushido principle to kill your enemy, regardless of his ability to defend himself, and that it was a duty to die for one's country. This was translated into the notion that to become a prisoner of war was to bring shame on one's family and so prisoners of war were treated abominably as a matter of official policy. For this, and General Tojo's condoning of affairs in China, he was ultimately tried for war crimes and executed in 1948.

HARRY S. TRUMAN

Truman was born in 1884 and grew up a farm boy in Missouri, moving from Lamar to Harrisonville to Belton, to Grandview and finally to Independence. Harry S. Truman (the 'S' was just an initial) was the only President of the US to serve his country in combat in the First World War; he was a captain, in command of Battery D, 129th Field Artillery, 60th Brigade of the 35th Infantry Division. The men of his battery had a poor record of discipline and at one time were ready to abandon an action when Truman gave them the dressing-down of their lives and terrified them back into action.

Harry S. Truman, who became President after the sudden death of Roosevelt.

A Colonel Douglas MacArthur confronted Truman in one action, the Hundred Days Offensive, and reprimanded him for failing to provide artillery support.

Politics came into Harry Truman's life during the Great Depression and he entered the US Senate in 1935, representing the State of Missouri. He was then selected to be President Roosevelt's running mate in 1944 to take office in January 1945. Becoming the 33rd President by inheritance in April 1945, he stood in his own right for election in 1948 and won, holding office until January 1953, when he handed over the power of the Presidency to Republican Dwight D. Eisenhower, the former Supreme Allied Commander in Europe.

The heaviest burden of decision in his Presidency was his approval for the dropping of the atom bombs on Hiroshima and Nagasaki and before making that decision, he sought the counsel of the four most trusted senior officers in his Pacific Command: Admirals Nimitz and Halsey and Generals MacArthur and Smith. Their combined forecast of four more years of battle and at least four million dead, convinced President Truman that using the atom bomb was the right decision.

ADMIRAL ISOROKU YAMAMOTO

Isoroku Tanako was born in 1884 in a small village on Hokkaido, the son of an intermediate samurai of the Nagoaka Domain. In 1896 he enrolled in the Naval Academy at Hiroshima. After graduation, he served in the Russo-Japanese War and later on board several Imperial Navy ships until he entered the Naval Staff College in 1913, from where he graduated in 1916. It was at this time that he took the name 'Yamamoto', having been adopted, in Japanese custom, into the Yamamoto family – another Nagoaka samurai family.

Between 1919 and 1921, Yamamoto studied at Harvard University, and learnt a great deal about American culture and attitudes to war. After graduating he returned to Japan, then came back to the US as naval attaché in Washington DC. He served two terms and in 1924, transferred from the Gunnery Division of the Imperial Navy to the Aviation Division. His first ship's command was the *Isuzu* in 1928, followed by the aircraft carrier *Akagi*. On his return to Tokyo, he was promoted to naval major-general (rear-admiral) and was vocal in his opposition to General Tojo's annexation of Manchuria. He was a political 'dove' and was also opposed to going to war with the US.

By 1941, General Tojo was Prime Minister of Japan and many thought that Yamamoto's influence would wane. However, his adoptive family was well connected with the Emperor and Hirohito knew and liked Yamamoto, so he remained in the 'inner circle' and was promoted to naval general (admiral) in November 1940. When the decision was made to attack Pearl Harbor, Yamamoto, as Commander-in-Chief of the Combined Fleet, was given the task of commanding the attack. Strategically and tactically it demonstrated his remarkable skills, for the attack was a master stroke. He was later reported to have said 'I fear we have awoken a sleeping giant'; in fact he wrote, in a letter from 1942, 'A military man can scarcely pride himself on having smitten a sleeping enemy – it is more a matter of shame, simply, for the one smitten. I would rather you made your appraisal after seeing what the enemy does, since it is certain that, angered and outraged, he will soon launch a determined counterattack'. The US was indeed angered and outraged.

Yamamoto was travelling across the Pacific on a morale-boosting tour after the collapse of Guadalcanal, when the Mitsubishi G4M aircraft in which he was flying out of Rabaul was intercepted and shot down by a US squadron of P-38 Lightnings, after Japanese codes had been broken and the Americans discovered where he was. He died on 18 April 1943, exactly a year after the Doolittle Raid.

Appendix 2

Ships

USS *HORNET* (CV-8)

The USS *Hornet* was a Yorktown Class aircraft carrier, the seventh ship of the US Navy to carry that name and the first aircraft carrier named *Hornet*. She was 824 feet 9 inches long and 114 feet wide. Fully laden, she weighed in at 29,581 tons and was capable of 33.8 knots during sea trials off the Virginia coast. Ordered to be built at the Newport News Shipping Company at Norfolk, Virginia, the ship was sponsored by Mrs Frank Knox, wife of President Roosevelt's Secretary of the Navy (and an avid supporter of assistance to Great Britain in the Second World War). Laid down in September 1939, the *Hornet* was commissioned in December 1941 and began sea trials before Christmas.

The USS *Hornet* undergoing sea trials in December 1941. She carried the Doolittle Raiders towards their destination in April 1942.

After Captain Francis Low's suggested trial of twin-engined bombers taking off from the deck of a carrier, Jimmy Doolittle's selected aircraft, the B-25 was test flown from the *Hornet* successfully in February 1942. The *Hornet* was then ordered to sail for Alameda Navy Yard in San Francisco Bay, to rendezvous with Jimmy Doolittle's sixteen specially prepared B-25 bombers.

Hornet, commanded by Captain Marc Mitscher, formed part of Task Force 16, which sailed towards Japan in April 1942. She was accompanied by USS *Enterprise*, another carrier, which provided air cover and advance reconnaissance for the Task Force as it approached Japanese waters.

After the Doolittle Raid launch, *Hornet* took part in the Battle of Midway and then the Solomons campaign, where the US carrier fleet was reduced to one, the *Hornet*. The Battle of the Santa Cruz Islands ended her career when three bombs truck her deck and a Japanese aircraft was flown directly into the deck, before two torpedo hits put her out of action. The USS *Northampton* was ordered to tow *Hornet* to safety, but two more Japanese hits caused the stricken carrier to be scuttled.

USS *INDIANAPOLIS* (CA-35)

The *Indianapolis* was a Portland Class cruiser, built by New York Shipbuilding in Camden, New Jersey. Launched on 7 November 1931, the ship was sponsored by Miss Lucy Taggart, the daughter of a former mayor of Indianapolis and US Senator, Thomas Taggart.

Commissioned at Philadelphia Navy Yard, the first captain was Captain John M. Smeallie. Sea trials and shakedown took place in the Atlantic and in Guantanamo Bay. After acceptance, the ship served in the Panama Canal Zone and in the Pacific off Chile.

On two occasions the *Indianapolis* hosted President Roosevelt on formal visits before the Second World War and then went into action in the South Pacific.

Action began south of Rabaul, New Britain in February 1942, when the task force of which the *Indianapolis* was a part came under attack from 18 Japanese bombers, 16 of which were shot down by a combination of anti-aircraft fire from the ships and aircraft taking off from the deck of the USS *Lexington*. March saw the task force in operation in New Guinea, then a brief respite for an overhaul and modifications at Mare Island Navy Yard. The Indianapolis went back into action for a convoy escort to Australia, followed by a confrontation with the Japanese in the Aleutian Islands. Action at Kiska Island, Adak Island and the Dutch harbor on Unalaska Island saw out 1942.

1943 saw the *Indianapolis* in action with Admiral Spruance's 5th Fleet, in Operation *Galvanic* at the Gilbert Islands and in the Battle of Makin, then Tarawa and the Marshall Islands. In 1944, Kwajalein followed, then the Western Carolines and the Palau Islands. The Battles of Saipan and Tinian, the Battle of the Philippine Sea, Guam and Pelelieu are in the *Indianapolis* battle honours.

In November 1944 Captain Charles McVay took command. He took the ship, after refit, into action at Iwo Jima, where the *Indianapolis* gave massive support to the carrier force. Okinawa followed and then *Indianapolis* returned to the US for overhaul. Back to sea from San Francisco, the *Indianapolis* made that momentous journey to Tinian Island to deliver components of the 'Little Boy' atomic bomb. Leaving San Francisco on 16 July 1945, the delivery was made at Tinian ten days later. After a minor crew change at Guam, the *Indianapolis* left on 28 July for Leyte, in the Philippines. She never reached Leyte, being sunk by the Japanese submarine I-58 fourteen minutes after midnight on 30 July.

IJN SUBMARINE I-58

Submarine I-58 was completed at Kure in September 1944 and commissioned in December of that year. It was built as a dual purpose vessel with a capacity to carry up to six 'Kaiten' miniature manned torpedo/submarines, as well as torpedoes. Its commander was Lieutenant Commander Mochitsura Hashimoto and it was initially assigned to patrols around Okinawa.

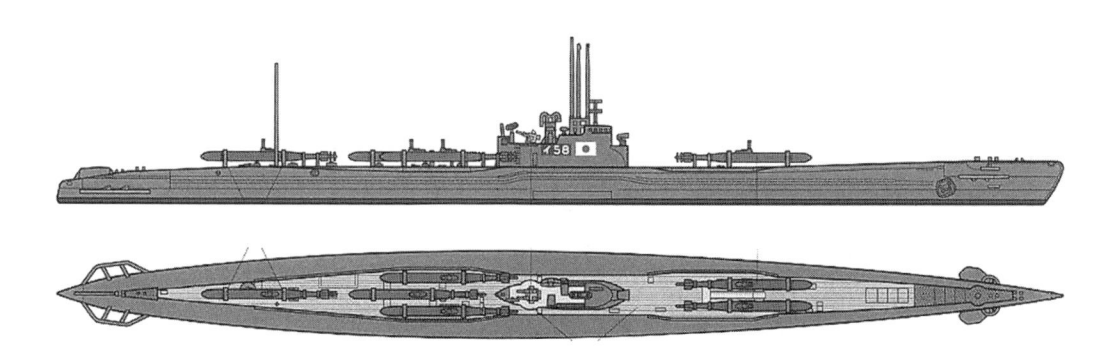

After the American victory at Okinawa, I-58 returned to Kure in April 1945 and then transferred to the patrol group around the Philippine Islands, commencing patrols on 15 July. During this duty, the commander spotted a large US battlecruiser, unescorted. It was the USS *Indianapolis*. Surprised that it had no escort, and making sure that no other ship was in sight before closing in on his quarry, Commander Hashimoto set the *Indianapolis* up in his sights and fired six torpedoes into its hull, sinking the vessel in twelve minutes.

When Japan surrendered on 2 September 1945, I-58 was back in Kure. She was scuttled near the Goto islands on 1 April 1946 as part of Operation *Road's End*, after being stripped of all usable materials and equipment.

IJN BATTLESHIP *HARUNA*

During the Second World War the battleship *Haruna* was the Japanese Navy's premier battleship. It had a displacement of 37,200 tons and was designed by the British naval architect/engineer George Thurston. It was built as a battle cruiser in Kobe Naval Dockyard between 1912 and 1915, the fourth and last of the Kongo Class, in which role it served between 1915 and 1926. Laid down in 1912 and launched at the end of 1913, the *Haruna* was commissioned into the Imperial Japanese Navy in April 1915 and her first captain was Captain Kajishiro Funakoshi.

Re-fitted in 1926, the *Haruna* was re-launched as a battleship and served in that role until 1933, when it was re-designated a fast battleship. During the Sino-Japanese War, the *Haruna* transported Japanese Army troops to mainland China, before being redeployed to the Third Battleship Division in 1941. On the eve of the Second World War, the *Haruna* sailed as part of the Southern Force, in preparation for the Japanese invasion of Singapore.

As part of the Third Battleship Division, the *Haruna* fought in almost every major naval action of the Pacific War, covering landings in Malaya and the Dutch East

The *Haruna* under attack on 28 July 1945.

The Japanese battleship *Haruna*.

Indies in 1942, before engaging the US Navy at the Battle of Midway and during the Guadalcanal Campaign. Throughout 1943, the *Haruna* primarily remained at the harbours of Truk Lagoon, Kure Naval Base, Sasebo Naval Base, and Lingga, deploying on several occasions in response to American air strikes on Japanese island bases. *Haruna* also took part in the Battle of the Philippine Sea and the Battle of Leyte Gulf in 1944, the greatest naval battle in history, against the Allied fleets. In 1945 she was transferred to Kure Naval Base, before being sunk by aircraft of Task Force 38 on 24 July 1945, after an abortive attempt by aircraft of the 494th Bombardment Group earlier in the same day.

Appendix 3

Aircraft

AIRCO DH-4

The DH-4 was designed by Geoffrey de Havilland, who was commissioned to produce a two-seat light bomber. Being designed in Great Britain, de Havilland clearly thought of a British engine first and so the aircraft was powered by a Rolls-Royce Eagle engine, which delivered 250 horsepower, a very powerful engine for its time. The result was that the DH-4 could carry its own weight as a load, which typically would have included the pilot, the gunner/bomb aimer and a significant payload of bombs. Versions of the DH-4 were built in Britain and America, with just under 1500 being built in Britain and almost 5000 in the US. The American version was fitted with the 400hp Liberty engine and remained in service with the Air Service and the Army Air Corps.

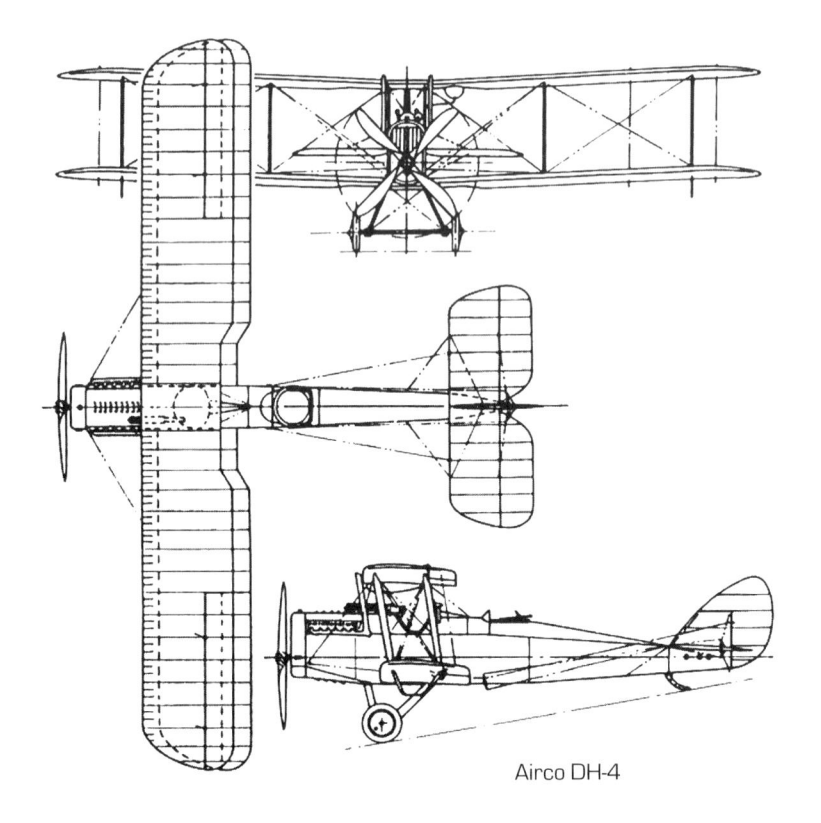

Airco DH-4

Flying up until the 1930s, the DH-4 was to the US what the Bristol F-2B was to Britain. It served America well on border patrols and later as a civilian mail carrier. Famously Lieutenant Jimmy Doolittle flew a DH-4 on the first-ever trans-America overland flight in 1922 and operationally until 1925.

BOEING B-17 FLYING FORTRESS

The Boeing B-17 Flying Fortress was a four-engine heavy bomber aircraft developed in the 1930s for the then-United States Army Air Corps (USAAC). The prototype, Model 299, first flew on 28 July 1935, during which a journalist coined the name 'Flying Fortress'. It could carry 4800lbs of bombs, had five machine guns (one of which was installed in the nose), and was powered by Pratt and Whitney R-1690 Hornet radial engines producing 750hp each. The B-17 went through several variants during the late 1930s and early 1940s.

During the Second World War the B-17 was flown by the RAF in 1941, and later the US Eighth and Fifteenth Air Forces. It was used primarily in the strategic bombing campaign against German military and industrial targets, and later in the Pacific against Japanese airfields and shipping. In all 32 US combat groups were equipped with the B-17; in August 1944 there were 4574 B-17 in USAAF service.

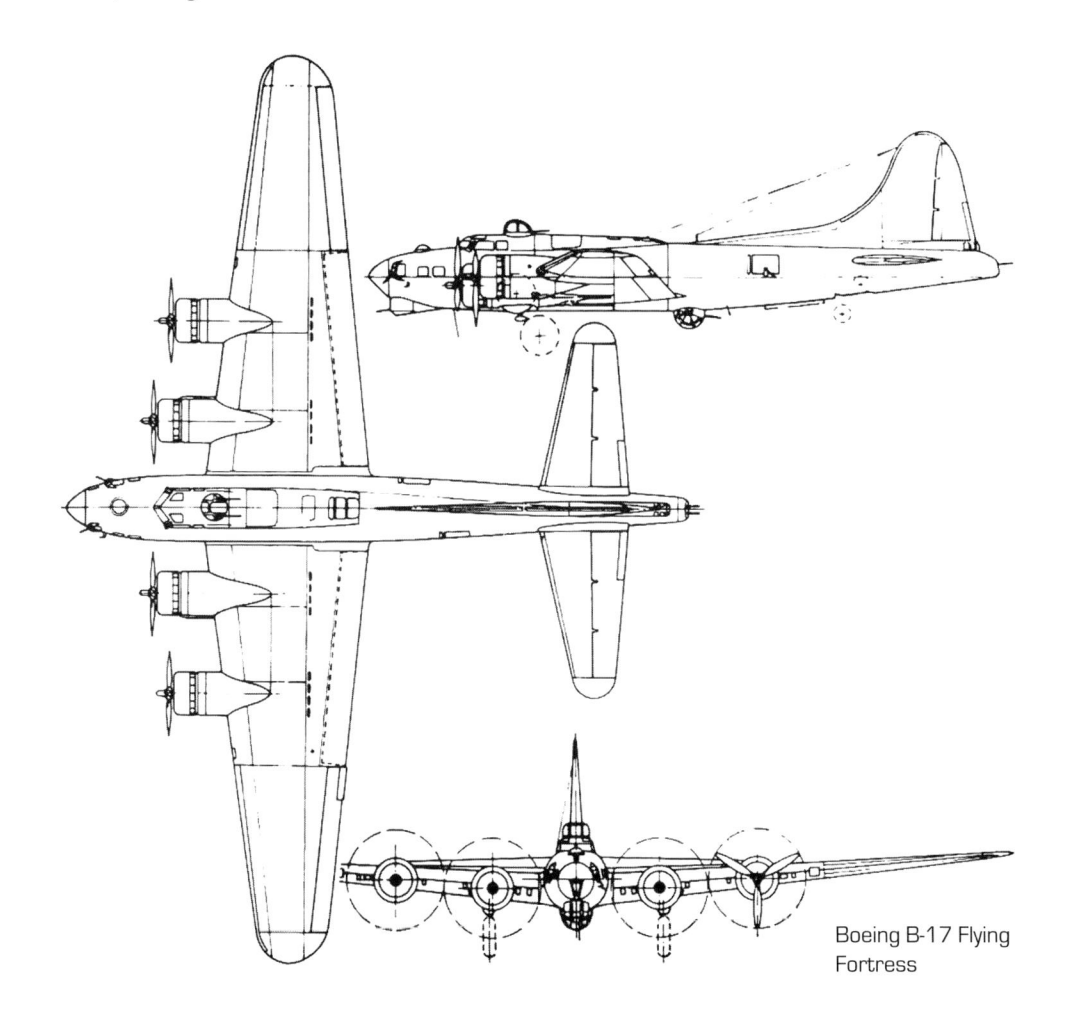

Boeing B-17 Flying Fortress

BOEING B-29 SUPERFORTRESS

The B-29 prototype, Model 345, was submitted by Boeing on 11 May 1940, after a US Army Air Corps request for the development of long-range bombers in 1938. The result was to be the largest bomber used during the Second World War. The formal specifications issued in December 1939 were for a 'superbomber' capable of carrying 20,000lbs with a range of 2667 miles and a speed of 400mph. The B-17 was first flown on 21 September 1942 and introduced for military use on 8 May 1944, after Boeing ran into test difficulties following several accidents, and the test flight programme being taken over by USAAF.

The most famous B-29 was the *Enola Gay*-the aircraft piloted by Colonel Paul W. Tibbets to drop the world's first atomic bomb on Hiroshima. B-29 *Enola Gay* was built by the Glenn L. Martin Company at its Omaha facility, as were all the aircraft operated by the 393rd Bombardment Squadron.

Another type which grew out of the B-29 was the B-50, 371 examples of which were built with a much larger fin and powered by the Pratt & Whitney R-4360 engine. This version was capable of flying at just under 400mph and it was a B-50 that became the first-ever aircraft to fly non-stop round the world.

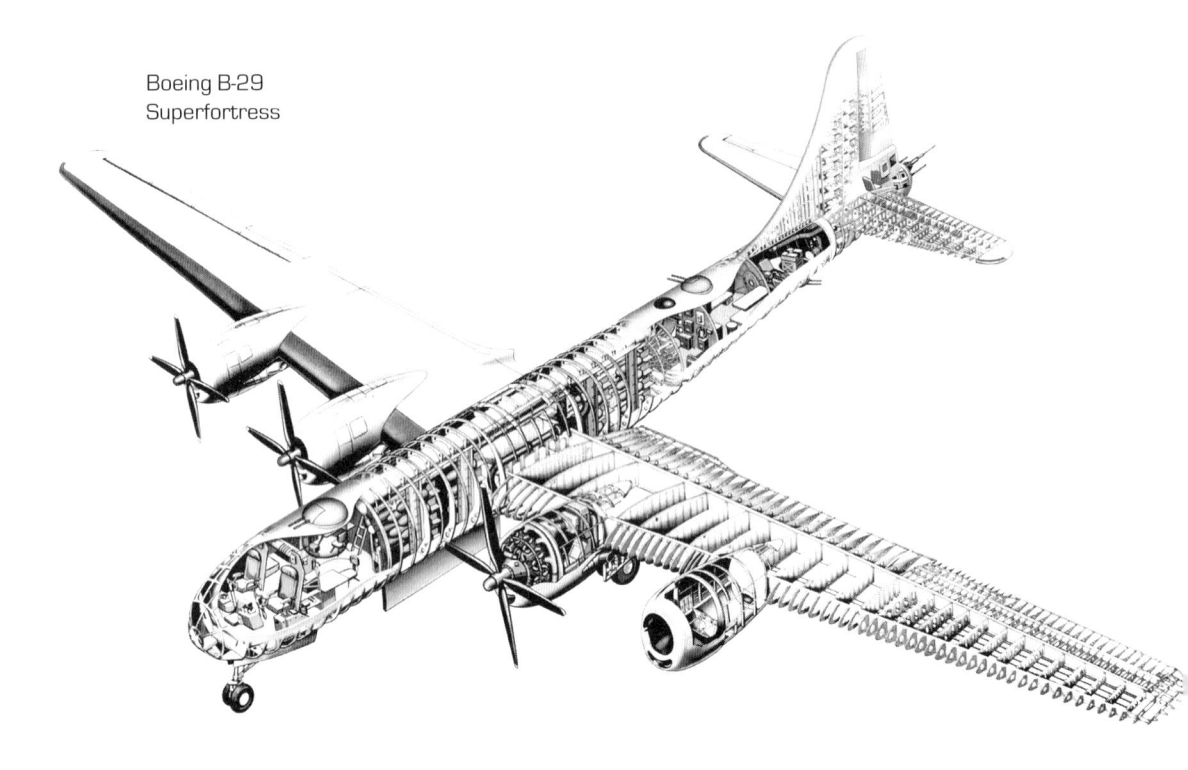

Boeing B-29 Superfortress

BOEING B-47 STRATOJET

The B-47 was a six-engined, jet-powered, long-range medium bomber designed to fly at high altitudes at subsonic speeds. It was designed following a USAAF informal request in 1943, the result being the prototype Model 424. The later formal request was for a bomber with a range of 3500 miles, maximum speed of 550mph, a cruise

AIRCRAFT

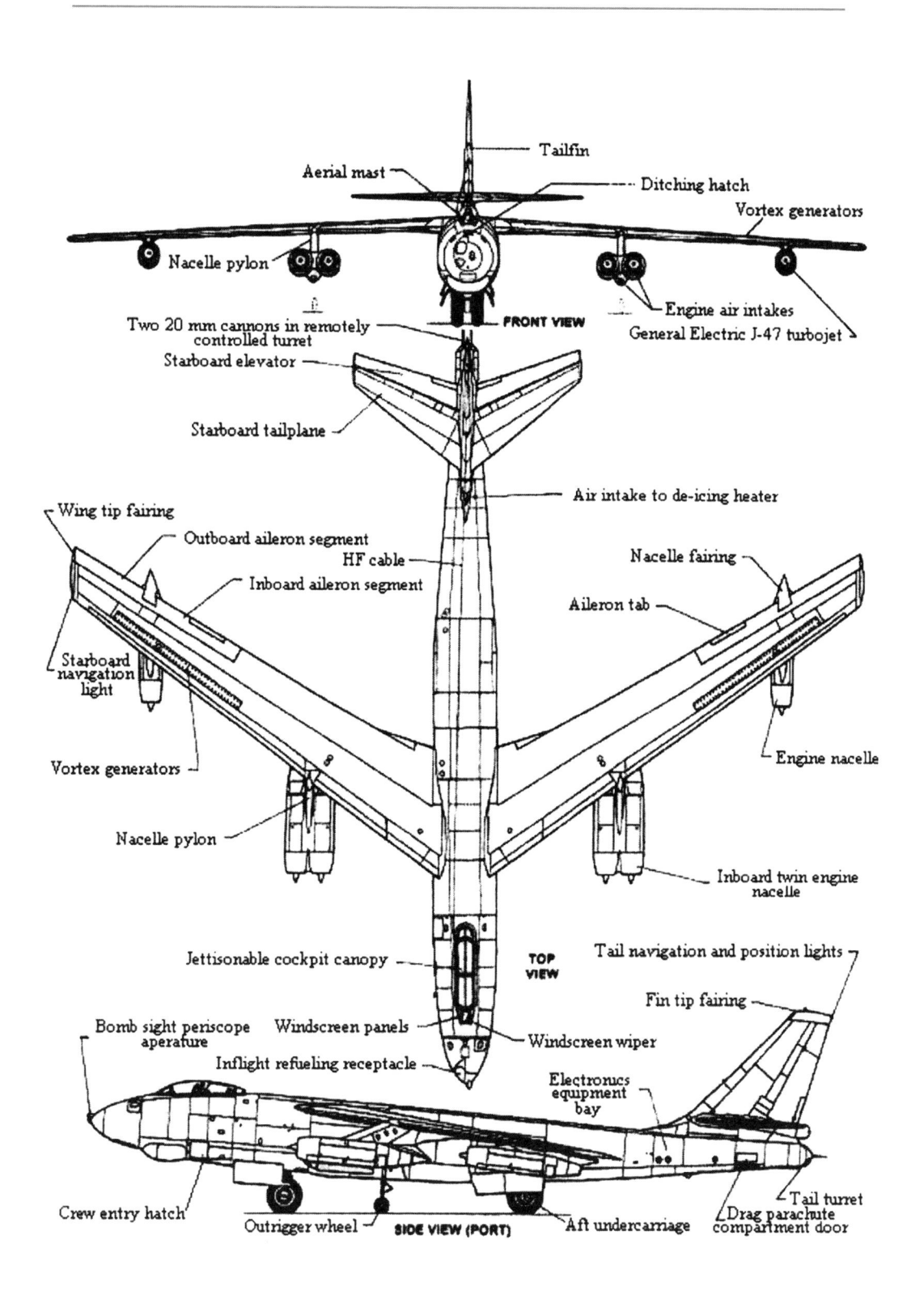

217

Boeing B-47 Stratojet

speed of 450mph and an altitude capacity of 45,000 feet. The thinking behind it was for the US to have to ability to drop nuclear bombs on the USSR if the need arose, thus the B-47 was not just an advanced bomber but a political statement.

The B-47 was Paul Tibbets' last operational type; he flew one aircraft for 1000 hours. The B-47 eventually went into service in 1951 with Strategic Air Command and some 2032 examples were built. The aircraft remained in service into the 1970s, although it never saw combat. Some aircraft were modified for photo and weather reconnaissance and electronic intelligence.

CONSOLIDATED NY

The Consolidated Model 2 was a PT-1 biplane trainer that was produced in the US as the NY, there being several variants. The basic model weighed 2145lbs, had a range of 182.5 miles, a 40 foot wingspan and a maximum speed of 90mph. The NY-1 had provision for the landing gear to be replaced by floats, the weight countered by a larger vertical tail. The NY-2 had a longer wing span and was powered by a R-790-8 Wright Whirlwind J-5 engine producing 220hp, while the NY-3 was powered by a R-760-94 Wright engine.

Consolidated NY-2

Doolittle aboard his blind flying aircraft; it is clearly not a PT-1. Note also the Sperry artificial horizon and the gyro-compass in front of him.

The NY-1 was first flown in November 1925, the NY-2 in October 1926. The US Navy had 108 in active service in 1929, and in that year Jimmy Doolittle chose to use an NY-2 for his blind-flying experiments, which were run by the Massachusetts Institute of Technology and the Army Air Corps. There is some debate over the actual aircraft type used for this programme; many early documents giving the aircraft designation as the PT-1. However, the PT-1 had a quite different airframe from the aircraft flown by Doolittle and close examination of original photographs clearly identify it as the NY-2 (PT-3).

CURTISS JN-4 JENNY

The Curtiss JN-4 Jenny was the first aircraft Aviation Cadet James H. Doolittle ever flew. It was the standard flying training aircraft of the US Army Signal Corps Aviation Section in the First World War and almost 7000 examples were built. It was quite a large aircraft, having a wing span of 43 feet 8 inches.

Powered by the Curtiss OX-5 vee-eight engine of 95 horsepower, the Jenny was found to be a most reliable aircraft, capable of carrying over 1000lbs. Interestingly, the Curtiss OX-5 has the distinction of being the first-ever mass-produced aero engine in the US and the Jenny went on to be the backbone of America's flying circuses in the 1920s and 1930s.

Curtiss JN-4 Jenny

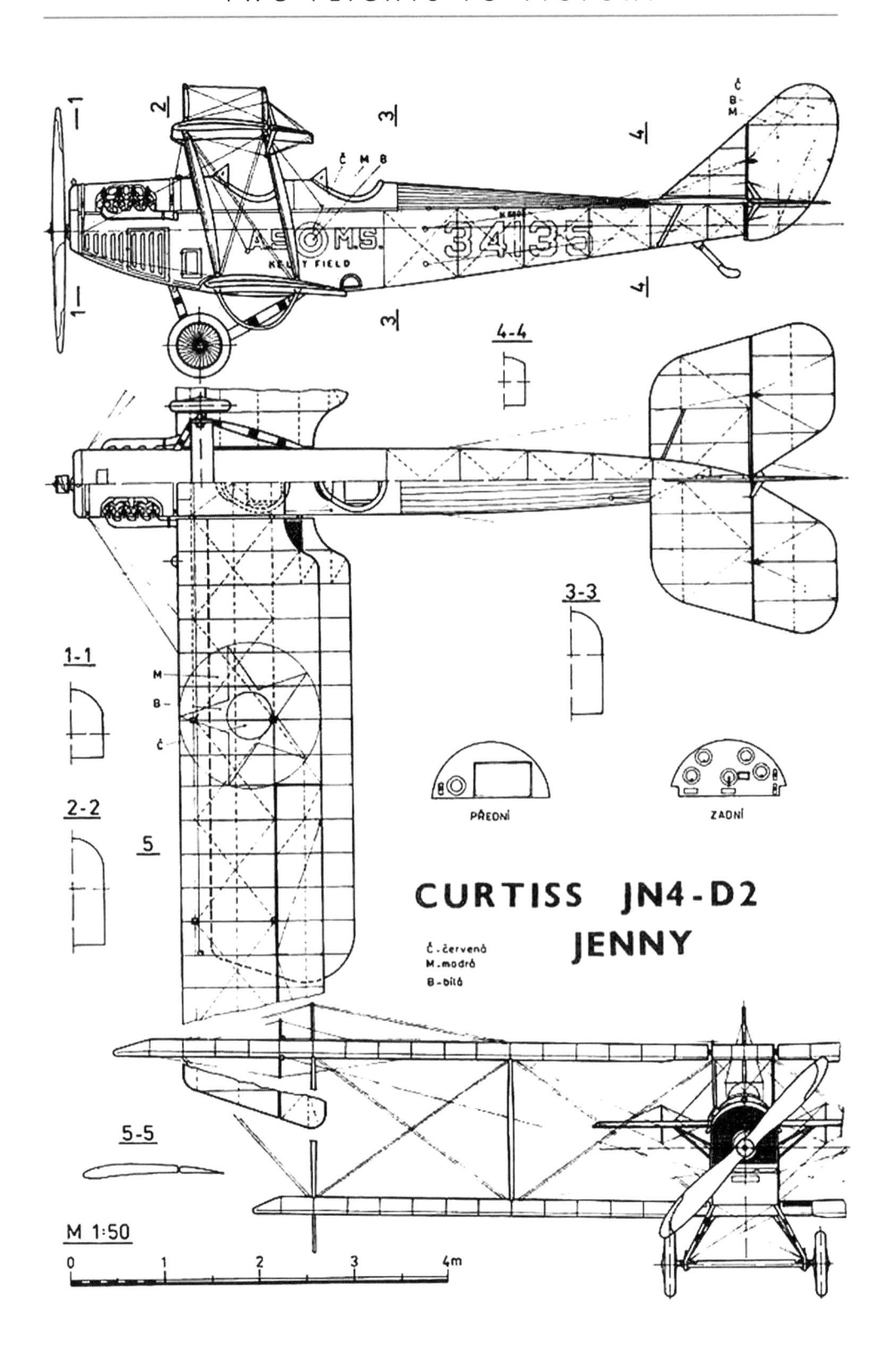

CURTISS P-1 PURSUIT

The Curtiss P-1 was the first of a long line of highly successful pursuit aircraft built by the Glenn L. Curtiss Company. It was an open cockpit biplane with a weight of 2195lbs, a wingspan of 31.5 feet, was 23 feet long and had a maximum speed of 155mph.

In a bid to sell the aircraft to South American countries, Curtiss acquired Jimmy Doolittle to demonstrate the aircraft. This he did with great success, and used a P-1 to make the first cross-Andes flight. He later used a Curtiss P-1B to fly the first outside loop in 1927, a manoeuvre previously thought to be highly dangerous.

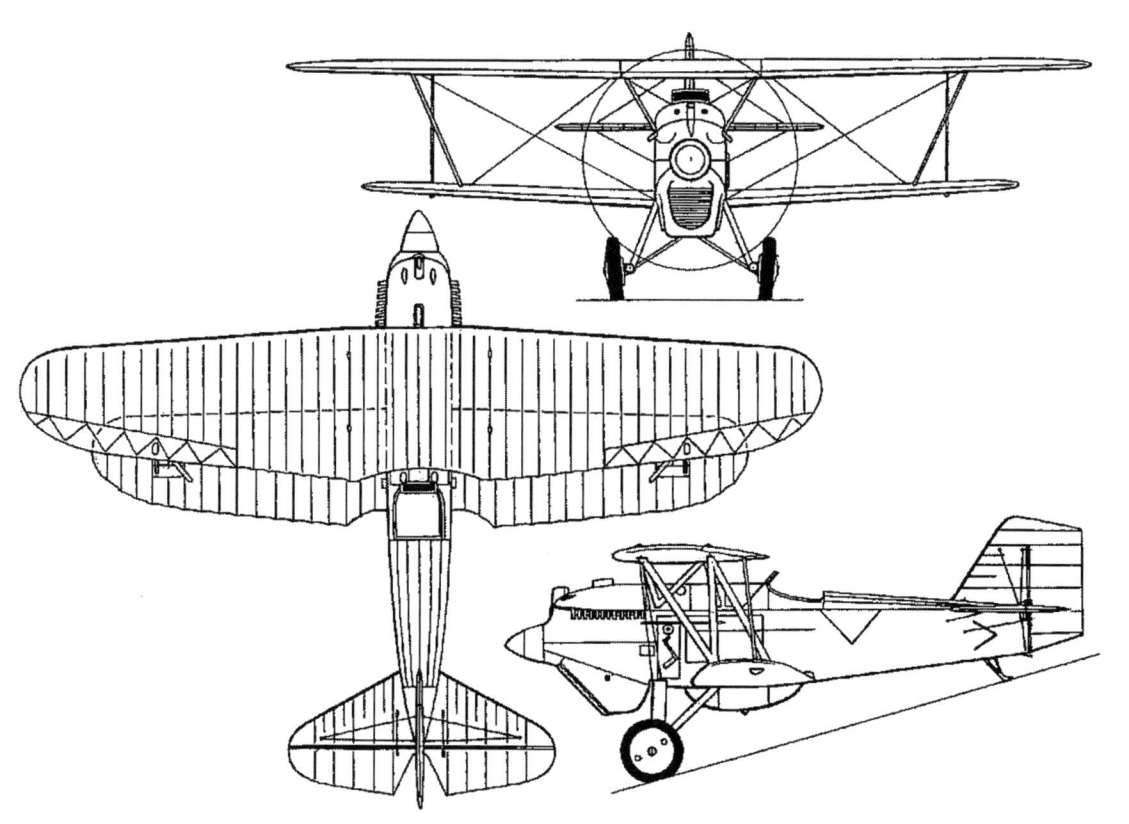

Curtiss P-1 Pursuit

CURTISS P-40 WARHAWK

The Curtiss P-40 was a development from the radial engined P-36. A much smoother airframe and faster machine was the result, though many ground crew working on the P-40B were critical of its engine, the Allison V-12, because of varied reliability in different theatres of operation. It was a single-engined fight, first flying in 1938 and remaining in service until the end of the Second World War. By the end of production 13,738 had been built. It weighed 6350lbs, was 31.67 feet in length, had a maximum speed of 360mph and a range of 650 miles.

The most famous two users of the P-40 were the American Volunteer Group, operating in Burma and South West China, and Number 112 Squadron of the Royal Air Force in the Western Desert of North Africa. Commanded by Major-General Claire Lee Chennault, the 'Flying Tigers' pilots included such legendary names as Lieutenant Gregory Boyington, a US Marine Corps pilot who later commanded VMF 214 the 'Black Sheep' squadron.

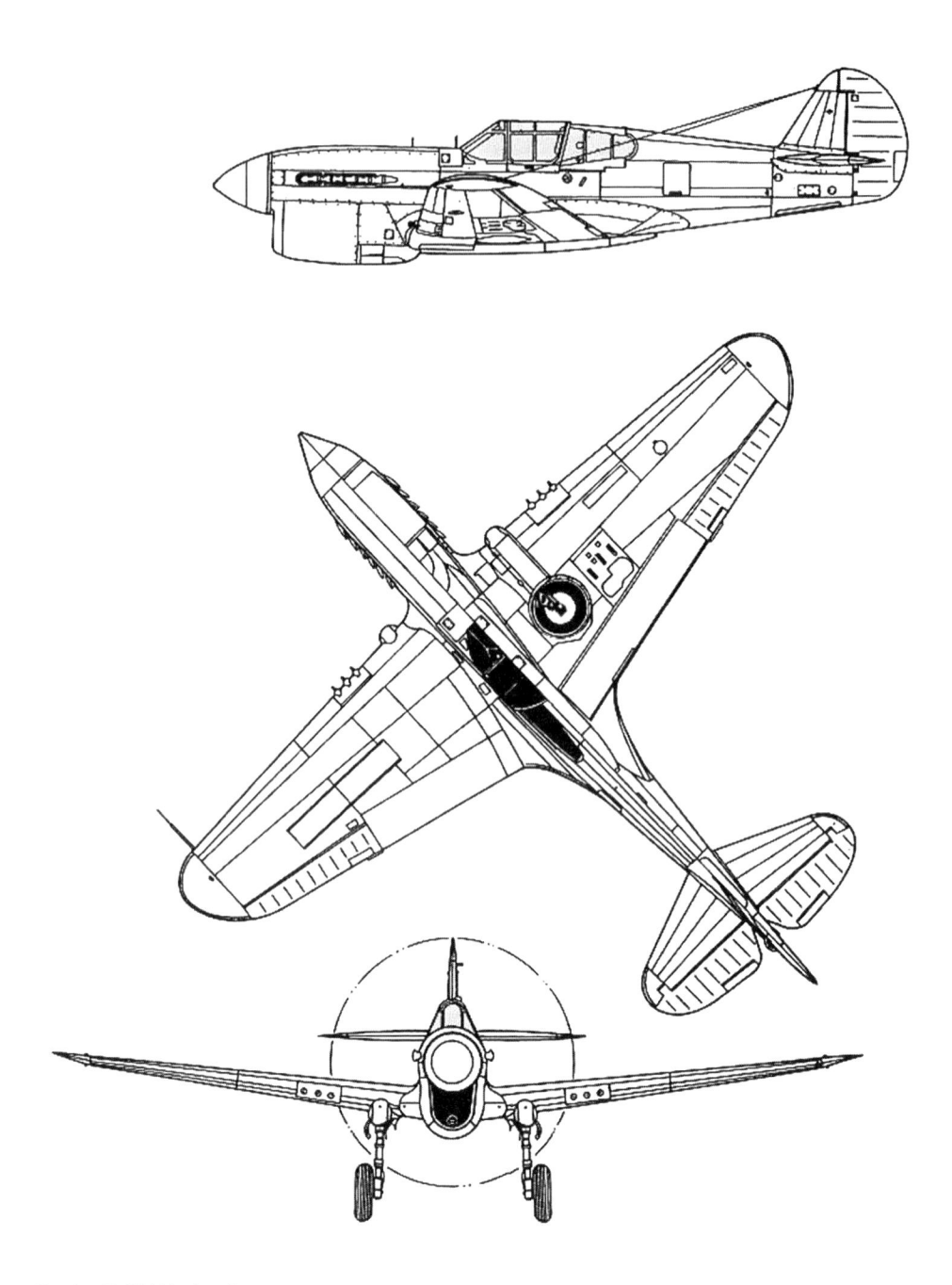

Curtiss P-40 Warhawk

CURTISS R-3C

The Curtiss R-3C was a floatplane with a wingspan of only 21 feet 9 inches and a length of just under 20 feet, weighing 2150lbs. It was powered by the Curtiss D-12 V-12 engine, giving 635hp, and was reckoned to be capable of 254mph in perfect conditions. The airframe was built from a combination of spruce longerons and laminated ply structure.

The R-3C was flown by Jimmy Doolittle in the Schneider Trophy Race in 1925. At the time European planes had the edge technologically on American aircraft, but Doolittle's hairpin turns and expert flying gave the US its second win, with an average speed of 232.6mph. A year after winning the Schneider Trophy, Jimmy Doolittle was awarded the Mackay Trophy for this feat, acknowledging that this was the fastest a seaplane had ever flown.

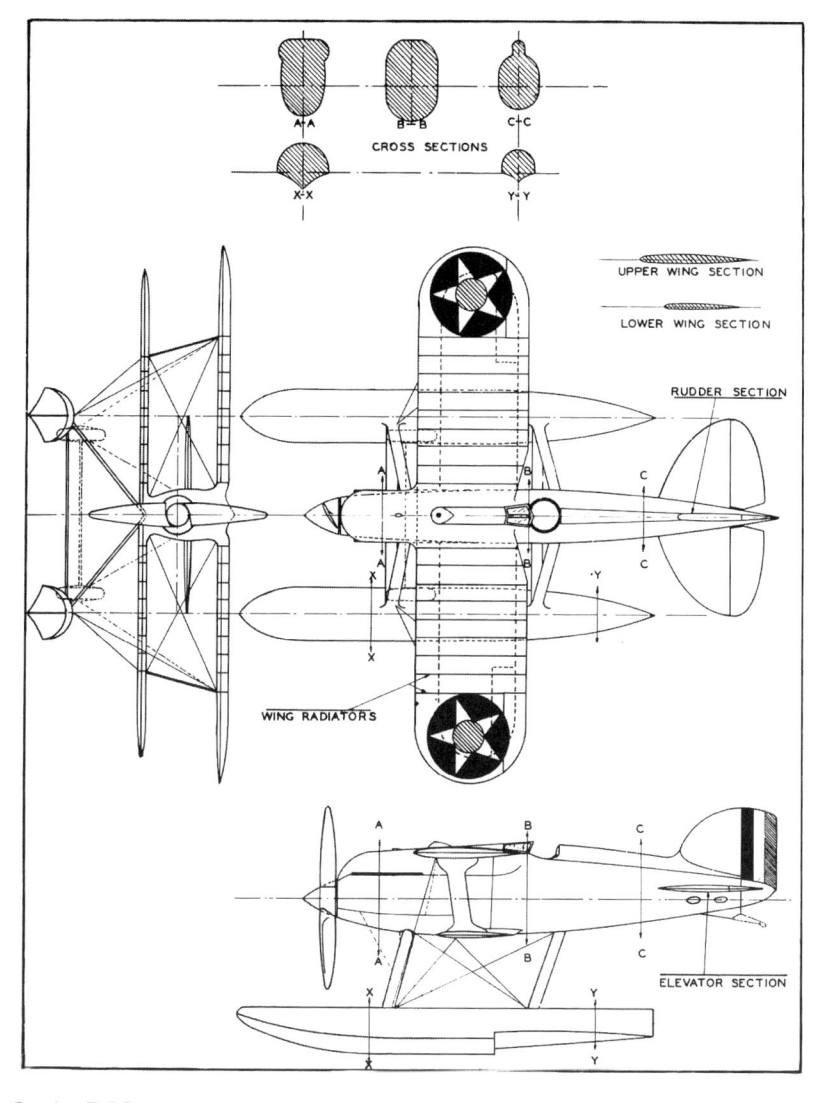

Curtiss R-3C

DOUGLAS A-20 HAVOC

The A-20 was a light attack bomber, the result of a US Army Air Corps specification issued in 1937. The first models were not picked up in the US, but orders did come from France. Improvements in France and Britain encouraged the Army Air Corps to order the A-20 for high-altitude bombing and the A-20A for lower-altitude work. They were powered by turbosupercharged Wright R-2600-7 engines, but these were bulky and the prototype suffered cooling problems, which Paul Tibbets was instrumental in solving.

The aircraft was considered for use by the Doolittle Raiders, as it had a 4000lb bomb load and a speed of 340mph, together with long range. In the event Jimmy Doolittle rejected it on the basis that it had no co-pilot seat, and thus one man would have to fly the entire mission. Given the distances involved this was impractical.

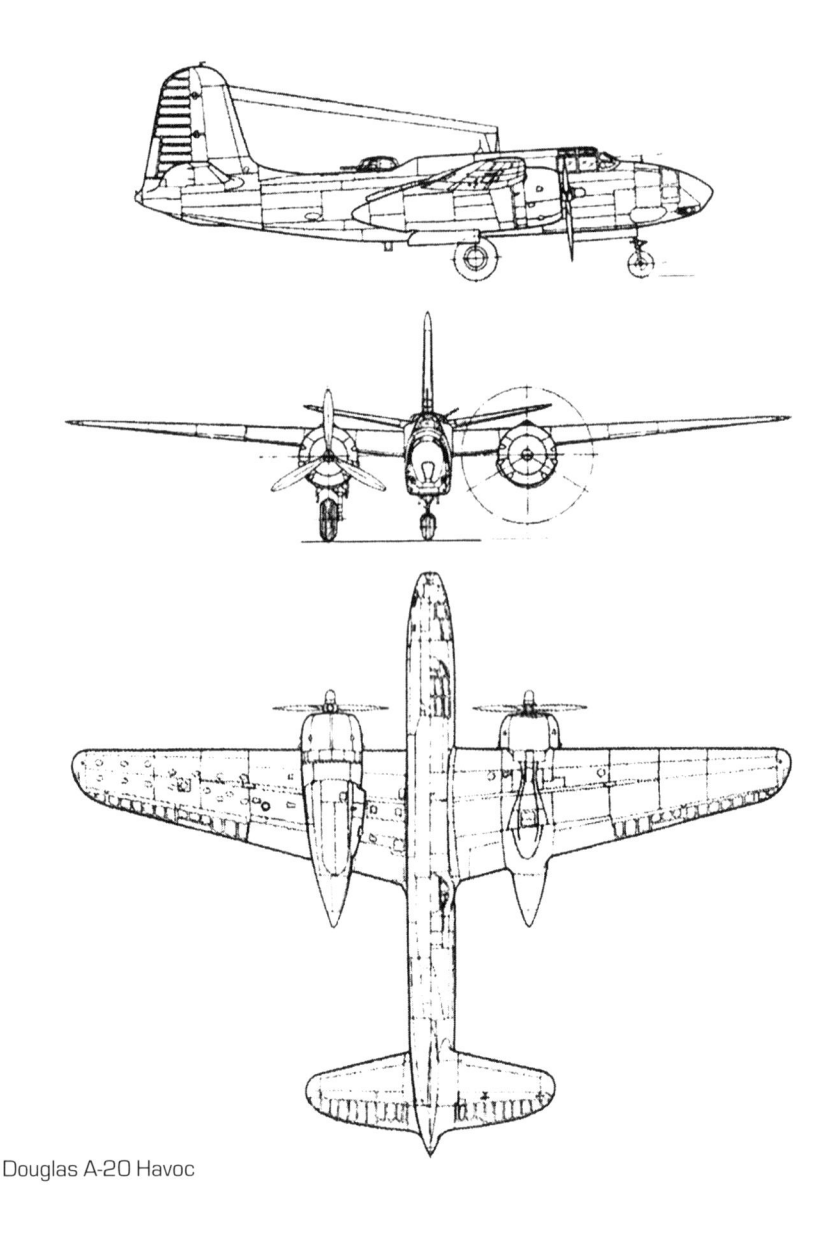

Douglas A-20 Havoc

DOUGLAS B-18 BOLO

The B-18 'Bolo' was a new-generation twin-engined bomber which came to the US Army Air Corps to replace the obsolescent Martin B-10. The B-18 was pretty quick off the drawing board because it used the wings and tail surfaces of the DC-2 medium airliner. 350 were built and spread through most bomb groups in the US Army Air Corps. Two bomb groups, the 5th and 11th, were decimated in the Japanese attack on Pearl Harbor and while Captain Paul Tibbets was waiting for his transfer to the new-to-be-formed B-17 bomb group, the 29th, he was assigned to East Coast patrol activities with the B-18, while the 29th Bombardment Group was transferred to Hickam Field in Hawaii.

The B-18 was totally unsuited to the strategic bombing role, with a cruise speed of only 130 miles an hour and an operational ceiling of only 12,000 feet, but it was an excellent patrol aircraft, being highly forgiving and very gentle in flight.

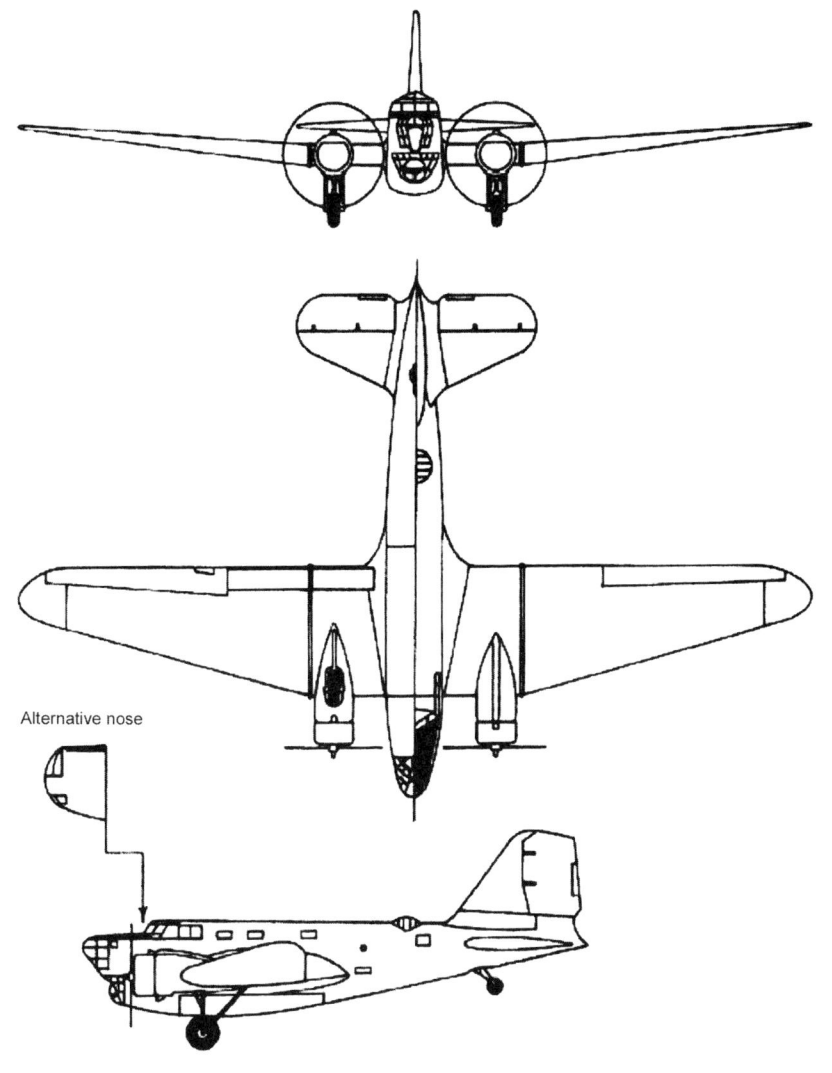

Alternative nose

Douglas B-18 Bolo

DOUGLAS B-23 DRAGON

The Douglas B-23 was a twin-engined medium bomber – developed as a successor to the B-18 Bolo – which entered service with the US Army Air Corps in 1939. Only 38 were manufactured between July 1939 and September 1940. It was the first US bomber equipped with a glazed tail gun position and could carry a crew of six. It weighed 19,089lbs, had a top speed of 282mph, had a range of 1400 miles (with 4000lb bomb load) and was powered by two Wright R-2600-3 radial engines producing 1600hp each.

The B-23 it was initially one of the contenders for the Doolittle Raid. However, its wingspan of 98 feet made it a very precarious contender, on the basis that the USS *Hornet*'s deck width (beam) was only 114 feet. The B-26 also put itself out of contention because its takeoff speed was higher than the B-25 and so the takeoff distance was longer.

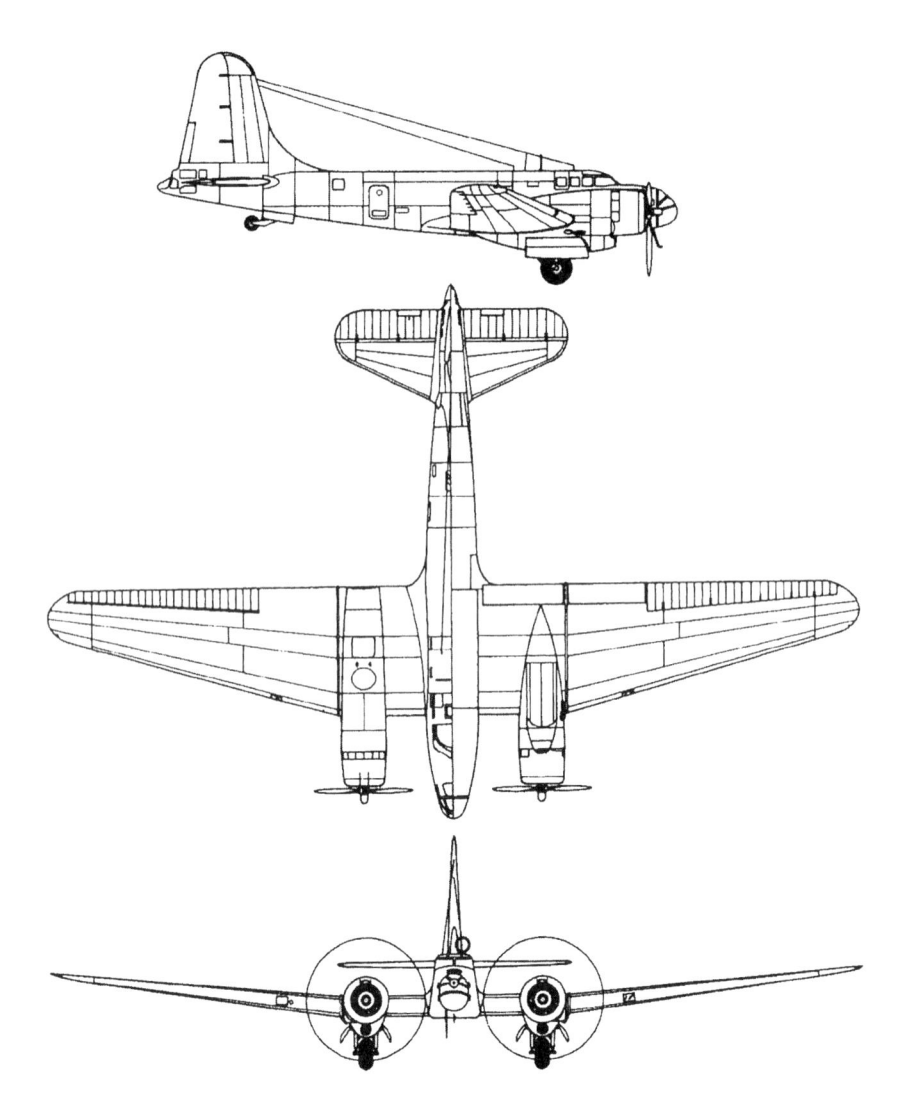

Douglas B-23 Dragon

AIRCRAFT

DOUGLAS DC-6/C-54 SKYMASTER

The C-54 was a four-engined military transport aircraft airliner derived from the civilian Douglas DC-4. It weighed 38,930lbs and could carry 50 troops. It had a maximum speed of 275mph, a range of 4000 miles, was 93 feet 10 inches long and was powered by four Pratt & Whitney R-2000-9 radial engines producing 1450hp.

The C-54 was the most widely used four-engined transport in the US Army Air Force's inventory, despite only 1170 being built. It equipped the 320th Troop Carrier Squadron as part of the 509th Composite Group, and Tibbets used one to travel between Wendover Field, Tinian, Alamogordo and Washington DC. The civil version, the DC-6, along with several hundred surplus C54s, formed the backbone of international air transport for a number of years after the war's end.

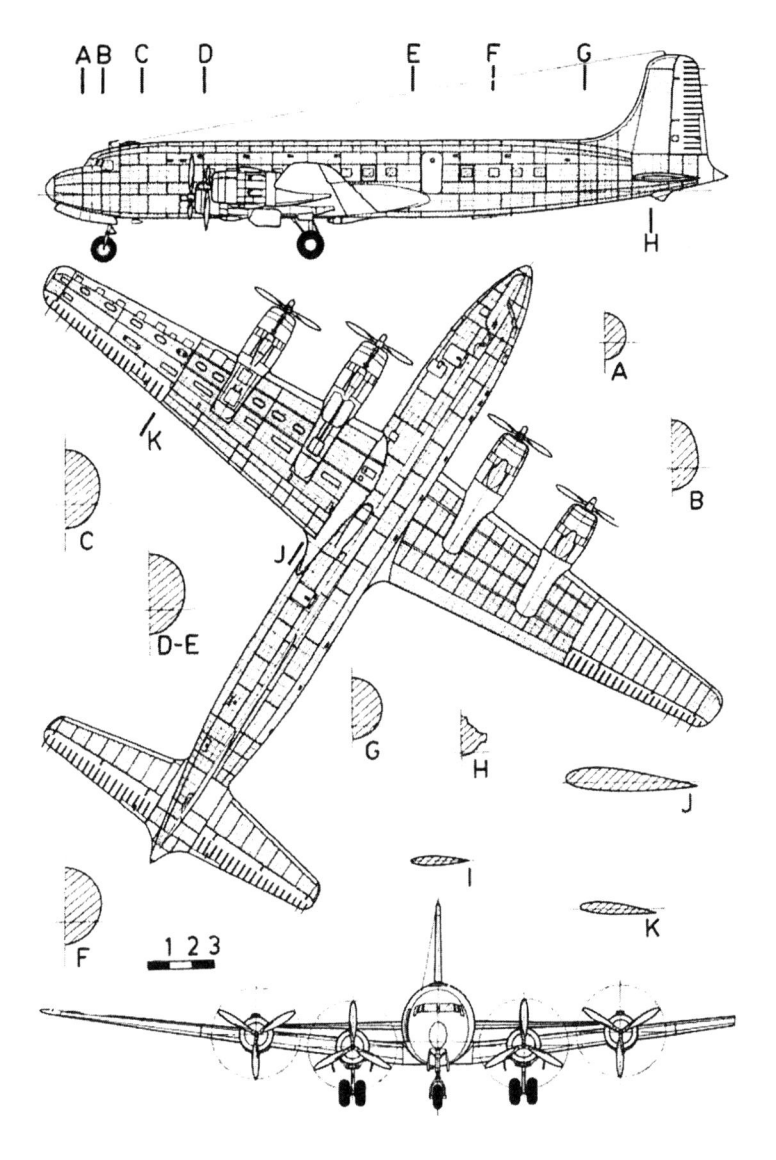

Douglas DC-6/C-54 Skymaster

DOUGLAS O-46A

The Douglas O-46 was the last in a line of observation monoplanes built by Douglas between May 1936 and April 1937, a development of the O-43. It weighed 4776lbs, had a maximum speed of 200mph and a range of 435 miles.

The US Army Air Corps decided the O-46 was too big and heavy for soft-field observation activities, despite its British counterpart, the Westland Lysander, having four feet more wingspan. It was the first operational aeroplane flown by Lieutenant Paul Tibbets at Fort Benning. However, since the Army Air Corps had made its decision to withdraw the O-46 from front-line service, it was to be re-designated L-46 and while a few of the total 90 ordered in 1935 were in service at the start of the war, they were soon relegated to a training role. One O-46 survives in the USAF Museum at Wright Patterson Air Force Base in Ohio.

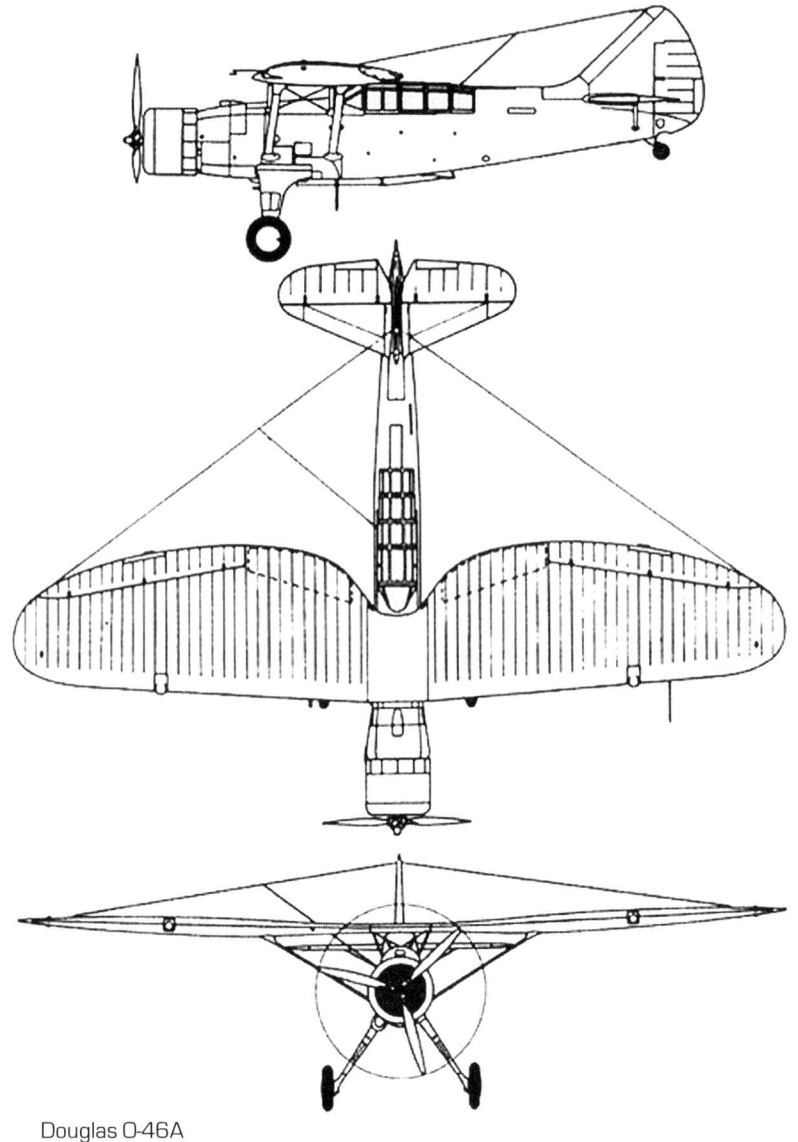

Douglas O-46A

GEE-BEE R-1 RACER

The 'Gee-Bee' Racer was designed by the Granville Brothers and was essentially a Pratt & Whitney 'Wasp' engine fitted with enough cowling, fuselage and flying surfaces to get it into the air and keep it there at its maximum speed of 294.38mph. It weighed 1840lbs, had a range of 925 miles and was 17 feet 8 inches in length. It was the successor to the Model Z, fitted with a bulletproof windscreen and internal fuel caps, modifications made after a Model Z crashed and the fuel cap being propelled into the pilot's face was blamed. The R-1's had a teardrop-shaped fuselage, designed to lower drag after wind tunnel testing. The fuselage acted as an airfoil, allowing for tight turns without a drop in altitude. Jimmy Doolittle flew the Racer in the 1932 Thompson Trophy Race, which he won, after his Laird 'Super Solution' was damaged.

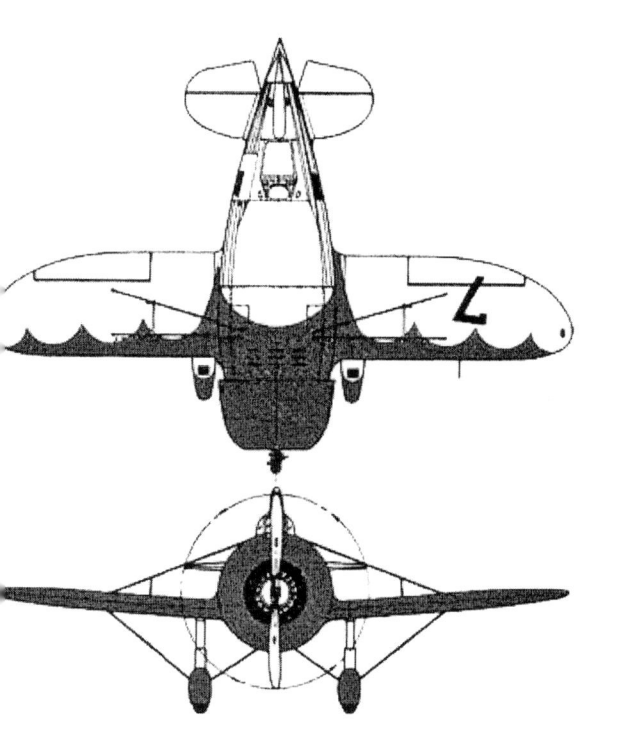

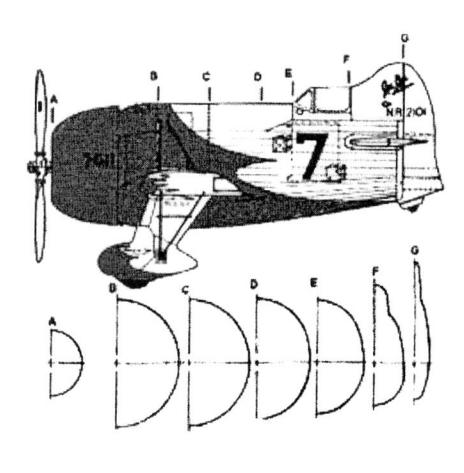

Gee-Bee R-1 Racer

LAIRD LC-DW500 SUPER SOLUTION

The Laird Super Solution was a racing biplane built by Mattie Laird; work began on 8 July 1931 and it was first flown on 22 August. It was similar in appearance to the Gee Bee and had a large radial engine. Its aerodynamic construction and tight engine cowling made it an advanced design, and it was 200lbs heavier than the early DW300 as it carried instruments for cross country and blind flying.

Jimmy Doolittle flew a Super Solution named *Sky Buzzard* in the Bendix Trophy. His aircraft was painted green, with yellow wings and carried the racing number 400. After winning the Bendix Trophy in record time, Doolittle went on to Newark in New Jersey to set a new trans-continental record, arriving just eleven hours, sixteen minutes and ten seconds after he had taken off from Burbank.

Laird LC-DW500
Super Solution

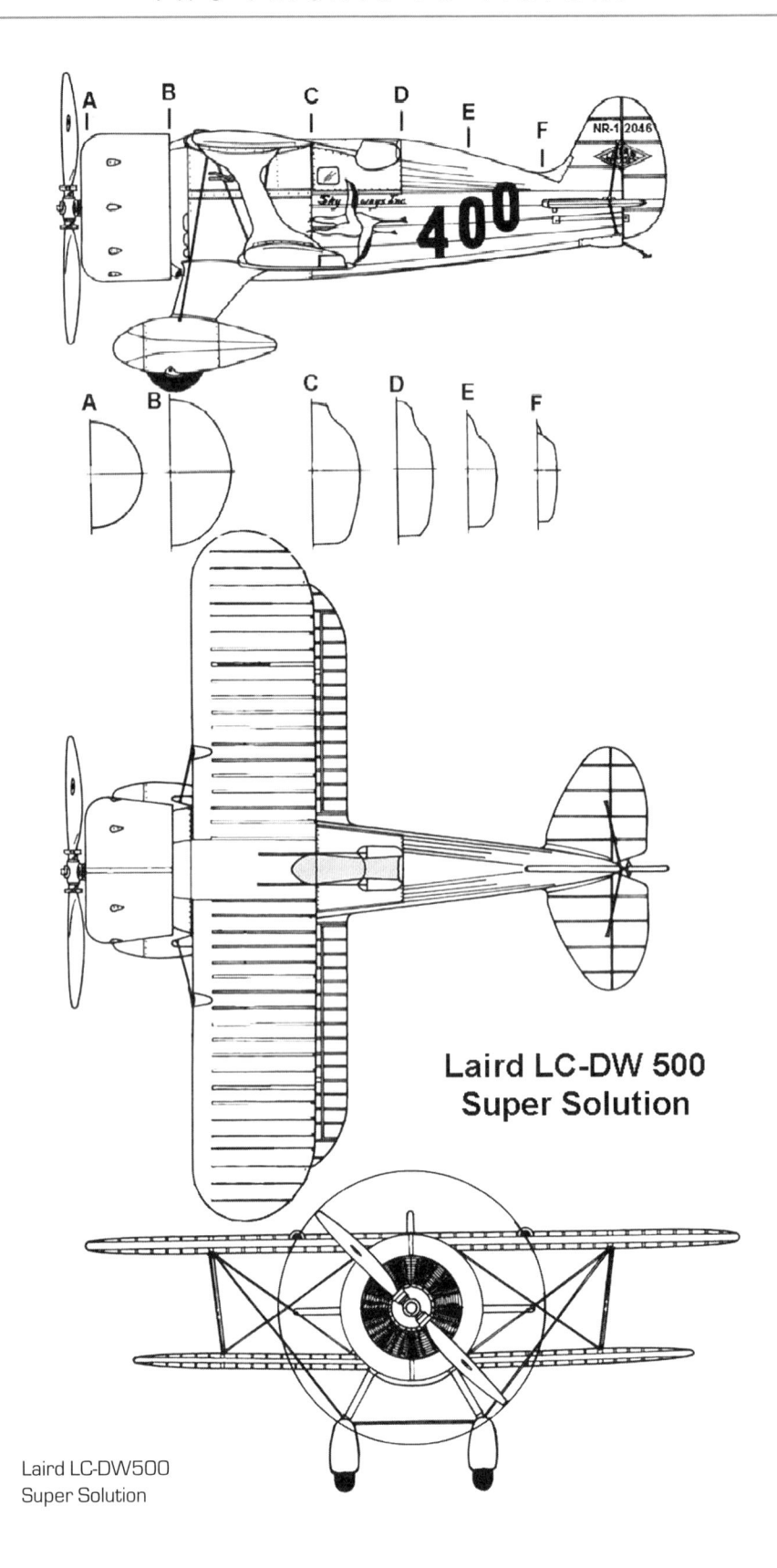

MARTIN B-10

The B-10 was the first all-metal bomber in service with the Army Air Corps, first flying in 1932 and entering service in June 1934. It introduced fully cowled engines to bombers and was considered well ahead of its time. Its odd profile was the result of two separate glazed cockpit canopies and a large glazed gunner's turret at the nose. It weighed 9681lbs, had a maximum speed of 213mph and a range of 1240 miles. It was 44 feet 9 inches long and could carry a crew of three.

A squadron of these aircraft was located at Fort Benning and Lieutenant Paul Tibbets developed his bombing skills on this type. It was an easy aircraft to fly and whilst Tibbets didn't fly it for long, it was good experience for him before converting to the Douglas B-18 'Bolo'.

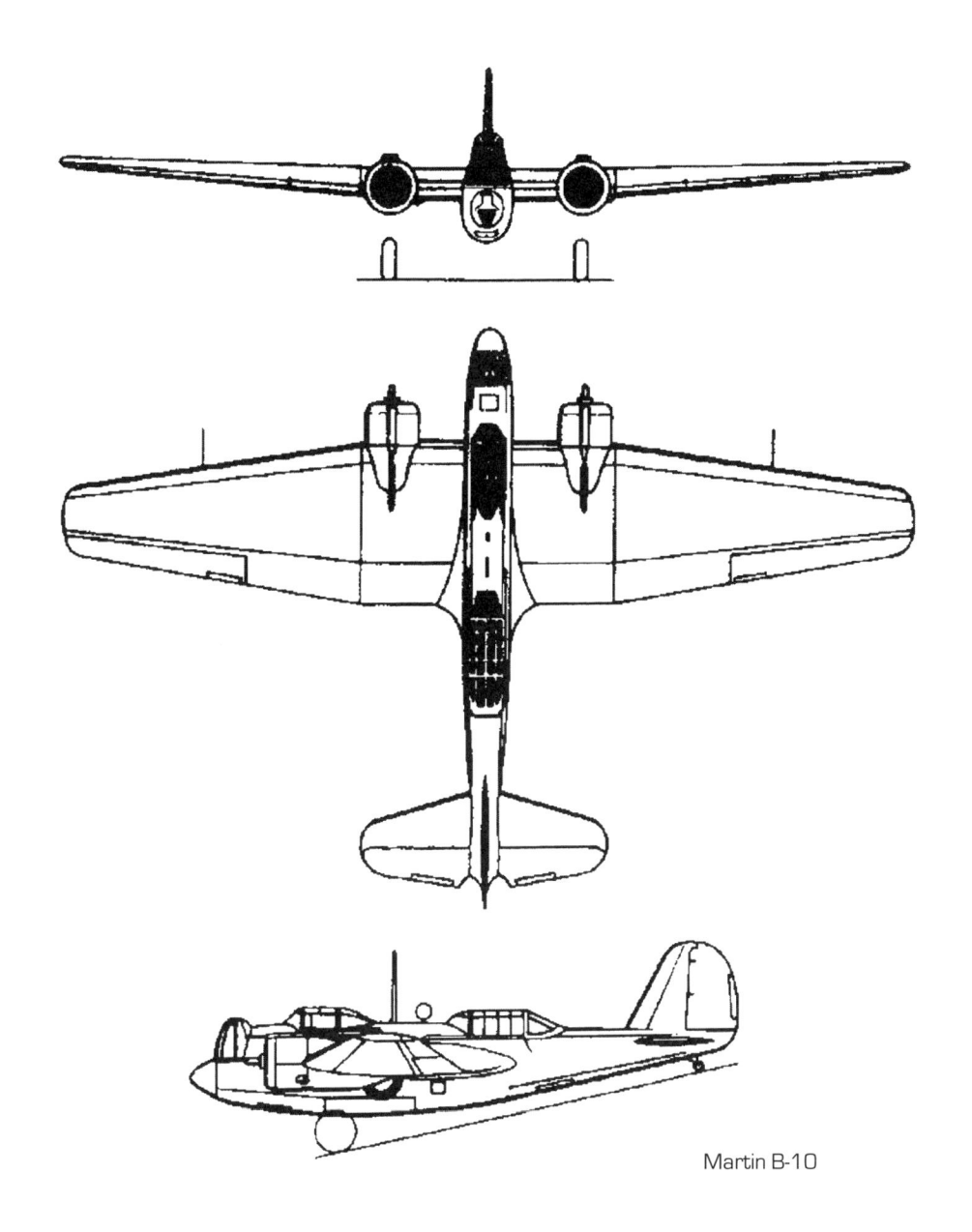

Martin B-10

MARTIN B-26 MARAUDER

The Martin B-26 Marauder was a twin-engine medium bomber built by the Glenn L. Martin Company. It was designed in response to the March 1939 US Army Air Corps specifications, a maximum speed of 350mph, a range of 3000 miles and a bomb load of 2000lbs. The Glenn L. Martin design was submitted on 5 July 1939 and an operational model was in service within two years. The resulting B-26 weighed 24,000lbs, had a maximum speed of 287mph and a range of 2850 miles. It was 58 feet 3 inches long and was powered by two 2× Pratt & Whitney R-2800-43 radial engines producing 1,900hp.

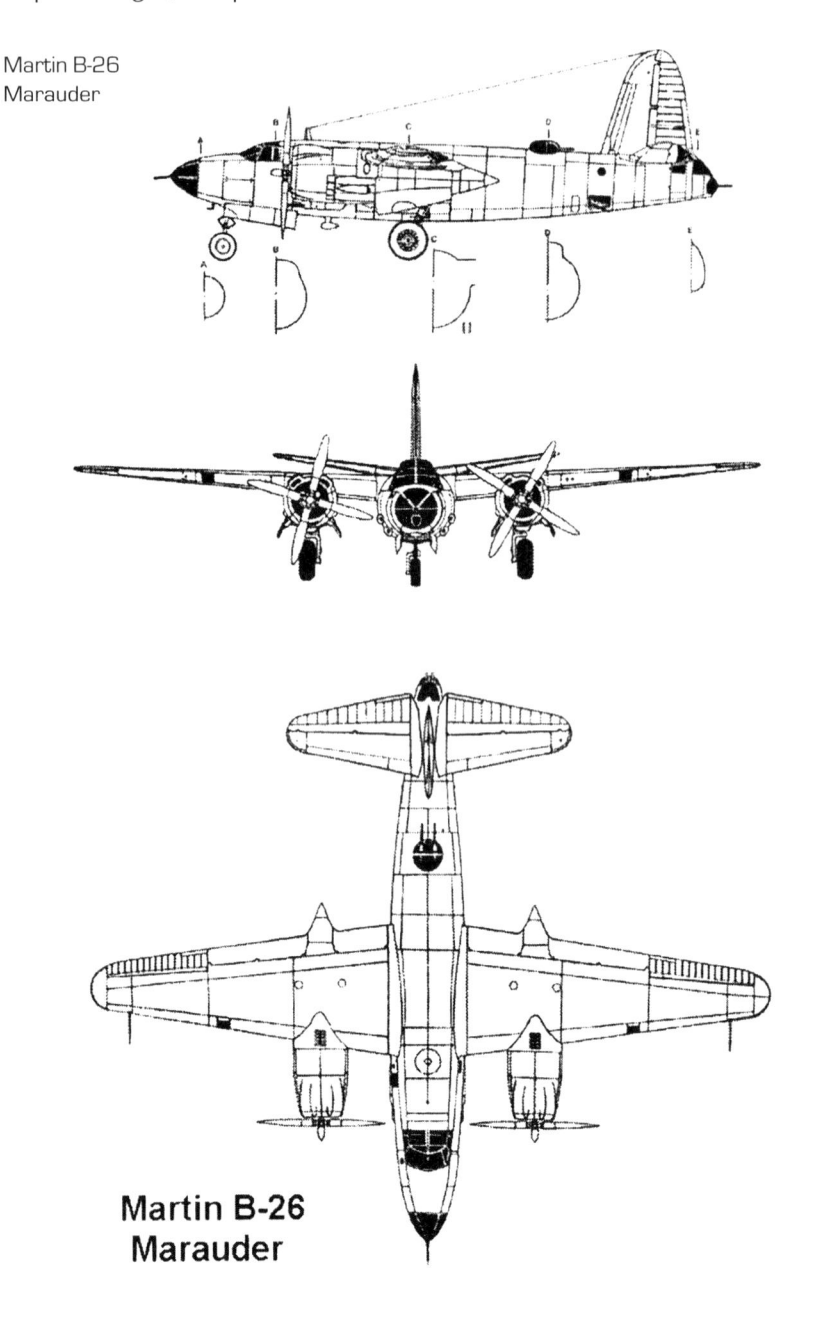

Martin B-26 Marauder

Martin B-26 Marauder

Shortly after joining the staff of General Henry H. Arnold at Army Air Corps Headquarters in Washington DC, Major Jimmy Doolittle was called upon to perform a validation test and production examination for the then-new Martin B-26. It had been ordered into production straight from the drawing board with no pre-production prototypes built or evaluated. In principle, the B-26 was a high-performance medium bomber and had already gone into service with the Royal Air Force in Great Britain and with the South African Air Force. But it quickly acquired for itself the reputation of 'widow-maker' and Doolittle's task was to identify why and to recommend such rectifications as might restore it to a safe and useful weapon, or to terminate its production.

Doolittle concluded that the Marauder was a viable aircraft, but it needed a number of modifications to make it safe and crews flying it needed extended flying training to learn to handle a tricycle undercarriage, as most pilots had come from single engined 'tail-draggers'. His first task was to relocate the battery master switch to a position on the flight deck from just inside the crew entry hatch. Next, he recommended the extension of the wingspan by about seven feet to increase stability in a turn, especially if an engine went dead in flight. After these and some other minor modifications, the aircraft was allowed to continue in production.

NORTH AMERICAN B-25B MITCHELL

The North American B-25 Mitchell was a twin-engined medium bomber manufactured by North American Aviation. It was named for General Billy Mitchell, the only US military aircraft named for a person. It served in every theatre of the Second World War and by the end of its production nearly 10,000 B-25s of various models had been built. It weighed 21,120lbs, had a maximum speed of 275mph, a range of 2700 miles and was powered by two Wright R-2600 Cyclone 14 radial engines, producing 1850hp.

The Mitchell was one of the aircraft considered by Jimmy Doolittle when he was choosing the aeroplanes to be used for the Doolittle Raid. In the event, while the B-26 had an acceptable wingspan of only 71 feet, its takeoff distance and speed quickly put it out of contention.

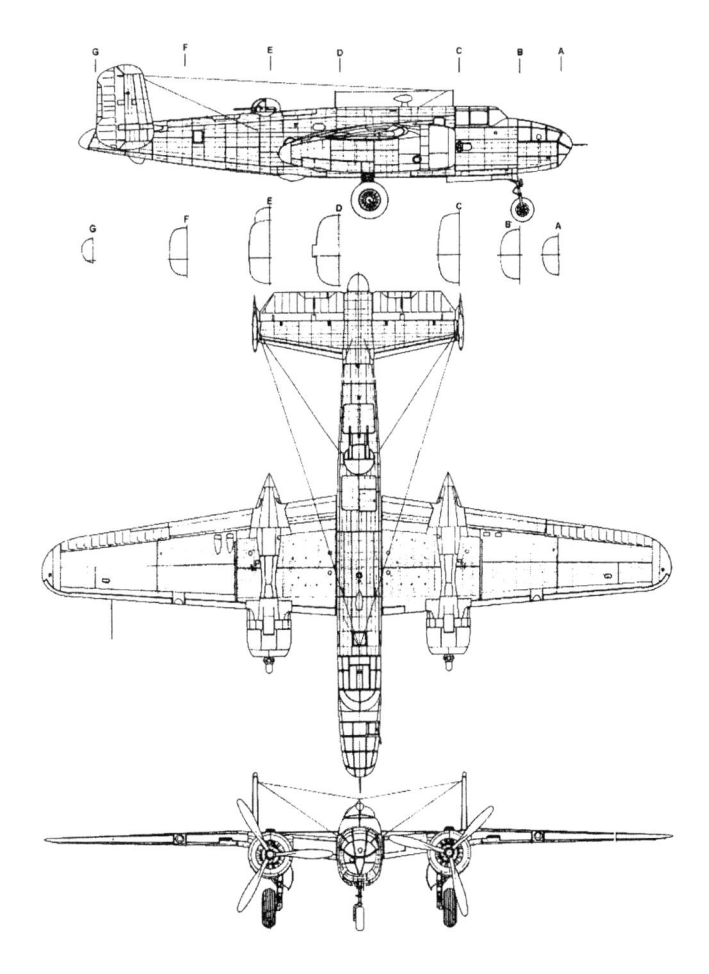

North American B-25B Mitchell

NORTH AMERICAN O-47

The North American O-47 was an observation fixed-wing aircraft monoplane, fitted with retractable landing gear, a low-wing configuration and a three-blade propeller. It weighed 5980lbs, had a maximum speed of 221mph and a range of 840 miles.

The O-47 was Lieutenant Tibbets' second operational type at Fort Benning and whilst this type was no smaller and no more suitable to soft-field operation, it was a more modern design and, with its retractable landing gear, was better able to avoid enemy fighters in the right circumstances. It carried up to four crew members – a pilot, an upper observer, a gunner in the upper glazed cockpit, then a photographer/observer in the underbelly glazed area, though the aircraft could operate with a fixed vertical camera operated by the upper observer if a crew of only three was available or required.

A total of 238 O-47s were built, but like the O-46, it was found to be too heavy and too cumbersome for forward field operations and was ultimately replaced with lighter aircraft, such as the Vultee Vigilant, the Stinson Sentinel and the Piper Cub/Grasshopper.

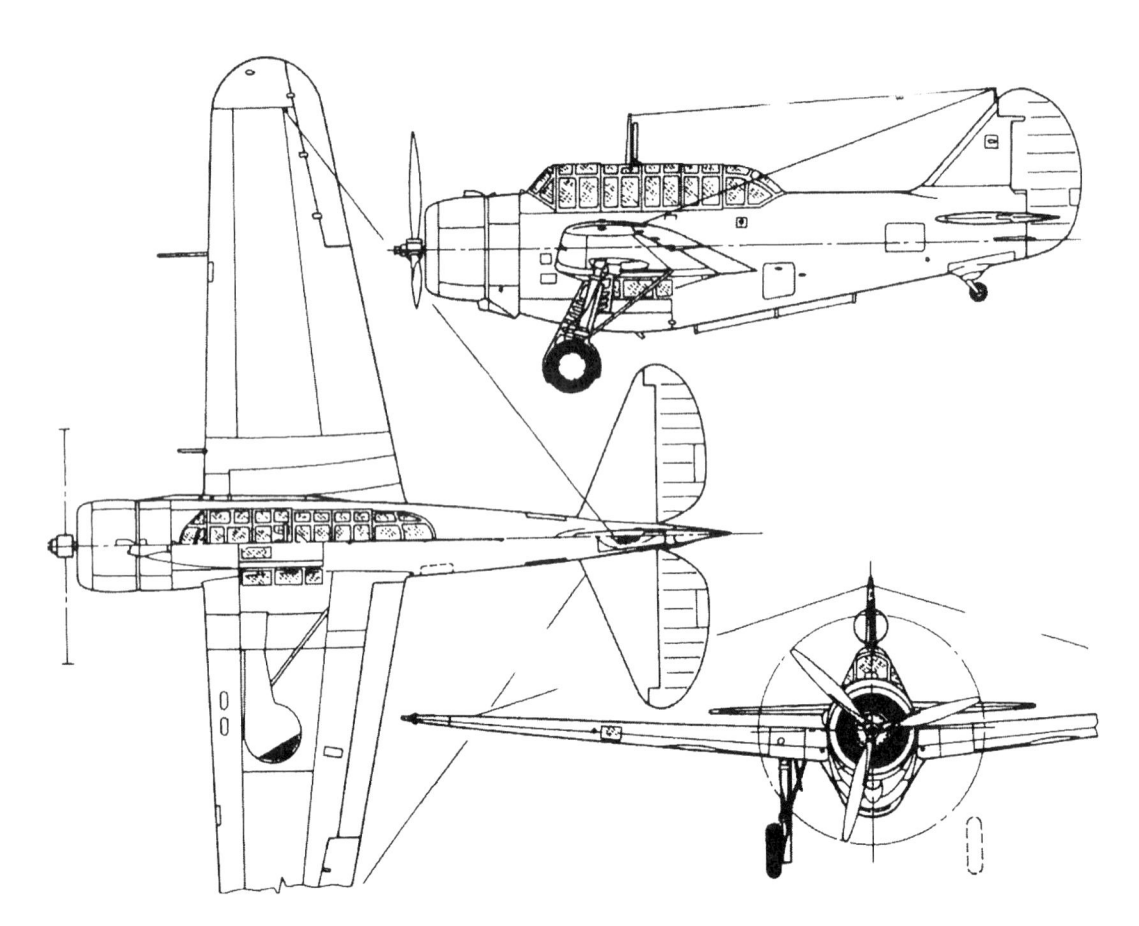

North American O-47

Appendix 4

Military Organisations

EIGHTH US ARMY AIR FORCE

The Eighth US Army Air Force was activated at Savannah, Georgia on 2 January 1942, initially under the command of Major-General Carl Spaatz. It was the first significant step by the US to become involved in the War in Europe. General Spaatz assumed command on 5 January and established his provisional Eighth Air Force Headquarters at Bolling Field in Washington DC. Three days later, the order activating the US Forces in the British Isles (USAFBI) was announced and on 15 June General Spaatz arrived in England to bring his Eighth Air Force Headquarters to RAF Bushey Park.

The operational elements of the Eighth Air Force consisted of VIII Bomber Command, under Brigadier-General Ira Eaker, which was established in company with VIII Fighter Command. Both were established on 19 January 1942 and their tasks were to conduct strategic bombardment over Europe with four-engined bombers and to provide fighter escort to those bombers where they needed it. VIII Air Support Command was formed on 24 April to provide troop transport, reconnaissance and tactical bombardment using twin-engined bombers.

The first operational unit of the 'Mighty Eighth' was the ground echelon of the 97th Bombardment Group (H), located at RAF Polebrook in Northamptonshire, under the command of Colonel Frank A. Armstrong on 9 June. The first bombing raid over Europe was carried out on 17 August and the lead aircraft on that raid was a Boeing B-17E named *Butcher Shop*. It was the personal aircraft of the Group Commander, but Colonel Armstrong had not yet achieved operational status in flying the B-17, so the pilot was Major Paul W. Tibbets, commander of the 340th Bombardment Squadron. Brigadier-General Eaker was a passenger in an accompanying aircraft, *Yankee Doodle*. That first raid was escorted by Royal Air Force Spitfires and the target was the Rouen-Sotteville railway marshalling yards in northern France.

The Eighth Air Force went on to bomb targets in Europe by day, while RAF Bomber Command did so at night. In January 1944, a new commander of the Eighth Air Force was appointed – Lieutenant-General James H. Doolittle – and in June 1945 he took the Mighty Eighth to Okinawa to re-equip with B-29s in support of General Curtis LeMay's Twentieth Air Force. However, the bombing of Hiroshima and Nagasaki brought the war to its end before the Eighth could become operational in the Pacific.

TWELFTH US ARMY AIR FORCE

At the time that Brigadier Jimmy Doolittle was doing his nationwide recruitment tour of the US in the summer of 1942, the involvement of the US in the Second World War in North Africa and Europe was being debated by the Chiefs of Staff in Washington. In August, the first USAAF launched bombing raid over Europe took place and the involvement of US forces in the North African campaign already being fought by the British forces was under discussion. This led to the creation and planning of Operation *Torch*, the invasion of North Africa's western reaches of Tunisia and Morocco.

As early as the August raid over Europe, the decision had been made that the US would become involved in North Africa and would mount an invasion. Major-General George S. Patton was to launch the invasion on Casablanca and Brigadier-General James H. Doolittle was to head up the newly formed Twelfth Air Force. Because this extensive operation required a new organisation to provide enough manpower and equipment, Twelfth Air Force activation plans were prepared simultaneously with the invasion strategy.

On 20 August 1942, Twelfth Air Force was activated at Boiling Field in Maryland. On 23 September 1942, General Doolittle formally assumed command of Twelfth Air Force, with Colonel Hoyt S. Vandenberg as his chief of staff. Barely four months after it was conceived, Twelfth Air Force made its first contributions to the Second World War; when the North Africa invasion D-Day arrived on 8 November 1942, Twelfth Air Force, which included Royal Air Force squadrons as well as USAAF units, more than met its assigned missions.

After North Africa, Twelfth Air Force saw action in Sicily, Italy and southern France. By VE Day it had flown 430,681 sorties, dropped 217,156 tons of bombs, claimed destruction of 2857 enemy aircraft and lost 2667 of its own aircraft. Twelfth Air Force was deactivated in Florence, Italy on 31 August 1945. It was reactivated at March Field, California on 17 May 1946, and was assigned to Tactical Air Command.

Command Structure of the Northwest African Strategic Air Force 1943–1944, NASAF Organisation for Operation Husky

Commanding General Major-General James H. Doolittle

5th Bomb Wing   Brigadier-General Joseph H. Atkinson

2nd Bombardment Group (B-17)   Lieutenant-Colonel Joseph A. Thomas
20th Bombardment Squadron
49th Bombardment Squadron
96th Bombardment Squadron
429th Bombardment Squadron

MILITARY ORGANISATIONS

97th Bombardment Group (B-17)   Colonel Leroy A. Rainey

340th Bombardment Squadron
341st Bombardment Squadron
342nd Bombardment Squadron
414th Bombardment Squadron

99th Bombardment Group (B-17)   Colonel Fay R. Upthegrove

346th Bombardment Squadron
347th Bombardment Squadron
348th Bombardment Squadron
416th Bombardment Squadron

301st Bombardment Group (B-17)   Lieutenant-Colonel Samuel Gormly Jr

32nd Bombardment Squadron
352nd Bombardment Squadron
353rd Bombardment Squadron
419th Bombardment Squadron

1st Fighter Group (P-38)   Major Joseph S. Peddie

Headquarters Squadron
27th Fighter Squadron
71st Fighter Squadron
94th Fighter Squadron

14th Fighter Group (P-38)   Colonel Oliver B. Taylor

Headquarters Squadron
37th Fighter Squadron
48th Fighter Squadron
49th Fighter Squadron

55th Fighter Group (P-38)   Lieutenant-Colonel Frank B. James*

Headquarters Squadron
38th Fighter Squadron
338th Fighter Squadron
343rd Fighter Squadron

47th Bomb Wing   Brigadier-General Carlyle H. Ridenour

310th Bombardment Group (B-25)   Colonel Antony G. Hunter
379th Bombardment Squadron
380th Bombardment Squadron
381st Bombardment Squadron
425th Bombardment Squadron

321st Bombardment Group (B-25)   Colonel Robert D. Knapp

445th Bombardment Squadron
446th Bombardment Squadron
447th Bombardment Squadron
448th Bombardment Squadron

17th Bombardment Group (B-26)   Lieutenant-Colonel Charles R. Greening

34th Bombardment Squadron
37th Bombardment Squadron
95th Bombardment Squadron
432nd Bombardment Squadron

319th Bombardment Group (B-26)   Colonel Gordon H. Austin

437th Bombardment Squadron
438th Bombardment Squadron
439th Bombardment Squadron
440th Bombardment Squadron

320th Bombardment Group (B-26)   Colonel Karl Baumeister

441st Bombardment Squadron
442nd Bombardment Squadron
443rd Bombardment Squadron
444th Bombardment Squadron

82nd Fighter Group (P-38)   Colonel John W. Weltman

Headquarters Squadron
95th Fighter Squadron
96th Fighter Squadron
97th Fighter Squadron

325th Fighter Group (P-40)   Lieutenant-Colonel Robert L. Baseler

Headquarters Squadron
317th Fighter Squadron
318th Fighter Squadron
319th Fighter Squadron

No. 205 Group RAF   Acting Air Commodore John H.T. Simpson

No. 231 Wing RAF (Wellington)
No. 37 Squadron
No. 40 Squadron
No. 70 Squadron

No. 236 Wing RAF

No. 104 Squadron (Wellington)
No. 462 Squadron (Halifax)

No. 330 Wing RAF (Wellington)

No. 142 Squadron
No. 150 Squadron

No. 331 Wing RCAF (Wellington)

No. 423 Squadron
No. 424 Squadron
No. 425 Squadron

3rd Photographic Reconnaissance Group Lieutenant-Colonel Frank L. Dunn**

Headquarters Squadron
5th Photographic Reconnaissance Squadron (P-38 F-5 Mosquito PRIX)
12th Photographic Reconnaissance Squadron (P-38 F-5)
15th Photographic Mapping Squadron (B-17 F-9)

332nd Fighter Group (P-40) (Tuskegee Airmen)   Lieutenant-Colonel Benjamin O. Davis***

99th Fighter Squadron
100th Fighter Squadron
301st Fighter Squadron
302nd Fighter Squadron

* The 55th Fighter Group was training at McChord Field, Washington and scheduled to arrive in the MTO, but the group was eventually sent to England and assigned to the Eighth Air Force.

** The 3rd Photographic Reconnaissance Group was detached to NASAF for Operation Husky.

*** The 99th Fighter Squadron was the only Tuskegee Airmen unit until after the Anzio Landings when the 100th, 301st and 302nd Squadrons joined it to form the 332nd Fighter Group.

FIFTEENTH US ARMY AIR FORCE

The Fifteenth Air Force was formed on 2 November 1943, under the command of newly promoted Major-General James H. Doolittle, who had just transferred from the Twelfth Air Force. In the 18 months of its existence the Fifteenth Air Force, operating primarily from the complex of airfields in southern Italy, destroyed all fuel production within its range in southern Europe, knocked out all the major aircraft factories in its sphere and destroyed 6282 enemy aircraft. The Fifteenth crippled the enemy's transportation system over half of once-occupied Europe with repeated fighter and bomber attacks. On occasion it helped disperse enemy counter attacks and spearheaded the advances of the Allied armies.

In nine countries of Europe, the Fifteenth dropped 303,842 tons of bombs on enemy targets, including military installations in eight capital cities. Its combat personnel made

148,955 heavy bomber sorties and 87,732 fighter sorties against the enemy. It lost 3364 aircraft and 21,671 personnel killed, wounded, missing and taken prisoner – 20,430 bomber crewmen and 1187 fighter pilots.

The Fifteenth fought four broad campaigns: against enemy oil, enemy air force, enemy communications and enemy ground forces. Most vital of the Fifteenth's oil targets was the Ploesti complex of refineries, which contributed about 30 per cent of the Axis oil supply and an equal amount of petroleum spirit. Ploesti was protected by 150 fighters and 250 heavy flak guns when the Fifteenth, with the cooperation of the Royal Air Force's 205 Group of night bombers, began a series of attacks against it on 5 April. The campaign continued until 19 August. Fifteenth and RAF bombers flew 5287 sorties, dropping 12,870 tons of bombs. The cost was 237 heavy bombers (15 of them RAF), 10 P-38 dive bombers and 39 escorting fighters. More than 2200 American airmen were lost. However, by the end of the campaign the refineries were reduced to only 10 per cent of their normal rate of activity and during the entire period from April to August the average production rate was reduced by 60 per cent.

The Fifteenth followed up the Ploesti attacks by dropping 10,000 tons of bombs in attacks on three synthetic oil plants in Silesia and one in Poland, reducing their combined production by February 1945 to 20 per cent of what it was in June 1944. Through devastating attacks on Weiner Neustadt and Regensburg – two of the three main enemy fighter manufacturing complexes – the Fifteenth helped achieve European air supremacy. By May 1944, estimated actual production stood at 250 aircraft a month within range of the Fifteenth against a contemplated production of 650 aircraft per month.

During the counter-air force and oil campaigns, the Fifteenth was also attacking enemy communications and transportation systems far behind the front lines, disrupting supply movements from industrial centres over an 800 mile radius from the Italian airfields. It also supplied Allied army cooperation bombing targets at Salerno, Anzio, and Cassino in the Rome campaign. On 15 April 1945 the Fifteenth put up a record 93 per cent of its available aircraft to soften up the approaches to Bologna in one of the final missions of the Italian campaign.

A unique sideline in the Fifteenth's operations was the rescue and repatriation of air crews shot down in enemy territory; no other air force has undertaken escape operations in so many countries. The Fifteenth returned 5650 personnel by air, surface vessel and on foot through enemy lines. In more than 300 planned 'reunion' operations, men were brought back safely from Tunisia, Italy, France, Switzerland, Greece, Albania, Bulgaria, Rumania, Hungary, Yugoslavia, Austria and Germany.

TWENTIETH US ARMY AIR FORCE

On 4 April 1944, the Twentieth Air Force was created at the behest of General Henry H. Arnold, Chief of Staff of the US Army Air Force. Its objective was to bring the war in the Pacific directly to Japan. The major power of the Twentieth were huge numbers of Boeing B-29 four-engined bombers; seventeen bombardment wings, each consisting of four groups and each group consisting of four squadrons equipped with twelve to fifteen B-29s created a formidable force of almost 1000 bombers under one command, to say nothing of the massive accumulation of B-24 Liberators and other aircraft types. It was initially under the command of Arnold himself, then later General Curtis LeMay and General Nathan Twining. When the Twentieth came under the US Strategic Air Forces in the Pacific in August 1945, it was commanded by General Carl Spaatz.

From mid 1944 the Twentieth's bombers operated from bases in India and China as part of Operation *Matterhorn*, the offensive against the Japanese Home Islands. However, supply problems and the cost in terms of men and materiel meant that aircraft were relocated to the newly-captured Mariana Islands, the last raid from China taking place on 15 January 1945. The Marianas (including the islands of Saipan, Tinian and Guam) were a far better location for bombing Japanese targets, being 1500 miles from Tokyo and therefore within the range of most B-29s. The first raid against Japan from the Marianas took off from Saipan on 24 November 1944, targeting an aircraft engine factory outside Tokyo, but was not a success; 111 B-29s took off but 17 aborted due to engine problems and only 24 dropped bombs on the target, due to it be obscured by cloud. One B-29 was destroyed by a Japanese fighter and by day's end the target had been hardly damaged.

Following several more unsuccessful raids, the newly installed commander, General LeMay, changed tactics to target the smaller industries that supplied the large installations that the Twentieth had been unable to seriously damage. M69 incendiary bombs rather than high-explosive bombs were used in the hope of starting fires. LeMay also ordered that the high altitude daylight raids be replaced with low altitude night raids to limit the effect of cloud cover, and the aircraft were to attack individually to save on fuel (pilots would not be required to assemble in the air). The first raid using these tactics took place on 9/10 March on Tokyo, carried out by the 314th Bombardment Wing, and was a great success, as the individual fires created by the M69 bombs joined to start a firestorm. Other attacks on Nagoya, Osaka and Kobe in March led to the deaths of over 120,000 Japanese at the cost of only 20 B-29s. The Twentieth continued its work until August 1945, when its 509th Composite Group conducted the atomic bombings of Hiroshima and Nagasaki, bring an end to war in the Pacific.

17TH BOMBARDMENT GROUP (M)

The 95th Aero Squadron was formed on 17 August 1917 at Kelly Field, Texas, under command of First Lieutenant Fred Natcher, by transferring enlisted men from organisations already in existence. It was to take part in the First World War and its aircraft initially came under British command, as did the pilots, flying Sopwith Camels. The crest of the 17th (as the 95th became) reflects the part it played in the conflict, having seven Maltese crosses in the style of those applied to German aircraft of the time, representing the campaigns in which the units of the 17th took part: Lorraine, Ile-de-France, Champagne-Marne, Aisne-Marne, Oise-Marne, St Mihiel and Meuse-Argonne. On 5 May it was assigned to the 1st Pursuit Group, and was demobilised on 18 March 1919.

On 18 October 1927 the 17th was revived as the 17th Observation Group, but did no flying and was re-designated as the 17th Pursuit Group in 1929. Even then, it took almost two more years to do any serious flying. Then, with Boeing P-12 biplane fighters and Boeing P-26 'Peashooter' monoplane fighters, the new group was activated on 15 July 1931. By 1935, it had been re-designated again, this time as the 17th Attack Group and equipped with Northrop A-17 aircraft. The 17th Bombardment Group (Medium) was formed in 1939 and equipped with the Douglas B-18 'Bolo' medium bomber.

In February 1941, President Roosevelt ordered the build up of the US armed forces, in preparation for a likely entry in the war. At this time the 17th Bombardment Group consisted of the 34th, the 37th and the 95th Bomb Squadron with the 89th Reconnaissance Squadron attached. The 17th began intensive training with their B-18s and B-23s, and were the first Group to receive the B-25 Mitchell; by September all four bomb squadrons were equipped with B-25s. As the 17th became more

Martin B-26 Marauders over Germany during the Second World War.

A Douglas A-26 Invader over Korea.

proficient, it was called upon to provide cadres of personnel to other bomb groups and from September until November 1941, the 17th participated in the Louisiana and the Carolina manoeuvres, after which the Group was transferred to March Field, in California, arriving there on 5 December.

After the attack on Pearl Harbor the 17th was despatched to Pendleton in Oregon for coastal patrol against Japanese attacks on the West Coast. On 25th December a plane from the 95th Squadron made the first 'kill' of an enemy submarine in US waters, when it engaged and sank a Japanese submarine at the mouth of the Columbia River. In early February 1942 the Group was transferred to Columbia Army Air Field, Owens Field initially, in South Carolina. Patrol duty on the East Coast continued for a while and during these patrols, the 17th sank a German U-boat, becoming the first group to sink a submarine on both coasts. As the Doolittle Raid was being planned by commanders, a select group of 120 men flew to Eglin Field to train for what turned out to be the Doolittle Raid.

The 17th Bombardment Group (Medium) was returned to the US after the Doolittle Raid and transferred to North Africa, coming under the command of their old leader Brigadier-General James H. Doolittle. In December 1942, the 17th Bombardment Group went to Telergma in Algeria, to take part in Doolittle's North Africa campaign.

As the ground campaign advanced, with George Patton's II Corps on the west and

A Martin B-57B Canberra in the 1950s.

The last flying machine of the 17th Bombardment Wing – the mighty B-52. The world's largest strategic bomber still, after over 50 years.

Bernard Montgomery's 8th Army in the East, the Afrika Corps was driven out of Africa and across to Sicily by May 1943. The 17th Bombardment Group had been transferred to Sedrata in Algeria to strike at the Mediterranean island of Pantelleria, an important Axis airfield. The 17th continued then into the Italian campaign, striking at Anzio, for which it was awarded a Distinguished Unit Citation.

The next event of particular note was the raid on Schweinfurt in Germany, for which another Distinguished Unit Citation came its way. Added to that was the French Croix de Guerre for the 17th's part in the invasion of southern France. Part of the Mighty Eighth by July 1945, when Jimmy Doolittle took his Eighth Air Force to the Pacific, the 17th Bombardment Group did not go with him. It returned to the US on 26 November and was disbanded. In all, the 17th Group had flown 624 missions and taken part in eleven campaigns of the War.

Revived in 1952 to take part in the Korean War, the 17th Bombardment Group flew Douglas B-26 'Invaders'. After the war the Group transferred to Miho Air Base in Japan and was eventually equipped with the Martin B-57 'Canberra' twin-jet bomber. Progressing through the jet bomber era, the 17th Bombardment Wing (Heavy) was flying B-52 Bombers from Wright-Patterson Air Force Base until 1975, then transferred to Beale Air Force Base in California. It was disbanded in 1976 and then re-formed as the 17th Training Wing at Goodfellow Air Force Base in Texas, where it still operates under the control of the Air Education and Training Command.

509TH COMPOSITE GROUP

The 509th Composite Group, under the command of Lieutenant-Colonel (later Colonel) Paul W. Tibbets, consisted of a personnel complement of 1767 men and eight individual military units. Its most famous squadron was the 393rd Bombardment (VH) Squadron, which is discussed in detail below. The other 509th flying squadron was the 320th Troop Carrier Squadron (initially commanded by Major Hubert W. Konopacki, then Major Charles W Sweeney). The other six units were support units, including the Headquarters and Base Service Squadron commanded by Major George W Westcott, the 390th Air Service Group (not a 'group' in the accepted sense of the word) commanded by Lieutenant-Colonel John W Porter, the 1027th Air Materiel Squadron commanded by Major Guy Geller, the 603rd Air Engineering Squadron commanded by Captain Earl O. Casey, the 1395th Military Police Company commanded by Captain Louis Schaffer and the 1st Ordnance Squadron (Special, Aviation) commanded by Major Charles F. Begg.

We tend to forget that there was a second flying squadron in the 509th Composite Group and Colonel Tibbets regularly flew its aircraft on his flights to meetings with his commanders and colleagues at the Pentagon. The 320th operated six Douglas C-54 four-engined 'Skymaster' transports, though the aircraft inventory was actually only five, so there was clearly an exchange of two aircraft at some time. There were two 'old' C-54s, BuAer Numbers 42-72594, 42-72605 and four 'new' ones – 44-9007, 44-9009, 44-9019 and 44-9027. The aircraft were capable of not only transporting troops but also foodstuffs, medical supplies, bomb parts and even light motor vehicles. Indeed, without the facility and high level of efficiency provided by the 320th the 393rd Bomb Squadron and the 509th Composite Group itself could not have operated. The 320th was known to all as 'The Green *Hornets*', although the emblem on the sides of the aircraft showed a winged pack mule hopping from one island to another. The 320th had a manpower complement of 152. Twelve of those were pilots/co-pilots, 7 navigators, 7 flight engineers, 10 flight loadmasters and the rest were ground crew technicians and administrators/clerks.

Lieutenant-Colonel Tom Classen commanded the 393rd Bombardment Squadron when it was equipped with Boeing B-17s, ready for assignment to Europe. This shot was taken of the 'Crew of the Week' before they were told they would lose the B-17 in favour of the much bigger B-29, and would be going to the Pacific.

A 320th Troop Transport Squadron C-54 on its way in to Tinian, escorted by a B-29. The 'Green Hornets' ran flights back and forth between Tinian and Wendover while the 509th was stationed at Tinian.

The unsung, hard-worked photographic crew of the 509th Composite Group. In charge of the team was Lieutenant Jerry Ossip (front centre).

The Headquarters and Base Service Squadron provided a multiplicity of services: the documentation for air movements of men and machinery, supplies and spare parts; the base administrative services; medical and dental services; recreational services; and welfare services. It worked closely with the 1027th Air Materiel Squadron and the 390th Air Service Group. These latter two units were primarily concerned with ensuring the availability of essential maintenance components for aircraft and their installation when available. The 390th was also responsible for the maintenance and repair of all the 509th ground vehicles and aircraft ground support equipment, as well as providing all the other miscellaneous services needed for a group the size of the 509th Composite Group.

The 603rd Air Engineering Squadron was basically a machine shop facility that would make any component not available from a standard aircraft parts inventory. This was an essential service as the 509th bombers had to be modified to carry a new weapon, and the C-54s had to be prepared to carry components; while some components of the first bomb were transported on USS *Indianapolis*, the remainder travelled with the 320th. It worked closely with the 1st Ordnance Squadron, which had the task of receiving the components of the atom bombs and making them fit to install and operate.

Captain Louis Schaffer's 1395th Military Police Company was a very important part of preserving the anonymity of the 509th Composite Group and maintaining the level of security. It worked closely with William 'Bud' Uanna's special security agents, all 30 of whom blended into the 1395th without trace. The dual role of the Military Police Company was firstly to preserve basic law and order and secondly, to preserve the secrecy essential to the operation of the 509th.

When first assigned to the 509th Composite Group, the decision was taken to maintain a home base location for the 320th at Wendover Field, so the majority of its maintenance section was based there also, though clearly there had to be some support

Two members of the 603rd Air Engineering Squadron, which provided a great deal of the ordinary engineering needs of the 393rd Bombardment Squadron and the 320th Troop Carrier Squadron.

crew located at Tinian. Its own maintenance team was headed by Lieutenant Richard B. Smith, with back-up stand-in from Warrant Officer Clarke Mathison. Mathison was a seasoned technician and most probably would have been the man on the ground at Tinian. This team was responsible for all first-line maintenance. Major repair and overhaul work was carried out at Wing level under the supervision of the 313th Bomb Wing, though with the establishment of the independent 320th local maintenance facility, Lieutenant Smith was succeeded by Captain Matthew H. Canjar, the higher rank justifying the additional responsibility.

393RD BOMBARDMENT SQUADRON, 509TH BOMB WING

The formation of the 393rd Bombardment Squadron (Heavy) was authorised for activation on 28 February 1944. It was to be equipped with the Boeing B-17G four-engined bomber, and on 11 March the squadron was declared active and assigned to become one the

504th Bombardment Group's squadrons and destined for Lieutenant-General Jimmy Doolittle's Eighth Air Force – 'The Mighty Eighth' – targeting German industry.

The 504th was based at Dalhart Army Airfield in Texas and the 393rd's first commander was Lieutenant-Colonel Thomas J. Classen. The squadron worked up to operational status and was ready for transfer to England when, while it was located at Fairmont Field in Nebraska, a decision was made by General Henry Arnold to allocate that squadron to the 509th Composite Group at Wendover Field in Utah. That transfer took place on 10 September 1944 and the squadron began its relocation the same day. Arnold chose the 393rd on the basis of its bombing scores and many hours in the air; under Classen's leadership the Squadron was highly disciplined and efficient. The 700 men of the 393rd transferred en bloc to the 509th, though its B-17s were to be left behind, to be replaced by the B-29, which had been made operationally efficient by the test flight team led by Lieutenant-Colonel Paul W. Tibbets.

Colonel Tibbets was commander of the 509th Composite Group into which the 393rd Bombardment Squadron was integrated as the key unit. For this reason he decided to assume command of the 393rd in the workup stage of the B-29. Lieutenant-Colonel Classen accepted this and graciously accepted the role of Deputy Squadron Commander, though in effect he retained his previous position as Tibbets was frequently absent taking part in Manhattan Project and Pentagon meetings.

After the bombings of Hiroshima and Nagasaki, the 393rd remained at North Field on Tinian until 17 October 1945, at which point the 509th returned to the US, taking up quarters at Roswell Army Air Field (later Walker Air Force Base) in New Mexico. With its expertise with atomic bombs, the unit became the core organisation for the Strategic Air Command (SAC) on its creation on 21 March 1946. The Squadron remained at Roswell until the Army Air Force directed the 509th to Kwajalein in the Marshall Islands, for Operation *Crossroads*, a nuclear test programme.

In 1952, the 393rd converted to the Boeing B-50 and in 1955, rejoined its old parent, the 509th, though now the 509th was a bombardment wing and was the first USAF unit to receive the USAF's first all-jet bomber, the six-engined Boeing B-47 'Stratojet', which it took to Pease Air Force Base in New Hampshire in 1958. In 1965, the decision was made to retire the now ageing B-47 and the 393rd received its first B-52 in March 1966, relocating a component of the Squadron to Anderson Air Force Base on Guam in November that year. By April 1968, the whole of the 393rd was operating from Guam.

Into the modern age comes the swing-wing FB111.

The remarkable Northrop-Grumman B-2 'Spirit'.

With the end of the Vietnam conflict, the 393rd returned to Pease Air Force Base and in November 1969, relinquished its last B-52 and re-equipped with the FB-111A. For a number of years the squadron contributed significantly to the 509th winning virtually every major bomber award in the Eighth Air Force and Strategic Air Command. Then came the news of the FB-111's retirement from service.

It was to be 1993 before the 393rd Bombardment Squadron came back to life, as the unit flying the world's most advanced strategic bomber, the Northrop B-2 'Spirit' from Whiteman Air Force Base in Missouri. On 17 December 1993, the first B-2, 'Spirit of Missouri' arrived at Whiteman and the 393rd Bombardment Squadron was alive once more, as a component of the 509th Bomb Wing.

Within two short years, members of the 393rd would again prove their mettle as the unit tasted combat for the first time in almost 30 years. On 24 March 1999, the 393rd Tigers played a key role in taking the B-2 into its first combat engagement when two of the aircraft attacked targets in the Former Republic of Yugoslavia. The 393rd Tigers would participate in and support the attacks until the end of hostilities. The unit also operated over Iraq in 2003 and has proved itself a truly global operational unit. One of its recent commanders was Colonel Paul W. Tibbets IV, grandson of the man who dropped the world's first atom bomb.

Appendix 5

The Doolittle Targets

In April 2011, a cache of documents and pictures was discovered in the home of the late Commodore Stephen Jurika who sailed aboard the USS *Hornet* and briefed Lieutenant-Colonel Doolittle and the crews of his sixteen B-25s prior to the raid. In 1939 at the age of 29, the then Lieutenant Jurika had been assigned to the US Embassy in Tokyo as Naval Attaché (Air). In 1940 relations between Japan and the US were deteriorating as Japan extended its grip on China.

At this time, Japan was importing oil from the US and the Dutch East Indies (now Indonesia) but after the Rape of Nanking in 1937 foreign trade into Japan was restricted. The US began to limit oil exports, which had a negative impact on the Japanese military, and Japan became more dependent upon its imports from the Dutch East Indies, through Royal Dutch Shell.

Lieutenant Stephen Jurika,
US Naval Attache to Japan,
1939–1941.

There is a letter which Jurika wrote to Colonel Harry Locke Smith USMC, his father-in-law (overleaf). Smith was commander of the Marine Barracks at Portsmouth Navy Yard at the time, and went on to command the Recruit Depot at Parris Island, in South Carolina during the war. In the letter Jurika detailed how the families of western businessmen and military personnel, including certain female embassy staff, were being shipped home for their own safety as war with Japan became more likely.

While at the US Embassy, Jurika was charged with the task of discreetly travelling through Japan and identifying potential military targets, such as armament and engineering factories, aircraft manufacturing plants, shipyards, oil refineries and storage areas, military arsenals, airfields and navy dockyards. He used his connections at Shell Oil to discover the levels of petroleum spirit being delivered to the Japanese Armed Forces and discovered that by 1940, their consumption had increased hugely. Over a period of almost two years, Jurika went unnoticed, carrying out his surreptitious activities.

Colonel Harry Locke Smith USMC, with his daughter, Lillian Jurika.

> **AMERICAN EMBASSY**
> OFFICE OF THE NAVAL ATTACHÉ
> TOKYO
>
> Sunday, 27 October, 1940.
>
> Dear Colonel,
>
> Thought I'd write and give you the latest news from out our way. Also more definite news on Lil's and Pat's trip.
>
> Today, a cable came in from the State Department telling all wives to get out. Now, the first cable only authorized the transportation of wives but did'nt require them to leave. This latest piece of news means business, so I changed Lil's booking from the President Cleveland on 12 December to the President Taft on November 24th. That is the best I could do, as I don't want her to go on a refugee ship, which may have an epidemic of Chinese diseases break out on the voyage. So, instead of arriving after Christmas, Lil will be home long before. I have reservations with United Air Lines for them to fly from San Francisco to Boston, as I think fifteen hours by air is better than four days and four nights on a train. Lil will keep you informed of her movements, and I shall call you on the 'phone from time to time and keep you posted from this end.
>
> All our furniture, silver etc is packed and ready for shipment on the Tawata Maru, sailing on 13 Novemebr. We shall both breathe more freely when the possessions are out of the country. We have spent a mint of money and hard work acquiring our small belongings and would hate to see them be lost out here. The house has a bare, barnish air about it, but we don't care.

The detail to which Jurika went was amazing. He not only located potential targets, he also noted the surrounding landscape and plotted approach directions into those targets and the best departure points to minimise the risk of attack and aircraft being shot down by Japanese defenders. He could not possibly have known the real significance of his efforts, or the path that information would take him along.

THE DOOLITTLE TARGETS

When the Doolittle Raid went into the planning stage after Pearl Harbor, Jurika was brought in by Captain Donald Duncan, Admiral King's Air Adviser. He worked with fellow US Navy Lieutenant Henry Miller, who was to train Doolittle and his pilots to get a B-25 bomber off a carrier deck. Duncan's objective was to make use of the information Jurika had gathered over a year before, so as maximise target strikes and minimise the risk of aircraft damage or loss.

We still have the wicker furniture on the sun porch, and have borrowed a double bed to sleep in. We're giving a " barn dance" party next week, to which all guests will bring their own settees, chairs etc. The radio still blares American music, and the kitchen is fully equipped as we don't care much about the Japanese utensils. I sold our GE refrigerator, camera, small radio, am selling the Buick, some old clothes and all the odds and ends we don't care to cart about with us.

Tokyo is really a city of the living dead; so different from last year! Most of the American and British women and some of the men have gone, and now everyone else is packing or about to pack. We still go to impromptu parties in our falling down clothes, no more white tie and black tie affairs. I was over at the Japanese Navy Club for lunch on Saturday-- probably our last visit to the beautiful spot. The Japanese Navy does not want to tangle horns with us or the British but the dammed Army is running this country and a more ignorant, provincial outfit you have never seen or heard. I also attended an Imperial Review of the Navy (without permission) and another Army Review by request. About fifty thousand troops on one huge parade ground, with their latest mechanized equipment, AA guns, big guns and lots of tanks, tractors etc. It failed to impress any of us as some of the latest equipment broke down directly before the Emperor while passing in review. The review lasted from 8;30 in the morning to after midday-- simply collossal.

Since this is going in the diplomatic pouch, I shall tell you abit of what I've been doing. For the past four months I've been drawing up bombing maps of Japan, by main manufacturing

> districts, a job which has never been done in this office. Also plans for bombing Tokyo, its powder factories, munitions factories, government buildings; collecting and evaluating information on Jap bases in South China, Indo China, the South Seas, and getting down to business on every phase of the possible war. As a result, the Naval Attache has requested that I be sent, for War station, to the staff of Commander Aircraft, Battle Force as an assistant operations officer. I don't know what will come of the matter but am not inclined to worry. Still plenty of work to do here, and I hope we get another two months grace.
>
> Your selection board met on October 15th, and we are awaiting telegraphic news (via the Fourth Marines in Shanghai) of your selection. We know you will make the grade and are not losing any sleep over the problem, even though you may be. You tell Momie for me that I don't want to hear her yell, " March 'em around again, Harry! " when you receive those stars in place of the eagles.
>
> Both Lil and Pat are the picture of health, and you will be very much surprised at Pat's size. She is the image of Lil, with the cutest way of " nice nicing" (caressing) your face. She talks all day long, mostly Japanese, but says " Good Night Baby and Goodbye , along with a few other expressions in English. She's a regular mimic, repeating everything she hears. One thing I'd better tell you. When she says " Sampo," she means she wants to go for a walk, even if its just around the room. She must take after Momie, for she wants to walk ALL THE TIME.
>
> Must stop and get back to work, Colonel, so with best regards to you both,   *Yours, Steve*

Many Raiders have told interviewers that they were given a choice of targets before they took off from the *Hornet* – and they may have been. But the targets they chose were pre-selected by Lieutenant Stephen Jurika and then by Lieutenant-Colonel Jimmy Doolittle. It is certain that each crew would have been briefed on their individual target, the approach direction they would take and the escape route. That each aircraft escaped is testament to the care and detailed attention given to his task by Lieutenant Jurika, to say nothing of the quality of information he gathered while he was located in Japan.

After the Second World War was over, Stephen Jurika remained in the US Navy and, over the fifteen years that followed the Doolittle Raid, was appointed to a number of diplomatic and command appointments, retiring in the rank of Commodore. In 1957 he completed a master's degree at George Washington University and then became a professor of naval science at Stanford University. He also was appointed Commander of that University's Navy ROTC unit. Within five more years, he had secured doctoral degrees in both political science and geography from Stanford. He also served as vice president of the Missiles Division at the Lockheed Missiles and Space Company. In later years he was appointed a professor at Santa Clara University and the Naval Postgraduate School in Monterey, California. He died at the age of 82 in 1993.

Appendix 6

The Doolittle Raiders

The following are brief histories of the men who flew the 16 B-25s of the Doolittle Raid, listed by crew. The aircraft are presented in the order they took off from the USS *Hornet*, under the number allocated by the Bureau of Aeronautics, a unit of the Department of Defense which orders all military aircraft for all three (or four) armed services of the US. The 'BuAer' number is allocated at the order stage for new aircraft and consists of two elements – the prefix is the last two digits of the year of order and the second set of the digits is the sequential number, i.e. '40-2344' was the 2344th aircraft ordered in 1940. 40-2344 was, in fact, the oldest B-25 of the 16 taken on the Doolittle Raid. This original aircraft was replicated by North American Aviation, the original manufacturer of the B-25, after the Second World War, and presented to the US Air Force Museum, where it is still on display today.

B-25 40-2344 (37TH BOMBARDMENT SQUADRON)

This aircraft was piloted by Jimmy Doolittle himself, with his co-pilot Lieutenant Richard E. Cole. Dick Cole was born on 7 September in 1915 and enlisted in the Army Air Corps on 22 November 1940. He was commissioned as a second lieutenant pilot in July 1941. He remained in the China-Burma-India Theatre after the Raid until June 1943, and served there again from October, 1943 until June 1944. Captain Cole was relieved from active duty in January 1947, but returned in August that same year. He was Operations Advisor to the Venezuelan Air Force from 1959 to 1962. He saw peacetime service in Ohio, North Carolina and California. He was rated as a command pilot, retiring as a Colonel in 1962.

Navigator Lieutenant Henry A. 'Hank' Potter completed navigator training and was commissioned as a second lieutenant in June 1941. He served in the US after the Raid in Michigan, Colorado, Washington DC, Florida and California. He served overseas in Germany from 1954 to 1958. He was rated a master navigator and retired in the rank of Colonel.

Bombardier Staff Sergeant Fred Braemer enlisted at the age of just seventeen years and eight months, attending Military Intelligence, Bombardier and Navigator Schools. He was released from active duty as an officer on 1 November 1945 and re-entered service in enlisted status during the Korean War, retiring as a Captain in 1968.

Staff Sergeant Paul Leonard, the engineer/gunner, was born in Roswell, New Mexico. He enlisted in the Army in 1931 and was trained as an aircraft mechanic, joining the 37th Bombardment Squadron in May 1941. He was killed in action by enemy aircraft at Youks-Les-Bains in Algeria on 5 January 1943.

B-25 40-2292 (34TH BOMBARDMENT SQUADRON)

The pilot Lieutenant Travis Hoover came from Melrose, New Mexico and enlisted in the California National Guard in November 1938, transferring to the US Army in August 1939. He completed pilot training and was commissioned as a second lieutenant in May 1940. He remained in the China-Burma-India Theatre after the Raid until June 1942. He served as a bomber pilot in England, North Africa and Italy from July 1942 until September 1944. Peacetime overseas service was on Okinawa. US home assignments included Washington DC, Texas, California, Mississippi and Kansas. He was rated as a command pilot and retired in the rank of Colonel.

Co-pilot Lieutenant William N. Fitzhugh, came from Temple, Texas. He joined the Army in November 1940 and completed advanced flying training in July 1941 at Stockton Field in California. After the raid he remained in the China-Burma-India Theatre until June 1943. He served as a test pilot and maintenance officer at Brookley Field, Alabama until release from active duty in July 1946 as a major.

Navigator Lieutenant Carl Wildner, was born in Holyoke, Massachusetts and was commissioned into the Cavalry Reserve in June 1937, entering the regular service as a flight cadet in November 1940, being rated as a navigator in July 1941. After the raid he remained in India until July 1943. He returned to the US and served at various bases as a navigation instructor. In 1946 he was assigned to Alaska and subsequently served in Newfoundland and Germany. He retired from active duty in 1954, then from the Air Force Reserve in 1962 as a Colonel.

Bombardier Lieutenant Richard Miller came from Fort Wayne, Indiana and enlisted in February 1939 but was eliminated from pilot training in April that year. In May 1941 he re-enlisted, was rated as a bombardier and commissioned as a second lieutenant in December 1941. Captain Miller died from wounds received in the air over North Africa on 22 January 1943.

Staff Sergeant Douglas Radney (engineer-gunner) was born in Mineola, Minnesota. He enlisted in the Army in January 1936 as an aircraft mechanic. He was commissioned in 1945 and subsequently completed pilot training. He served overseas in Alaska as a cold weather test pilot and maintenance officer. He retired in May 1959 as a senior pilot in the rank of Major.

B-25 40-2270 *WHISKEY PETE* (95TH BOMBARDMENT SQUADRON)

Pilot Lieutenant Robert M. Gray enlisted as a flying cadet in June 1940 at Dallas, Texas. He graduated with rating of Pilot and was commissioned as second lieutenant at Kelly Field, Texas in February 1941. He was assigned to the 34th Bomb Squadron and then 95th Bomb Squadron of 17th Bomb Group at McChord Field, Washington. He remained in the China-Burma-India Theatre after the raid. He was killed in action on 18 October 1942 while on a combat mission near Assam India. Gray Air Force Base in Texas is named in his honour.

Co-Pilot Lieutenant Jacob E. Manch was appointed second lieutenant in the Infantry Reserve in May 1940. He enlisted as a flying cadet in February 1941 and graduated from the Advanced Flying School, Stockton, California, with rating as pilot in September, 1941. He was assigned to 17th Bomb Group at Pendleton Field, Oregon. He remained in China-Burma-India Theatre after the raid until June 1943. He was assigned to US bases in California, Utah and New Jersey during the rest of the war. He served in Japan and Korea as Air Liaison Officer with 7th US Infantry Division during the Korean War. He returned to the US in September 1953 and was stationed at Nellis Air Force Base,

Nevada. He was killed in a bail out of a T-33 aircraft near Las Vegas, Nevada on 24 March 1958.

Navigator Lieutenant Charles J. Ozuk enlisted in November 1939 at Chanute Field, Illinois. He attended Radio and Mechanics School at Chanute Field before pilot training. He was eliminated from pilot training in June 1940, but then accepted for navigation training in November 1940 and graduated with rating of navigator and commissioned as second lieutenant at McChord Field, Washington in June 1941. He remained in China-Burma-India Theatre after the raid until July 1942. He subsequently served in North Africa until April 1945, when he was relieved from active duty.

Bombardier Sergeant Aden E. Jones joined the Army Air Corps in September 1939 at Fort MacArthur, California. He was stationed at March and McChord Fields with the 95th Bomb Squadron. He remained in China-Burma-India Theatre after the raid until July 1943. He graduated as bombardier. He held various US home assignments at bases in South Carolina, Louisiana and California. He served briefly in Japan after the war and was discharged in December 1948.

Engineer Gunner Corporal Leland D. Faktor enlisted at Fort Des Moines, Iowa in August 1940. He completed Airplane Mechanic's School at Chanute Field, Illinois in April 1941. He was then assigned to the 95th Bomb Squadron, 17th Bomb Group at McChord Field, Washington. He died at Sui-chang, Chekiang Province in China on bail-out from the aircraft after the raid, when his parachute harness was caught in the escape hatch. He was interred at Wan Tsuen in China.

B-25 40-2282 (95TH BOMBARDMENT SQUADRON)

The pilot Lieutenant Everett 'Brick' Holstrom came from Cottage Grove, Oregon and graduated from flight school at Kelly Field in Texas in 1941. He went on to reach the rank of Brigadier-General and had the distinction of flying every multi-engined jet type in the Strategic Air Command inventory before his retirement in 1969.

Co-pilot Lieutenant Lucien Youngblood came from Pampa, Texas. He graduated from advanced flight school at Stockton Field, California in July 1941. Major Youngblood was killed in a flying accident over the Serranias Delburro Mountains, Mexico on 28 February 1949.

Lieutenant Harry McCool from La Junta, Colorado was the navigator. He entered military service in March 1940 at Oklahoma City. He completed navigator training and was commissioned as a second lieutenant in June 1941. After the raid he served in the European Theatre of Operations as a B-26 and B-17 navigator from August 1942 until April 1945. He later served overseas in North Africa with Strategic Air Command. He was also rated as a bombardier and served as an Intelligence Officer, retiring in the rank of Lieutenant-Colonel.

Bombardier Sergeant Robert Stephens was born in Hobart, Oklahoma and entered military service as a private in November 1939 at Fort Riley, Kansas. He completed Bombardier School in June 1940 and Mechanics School in February 1941. He remained in the China-Burma-India Theatre after the raid as a bombardier until July 1943. He served in various US home assignments for the remainder of his service. He was commissioned as a Flight Officer in February 1944 and was then rated as Aircraft Observer. He retired through physical disability in December 1944 and died on 13 April 1959.

The gunner was Corporal Bert Jordan, who entered the Army Air Corps in November 1939. He completed the aircraft and engine mechanic's course in April 1941 and was rated as engineer-gunner in February 1942. After the raid he returned to the China-Burma-India Theatre in 1943 and in 1945 served in Asiatic Pacific Theatre. After the war he served overseas in Germany, England, Japan, Guam and Canada as an aircraft maintenance technician. He served in the Korean War and in Vietnam and ended his service as a Chief Master Sergeant.

B-25 40-2283 (95TH BOMBARDMENT SQUADRON)

The pilot was Captain David M. Jones from Marshfield, Oregon. He enlisted in the National Guard in June 1932 and served on active duty as a second lieutenant with the 8th Cavalry for a year before entering pilot training in June 1937. He gained his rating as pilot in June 1938 and served with the 17th Bomb Group at March and McChord Fields. After the raid he served in North Africa with the 17th Bombardment Group, and was shot down over Bizerte on 4 December 1942. He spent two and a half years as a prisoner of war in Stalag Luft III. After the war he was based in Louisiana, Virginia, North Carolina, Texas and Ohio. He served overseas as 47th Bomb Wing Commander in Sculthorpe, England. He retired in the rank of Major-General.

Co-pilot Lieutenant Rodney 'Hoss' Wilder came from Taylor in Texas. He entered military service in November 1940 as a flying cadet. He graduated from flying training and was commissioned as a second lieutenant in May 1941. He was the co-pilot on the B-25 that sighted and sank a Japanese submarine on 24 December 1941 at the mouth of the Columbia River. After the raid, he served as a Bombardment Squadron Commander in England, North Africa, Italy and Corsica. He returned to the US in May 1944 and served as base commander at bases in Texas and Oklahoma. He reverted to inactive status in June 1947 and retired as Regional Director of General Services Administration.

Navigator Lieutenant Eugene McGurl came from Belmont, Massachusetts. He completed navigation training and was commissioned as a second lieutenant in December 1941. He remained in the China-Burma-India Theatre after the raid and was killed in action on 3 June 1942 when his plane crashed into a mountain after bombing Lashio, Burma en route to Kunming, China.

Lieutenant Denver Truelove was the bombardier and came from Clermont, Georgia. He entered military service in May 1940 at Atlanta, Georgia. He completed bombardier and navigator training in April 1941. After the raid he served in North Africa. He went on to fly with the 428th Bombardment Squadron in Italy and was killed in action on 5 April 1943.

Sergeant Joseph Manske was the engineer/gunner. He entered service in September 1939 at Chanute Field, Illinois. He completed the aircraft mechanics course. After the raid, he attended OCS and was commissioned a second lieutenant in December 1942. He served in Africa and Italy as an Aircraft Maintenance Officer from October 1943 to August 1945. He was relieved from active duty in April 1946. He was recalled to active duty as Special Assistant for National Guard Affairs in March 1957 and retired in the rank of Colonel.

B-25 40-2298 *GREEN HORNET* (95TH BOMBARDMENT SQUADRON)

Pilot Lieutenant Dean Hallmark was born in Robert Lee, Texas. He completed advanced pilot training in July 1941 at Stockton Field, California, and joined the 95th at Pendleton Field in Oregon. He was captured by the Japanese and executed on 15 October 1942 at Kiangwan Prison, Shanghai, China.

Co-pilot Robert Meder came from Cleveland, Ohio. He joined the 95th Squadron on completion of flight training in July 1941, also graduating from Stockton Field in California. He entered the service in November 1940 at Fort Hayes, Ohio. After training, he was assigned to the 95th Bomb Squadron. He was captured after the raid and was a prisoner of war from April 1942 until his death from beri-beri and dysentery on 1 December 1943.

The navigator was Lieutenant Chase Nielsen from Hyrum, Utah. He enlisted as a flying cadet at Fort Douglas, Utah in August 1939. He was commissioned and rated navigator in June 1941. He later earned ratings as Senior Aircraft Observer and Master Navigator. He was captured after the raid and held from April 1942 until August 1945. Captain Nielsen was the only Raider who returned to testify at the Japanese War Crimes Trials. He remained in the service with various units of Strategic Air Command until his retirement in November 1961 in the rank of Colonel. He was the only survivor of the crew, giving Green Hornet the highest casualty rate of all the raid aircraft.

Sergeant William J. Dieter, the Bombardier, was born in Vail, Iowa. He enlisted in October 1936 at Vancouver Barracks, Washington. He graduated from Coast Artillery Motor School, Fort Lewis, Washington in 1938. Then he re-enlisted in December 1940 and was assigned to the 95th Bombardment Squadron at McChord Field, Washington. He drowned offshore from China when his aircraft ditched in crash landing after the Doolittle Raid. He was interred by local Chinese at Shatow, China.

Corporal Donald Fitzmaurice was from Lincoln, Nebraska. He enlisted in August 1940 at Chanute Field, Illinois and attended the Airplane Mechanic's School there. He graduated in March 1941 and was assigned to the 95th Bomb Squadron. Corporal Fitzmaurice also drowned when Lieutenant Hallmark ditched the bomber in the ocean just off the coast of China. He too was interred by the Chinese at Shatow, China.

B-25 40-2261 *RUPTURED DUCK* (95TH BOMBARDMENT SQUADRON)

The pilot was Lieutenant Ted W. Lawson. Lawson joined the Army Air Corps in March 1940 and received his wings and commission in November that year, graduating from Stockton Field, California. He was seriously injured and had a leg amputated as the result of crash landing after the raid. He was the author of *30 Seconds Over Tokyo* which was the story of his crew. After leaving hospital he served as Liaison Officer at the US Air Mission in Santiago from May 1943 until April 1944. He was retired due to physical disability on 2 February 1945.

The co-pilot was Lieutenant Dean Davenport, who enlisted as a flying cadet in February 1941. He graduated from Advanced Flying School at Stockton Field in California, and was commissioned as a second lieutenant in September 1941. He returned from India in October 1942. He was the technical advisor for the film *Thirty Seconds Over Tokyo*, based on Ted Lawson's book. He served in Alaska flying P-40, P-38 and P-51 aircraft from 1944 until 1947. He was commanding officer of several fighter units and also commanded an Air Defense Command unit flying F-106 interceptors. He served in Korea and flew 86 combat missions. He retired in the rank of Colonel.

Lieutenant Charles L McClure was the navigator. He enlisted as a flying cadet in October 1940 at Jefferson Barracks, Missouri. He graduated from navigator training and was commissioned as a second lieutenant in December 1941. He was injured during the Doolittle Raid was was hospitalised until June 1943. He was then assigned duties as a navigator instructor but was again hospitalised from February to June 1945. He retired due to physical disability in June 1945 in the rank of Captain.

The bombardier was Lieutenant Robert L. Clever. He enlisted as an aviation cadet at Vancouver Barracks, Washington in March 1941. He was commissioned as a second lieutenant with rating of bombardier in December 1941 at Pendleton Field, Oregon. He was injured during the Doolittle Raid. He was stationed at Baer Field, Fort Wayne, Indiana when he was killed in an airplane crash near Versailles, Ohio on 20 November 1942.

Engineer/gunner David Thatcher enlisted in military service in December 1940. He completed Airplane and Engine Mechanic Course at Lincoln, Nebraska in December 1941. After the raid he served in England and Africa until January 1944. He was discharged from active duty in July 1945 after a home-based assignment in California. He received the Silver Star for his courageous support of his wounded crewmates, although Ted Lawson had actually recommended him for the Distinguished Service Cross.

B-25 40-2242 (95TH BOMBARDMENT SQUADRON)

Pilot Captain Edward 'Ski' York enlisted in the US Army (Infantry) in July 1930. He served at several locations before winning an appointment to the US Military Academy. He was commissioned as a second lieutenant upon graduation and was assigned to pilot training at Randolph and Kelly Fields where he received his wings in August 1939. He and his crew were interned in Russia after the raid for thirteen months. Shortly after returning to the US in 1943 he was reassigned to a B-17 unit in Italy. Following the Second World War he was sent to Warsaw as Air Attaché, and after returning to the US in 1947 he was assigned as Commandant of Air Force Officer Candidate School. He later served in Korea and Vietnam. He graduated from the Air War College and spent time at the Pentagon before becoming Chief of Staff of USAF Security Service, San Antonio, Texas. He retired in 1968 in the rank of Colonel.

The co-pilot was Robert Emmens from Medford, Oregon. He graduated from Flying Training School with a rating of pilot in February 1938 and was assigned to the 17th Bomb Group at March Field, California. He joined the Tokyo mission just before boarding the *Hornet* without training at Eglin. Before retiring in 1965, in the rank of Colonel, he served in Europe and Japan on intelligence assignments.

The navigator Lieutenant Nolan Herndon was from Columbia, South Carolina. He entered the service on 27 July 1940 at Dallas, Texas. Graduating from navigator training and being commissioned as a second lieutenant in June 1941, he then completed bombardier training. He was interned in Russia after the raid for thirteen months and returned to the US in May 1943. He held various US assignments until the end of the war, then retired from active duty in the rank of Major in November 1945.

Bombardier Staff Sergeant Theodore Laban came from Kenosha, Wisconsin. He entered military service in October 1935. He completed aircraft maintenance courses on B-25, B-26, and B-29 aircraft. After his release from Russia he served overseas in England, the Philippines and Guam. He retired as a Master Sergeant in November 1956. After retirement, he earned a Bachelor of Science degree in electrical engineering and worked as a research engineer.

Engineer/Gunner Sergeant David Pohl, from Boston, Massachusetts, entered military service in January 1940. He was the youngest of the 80 Doolittle Raiders. After release from Russia he completed pilot training in August 1945 and subsequently served with Training Command and Caribbean Defense Command in the Panama, Canal Zone. He left the service in December 1947as a First Lieutenant. He received a Bachelor of Science degree in 1951 in business administration from Babson Institute, Boston, Massachusetts.

B-25 40-2303 *WHIRLING DERVISH* (34TH BOMBARDMENT SQUADRON)

Lieutenant Harold F. Watson was the pilot of this aircraft. He entered military service in August 1940. He completed flying training and was commissioned as a second lieutenant in September 1940. He was severely injured in bail-out and was a patient in Walter Reed Hospital, Washington DC until July 1944. He remained in service after the war and served at bases in Colorado, Washington, Alabama, Georgia, Louisiana, Oklahoma and California. He served in Japan from May 1954 until October 1955. He retired as a lieutenant-colonel in October 1961.

Lieutenant James Parker from Houston, Texas, was the co-pilot. He enlisted at Houston in November 1940 and graduated from Advanced Flying School as a pilot in July 1941. After the raid he served in North Africa as a pilot of light bombardment aircraft. He subsequently served in Europe in the Army of Occupation. He left the service as Major Parker in June 1947.

Lieutenant Tom Griffin, from Green Bay, Wisconsin, was the navigator. He entered the service in July 1939 as second lieutenant, Coast Artillery, but requested relief from active duty in 1940 to enlist as a flying cadet. He was rated as a navigator and re-commissioned on 1 July 1940. After the raid, he served as a navigator in North Africa with the 17th Bombardment Group, until he was shot down and captured by the Germans in July 1943. He remained a prisoner of war until his release in April 1945. He left the service in the rank of Major.

Sergeant Wayne Bissell from Walker, Minnesota was the bombardier. He enlisted in the Army in September 1939 and completed bombardier training. After the Doolittle Raid he returned home to take pilot training and earn his wings and a commission in 1943. He served as a B-25 pilot in Southwest Pacific. He left eh service in July 1945.

Staff Sergeant Eldred Scott from Atlanta, Georgia, enlisted in the Infantry in September 1924. He transferred to the US Army Air Corps and graduated from Mechanics School. After the raid he served in England and France from February 1944 until February 1945.

B-25 40-2250 (89TH RECONNAISSANCE SQUADRON)

The pilot was Lieutenant Richard Joyce, who entered the service in July 1940 and received his pilot wings and commission at Kelly Field, Texas in March 1941. He was then assigned to the 89th Reconnaissance Squadron at McChord Field, Washington. He remained in China-Burma-India Theatre until December 1942. He held various US home assignments until relieved from active duty in the rank of Lieutenant-Colonel in March 1946.

Co-pilot was Lieutenant Royden Stork from Frost, Minnesota. He entered military service in November 1940. He graduated from Advanced Flying Training in April 1941 at Stockton Field, California. He remained in India after the raid for 16 months, piloting B-24s. After his return to the US he was assigned to Foreign Equipment Evaluation duties and then as a ferry pilot for Air Transport Command. He was released from active duty in January 1946, then became a make-up artist in Hollywood.

The navigator/bombardier was Lieutenant Horace 'Sally' Crouch from Columbia, South Carolina. He first served in South Carolina National Guard from 1937 until 1940. He accepted a commission as second lieutenant in July 1940, then attended bombardier, navigator and radar training to become 'Triple Rated'. He remained in the China-Burma-India Theatre after the raid until June 1943. After the war he served three tours in the Pacific and one tour each in England, North Africa and Germany. He retired as a lieutenant-colonel in April 1962. He then taught mathematics at Columbia High School in South Carolina.

Engineer/gunner Sergeant George E. Larkin Jr came from New Haven, Kentucky and entered military service on 27 November 1939 at Fort Knox, Kentucky. He graduated from Airplane Mechanic's School and was assigned to 89th Reconnaissance Squadron, McChord Field, Washington. He remained in the China-Burma-India Theatre after the raid and was killed on 18 October 1942 in airplane crash near Assam, India while assigned to 11th Bomb Squadron on detached service with the 26th Fighter Squadron.

Gunner Staff Sergeant Edwin 'Ted' Horton was born in North Eastham, Massachusetts. He entered the service in September 1935 at Providence, Rhode Island. He served overseas with Field Artillery at Schofield Barracks, Hawaii from 1935 to 1938 before re-enlisting and serving with the 95th Bomb Squadron at March Field, California. He completed Gun Turret-Maintenance School, Aircraft Armorer and Aircraft Mechanics Schools. He remained in China-Burma-India Theatre after the raid until July 1943. He held various US home assignments in Oklahoma and Florida and served overseas at Wheelus Field, Tripoli, Libya and retired from the service as a Master Sergeant in 1960.

B-25 40-2249 *HARI-KARI-ER* (89TH RECONNAISSANCE SQUADRON)

The pilot was Captain C. Ross Greening, from Carroll, Iowa. He entered military service in June 1936 at Fort Lewis, Washington and graduated from Advanced Flying School at Kelly Field, Texas in June 1937. He served at bases in Louisiana and California before joining the 17th Bomb Group at Pendleton, Oregon in June 1940. After the raid he was assigned to the B-26-equipped 17th Bombardment Group in North Africa and was shot down in July 1943 during a raid on Naples. He was captured by the Germans but escaped after two months. After evading capture for six months he was recaptured and spent the rest of the war in Stalag Luft I at Barth, Germany. After the war he had US assignments until 1955 at which time he was assigned for a brief period as Air Attaché to Australia and New Zealand. He died on 29 March 1957 at Walter Reed Hospital, Washington DC.

Co-pilot Lieutenant Kenneth Reddy was from Bowie, Texas. He enlisted as a flying cadet at Fort Worth, Texas in November 1940. He was rated as pilot and commissioned as a second lieutenant in July 1941. He returned to the US after the raid in June 1942. He was killed in an aircraft accident near Little Rock, Arkansas on 3 September 1942.

Lieutenant Frank Kappeler, from San Francisco, California, was the navigator. He transferred to aviation cadet training in December 1939 and was commissioned a second lieutenant in June 1941 at McChord Field, Washington with a rating as navigator. He later received training as a bombardier. He remained in China-Burma-India Theatre after the raid until August 1942. He served in the European Theatre of Operations from November 1943 until June 1945. His US assignments after the war included bases in Texas, Ohio and California before returning overseas to Japan where he served from May 1951 until February 1952. He was Deputy Commander of the Minuteman Site Activation Task Force at Minot Air Force Base in North Dakota. He retired in the rank of Lieutenant-Colonel.

Staff Sergeant William L. Birch from Galexico, California was the bombardier. He entered the service in September 1939 at March Field, California. He graduated from Bombsight Maintenance School at Lowry Field in Colorado. After the raid he attended Pilot Training School and graduated from Advanced Flying School, Lubbock, Texas in June 1943. He was commissioned as second lieutenant. He left the service after various US assignments on 7 December 1945.

Sergeant Melvin Gardner from Mesa, Arizona was the engineer/gunner. He enlisted in the service at Fort Bliss, Texas on 5 October 1939. He attended the airplane mechanic's course at Chanute Field, Illinois and was assigned to the 34th Bomb Squadron at March Field, California. He remained in China-Burma-India Theatre after the raid. He was killed in action on 2 June 1942 while en route to Kunming, China after a bombing mission on Lashio, Burma.

B-25 40-2278 *FICKLE FINGER* (37TH BOMBARDMENT SQUADRON)

The pilot was Lieutenant Bill Bower from Ravenna, Ohio. He was commissioned in October 1940 and rated as pilot. After the raid he served in England with Eighth Air Force bomber units from September 1942 until September 1945. He was a graduate of Air Command and Staff College. He had post-war assignments in California, Washington DC, Colorado and Georgia as well as Newfoundland. He retired as a Colonel in 1966.

Co-pilot was Lieutenant Thadd Blanton from Archer City in Texas. He entered the service in November 1940 at Dallas, Texas. He completed flight training in July 1941. He remained in China-Burma-India Theatre after the raid until July 1943. He was stationed in Alaska, the British West Indies and the Philippines after the war. He retired due to physical disability in November 1960 as a lieutenant-colonel. He died in Orlando, Florida on 27 September 1961.

The navigator was Lieutenant William Pound Jr from Milford, Utah. He joined the service in May 1940 at March Field, California and was commissioned and rated as navigator in June 1941. After the raid he flew 50 missions in the European Theatre of Operations between September 1942 and March 1944. He was released from active duty in August 1948 in the rank of lieutenant-colonel.

Technical Sergeant Waldo Bither was the bombardier and came from Houlton, Maine. He enlisted in January 1925 and served in the Coast Artillery in the Philippines from 1925 until 1928. He enlisted in the Army Air Corps and completed armourer and bombardier-navigator training. After the raid he was commissioned and served as an Aircraft Maintenance Officer in Europe and Japan, in addition to home service in the US. He retired in January 1954 as a major with over 28 years of service and was later employed by the General Services Administration.

Staff Sergeant Omer Duquette, from West Warwick, Rhode Island made up the crew as engineer/gunner. He enlisted in February 1938 at Providence, Rhode Island and served at Fort Slocum, New York and Albrook Field, Canal Zone before joining the 37th Bomb Squadron at Pendleton. He remained in the China-Burma-India Theatre after the raid and was killed on 3 June 1942 when his plane crashed into a mountain after bombing Lashio, Burma while en route to Kunming, China.

B-25 40-2247 *THE AVENGER* (37TH BOMBARDMENT SQUADRON)

The pilot was Lieutenant Edgar McElroy, who entered military service in November 1940. He completed pilot training and was commissioned as a second lieutenant in July 1941. He remained in China-Burma-India Command after the raid until June 1943. He subsequently served in many operational assignments at squadron, group and wing level. He was rated as a command pilot and his post-war service locations included Japan, Korea, the Mariana Islands, England, Germany and Laos. He retired in June 1962 as a lieutenant-colonel.

The co-pilot was Lieutenant Richard Knobloch, from Milwaukee, Wisconsin. Entering military service in November 1940 at Randolph Field, Texas, he graduated from pilot training and was commissioned as a second lieutenant in July 1941. After the raid he remained in China-Burma-India Theatre and completed more than 60 bombing missions before returning to the US in 1943. After various assignments he reported to England for duty with the RAF. He served as deputy commander of a Tactical Reconnaissance Wing, then as Air Attaché to Italy, deputy commander, AF Personnel Centre and Wing Commander, and Commander of Andrews Air Force Base in Maryland. He was a graduate of the Industrial College of the Armed Forces. He retired as a brigadier-general in 1970.

The navigator was Lieutenant Clayton Campbell who was born in St Manes, Idaho. He joined the service in June 1940 at Fort Wright, Washington. He was commissioned and rated as navigator in June 1941. He remained in China-Burma-India Theatre after the raid and flew 250 combat hours. He was released from active duty in the rank of lieutenant-colonel in December 1945.

The bombardier was Sergeant Robert Bourgeois from Lecomte, Louisiana. He entered the service in October 1939 at New Orleans. He graduated from Bombsight Maintenance School at Lowry Field in Colorado. He remained in China-Burma-India Theatre after the Doolittle Raid until July 1943. He left active duty as a Flight Officer in March 1946.

The engineer/gunner was Sergeant Adam Williams from Gastonia, North Carolina. He enlisted in September 1938 at Charlotte, North Carolina and served with Field Artillery before transferring to the Army Air Corps in 1939. He was assigned to the 37th Bomb Squadron at Barksdale Field, Louisiana. After the raid he remained in China-Burma-India Theatre until June 1943. He was discharged in the rank of Master Sergeant in July 1945.

B-25 40-2297 (89TH RECONNAISSANCE SQUADRON)

The pilot was Major John A. Hilger, from Sherman, Texas. He was commissioned as a second lieutenant in the infantry, but resigned that commission to enter the Army Air Corps as a flying cadet in February 1933. He received his wings and was placed on active duty in February 1934. He was commissioned as a second lieutenant in February 1935. He was commanding officer of the 89th Reconnaissance Squadron during the raid, after which he returned to the China-Burma-India Theatre as a commander of a bomber group. During the last eighteen months of the war he served on the staff of Admiral Chester A. Nimitz, Commander-in-Chief, Pacific Area. He attended Air War College and National War College and served in several operational and staff assignments. During the Korean War he was commander of the 307th Bomb Wing located on Okinawa. He also served in Turkey and Norway. He was assigned Chief of Staff, Air Training Command, Randolph Air Force Base, Texas, retiring in the rank of brigadier-general in August 1966.

His co-pilot was Lieutenant Jack Sims from Kalamazoo, Michigan, who entered military service in June 1940. He was rated as pilot at Stockton Field in California and commissioned as a second lieutenant in July 1941. After the raid he was stationed in India flying submarine patrols. In August 1942 he was assigned to one of the 17th Bombardment Group's B-26 units and served in North Africa where he completed 40 combat missions, on the last of which he was shot down over Salerno, Italy. He graduated from Air Command and Staff College and Air War College. He served in various US home assignments, as well as Japan and England after the Second World War. He retired as a colonel in July 1968.

Lieutenant James Macia was the bombardier and navigator, born in Tombstone, Arizona, entering military service in June 1940. He completed navigator training and was commissioned second lieutenant in June 1941. After the Doolittle Raid he served two combat tours (80 missions) in B-26s with the 320th Bomb Group in Europe from March 1943 until April 1945. Relieved from active duty in February 1946, he returned to Arizona to pursue opportunities in mining. Recalled in March 1951, he served in Europe, Washington DC, Barksdale Air Force Base and Kelly Air Force Base. He retired as Chief of Staff, Air Force Security Service in 1973 as a colonel. He was the last Raider to retire from active duty.

Flight engineer/gunner was Staff Sergeant Jacob Eierman from Baltimore, Maryland. He entered the service on 20 August 1936. He graduated Radio Repair and Operator School, Chanute Field, Illinois and served in North Africa after the raid.

The radio operator/gunner was Staff Sergeant Edwin 'Ed' Bain, a native of Greensboro, North Carolina. He joined the Service in August 1936. He graduated from Radio Repair and Operator School, Chanute Field, Illinois. He killed in action on 19 July 1943 when his plane crashed in the Tyrrhenian Sea while returning from a combat mission near Rome.

B-25 40-2267 *TNT* (34TH BOMBARDMENT SQUADRON)

The pilot was Lieutenant Donald Smith from Oldham, South Dakota. He was commissioned as a second lieutenant in the infantry, then entered the regular service as a flying cadet in July 1940. He completed flight training and was rated as pilot in March 1941. He returned to the US after the raid and was assigned to the 432nd Bomb Squadron at Barksdale, Louisiana. Captain Smith was killed in western Europe as result of injuries sustained in an airplane crash on 12 November 1942.

The co-pilot was Lieutenant Griffith Williams of Chicago, Illinois, who enlisted as a flying cadet in November 1940 at Hemet, California. He was commissioned as a second lieutenant and rated as pilot in July 1941 at Stockton Field, California. He was then assigned to the 89th Reconnaissance Squadron. He remained in the China-Burma-India Theatre until July 1942. He was later assigned to Twelfth Air Force (17th Bombardment Group under Jimmy Doolittle's command) in North Africa and was shot down in July 1943. He was a prisoner of war from July 1943 until April 1945. He retired as a major in January 1952.

The navigator/bombardier was Lieutenant Howard Sessler of Boston, Massachusetts. He entered military service in December 1940. He graduated from bombardier training and was commissioned as a second lieutenant in August 1941. He then completed navigator training in December 1941. He remained in China-Burma-India Theatre after the raid until July 1942. He served in the European Theatre from September 1942 until September 1943 and the Mediterranean Theatre from September 1944 until June 1945. He was relieved from active duty in November 1945 in the rank of major. He graduated from the University of Southern California in 1950 with a Bachelor of Engineering (Civil) degree and ultimately became the president of a construction firm.

The gunner was Lieutenant Doctor Thomas White MD, from Maui, Hawaii. He joined the US Army Air Corps in June 1941. After the raid he served in England, North Africa, Sicily and Italy, leaving the service as a major and returning to private practise.

Engineer/gunner Sergeant Edward Saylor came from Brusett, Montana and enlisted in December 1939 at Fort George Wright, Washington. He attended the Air Corps Training School at Chanute Field, Illinois and served throughout the Second World War in enlisted status both in the US and overseas until March 1945. He accepted a commission in October 1947 and served as Aircraft Maintenance Officer at bases in Iowa, Washington, Labrador and England, retiring in the rank of major.

B-25 40-2268 *BAT OUT OF HELL* (89TH RECONNAISSANCE SQUADRON)

The pilot was Lieutenant William Farrow from Darlington, South Carolina. He entered the service in November 1940 at Fort Jackson, South Carolina and completed flight training at Kelly Field, Texas and commissioned as second lieutenant in July 1941. He was captured by the Japanese after the raid and executed on 15 October 1942 in Shanghai, China.

The co-pilot was Lieutenant Bob Hite from Odell, Texas. He enlisted as an aviation cadet in September 1940 at Lubbock, Texas. He was commissioned as second lieutenant and rated as pilot in May 1941. He was captured after the raid and imprisoned by the Japanese for 40 months. Liberated by US troops in August 1945, he remained on active duty until September 1947. He returned to active duty during the Korean War in March 1951 and served overseas before relief from active duty in November 1955 in the rank of lieutenant-colonel.

Lieutenant George Barr was the navigator. He entered the service in February 1941. He completed training as a navigator and was commissioned a Second Lieutenant at Pendleton, Oregon in December 1941. He was a prisoner of war of the Japanese from April 1942 until August 1945. He retired in the rank of captain due to physical disability in September 1947.

The bombardier was Corporal Jacob de Shazer, who was born in West Stayton, Oregon. He enlisted in February 1940 at Fort McDowell, California. He attended bombardier and airplane mechanics schools. He was captured by the Japanese after the raid and spent 40 months as a prisoner of war. He was released in August 1945 and left the service on 15 October 1945. He then graduated from Seattle Pacific College, Washington, in June 1948 with a Bachelor of Arts degree in preparation for a life as a missionary. After completion of his missionary training, he returned to Japan on 28 December 1948.

The engineer/gunner was Sergeant Harold Spatz from Lebo, Kansas. He entered military service in November 1939 at Fort Riley, Kansas. He received training as an aircraft mechanic at Glendale, California from September 1940 until March 1941. He was captured by the Japanese after the raid and executed by firing squad on 15 October 1942 at Kiangwan Cemetery, Shanghai, China.

Lieutenant Farrow, Sergeant Spatz and Lieutenant Dean Hallmark were all cremated and their remains taken to the International Funeral Home in Shanghai, from whence they were recovered in 1945.

Appendix 7

The B-29s of the 393rd

The aircraft detailed here are those which equipped the 393rd Bombardment (VH) Squadron on Tinian as the final allocation of B-29s ordered in February 1945 to be allocated as the replacements for the training machines that the crews had worn out in the work-up programme. Some of these aircraft didn't actually reach Tinian until June 1945. Each aircraft had a 'Victor' number, a radio call sign; 'Victor 82' was the call sign of Colonel Tibbets' own aircraft, *Enola Gay*.

There has been considerable debate about when individual aircraft were given their nose art and it has been suggested that only *Enola Gay* carried its nose art before its atomic mission. We do know that a couple of others could not have been decorated until after the event – notably *Bock's Car*. This aircraft carries the 'Salt Lake – Nagasaki' inscription, which could not have been applied until after the event, because Nagasaki was only chosen as the target on the morning of 9 August. However, most of the photographs of the aircraft in this book show them with nose art at Tinian, so many were clearly decorated soon after the atomic attacks.

VICTOR 71 *JABIT III* B-29-36-MO 44-27303

Crew B-6

Major John A. Wilson

Delivered 3 April 1945, it departed Wendover for Tinian on 5 June, arriving on 11 June. It was originally assigned the Victor number 1 but on 1 August, was given the large 'A' tail markings of the 497th Bomb Group as a security measure and so had its Victor changed to 71 to avoid being mistaken for a genuine 497th Group aircraft. *Jabit III* was used by the group commander, Colonel Paul Tibbets, on 24 and 25 July to drop two dummy 'Little Boy' atomic bomb assemblies into the ocean off Tinian to test fire their radar altimeter components. In addition to the Hiroshima mission and two test flights, *Jabit III* was flown by Major Wilson and crew B-6 on ten training and practice missions and three combat missions, dropping pumpkin bombs on industrial targets in Taira, Ube and Uwajima. Captain Ralph Devore and crew A-3 also flew *Jabit III* on a pumpkin bomb mission to Osaka. The plane and crew B-6 were one of two sent back to Wendover on 9 August 1945, to stand by to the plutonium core and initiator for a third atomic bomb to Tinian, but the war ended before that was necessary. The aircraft was not marked with its nose art whilst on Tinian, but it has been said that it was named before it left and by the time it flew as the weather reconnaissance aircraft on 6 August over Kokura, the secondary target on that day. *Jabit III* was damaged in a landing accident in Chicago on 29 September 1945 whilst on a training flight and was scrapped in April 1946.

VICTOR 72 *TOP SECRET* B-29-36-MO 44-27302
Crew B-8

Captain Charles F. McKnight

Top Secret was built at the Martin Plant at Omaha as a Block 35 aircraft. It was one of ten modified as a 'Silverplate' machine and re-designated 'Block 36'. Delivered on 2 April 1945, it left Wendover for Tinian on 5 June, arriving on 11 June. It was originally assigned the Victor number 2 but, like *Jabit III* was given the large 'A' tail

Top Secret, Victor Number 72, flown by Crew B-8 under Captain Charles F. McKnight.

markings of the 497th Bomb Group and had its Victor number changed to 72. While at Tinian, McKnight and crew B-8 flew *Top Secret* on 13 practice bombing missions and four combat pumpkin bomb missions against Japanese industrial targets at Otsu, Yokkaichi, Ube and Toyoda. The plane flew two other pumpkin bomb missions to Taira under the command of Captain Joseph E. Westover, and Major Claude Eatherly with crew C-11 flew a mission over Yokkaichi. On 6 August, it was assigned as the strike spare for the first atomic bomb mission but did not follow it through, landing at Iwo Jima as planned when *Enola Gay* was able to complete its assignment. In November 1945, *Top Secret* returned with the 509th to Roswell Field in New Mexico.

VICTOR 73 *STRANGE CARGO* B-29-36-MO 44-27300

Crew A-4

Captain Joseph E. Westover

Strange Cargo left Wendover on 5 June for Tinian, arriving on 11 June. It was originally assigned the Victor number 3, then given the large 'A' tail markings of the 497th Bomb

Strange Cargo, Victor 73, Captain Joseph Westover's Crew A-4.

Group and had its Victor number changed to 73. Whilst at Tinian, Captain Westover and crew A-4 flew *Strange Cargo* on 11 practice bombing missions and three combat pumpkin bomb missions against Japanese industrial targets at Nagasaki, Tsuruga and Toyoda. The plane flew one other pumpkin bomb mission to Fukushima under Captain Frederick C. Bock and crew C-13. In November 1945 it returned with the 509th to Roswell, New Mexico. From March to August 1946 it was assigned to the Operation *Crossroads* task force, then rejoined the 509th Bomb Group at Roswell. In June 1949 *Strange Cargo* was transferred to the 97th Bombardment Group at Biggs Air Force Base, Texas, then sent to McClellan Air Force Base in August 1949 for modification to WB-29 specifications at the Sacramento Air Materiel Area.

VICTOR 77 *BOCK'S CAR* B-29-36-MO 44-27297

Crew C-13

Captain Frederick C. Bock

Bock's Car left Wendover on 11 June 1945 for Tinian and arrived on 16 June. It originally had the Victor number 7 but was given the triangle N tail markings of the 444th Bomb Group and had its Victor number changed to 77. *Bock's Car* was the B-29 used to drop the atomic bomb 'Fat Man' on Nagasaki on Thursday 9 August, flown by Major Charles W. Sweeney with Crew C-15. It was also used in 13 training and practice missions from Tinian, and three combat missions in which it dropped pumpkin bombs on industrial targets. Crew C-13 bombed Niihama and Musashino, and Lieutenant Don Albury and crew C-15 bombed Toyama. *Bock's Car* returned to the US in November 1945 and served with the 509th at Roswell Army Air Field, New Mexico. It was nominally assigned to the Operation *Crossroads* task force but there are no records indicating that it deployed for the tests. In August 1946 it was assigned to the 4105th Base Unit at Davis-Monthan Army Air Field, Arizona, for storage. It is today on display in the US Air Force Museum at Wright-Patterson Air Force Base in Ohio.

VICTOR 82 *ENOLA GAY* B-29-45-MO 44-86292

Crew B-9

Captain Robert A. Lewis

Accepted on 18 May 1945 and flown from Omaha to Wendover on 14 June. Thirteen days later, the aircraft left Wendover for Guam, where it received a bomb bay modification and flew to Tinian on 6 July. *Enola Gay* was originally given the Victor number 12, then took on the circle R tail markings of the 6th Bomb Group, taking a Victor number change to 82. During July, after flying eight training missions and two combat missions dropping pumpkin bombs on industrial targets at Kobe and Nagoya, *Enola Gay* did a rehearsal flight for the actual mission with a dummy 'Little Boy'. On 5 August 1945, during preparation for the first atomic mission, pilot Colonel Paul Tibbets assumed command of the aircraft and named it after his mother, Enola Gay Tibbets.

VICTOR 83 *FULL HOUSE* B-29-36-MO 44-27298

Crew A-1

Major Ralph R. Taylor
Full House was delivered on 20 March 1945, left Wendover for Tinian on 11 June and arrived on 17 June. It started with Victor number 13, but was given the square P tail markings of the 39th Bomb Group and the revised Victor number of 83. In addition to its roles on the Hiroshima and Nagasaki missions, Major Taylor and crew A-1 flew the bomber on 12 practice and training missions, and four combat missions in they dropped pumpkin bombs on industrial targets at Toyama, Niihama, Yaizu and Ube, Yamaguchi. Captain Frederick C. Bock and crew C-13 flew *Full House* on a pumpkin bomb mission to Komoro. In November 1945 the aircraft returned to the US with the 509th Composite Group to Roswell. In June 1949 it was transferred to the 97th Bomb Wing at Biggs Air Force Base, Texas, then reconfigured as a TB-29 trainer in April 1950 by the Oklahoma City Air Materiel Area at Tinker Air Force Base.

VICTOR 84 *SOME PUNKINS* B-29-36-MO 44-2729

Crew B-7

Captain James N. Price Jr
Received at Wendover on 19 March 1945, it arrived on Tinian on 14 June and was originally assigned the Victor number 4, which changed to 84 when it took on the large 'A' tail markings of the 497th Bomb Group. Some sources credit the name to a 1930s comic strip, but a close look at the nose art suggests it might have more to do with the nickname for the egg-shaped bombs these aircraft carried. *Some Punkins* flew 13 training and practice missions and five combat missions with pumpkin bombs on industrial targets on Toyama, Ogaki, Shimoda, Yokkaichi and Nagoya. It was the only B-29 of the 393rd Bomb Squadron to be flown exclusively by its assigned crew on all operational missions. In November 1945 it returned with the rest of the 509th to Roswell. On 1 March 1946, while at Kirtland Army Air Field in preparation for assignment to Operation *Crossroads*, it was struck while parked by a taxiing B-29, incurring severe damage to its forward fuselage. The aircraft was transferred to the 428th Base Unit at Kirtland in April 1946 and declared damaged beyond economical repair. In August it was deliberately set alight as part of fire fighting training and destroyed.

VICTOR 85 *STRAIGHT FLUSH* B-29-36-MO 44-27301

Crew C-11

Major Claude Eatherly
Flown from Omaha to Wendover on 2 April, it arrived on Tinian on 13 June. Originally assigned Victor number 5, it was given the triangle N tail markings of the 444th Bomb Group and Victor number 85. The aircraft was named *Straight Flush*, apparently inspired by Eatherley's gambling habit. From June to August it flew 11 training missions and six combat missions in which pumpkin bombs were dropped on Japanese industrial

targets. Eatherly's crew bombed Tokyo, Otsu, Taira and Maizuru, while Captain Charles D. Albury and crew C-15 used *Straight Flush* to bomb Koromo. On 6 August *Straight Flush* flew a mission over Japan as a weather patrol aircraft for the Hiroshima bombing; two days later, it made its final combat flight, a bombing raid on Yokkaichi. One source has it that on the first pumpkin mission, on 20 July, Major Eatherly attempted to bomb the Imperial Palace through an overcast sky as a 'target of opportunity' but missed, hitting a bridge called Gofukubashi. The attack was contrary to bombing restrictions (to protect the person of Emperor Hirohito) but apparently went unpunished. In November 1945 the aircraft returned with the 509th to Roswell Field, New Mexico. From March to August 1946 it was assigned to the Operation *Crossroads* task force, then rejoined the 509th at Roswell. While stationed there, *Straight Flush* is alleged to have played a part in the 1947 UFO incident at Roswell. On 9 July 1947 the crew of *Necessary Evil*, another B-29 which had participated in the Hiroshima mission, was ordered to fly *Straight Flush* from Roswell to Fort Worth, Texas to deliver a 'large wooden crate' believed to contain parts of the crashed UFO. Due to confusion over the aircraft tail numbers, there is some uncertainty as to which aircraft was actually involved in this flight. In June 1949 *Straight Flush* was transferred to the 97th Bombardment Group at Biggs Air Force Base, Texas, then sent to Tinker Air Force Base in April 1950 to become a TB-29 trainer.

VICTOR 86 *NEXT OBJECTIVE* B-29-36-MO 44-27299

Crew A-3

Captain Ralph N. Devore

Next Objective arrived at Wendover on 20 March and moved to Tinian on 17 June 1945. Originally assigned the Victor number 6, it was given the triangle N tail markings of the 444th Bomb Group and the Victor number 86. While at Tinian, Captain Devore and his crew flew *Next Objective* on 12 practice bombing missions and three pumpkin bomb missions against industrial targets at Toyama, Niihama and Nagoya. One other mission was aborted. Major Charles Sweeney, by this time commanding officer of the 393rd Bomb Squadron, used *Next Objective* to rehearse procedures with a dummy 'Little Boy' on 26 and 29 July. On the second of these missions *Next Objective* landed on Iwo Jima where the inert bomb was unloaded, then reloaded to practice a contingency in which a spare aircraft would take over 6 August mission if *Enola Gay* were to abort. In November 1945, *Next Objective* went back to Roswell. From March to August 1946 it was assigned to the Operation *Crossroads* task force, then returned to the 509th Bomb Group at Roswell. In April 1949, it was transferred to the 97th Bombardment Group at Biggs Air Force Base, Texas.

VICTOR 88 *UP AN' ATOM* B-29-36-MO 44-27304

It arrived at Wendover on 5 April 1945 and went on to Tinian on 17 June. Originally assigned the Victor number 8, it was given the triangle N tail markings of the 444th Bomb Group and the Victor number 88. Operating out of Tinian, Captain Marquadt, the crew B-6 leader, and his crew flew eight training and practice bombing missions and pumpkin bomb missions against targets in Taira and Hamamatsu. Captain Bob Lewis's crew B-9 flew it on a pumpkin bomb mission to Tokushima after the Hiroshima mission, and Lieutenant-Colonel James Hopkins and crew C-14 used it to attack Nagoya with a pumpkin bomb. *Up an' Atom* returned to the US with the 509th in November 1945 to

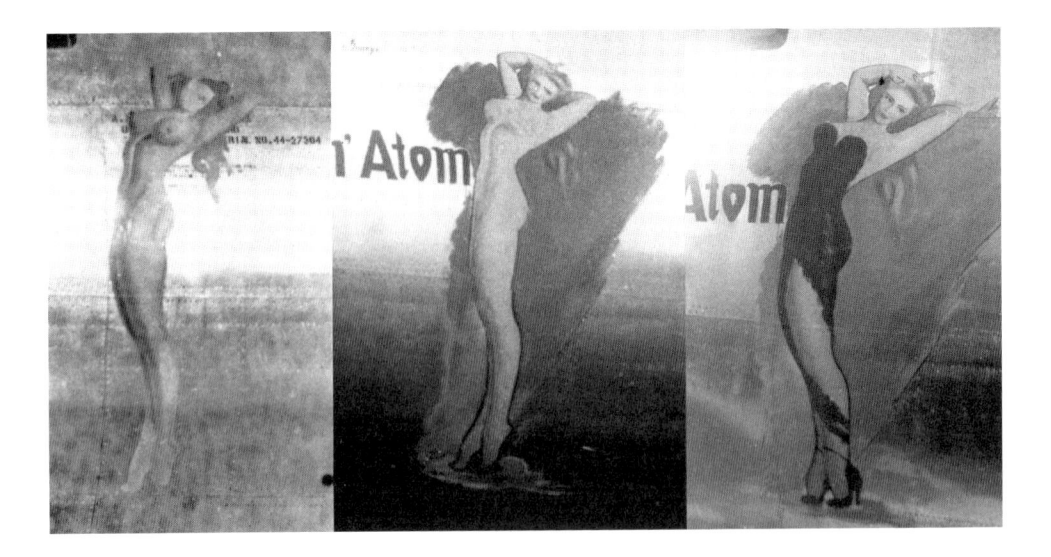

The nose art of *Up'n'Atom*. The first rendering was the only completely naked figure on any of 393rd's B-29s. It appears not to have met with approval in all circles, as it was made more 'demure' in the second rendering. Even this was not enough, for soon the lady appeared with all modesty restored.

Roswell. From April to August 1946 it was assigned to the Operation *Crossroads* task force. In August 1949 it became part of the 97th Bomb Wing at Biggs Air Force Base, Texas, and was reconfigured as a TB-29 trainer in April 1950 by the Oklahoma City Air Materiel Area at Tinker Air Force Base.

VICTOR 89 *THE GREAT ARTISTE* B-29-40-MO 44-27353
Crew C-15

Captain Charles Albury
The Great Artiste arrived at Wendover on 20 April 1945 and moved to Tinian on 28 June. Adorned with the Circle R mark of the 6th Bomb Group, it also was allocated the Victor number of 89 on 1 August. *The Great Artiste* was the only B-29 of the 393rd Squadron to take part in both atomic bombing missions, since it was fitted with the instruments to measure the explosions. *The Great Artiste* was to have been the aircraft to deliver the 'Fat Man' Bomb on Nagasaki, but various complications prevented the instrumentation being removed, so it flew the same task as it did over Hiroshima. *The Great Artiste* was flown by five different crews on 12 training and practice missions, and by Captain Albury and crew C-15 on two combat missions, one of which was aborted and the other in which it used a pumpkin bomb to attack the railway yards at Kobe. Captain Bob Lewis and his crew B-9 flew it to drop a pumpkin bomb on an industrial target in Tokushima. In November 1945 it returned with the 509th to Roswell. On 3 September 1948, *The Great Artiste* was on a polar navigation training mission but developed engine problems after takeoff from Goose Bay and ran off the end of the runway when trying to land. It was so heavily damaged that it never flew again and was finally scrapped at Goose Bay a year later, in September 1949.

VICTOR 90 *BIG STINK* B-29-40-MO 44-27354

Crew A-5

Lieutenant-Colonel Thomas J. Classen

Big Stink arrived at Wendover on 20 April 1945. It transferred to Tinian on 25 June and was allocated to the command of the original 393rd commander, Lieutenant-Colonel Classen. Its Victor number was changed from 10 to 90 on 1 August and it acquired the Circle R tail identification of the 6th Bombardment Group. On the Hiroshima mission *Big Stink* was a reserve aircraft, standing by at Iwo Jima, but it was not needed. On 9 August it flew as a photographic recording aircraft and carried international observers when commanded by Major James Hopkins, the Group's Operations Officer, flying with crew C-14.

Big Stink did not meet its rendezvous with the other aircraft of the strike flight, but it did arrive at Nagasaki in time to photograph the effects of the blast, then flew to Yontan Airfield on Okinawa to join *Bock's Car* and *The Great Artiste*, all the aircraft returning to Tinian together. *Big Stink* also flew 12 training and practice missions and two combat missions to drop pumpkin bombs on Nagaoka and Hitachi, both flown by Classen and crew A-5. *Big Stink* was flown by more crews (9 out of the 15) on operational missions than any other 393rd B-29. After the Second World War it joined the rest of the 509th at Roswell. In April 1946 it was assigned to Operation *Crossroads*, and renamed *Dave's Dream* by its crew in honour of Captain David Semple, a bombardier who had been killed in the crash of another B-29 on 7 March 1946, near Albuquerque, New Mexico. Semple had been a bombardier in many of the 155 test drops for the Manhattan Project. On 1 July 1946, *Dave's Dream* dropped the Fat Man-type atomic bomb used in Test Able of Operation *Crossroads* in the Bikini Atoll.

VICTOR 91 *NECESSARY EVIL* B-29-45-MO 44-86291

Crew C-14

Captain Norman Ray

Delivered to Wendover on 18 May 1945 and transferred to Tinian on 2 July, *Necessary Evil* was originally assigned the Victor number 11 but became Victor 91 and took on the tail marking of Circle R of the 6th Bombardment group. On 6 August, this aircraft was used as a camera plane to photograph the explosion and effects of the atom bomb over Hiroshima and to carry scientific observers. At the time of the attack the aircraft was not named and was known only by its victor number. That mission was flown by crew B-6, with Captain George Marquardt as the aircraft commander. In addition to the Hiroshima mission, *Necessary Evil* flew ten training and practice missions and three combat missions in which it dropped pumpkin bombs on targets in Kobe, Kashiwazaki and Koriyama, all flown by Captain Ray and crew C-14. In December 1945 it returned to the US with the 509th to Roswell. It was part of the Operation *Crossroads* task force from August 1946 until June 1949, when it was transferred to the 97th Bomb Wing at Biggs Air Force Base in Texas. *Necessary Evil* was converted to a TB-29 trainer by the Oklahoma City Materiel Area at Tinker Air Force Base in April 1950.

VICTOR 94 *SPOOK* B-29-50-MO 44-86346

Crew C-12

Captain Herman S. Zahn

It was flown to Wendover in early July, where it was briefly used in training and practice bombing missions. On 27 July 1945, Captain Zahn and his crew flew the aircraft from Wendover to Kirtland Army Air Field, Albuquerque, New Mexico, accompanied by another 509th B-29 and one from the Manhattan Project test unit at Wendover (216th Base Unit). There, they each loaded one of three Fat Man atomic bomb assemblies (without the plutonium core, which had left the day before by courier on one of the 509th's C-54 Skymaster transports) in its bomb bay for transport to Tinian. The three bombers flew to Mather Army Air Field, California on 28 July and took off for Hawaii on the 29th, finally reaching Tinian on 2 August. *Spook* was assigned the square P tail identifier of the 39th Bomb group and given Victor number 94. The aircraft was not given a name or nose art. It arrived too late to participate in any training, practice, or combat operations. After only a week on Tinian, *Spook* was reassigned to the group deputy commander, Lieutenant-Colonel Thomas J. Classen and his crew A-5. It left Tinian on 9 August and returned to Wendover accompanied by *Jabit III*, with the maintenance crews for both aircraft aboard, to await orders to transport components of the third bomb. *Spook* flew to Roswell in November 1945, where it rejoined the 509th. Between April and August 1946 it was part of the Operation *Crossroads* task force based on Kwajalein. In June 1949 it was transferred to the 97th Bomb Wing at Biggs Air Force Base, Texas and in April 1950 was converted to a TB-29 trainer at Kelly Air Force Base, Texas and the Oklahoma City Air Materiel Area at Tinker Air Force Base.

VICTOR 95 *LAGGIN' DRAGON* B-29-50-MO 44-86347

Crew A-2

Captain Edward M. Costello

Flown to Wendover in early July and briefly used in training and practice bombing missions. On 27 July, Costello and his crew flew the airplane from Wendover to Kirtland Army Air Field in Albuquerque, New Mexico, accompanying two other B-29s, one from the Manhattan Project test unit at Wendover (216th Base Unit) and the other *Spook*, with the task of carrying a 'Fat Man' bomb assembly back to Tinian. During takeoff from Mather Field, a panel door on *Laggin' Dragon* enclosing the life raft compartment opened and ejected the raft, which wrapped around the horizontal elevator on the tail and fouled the aircraft's elevators. It struggled to stay aloft but the pilots managed to return to Mather safely. After removing and replacing major tail assemblies, *Laggin' Dragon* and its cargo continued to Hawaii, finally reaching Tinian on 2 August. Like *Spook*, *Laggin' Dragon* wore the square P tail identifier of the 39th Bomb group and had its Victor number changed to 95. It was too late to take part in other combat operations and took part in only two practice flights after the atomic attacks. This aircraft returned to the US in November 1945, based with the rest of the 509th at Roswell. In June 1946 it was part of the Operation *Crossroads* task force based on Kwajalein. In June 1949 it was transferred to the 97th Bomb Wing at Biggs Air Force Base, Texas, and in April 1950 was converted to a TB-29 trainer at Kelly Air Force Base, Texas and the Oklahoma City Air Materiel Area at Tinker Air Force Base.

Laggin' Dragon was Victor 95, flown by Captain Edward M. Costello and Crew A-2.

By the Same Author

Riley 75
Sixty Years of Naval Eight/208
As Old As the Industry: Riley (Winner of 1983 Society of Automotive Historians Cugnot Award)
Sporting Rileys: The Forgotten Champions (Winner 1989 SAH Award of Distinction)
Alfa Romeo: The Legend Revived
Seventy Five Years On: The Flying Shuftis
Alfa Romeo: The Spyder, Alfasud and Alfetta GT
Porsche: The Road, Sports and Racing Cars (with J. McNamara, M. Cotton & J. Snook)
Aston Martin & Lagonda Vee-Engined Cars
MGA: The Complete Story (Winner, International Automotive Media Conference Moto Award 1996)
Datsun Z-Series: The Complete Story (Winner IAMC Moto Award 1997)
Riley: A Centennial Celebration (Winner IAMC Silver Medal 1997)
All the Eights: Eight Decades of Naval Eight/208
Porsche 356: The Flat-Four Engined Cars (IAMC Silver Medal Winner 1999)
Riley: Beyond the Blue Diamond (Winner 2 x IAMC Silver Medals 1999)
Alfa Romeo: Spirit of Milan (Winner IAMC Silver Medal 2000)
Moto Guzzi: Forza in Movimento (Winner IAMC Silver Medal 2001)
Volvo 1800 - The Complete Story
Doolittle Tales
Volvo Tech for Parts People (Winner IAMC Bronze Medal 2010)
BTEC National Diploma Unit 15, Heavy Vehicle Brakes (Winner IAMC Silver & Bronze Medals 2011)

Bibliography

Atkinson, Rick, *An Army at Dawn: The War in North Africa, 1942–1943* (2004)
Chang, Iris, *The Rape of Nanking: The Forgotten Holocaust of World War II* (1998)
Cohen, Stan, Jim Farmer and Joe Boddy, *Destination Tokyo* (1992)
Cooper, Norman V., *Fighting General: A Biography of General Holland M. Smith* (1987)
Davis, Benjamin O., *Benjamin O. Davis Jnr., American: An Autobiography* (1991)
d'Este, Carlo, *Patton: A Genius for War* (1995)
Doolittle, James H. and Carroll V. Glines, *I Could Never be so Lucky Again* (1991)
Doolittle, James H., 'The Halsey-Doolittle Raid, April 1942' (report) (9 July 1942)
Glines, C.V., *Four Came Home* (1996)
Glines, C.V., *The Doolittle Raid* (2000)
Greening, C. Ross, *Not As Briefed* (1946)
Homan, Lynn M. and Thomas Reilly, *The Tuskegee Airmen* (1998)
Lewis, Ted W., *Thirty Seconds Over Tokyo* (1943)
Lu, David J., *Agony of Choice: Matsuoka Yosuke and the Rise and Fall of the Japanese Empire, 1880–1946* (2002)
Mason, John.T. Jr, *The Pacific War Remembered* (1986)
Merrill, James M., *Target Tokyo: The Halsey-Doolittle Raid* (1964)
Miller, Merle, *Plain Speaking: An Oral Biography Of Harry S. Truman* (1973)
Mitter, Rana, *A Bitter Revolution: China's Struggle with the Modern World* (2004)
Thomas G. and M. Morgan-Witts, *Enola Gay: Mission to Hiroshima* (1995)
Tibbets, Paul W., *Flight of the Enola Gay* (1989)

Aeroplane Monthly 1968–2005
Air Force (US) 2001–2004
Flying 1962–2002
Model Airplane News 1972–2003
www.doolittleraider.com

Interviews with Doolittle Raiders

Bower William M. (2002/2003) Aircraft Number 12
de Shazer, Jacob (2002/2003) Aircraft Number 16
Griffin, Thomas C. (2002/2003) Aircraft Number 9
Herndon, Nolan A. (2002/2003) Aircraft Number 8
Hite Robert L. (2003) Aircraft Number 16
Hoover, Travis (2003) Aircraft Number 2
Nielsen, Chase J. (2002/2003) Aircraft Number 6
Sims, Jack A. (2002) Aircraft Number 14
Thatcher, David J. (2002/2003) Aircraft Number 7

Index

17th Bombardment Group 45, 49, 56, 57, 86, 87, 90, **90**, 91, 238, 241, 242, **242**, **243**, 243, 244, **244**, 245, 259, 260, 261, 263, 264, 265, 267, 268
34th Bombardment Squadron **8**, 45, 63, 67, 183, 238, 242, 259, 264, 266, 268
37th Bombardment Squadron 45, **65**, 65, 67, **90**, 90, 237, 238, 242, 258, 266, 267
89th Reconnaissance Squadron 45, 63, 67, 242, 264, 265, 267, 268, 269
90th Aero Squadron 15, 102, 178
95th Bombardment Squadron 45, 61, **62**, 62, 238, 241, 242, 243, 259, 260, 261, 262, 263, 265
97th Bombardment Group 82, **83**, **84**, 84, 85, 87, 91, 103, 104, **104**, 120, 179, 181, 235, 237, 238, 273, 275, 276, 277, 278
104th Aero Squadron 15
320th Bombardment Group 87, 91, 268
320th Troop Transportation Squadron **105**, 105, 121, **122**, 123, 128, **129**, 136, **227**, 227, 238, 245, **246**,
393rd Bombardment Squadron (VH) 120, 121, **122**, 123, 125, 128, **128**, 130, 131, **133**, 133, 138, **139**, 139, **140**, 140, 142, 143, **148**, 148, 216, **216**, 245, **246**, 246, 248, **249**, 249, 251, 270, 274, 275, **276**, 276, 277
494th Bombardment Group 7, 148, 213
509th Composite Group 7, 104, 106, **106**, 107, 115, 120, 121, 123, 124, 126, 127, 130, 131, 133, 134, 135, 136, 138, 139, **140**, 146, 155, 158, 175, 188, 196, 197, 227, 241, 245, 246, **247**, 247, 248, **249**, 249, 251, 272, 273, 274, 275, 276, 277, 278
Airco DH-4 15, **16**, 16, 22, 214, **214**, 215
Albury, Captain Charles 161, 276
Argus Camera 151, **152**, 152
Armstrong, Colonel/Lieutenant-General Frank A. 85, 87, 120, 126, 178, **178**, 179, 181, 183, 235
Arnold, General Henry H. 125, 27, **40**, 42, 49, 51, 57, 68, 80, 91, 93, 95, 140, 179, **179**, 180, 189, 233, 240, 241, 249
Atkinson, Colonel/Lieutenant-General Joseph H. **83**, 87, 88, 180, 181, 182, 236
Avenger, The 67, 266
Bat Out Of Hell 58, 67, 269
Beahan, Captain Kermit 132, 161, 162, 163
Bendix Trophy 22, 23, 229
Beser, Lieutenant Jacob 149, 160, 161, 163
Big Stink 162, 163, **163**, 277
Bock, Captain Frederick C. 160, 162, 273, 274
Bock's Car 160, **160**, 161, 162, **164**, 165, 176, 270, 273, 277
Boeing B-17 (Flying Fortress) **82**, 83, 84, **84**, 85, 87, 93, 95, 103, 104, **104**, 120, **123**, 123, 179, 180, 188, 215, **215**, 235, 236, 237, **246**, 260, 263
Boeing B-29 (Superfortress) **12**, 12, **91**, 91, 93, **94**, 105, 111, 115, **115**, **116**, 116, 118, **119**, 119,

INDEX

120, 121, **122**, 122, 124, **125**, 125, 126, **126**, 130, **133**, 133, 135, 136, **139**, 139, 144, **144**, **145**, 145, 146, 147, 151, 160, **160**, **163**, 163, 179, 180, 216, **216**, 240, 241, 246, 249, 263, 270, 271, **271**, **272**, 272, 273, 274, 275, **276**, 276, 277, 278
Boeing B-47 (Stratojet) 106, 179, 216, **217**, 218, 249
Boeing B-52 (Stratofortress) **177**, 177, **244**, **244**, 245, 249, 251
Boeing Airplane Company 91, 93, 95, 106, **117**, 118, 119, 120
Bower, Lieutenant William M. 65, 266
Braemer, Lieutenant Fred 60, 258
Burma 12, 35, 36, 182, 222
Cartwright, Lieutenant Thomas 148
Chance Vought F4U (Corsair) 76, **76**, 77
Chennault, Major-General Claire Lee 36, 182, **182**, 222
Chiang, General Kai-Shek 31, 36, 68, 172, 173, **173**, 182
Chile 18, 19
Chuchow, China 45, 59, 60, 61, 67, 73
Chuhsien 62, 64, 65, 67
Chungking 61, 72, 73
Classen, Lieutenant-Colonel Thomas J. 138, 139, **246**, 246, 249, 277, 278
Cleveland, OH 22, 23, 24, 25, 261
Columbia Army Air Field 45, 243
Consolidated NY-2 20, **21**, 96, 218, **218**, **219**, **219**
Consolidated B-24 (Liberator) 7, 93, **94**, **95**, 95, 147, **147**, **148**, 148, 185, 241, 264
Costello, Captain Edward M. 278, 279
Curtiss JN-4 (Jenny) 15, 219, **220**, 220
Curtiss P-1 (Hawk) 18, **19**, **221**, 221, **221**
Curtiss P-40 (Warhawk) 36, 91, **92**, 93, 221, **222**, 238, 239, 262
Curtiss R3C Racer **16**, 16, 233, **233**
Davis, Colonel Benjamin O. Jr **92**, 93, 239
Devore, Captain Ralph N. 270, 275
Doolittle, Lieutenant-Colonel/ Lieutenant-General James H. 7, 11, 14, **16**, 17, 18, 19, 20, **21**, 22, 23, 24, 25, 26, 43, 44, 45, 46, 47, 49, 50, 51, 53, 55, **56**, 57, **58**, 59, 60, 61, 63, **66**, 67, 68, **70**, 73, 80, **81**, **84**, 85, 86, 87, 88, 89, 90, 93, 96, 115, 183, 202, 215, **219**, 221, 223, 224, 229, 233, 235, 236, 239, 243, 245, 251, 255, 256, 258
Doolittle Raid 12, 44, 45, 51, 54, 68, 69, 74, 75, 86, 90, 177, 189, 194, 200, 208, 210, 226, 233, 243, 255, 257, 258, 262, 263, 264, 267, 268
Doolittle Raiders 7, 48, 51, 53, 58, 59, **59**, 60, 72, **72**, 194, 209, 224, 258, 263
Douglas A-20 (Havoc) 44, **44**, 102, **102**, 103, 224, **224**
Douglas B-18 (Bolo) **103**, 103, 178, 225, **225**, 226, 231, 242
Douglas B-23 (Dragon) 43, **43**, 45, 226, **226**, 242
Douglas B-26 (Invader) 243, **243**, 245
Douglas O-46 96, **99**, 228, **228**, 234
Douglas C-54 (Skymaster) **105**, 105, **122**, **129**, 129, 136, 227, **227**, 245, **246**, 278
Duncan, Captain Donald B. 42, 255
Dutch East Indies 77, 252
Eaker, Lieutenant-General Ira C. 85, 87, 178, 183, **183**, 202, 235
Eatherly, Major Claude R. 149, 272, 274, 275
Eisenhower, General Dwight D. 80, 84, 85, 87, 89, 180, 192, 199, 207
Eighth US Army Air Force 83, 84, 85, 87, 178, 183, 202, 215, 235, **235**, 239, 245, 249, 251, 266
Enola Gay 96, 107, 143, 144, **145**, 146, **147**, 149, 150, 151, 152, 153, 154, **156**, 156, **157**, 158, **159**, 159, 160, 176, 197, 216, 270, 272, 273, 275
'Fat Man' 127, **127**, 136, 140, 159, 160, 161, 162, **162**, 163, 171, 273, 276, 277, 278
Ferebee, Captain Thomas 106, **123**, 123, 129, 130, 131, 139, 149, 153
Fickle Finger 65, 266
Fifteenth US Army Air Force 93, 181, 215, 239, **240**, 240
First Ordnance Squadron, Special (Aviation) 130, **130**, **131**, 131,

132, **132**, 135, 136, 137, 138, 142, **143**, 143, 146, **146**, 152, 175, 245, 247
Full House 144, 149, **150**, 150, 274
Gee-Bee R-1 Racer 24, **25**, 25, **229**, 229
General Dynamics FB-111 **250**, 251
Goodyear 45, **52**
Gray, Lieutenant Robert M. 61, 259
Great Artiste, The **133**, 133, 142, 143, 144, **149**, 149, 151, 153, 154, 156, 158, 160, **161, 162, 163, 276, 277**
Greening, Captain C. Ross 47, 64, 238, 265
Groves, Major-General Leslie R. 109, **109**, 110, 111, 113, 127, 128, 133, 137, 139, 143, 156
Guggenheim 20
Hallmark, Lieutenant Dean E. 62, 67, 69, 73, 261, 262, 269
Halsey, Vice-Admiral William F. Jr 13, 54, 57, 58, 184, **184**, 207
Hari-Kari-er 64, 265
Haruna 148, 212, **212**, 213, 213
Hashimoto, Commander Mochitsura 137, 172, 184, **185**, 185, 211, 212
Hilger, Major John A. **50**, 51, **66**, 67, 68, 267
Hirohito, Emperor of Japan 142, 156, 166, 185, 186, **186**, 205, 208, 275
Hiroshima 7, 11, 12, 73, 104, 105, 107, 111, 121, 129, 136, 137, 140, 143, 144, 147, 148, 149, 153, **154**, 154, **156**, 156, 158, 159, 160, 161, 162, 163, 165, 166, **168**, 168, 169, **169**, **170**, 170, **171**, 173, 177, 180, 197, 203, 207, 216, 235, 241, 249, 270, 274, 275, 276, 277
Holstrom, Lieutenant Everett W. 62, 260
Hong Kong 35, 40
Hopkins, Major James 162, **163**, 163, 275, 277
Hoover, Lieutenant Travis M. 61, 259
I-58 (Japanese submarine) 137, 185, 193, 211, **211**, 212
Iwo Jima 12, 13, 77, **77**, **78**, 79, 143, 144, 149, **153**, 153, 165, 192, 202, 211, 272, 275, 277
Jabit III 144, 149, 150, **150**, 270, 271, 278

Jeppson, Lieutenant Morris 131, 132, 136, 145, 149, 152, 153
Jones, Captain David M. 62, 261
Joyce, Lieutenant Richard O. 63, 64, 264
Jurika, Lieutenant Stephen 252, **252**, 253, 254, **254**, **255**, 255, **256**, 256, 257
K-20 Camera 96, **151**, 151
King, Fleet Admiral Ernest J. 42, 57, 186, **186**, 187, 189
Kobe 54, 59, 67, 212, 241, 273, 276, 277
Korea 28, 29, 30, 31, 170, 243
Kwantung Army 33, 34, 186, 204
Laggin' Dragon 278, **279**
Laird LC-DW500 (Super Solution) 22, **23**, 23, 24, 229, **230**
Lawson, Captain Ted 50, 53, 57, 62, 69, 70, **71**, 71, 72, 262, 263
League of Nations 31, 33, 35
LeMay, Lieutenant-General Curtis E. 85, 105, 106, 137, 138, 139, 143, 149, 158, 159, 187, 188, **188**, 189, 235, 241
Lewis, Captain Robert A 131, 132, **133**, 133, 139, 142, 143, 144, 149, 156, 158, 273, 275, 276
Leyte Gulf, Battle of 13, 192, 195, 213
'Little Boy' 13, 121, **121**, 136, **136**, 140, **141**, 141, 145, **145**, 146, **146**, 147, **147**, 152, 153, **155**, 155, 157, 162, 171, 193, 197, 211, 270, 273, 275
Lonesome Lady **148**, 148
Low, Captain Francis S. 42, **189**, 189
MacArthur, General Douglas 13, 137, 138, 140, 169, 190, **190**, 192, 207, 260
Malaya 35, 40, 212
Manchuria 29, 30, 32, 33, 192, 208
Manhattan Project 93, 108, **110**, 115, 125, 127, 130, 133, 140, 147, 168, 196, 200, 249, 277, 278
Mao, Tse-Tung 172, 174, **174**, 192
Mark Twain Bomb Sight **47**, 47, 60
Marshall, General George C. **40**, 42, 57, 80, 105, 180, 199, 211, 249
Martin B-10 96, **99**, 225, 231, **231**
Martin B-26 (Marauder) 25, 26, **26**, 27, 43, 87, 89, **90**, 90, 91, 93,

INDEX

226, 232, **232**, 233, 238, 242, **242**, 260, 263, 265, 267, 268
Martin Aircraft Factory, Omaha, NE 122, 144, 216, 271
McClellan Field, CA 49, 50, 51, 53, 273
McCook Field, OH 17, 19, 20
McElroy, Lieutenant Edgar E. 67, 266
McKnight, Captain Charles A. 150, 271, 272
McVay, Captain Charles Butler III 185, 186, **186**, 192, 193, 195, 196, 211
Meiji, Emperor/Dynasty 28, 29, 29, 185, 204
Miller, Cook 3rd Class Dorie 38, **196**
Miller, Lieutenant Henry L. 47, 48, 51, 53, 196, 255
Mitchell Field, NY 17, 20
Mitchell, Brigadier-General William 'Billy' 15, 17, 20, 27, 180, 190, 233
Mitscher, Vice-Admiral Marc A. 54, 56, 57, 58, 194, **194**, 195, 210
Mountbatten Admiral the Earl 13
Nagasaki 28, 129, 137, 140, 149, 160, 161, 163, **164**, **165**, 165, 166, **167**, 167, 171, **171**, 173, 175, 177, 180, 203, 207, 235, 241, 249, 270, 273, 274, 276, 277
Nagoya 54, 59, 67, 241, 273, 274, 275
Nanking 12, 33, **33**, 34, **34**, 35, **35**, 252
Necessary Evil **150**, 153, 155, 156, 158, 275, 277
Next Objective 275
Nielsen, Captain Chase J. 7, 62, 69, 262
Nimitz, Admiral Chester W. 13, 137, 176, 195, 196, **196**, 207, 267
Nissan GT-1 Le Mans Car **172**
Norden Bomb Sight **46**, 47, 91, 126, 130, 153
North Africa 7, 81, 84, 85, 86, 87, 90, 93, 95, 104, 115, 121, 123, 129, 181, 183, 188, 189, 199, 222, 236, 243, 259, 260. 261, 264, 265, 267, 268
North American B-25 (Mitchell) **8**, 25, 27, 43, 44, **45**, 45, 47, **50**, 50, 54, 56, 59, **59**, 60, 61, **61**, **62**, 62, 63, **63**, 64, **64**, **65**, 65, 67, 69, **70**, 70,

73, 184, 210, 233, **233**, 237, 238, 242, 255, 258, 259, 260, 261, 262, 263, 264, 265, 266, 267, 268, 269
North American O-47 96, **99**, **234**, 234
Northrop-Grumman B-2 (Spirit) 176, **176**, 177, **250**, 251, 252
Okinawa 13, 78, 79, 165, 189, 192, 211, 235, 259, 267, 277
Parsons, Captain William S. 120, 132, 137, 143, 144, 146, 147, 148, 149, 151, 152, 155, 175, 196, 197, **197**
Patrick, Major-General Mason M. 15
Patton, General George Smith Jr 80, **82**, 85, 86, 91, 100, 101, 197, 198, **198**, 199, **199**, 236
Pearl Harbor 7, 11, 35, **36**, 36, 37, 38, 39, 40, 43, 56, 59, 102, 157, 180, 184, 186, 187, 195, 196, 205, 208, 225, 243, 255
Perry, Captain Charles 158
Philippines 13, 35, 79, 137, 179, 190, 192, 193, 195, 201, 211, 263, 266
Potsdam (Conference/Declaration) 140, 156, 166
Price, Captain James N. 274
Pu Yi, Emperor of China 30, **30**, 31, **31**, **32**, 33
Ray, Captain Norman 277
Rockwell Field, CA 15, 16, 51, 183
Roosevelt, President Franklin D. 7, 38, **39**, 39, **66**, 68, 73, 74, 87, 108, 111, 113, 133, 192, 195, **200**, 200, 201, 206, 211, 242
Saipan Island 79, 134, 202, 211, 241
Schneider Trophy 16, **16**, 17, 24, 223, **223**
Shanghai 7, 59, 65, 67, 69, 261, 269
Shell Oil 22, 24, 253
Sherman, Boyd 18
Sky Buzzard 22, **23**, 23, 24, 229
Smith, Captain Donald 67, 268
Smith, Colonel Harry Locke 253, **253**
Smith, Lieutenant-General Holland M. 13, 78, 134, **134**, 201. **201**, 202, 207
Some Punkins 274
Spaatz, General Carl A. 85, 106, 137, 143, **157**, 157, 158, 183, 188, 202, **203**, 203, 235, 241

Spatz, Sergeant Harold 67, 69, 73, 269
Spook 278
Stimson, Secretary Henry L. 39, 111, 140
Stinson L-5 (Voyager/Sentinel) 100, **100**, **101**, 234
Stockton Field, CA 53, **53**, 259, 260, 261, 262, 264, 267, 268
Straight Flush 144, 149, 150, **150**, 274, 275
Strange Cargo 142, 272, **272**, 273
Sweeney, Major Charles W. 132, 143, 151, 160, 161, 162, 163, **164**, 165, 245, 273, 275
Taloa **147**, 148
Taylor, Major Ralph R. 149, 274
Thatcher, Sergeant David J. 68, 70, 263
Thompson Trophy 22, 23, 24, 229
Tibbets, Colonel Paul W. Jr 7, 9, **83**, 85, 87, 88, 89, 90, 91, 93, 95, 96, **97**, **98**, 100, 102, 103, 104, 105, 106, **107**, 107, 111, 115, 118, 119, 120, 121, 122, **122**, **123**, 123, 124, 125, 126, 127, 128, 129, 130, 131, 132, 133, 135, 136, 137, 138, 139, 148, 149, 151, **151**, 152, 153, 154, 155, 156, 157, **157**, 158, 159, 160, 165, 175, 179, 180, 185, 188, 189, 196, 199, 203, 216, 218, 224, 225, 227, 228, 231, 234, 245, 249, 251, 270, 273
Tinian Island 13, 79, 104, 105, 123, 129, 133, 134, **135**, 136, 137, 138, 139, 142, 144, 146, 151, 152, 155, 156, **157**, 157, 158, 162, 164, 165, 188, 193, 197, 202, 211, 227, 241, **246**, 248, 249, 270, 271, 272, 273, 274, 275, 276, 277, 278
TNT 67, 70, 71, 268
Tojo, General Hideki 35, 74, 186, **204**, 204, 205, 208
Tokugawa Shogunate 28, 29
Tokyo 29, 35, 44, 51, 54, 57, 58, 59, 60, 61, 62, 63, 64, 67, 71, 73, 74, 148, 204, 207, 241, 252, 262, 263, 275
Top Secret **128**, 144, **150**, 150, 151, 153, **271**, 272

Truman, President Harry S. 12, 133, 140, 156, 157, 190, 192, 201, 205, **206**, 207
Tuskegee Airmen 87, **92**, 93, 239
Twelfth US Army Air Force 85, 86, 87, 88, 89, 90, 91, **92**, 92, 93, 202, **236**, 236, 239, 268
Twentieth US Army Air Force 85, 105, 137, 138, 139, 203, 235, 240, 241, **241**
U-234 **112**, 113, 114
Up An' Atom 275
US Army Air (Corps, Forces, Service) 25, 36, 44, 57, 80, 93, 102, 103, 111, 121, 123, 124, 140, 161, 182, 203, 216, 224, 225, 226, 227, 228, 232, 235, 236, 239, 240, 264, 268
USS *George H.W. Bush* 176, **177**
USS *Hornet* 7, **8**, 42, **42**, 43, 44, 47, 50, 51, **52**, 53, 54, 55, **55**, **58**, 58, 59, 60, 61, **61**, 62, 63, **64**, **65**, 65, 67, 69, 136, 184, 194, **209**, 209, 210, 215, 252, 256, 258, 263
USS *Indianapolis* 136, **136**, 137, 138, 146, 185, 192, 193, 195, 210, **210**, 211, 212, 247
von Schoenebeck, Count 19
Watson, Captain Harold F. 63, 264
Wendover Field, UT 105, 121, **121**, 122, 123, 124, 127, 128, 129, 130, 131, 132, 133, 175, 197, 227, 246, 247, 249, 270, 271, 272, 273, 274, 275, 276, 277, 278
Westover, Captain Joseph E. 272, 273
Whirling Dervish 63, 264
Whiskey Pete 61, 259
Willows Airport, CA 7, 51, 53
Wilson, Major John A. 149, 270
Wright R-3350 Double Cyclone engine 116, 118, **118**, **119**, 119
Yalu River 29, 30, 192
Yamamoto, Admiral Isoroku 7, 36, 75, 207, **207**, 208
Yokohama 54, 59, 65, 140, 162
Yokosuka 54, 57, 59, **60**, 60, 67, 143
York, Captain Edward Ski 51, 62, 63, 263
Zahn, Captain Herman S. 278